# ALL THE WOMEN
## *of the*
# BIBLE

# ALL THE WOMEN
## *of the*
# BIBLE

*M.L. del Mastro*

CASTLE BOOKS

This edition published in 2006 by
**CASTLE BOOKS** ®
A division of Book Sales, Inc.
276 Fifth Avenue, Suite 206
New York, New York 10001

Designed by Tony Meisel

ISBN-13: 978-0-7858-1896-0
ISBN-10:  0-7858-1896-0

Printed in the United States of America

# CONTENTS

# INTRODUCTION

*All the Women of the Bible* encompasses two books, really, *The Book of Names* and *The Book of Stories.* Using the lives of the women who appear in the Bible – the Hebrew Scriptures, the New Testament, the Deuterocanonical books and the Apocryphal books commonly accepted by the major Christian religions – these two books are meant to direct the reader back to their Source. Taken together, the two books offer a way in to the mysterious relationship between people and the God Who reveals Himself in the Bible as Creator, Redeemer and Lover/Beloved of each person who chooses to accept His invitation.

In both books, Biblical citations, with additional cross-references, appear in square brackets at the end of the entry or story. For the most part, in preparing entries, I have preferred to paraphrase the text, making use of the best of the modern translations, together with the scholarly notes, for the shape and intent of the material. In both books, direct Biblical quotations appear in *italics*, followed, in square brackets, by the Biblical citation and the identifying indicator of the Biblical translation from which the quotation is made. A list of Biblical translations used appears at the head of the Bibliography with the identifying indicator for each. For the sake of clarity, I have chosen to capitalize, throughout, pronouns referring to God, even in material quoted directly from Scripture.

*The Book of Names* is a biographical Scriptural dictionary. Entries are arranged alphabetically, except for the ***Jerusalem/Zion/Israel*** set, where the members are arranged in historical order of successive images (***Chosen Bride of the Covenant, Bride-Turned-Whore, Widowed Mother, Covenant Bride Restored***).

Each entry briefly identifies the woman who is its subject, summarizes her life as it is known to us in Scripture, lists, as Biblical citations, the places in the Bible where her story can be found, offers cross-references to other dictionary entries and, where applicable, indicates in *italics* the titles of her story and/or related stories in *The Book of Stories.*

Unlike Edith Deen (in her seminal work on the Hebrew Bible and New Testament, *All the Women of the Bible*), and Editor Carol Meyers (in the latest authoritative scholarly dictionary, *Women in Scripture*), I have chosen to create a single, alphabetical dictionary, rather than the three-section format they favored. I found the three section format — named women arranged alphabetically, unnamed women and allegorical women arranged according to the books of the Bible — an unnecessary complication and difficult to use in order to find a particular woman.

The single dictionary that is *The Book of Names* contains all the named and unnamed real women and all the fully developed "literary"(allegory/personification/metaphor/teaching parable or example), images of women found in the Bible.

Goddesses, though not "real" women, are included and described, not in their own right as Meyers' work treats them, but insofar as they affected the fidelity of Israel to the Only God. For it was by suffering the consequences of her repeated infidelity that Israel, repentant and restored, was grounded, once and for all, in the truth of Moses', "*Hear, O Israel! The Lord is our God, the Lord alone!*" [Deuteronomy 6: 4; NAB]

Unnamed women are identified and listed by any name usually attached to them (husband, son, territory, event) as, in my judgment, they are more likely to be recognized that way than under any more general description.

The uses of the word *woman* and all its relational and/or occupational forms (wife, mother, daughter, slave, harlot, queen, midwife, for example), singular or plural, as these appear in Scriptural laws and precepts, do not appear in *The Book of Names*.

"Generic" uses, indicating inclusiveness of a situation or a punishment or reward (for instance, "*And so the Lord will not spare their young men, will have no pity for their orphans and* widows," [Isaiah 9: 16; JB]; "*I will pour out My spirit on all mankind. Your sons and* daughters *shall prophesy ... Even on the slaves, men and* women, *will I pour out My spirit in those days,*" [Joel 3: 1-2; JB]) are also omitted.

Names and entries for "literary" images of women appear in *italics*. These include all developed feminine personifications, all women treated in allegorical or developed metaphoric fashion and all women who appear in parables or teaching stories.

Undeveloped feminine metaphors do not appear in the Dictionary. Among these are cities, peoples and nations referred to with feminine pronouns ("daughter Dibion," [Jeremiah 48: 18]; "daughter Edom" [Lamentations 4: 21, 22] for instance), but not otherwise displaying feminine characteristics. *Church,* for another example, is customarily personified as feminine; unless the personification is developed as a metaphor or an allegory, the reference does not appear in *The Book of Names*. However, the uses of stock phrases like "daughter of Abraham" to indicate *real* women [see Luke 13: 10-17] appear in *The Book of Names* in their proper place.

Similes, where the point of the comparison is not the woman's experience but whatever it is being used to illuminate, do not appear in the Dictionary. Among these are "like a woman in labor" [Psalms 48: 7; Isaiah 12: 14], describing general intense distress; "like a nursing mother" [1 Thessalonians 2: 7] and, "as a nurse carries her baby," [Isaiah 66: 12; Numbers 11: 12] indicating tender care.

Feminine metaphors applied to God, fully treated by Meyers, (though not by Deen) do not appear in *The Book of Names*. There are two reasons for my omission.

First, God, as He reveals Himself in the Bible, is neither male nor female but, in the fullness of His Life, *transcends* gender. Thus, no one-gender image can be considered an equivalent, or metaphor, for God.

Plainly, God, Sourcing, as He does, both male and female, must possess the qualities we assign to women as well as those more commonly used of men. Indeed, that point is made in the Biblical account of the creation of human beings in God's image: *"God created man in the image of Himself, / in the image of God He created him / male and female He created them."* [Genesis 1: 27; JB]

And certainly, God reveals Himself in the Bible as exercising equally qualities we consider "female" and "male."

For example, Moses' complaint to God about the difficulties of caring for stubborn Israel and the unfairness of the burden God has asked him to bear, *"Was it I who conceived all this people, was it I who gave them birth, that You should say to me, 'Carry them in your bosom like a nurse with a baby at the breast to the land that I swore to give their fathers'?"* [Numbers 11: 12; JB] points to God as the mother conceiving and bearing Israel, and the One Who ought to care for the "child." But God also pictures Himself as the male parent of Israel, for instance, in Moses' admonition, *"You forget the Rock Who begot you, / unmindful now of the God Who fathered you."* [Deuteronomy 32; 18; JB]

More often, however, parental care offered Israel is non-gender specific, indicating the transcendence of God, Who serves His children as both mother and father, and Who, as Creator, is infinitely superior to both, in His parenting, for He wills to heal and forgive even the unforgivable, pouring out all the love of both parents on His wayward child, Israel, as we see in Hosea…

God says, *"When Israel was a child, I loved him, / and I called My son out of Egypt. / But the more I called to them, the further they went from Me; / they have offered sacrifice to the Baals ... I Myself taught Ephraim to walk, / I took them in My arms; / yet they have not understood that I was the One looking after them. / I led them with reins of kindness, / with leading-strings of love. / I was like someone who lifts an infant close against his cheek; / stooping down to him I gave him his food.* [Hosea 11: 1-4; JB].

But then He continues, *"Israel, how could I give you up? / ... My heart recoils from it, My whole Being trembles at the thought. / I will not give rein to my fierce anger, I will not destroy Ephraim again, for I am God, not man: I am the Holy One in your midst / and I have no wish to destroy."* [Hosea 11: 8-9; JB].

The second reason for the omission of these images from consideration is more briefly stated. For Israel, the One God was never considered female; the Bible uses only male referential pronouns for God. Indeed, goddesses belonged to the surrounding people, those whom God had *not* chosen, and any interaction with those figures was likely to draw Israel into the infidelity of false worship for which severe punishment would inevitably follow! Plainly, then, the feminine metaphors in Scripture were intended to function, not as proper metaphors would do, that is, as equivalents of God, but rather as simple, effective descriptors of qualities found in God.

In *The Book of Stories,* I have chosen to retell the stories of fifty six women who appear in Scripture, and who face, during the course of their stories, a crisis which changes the course of their lives, and sometimes of their nation's life.

I've chosen the method of *retelling* for these stories, as opposed to summarizing them, using them as the basis for moral instruction, or simply quoting them directly from their Scriptural source(s), because *retelling* the story, of necessity, refocuses it to answer, in detail, the one question every good story answers as it raises, that is, "But *why?*"

For it is true of each of these stories (as, indeed, of every story) that it flows, almost inevitably, from who the central figure *is*. In the case of each of these stories, she is a woman and, as in our world, that makes a difference, but she is also unique. So the action in her story – the choices she makes, the deeds she does, her responses to what circumstances, or other people's choices, do to her and her plans – all emerge from *herself.*

*Herself,* that is, her character, her history and her consequent relationships with and shaping by the others in her story, are all affected, and sometimes effected, by her culture with its *mores* and expectations, and often, in the case of the woman in Scripture, by her involvement, internal or external, affirmative or negative, active or passive, with the Lord God and His chosen people.

It is these essential elements of *herself* that supply and shape her motivation and define her limits. And it is these elements that will determine *why* she will do, or not do, what she does, *why* she will see what she sees, or fail to notice a thing, *why* she will both act and react as she does and, ultimately, *why* her story will come to a happy ending for her, or will not.

These are things that we want to know when we come to read a good story, and these things form the heart and purpose of a good *retelling*.

Now, doing a *retelling* of the women's stories found in Scripture presents a problem in this regard, not because the stories are not there, for they are, in rather surprising abundance and variety.

The problem, I have found, is that Scripture does not often provide, *in the stories themselves*, the kind of rich detail on which *retelling* depends – of the people and their histories, of their motivations for actions, of the customs that shaped (and freed or hindered) their living, of the events and/or their consequences that provide the context for their choices. Nor do the women's stories in Scripture often answer the question, "Whatever was she *thinking* – (when she did that, said that, suffered that, took that deadly course, believed him …)?"

Those things are what we really want to know! And those things are at the heart of *retelling,* indeed, are its chief stock in trade. For some of these things, the notes and commentaries that accompany the various translations and presentations of Scripture are excellent sources. For others, there is nothing.

Obviously, if Scripture, in its text and/or notes and commentaries, provides these things, and sometimes, as in the case of Sarah, the haunted, seven-times widowed, untaken bride of the Book of Tobit, it does in abundance, the reteller says a quick prayer of thanks and uses them all with delight!

But when Scripture offers only the "bare bones" of the story, as in the case of Jephthah's daughter, or that of Jael, or even that of Bathsheba, what is the reteller to do?

In my case, the reteller starts strip mining! That is, I try to enter *in* to the sequence of events which Scripture relates and imagine what combination of the woman's personal qualities, history, relationships (human and Divine), experiences and constraints (religious or social), *might possibly* have resulted in the woman's (evident), seeing of *this* choice, or *that* course of action as her only option in the situation in which she found herself.

In other words, I ask myself, "If *I* had been in her place, what conditions would have *had* to be in operation for *me* to have made her choices?" The answer sets up the *retelling*.

Obviously, the danger in this tactic is that the reteller has to supply the missing emotional and motivational levels of the story solely from personal experience, actual or vicarious, and that can falsify the *retelling*. This is particularly true in the case of the stories which employ a first person narrator. But, that pitfall avoided, the technique affords a window in to the woman's mental processes, emotional responses and the all-important *motivations* that make the story the woman's own, and its course inevitable.

Sometimes Scripture offers a full cast of characters for a woman's story, as in the case of Eve in the Garden, or Hannah, with her husband, his other, jealous, wife, and Eli the priest, or that of Ruth, with Naomi, Boaz and his harvesters. That makes telling her story a lot simpler – she has someone to talk to, for one thing, and often, Scripture provides the dialogue!

But sometimes, there is only the woman herself – the patriot woman of Thebez, or Rizpah, for instance – and her action. Obviously, no one lives in an unpeopled vacuum and manages to stop a siege single-handed, or protects the bodies of her slain sons and nephews from vultures and scavengers for a season without help. There *had* to be someone around! *Retelling* allows the reteller to fill in those gaps, by filling in the servants, or friends, or messengers the story's Scriptural action obviously demands.

A variant of that supplying of characters occurs in the second story of Eve. We know from Scripture that she and Adam were alive when their first-born, Cain, killed his brother, Abel, and we know they survived the tragedy, with Cain's resultant, life-long exile, and conceived another son, Seth. Adam and Eve do not, however, appear in the Scriptural account of that first of all murders, either as participants or as respondents.

"But," says the reader, "they *must* have been there, *must* have known what happened, *must* have had some reaction! What was that all *like* for them? What did they make of it?"

The *retelling* that answers those questions is cast as a remembrance of Eve, baby-sitting with her grandson Enosh, Seth's son. It's what *might* have happened, *needed* to have happened, I think, to allow the shocked, grieving parents to integrate the experience of the loss of their children with their own failure in the Garden.

The *retelling* also allows for the expansion of the story line given in

Scripture by the supplying of incidents which illumine the character, motives, habits of thought and action and responses of the woman from whose actions the story is emerging. The appearance of the small dog in Martha's story is just such an addition. (Tobias' dog, on the other hand, is right there in the Book of Tobit).

That kind of invention isn't confined, in a *retelling,* just to filling in needed cast members or illuminating incidents. It may also be used, with care, in supplying supporting details to show *how* the woman got from *a* to, say *k*, when all Scripture mentions are *c, d, h* and *j*! The story of Rachel and Leah is a case in point. Scripture simply says Laban agreed to give Rachel to Jacob for his wife, and on the wedding night slipped Leah into the room, without mentioning such details as whether Rachel knew what was going on, or agreed to it, how the identity switch was actually arranged, and what both women, and later the duped Jacob, were *feeling* about the whole thing! The difficulty with such invention is that the reteller can over-elaborate. Used with discretion, however, it really helps to bring the story and the woman at its center to life.

Another thing *retelling* allows for is variety in the narrative voice. For some of the stories, I used the first person narrator – that is, the woman tells her own story, either directly to the reader, who becomes her listener, or to some other present, but silent, person (the dramatic monologue). That technique is sometimes the best way to get at what's going on inside the woman as she creates her story, when motivation and character are neither supplied nor otherwise easy to arrive at. Jephthah's daughter, uncomplainingly becoming her father's victory sacrifice, is a case in point.

In a variant, Judith's maidservant, companion and business manager serves as first person narrator for her mistress' daring and bloody elimination of Israel's enemy Holofernes. With her practical commonsense and natural "ordinary woman" responses, this old friend serves both as a foil for the heroic Judith and a lens for the true magnitude of her courage and faith in this action

The third person/omniscient narrator, the more usual narrative pattern, also works effectively in a *retelling*, and I discover, looking over the collection, that it seems to have been my method of choice. It allows for the supply of characters, supporting incidents and concrete details as well as the first person narration does, and seems to me to have been the best vehicle for incorporating such detail as Scripture has provided and blending this with the filling in that have seemed to me necessary.

The fifty-six women in the collection, among them, represent every phase of the story of any woman in this world. They range in age from the young (Mary, the mother of Jesus, at 15; Jephthah's daughter at about the same age), to the very old (Sarah, birthing Isaac at 90). Among them are virgins (like Tamar, Absalom's sister), widows (like Tamar, widow of Er and Onan), the orphaned (like Mahlah and her four sisters), and single women (like Martha of Bethany). Most of them are married, and most of them have the children all of them desire almost more than life itself, for marriage and mothering were seen as a woman's proper destiny. The barren, like Hannah, often storm heaven for a lifting of what they, and their people, see as the curse of the Lord God. Those in this group have their prayers answered.

For all of that, some of these women also lead effective lives outside their homes. There are three Queens (Athaliah, Esther and Jezebel), one Judge (Deborah, who also took an active advisory role in a successful war), four who contributed actively to the destruction of Israel's enemies (Jael, Judith, the quick-witted women of Abel and the patriot woman of Thebez) and leaders (Deborah), while one (Jehosheba), was instrumental in the overthrow of a tyrant and the restoration of the true heir to the throne of Judah.

Their personal lives are equally various. Some are cherished by their husbands (Rachel and Rebekah). Others are victims of rape (Dinah and the Ephraimite Levite's concubine), or political power (Bathsheba). Still others are prostitutes, some without apology (Rahab), others (the sinful woman anointing Jesus' feet), coming to see that life as flawed and rejecting it.

But all of them are fully alive, fully women, and in the course of their stories, becoming fully themselves.

The stories themselves each focus on a critical event or situation in the life of the woman who is its center. Each story attempts to show this living woman struggling with herself and those around her, to bring her vision of life and, often, her relationship with the Lord God, positive or negative, into fullest being. It's that struggle, with its pains, its illuminations, its joys or its frustrations that has made the stories worth the writing for me and, I hope, will make them worth the reading for you.

Now, for some "nuts and bolts" that might be helpful as you read *The Book of Stories*.

The title of each story begins with the name of the woman who is its center, and the stories are arranged alphabetically. At the end of each story, in square brackets, appear the Biblical citations for the woman, a reference to the woman's Dictionary entry, cross-references to other relevant entries in *The Book of Names* and, where applicable, *italicized* cross-references to related stories in the *Book of Stories.*

The major events in each story follow the Scriptural account, or accounts in cases where more than one source has told a woman's story, and the woman is not followed from her Scriptural appearance into other, further adventures.

Thus, Mary Magdalene, (who is seen by modern scripture scholars as neither Mary of Bethany nor the sinful woman who washed Jesus' feet with her tears, dried them with her hair, then kissed and anointed them with precious nard) is seen, as the *retelling* of her story opens, weeping at the tomb of Jesus. Her healing by Jesus, Who drove out seven devils in a miracle the Gospels do not describe, is presented as a memory; the details of her afflictions are an invention. That healing is seen as providing a motive and focus for her love of the Master, and an explanation, in part, for her attitudes and actions in the story. The story ends with her hurrying off, at Jesus' command, to tell the good news of His resurrection to His disciples and, though we might like to, we do not follow her from there. [Anyone seeking a clear, authoritative summary of the historical development of the Mary Magdalene story would do well to consult Carolyn Osiek's article, "Mary 3" in Carol Meyers' *Women in Scripture*]

Not all of these women received the approval, nor even the understanding, of their friends, their families, or the Biblical narrator. Some, like Mary, the Mother of Jesus, were honored as holy, while others, like Queen Jezebel, were condemned as enemies of Israel and the Lord God by their contemporaries.

But all were real women, vital, concerned and willing to pay whatever price was asked in order to find and possess their hearts' desire, and their struggles, successes and failures resonate with us in the twenty-first century. Among these women we may find companions, models, warnings – and, in the communion that links us with those who have gone before us, from life into Life, even friends.

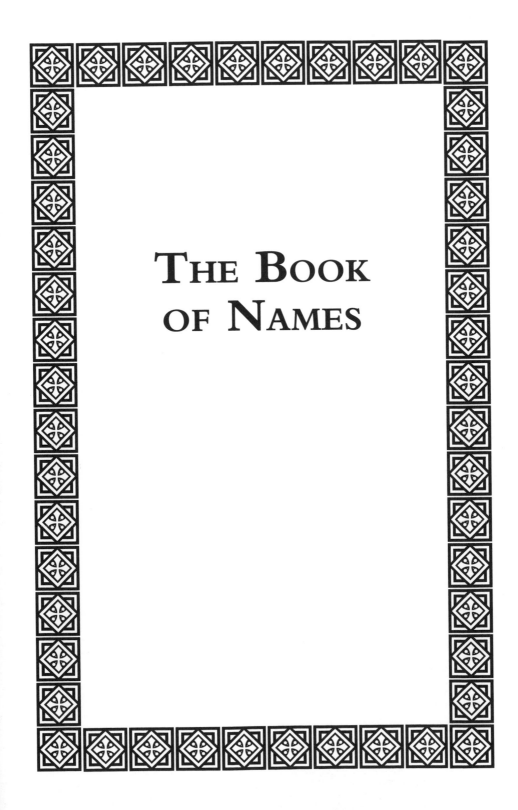

# THE BOOK
## OF NAMES

# A

**ABI** – Hebrew spelling; see **ABIJAH, daughter of Zechariah**

**ABIA** – alternate spelling for **ABI**; see also **ABIJAH, daughter of Zechariah**

**ABIAH** (also spelled **ABIJAH**), **daughter of Machir** – see also **EPHRATHAH, daughter of Machir**

**ABIGAIL, wife of King David (ca. 1010-970 BC)** – she was the wife of Nabal from Carmel; when Nabal refused to give David and his soldiers supplies in return for their protecting Nabal's shepherds and possessions from harm, she secretly prepared an offering and brought it to David; she thanked David for his care of their property, apologized for her husband and dissuaded David from seeking vengeance for Nabal's rudeness; on Nabal's death at the Lord God's hand, she accepted David's offer of marriage; Abigail was taken captive, together with Ahinoam of Jezreel and everyone else in the camp at Ziklag, by raiding Amalekites; all the captives were freed by David and his men; she was the mother of David's second son, Chileab, also called Daniel [**1 Samuel 25:** 2-44; **27:** 3; **30:** 3, 5, 18; **2 Samuel 2:** 2; **3:** 3; **1 Chronicles 3:** 1; see *ABIGAIL and the Sudden Smile*]

**ABIGAIL, daughter of Jesse** – she was the sister of King David (ca. 1010–970 BC), his seven older brothers and their sister, Zeruiah; she was the wife of Jether (also spelled Ithra) the Ishmaelite, and the mother of Amasa and the aunt of Abishai, Joab and Asahel [**2 Samuel 17:** 25; **1 Chronicles 2:** 16–17 (see also **NAHASH, ZERUIAH** and **King David's MOTHER**)]

**ABIHAIL, wife of Abishur** – she bore to Abishur (a descendant of Judah through Perez), two sons, Ahban and Molid [**1 Chronicles 2:** 29]

**ABIHAIL, wife of David's son, Jerimoth** – she was the daughter of Eliab, Jesse's son; she bore to Jerimoth a daughter, Mahalath; she was the grandmother of Jeush, Shemariah and Zaham [**2 Chronicles 11:18**]

**ABIJAH (Hebrew spelling, ABI; also spelled ABIA), daughter of Zechariah** – she was the wife of King Ahaz of Judah (ca. 736-716 BC) and the mother of Hezekiah, who succeeded Ahaz at twenty-five and ruled for twenty-nine years (ca. 716-687 BC) in Jerusalem [**2 Kings 18: 2; 2 Chronicles 29: 1**]

**ABIJAH (also spelled ABIAH), daughter of Machir** – see also **EPHRATHAH, daughter of Machir**

**Abijah's WIVES and DAUGHTERS** – King Abijah of Judah (911-870 BC) married fourteen wives, who bore him sixteen daughters along with twenty-two sons, a sign of his power and prosperity [**2 Chronicles 13: 21**]

**Abimelech's Concubine MOTHER** – see **Gideon's CONCUBINE**

**Abimelech of Gerar's SLAVE-GIRLS** – some were given to Abraham as recompense for Abimelech (innocent) taking into his tent Abraham's wife, Sarah, identified by Abraham as his sister; others, perhaps including these, were, along with Abimelech's wife, made barren by the Lord God for Abimelech's offense; their fertility was restored when the Lord God answered Abraham's prayer for Abimelech [**Genesis 20: 14-18** (see also **Abimelech of Gerar's WIFE**)]

**Abimelech of Gerar's WIFE** – she was made barren, together with all the women slaves in the house, by the Lord God, when her husband, King Abimelech, took Abraham's wife Sarah into his dwelling; warned by the Lord God in a dream that he would die for having taken Sarah, Abimelech hastily sent Sarah back with an offering of sheep, cattle, men and women slaves; Abraham prayed and the Lord God healed Abimelech, his wife and his slave-girls, freeing them from the barrenness with which He had cursed them on Sarah's account [**Genesis 20: 14-18** (see also **Abimelech of Gerar's SLAVE-GIRLS**)]

**ABISHAG** – she was a beautiful young woman of Shunem who was brought to King David (ca. 1010-970 BC), by his servants, to serve as his nurse and concubine (though he had no intercourse with her) when he was very old and failing in health; after David's death, Haggith's son Adonijah (who had previously tried to seize royal power), asked Bathsheba to ask her son, King Solomon, for Abishag as a bride; Solomon refused, seeing the request as another attempt at a coup, and had Adonijah executed [**1 Kings 1: 1-4, 15; 2: 13-25**]

**ABITAL** – she was one of the eight wives of King David (ca. 1010-970 BC); while in Hebron, she bore David a son, Shephatiah [**2 Samuel 3:** 4; **1 Chronicles 3:** 3]

**Abraham's CONCUBINES** – they were the mothers of sons by Abraham; during Abraham's lifetime, they saw their sons given gifts and sent eastward, away from the child of the Promise, Isaac, Abraham's son by Sarah [**Genesis 25:** 6 (see also **SARAH, wife of Abraham** and **HAGAR**)]

**"Abraham's DAUGHTER"** – see **WOMAN Who Suffered Eighteen Years**

**Achan's DAUGHTERS** – they were stoned by the community, along with their father and the rest of his family, whose possessions were burnt, because Achan had violated the ban proclaimed by Joshua and taken spoils dedicated to the Lord God from the conquered Jericho [**Joshua 7:** 1, 16-26]

**ACHSAH** – she was the daughter of Caleb, a descendant of Judah through Hezron; she was given as a prize by her father, to be the wife of the man who conquered and captured Kiriath-sepher (formerly Debir); the winner was Othniel, son of Kenaz, Caleb's brother; at her new husband's urging, she asked her father for a field; she then asked for some springs to go with the land (in the wilderness of the Negeb) to which this marriage and his gift had banished her; she obtained from Caleb the upper and lower springs [**Joshua 15:** 16-19; **Judges 1:** 12-15; **1 Chronicles 2:** 49]

**ADAH, daughter of Elon the Hittite** – she was the second Canaanite wife of Esau, the mother of Eliphaz; she became the grandmother of Teman, Omar, Zepho, Gatam and Kenaz, and of Amalek by Timna, concubine of Eliphaz [**Genesis 36:** 2, 4, 6, 10, 12, 16; called **BASEMACH (also spelled BASHEMATH)** in Genesis 26:34 (see also **OHOLIBAMAH, BASEMATH, daughter of Ishmael, TIMNA** and **Hittite and Canaanite women as WIVES**)]

**ADAH, first wife of Lamech** – she was a descendant of Cain through Enoch; she became the mother of Jabal, ancestor of the tent-dwellers and owners of livestock, and of Jubal, ancestor of all who play the lyre and the flute [Genesis 4:19-24 (see also ZILLAH and NAAMAH, daughter of Lamech)]

Adam's DAUGHTERS – they were women born during the eight hundred years that Adam lived after the birth (when Adam was one hundred thirty years old) of Seth, the son given Adam and Eve to comfort them for the death of Abel, who had been slain by his brother Cain; nothing more is known of them than this mention in the list of Adam's descendants before the Flood [Genesis 5: 4]

AGAR – alternate spelling; see HAGAR

AGIA (also spelled AUGIA) – identified, in 1 Esdras only, as a daughter of Barzillai; she married a man (perhaps Jaddus) who took Barzillai's name as his own; her descendants appear in the list of returnees from the Babylonian exile, among those whose claim to priestly status could not be supported by the records; her name does not appear in parallel lists of returning exiles in Ezra or Nehemiah, though her descendants do [1 Esdras 5: 38-40 (see also Barzillai's DAUGHTERS)]

AHINOAM, wife of King David (ca. 1010-970 bc) – a woman who came from Jezreel, she was married to David after Saul had given Michal, his daughter and David's wife, to Palti, son of Laish from Gallim; she was captured with Abigail when the Amalekites raided the Negeb and Ziklag, taking all the women and children; the women were rescued by David and his men, with all that the raiders had taken; she bore Amnon, David's first-born, at Hebron [1 Samuel 25: 43; 27: 3; 30: 1-20; 2 Samuel 2: 2; 3: 2; 1 Chronicles 3: 1]

AHINOAM, wife of King Saul (ca. 1030-1010 bc) – a daughter of Ahimaaz, she was the mother of four sons, Jonathan, Ishvi (also called Ishbaal and Ishbosheth), Abinadab and Malchishua, and of two daughters, Merab and Michal [1 Samuel 14: 49-50]

AHLAI – he or she was the only named child of Sheshan (a descendant of Judah through Perez and Hezron), who [1 Chronicles 2: 34] is listed as having only daughters; listed [1 Chronicles 2: 31] as a son; if Ahlai was a daughter, she might be the one given to the slave Jarha in marriage, and so be the mother of a son, Attai; though the list of Attai's descendants includes

Zabad, there is no indication that he is the "Zabad son of Ahlai" listed [1 Chronicles 11: 41b] among David's champions [1 **Chronicles 2:** 31, 34-35]

**AHOLAH –** alternate spelling; see *OHOLAH*

**AHOLIBAH –** alternate spelling; see *OHOLIBAH*

**AHOLIBAMAH –** alternate spelling; see **OHOLIBAMAH**

**Amaziah's DAUGHTERS –** these children of the priest of Bethel were to be slaughtered, with their brothers, when Israel went into exile; their fate was proclaimed by the prophet Amos when he spoke the word of the Lord God as an answer to Amaziah; Amaziah had been trying to discredit Amos with King Jeroboam of Israel (783-743 BC) and to send him back to Judah [**Amos 7:** 16-17 (see also **Amaziah's WIFE**)]

**Amaziah's WIFE –** she was married to Amaziah, priest of Bethel; Amaziah warned King Jeroboam of Israel (783-743 BC) that Amos was plotting against Israel and the King; Amaziah also told Amos to go back to Judah and prophesy there; in response, Amos gave him the Lord God's answer, prophesying that Amaziah would die on unclean soil, Israel would go into exile and Amaziah's own wife would be forced to become a prostitute, his children would be killed and his land would be portioned out [**Amos 7:** 16-17 (see also **Amaziah's DAUGHTERS**)]

**Amos' WOMEN of Samaria –** appearing in a diatribe against exploitation of the poor, religious hypocrisy and corruption, they were called "cows of Bashan" and pictured as simultaneously crushing the poor and asking their husbands for something to drink; they would be dragged out of the city with hooks and driven toward Assyria as a punishment of the Lord God [**Amos 4:** 1-3]

**ANAH –** she was formerly considered the daughter of Zibeon and mother of Oholibamah, first Canaanite wife of Esau; modern scholarship considers Anah to be the son of Zibeon and father of Oholibamah [**Genesis 36:** 2, 14, 18, 24, 25; **1 Chronicles 1:** 40]

**ANATH** – she was a warrior goddess; with Asherah and Astarte, she was one of three great goddesses worshipped by the Canaanites; she was seen as consort or sister of Baal; in the Bible, her name appears only in place names, possibly indicating that the goddess was worshipped there, and in three personal names, which may or may not refer to the goddess [**Joshua 15:** 59; **19:** 38; **21:** 18; **Judges 1:** 33; **3:** 31; **5:** 6; **1 Kings 2:** 26; **1 Chronicles 7:** 8; **8:** 24; **Nehemiah 10:** 19; **Isaiah 10:** 30; **Jeremiah 1:** 1; (see also **ASHERAH** and **ASTARTE**)]

**ANNA, prophetess** – she was the daughter of Phanuel of the tribe of Ashur; she was married for seven years, then widowed; at eighty-four years old, she never left the Temple but spent her time serving God day and night with fasting and prayer; she encountered the forty-day-old Jesus when Mary and Joseph brought Him to the Temple (as firstborn) to be redeemed, while Mary was purified according to the dictates of the Law; she praised God and spoke about the child to everyone who was waiting for the deliverance of Israel by the Messiah to come [**Luke 2:** 36-38 (see also **MARY, mother of Jesus, Son of God**)]

**ANNA, wife of Tobit** – she was the mother of Tobias; she earned the family living by spinning and weaving when Tobit, though he was faithful to the Lord God, was blinded; she rejoiced when Tobias returned home with a bride, and also in the healing of Tobit's eyesight; she survived Tobit and was buried beside him in Nineveh by Tobias [**Tobit 1:** 9, 20; **2:** 1, 11-14; **4:** 3-4; **5:** 17-22; **6:** 1; **10:** 4-7; **11:** 4-6, 9; **14:** 10, 12 (see also **EDNA, SARAH, wife of Tobias, Raguel's MAIDSERVANTS**); see *ANNA and the Homecoming* and *SARAH and the Bridal-Night Demon*]

**ANTIOCHIS** – she was a concubine of Antiochus IV Epiphanes, ruler of the Seleucid Empire (175-164/163 BC); his gift to her of the Cilician towns of Tarsus and Mallus caused their citizens to revolt, and his absence from Jerusalem (to calm the trouble) allowed Menelaus, the high priest, and Andronicus, the king's deputy, to conspire in the murder of Onias, the high priest faithful to the Lord God [**2 Maccabees 4:** 30]

**APAME** – in Zerubbabel's contest story answering the question, "What is the most powerful thing?" she was identified as the daughter of Bartacus and the concubine of Darius Hystaspis I of Persia (522-486 BC); in the story, she was pictured as taking Darius' crown, putting it on her own head and slapping his cheek without punishment; she was intended by the teller of the story to illustrate his proposition that women are more powerful than men, but less powerful than truth; the contest prize he asked and received was that Darius keep his oath to rebuild Jerusalem and its Temple, returning it sacred vessels [**1 Esdras 4:** 13-32]

**APPHIA** – she was the wife of one of Paul's converts, Philemon; Philemon owned Onesimus, a slave who had run away, met the Apostle Paul and been converted by him; Apphia was the mother of Archippus; a local church community met at their house [**Philemon 1:** 2]

**(The) ARAMITESS** – see **Manasseh's Aramaean CONCUBINE**

**Arpachshad's DAUGHTERS** – the girls born to Arpachshad, Shem's son and Noah's grandson, during the four hundred three years Arpachshad lived after the birth (when he was thirty-five years old) of Shelah (also spelled Salah); nothing more is known of them than this mention in the list of patriarchs after the Flood [**Genesis 11:** 13]

**ARSINOE** – she appears only in 3 Maccabees; she was daughter of King Ptolemy III Euergetes of Egypt (246-221 BC) and the consort-sister of Ptolemy IV Philopator (221-204 BC); in the fierce Battle of Raphia (217 BC) that followed the attempt by Theodotus (who had abandoned Ptolemy for the Seleucid King Antiochus III the Great of Syria (223-187 BC) to assassinate Ptolemy, Arsinoe, in tears and with her hair disheveled, rallied the troops, promising each two minas of gold if they won the battle, and thus gained the victory [**3 Maccabees 1:** 1-5]

**Artaxerxes' QUEEN** – the unnamed spouse of King Artaxerxes I Longimanus (465-423 BC), she may have been Queen Damaspia (d. 424 BC); she was present when her husband granted permission to Nehemiah, the kings cupbearer, to go to the land of Judah and help the exiles (returned home from Babylon) to rebuild Jerusalem; she took no part in the discussion and nothing further is known of her [Nehemiah 2: 1-8]

**ARTEMIS (also called DIANA), of the Ephesians** – she is the goddess worshipped in Ephesus as protector of the city; Demetrius the silversmith, fearing that the spread of belief in Jesus, as taught by the Apostle Paul, would ruin the local market for silver shrines of Artemis (bought by her worshippers), gathered his fellow-craftsmen and started a riot against the Christians, seizing two of Paul's Macedonian travel companions; the town clerk calmed the people and dismissed the assembly; no harm came to the Christians [**Acts 19:** 23-41 (see also **NANEA**)]

**ASENATH** – she was the daughter of Potiphera, priest of On, and the Egyptian wife of Joseph, the first son of Jacob by Rachel; she became the mother of Manasseh and Ephraim [**Genesis 41:** 45, 50-52; **46:** 20 (see also **Ephraim's WIFE** and **SHEERAH**)]

**ASHERAH (plural, ASHERIM)** – she was the mother goddess, who, with Anath and Astarte, was one of the three great goddesses of the Canaanites; in the Bible, her cult objects, shaped like poles or stylized trees, are called *asherah* (singular) or *asherim* (plural); she became a constant occasion of idolatry for Israel from the Exodus onward, and of consequent punishment by the Lord God each time the Israelites gave way and worshipped Asherah and other gods; when the Israelites repented, destroyed the altars and sacred poles set up to honor Asherah, and returned to the Covenant relationship with the Lord God as the only God, He received Israel back and restored the Covenant relationship [**Exodus 34:** 13; **Deuteronomy 7:** 3-6; **12:** 2-3; **16:** 21-22; **Judges 3:** 7-9; **6:** 25-32; **1 Kings 14:** 15, 23; **15:** 13; **16:** 33; **18:** 19; **2 Kings 13:** 6; **17:** 10-12, 16; **18:** 4; **21:** 3, 7; **23:** 4-7, 14-15; **2 Chronicles 14:** 3; **15:** 16; **17:** 6; **19:** 3; **24:** 18; **31:** 1; **33:** 3, 19; **34:** 3-4, 7; **Isaiah 17:** 8; **27:** 9; **Jeremiah 17:** 2; **Micah 5:** 9-14 (see also **ANATH, ASTARTE, WEAVERS of Clothes for Asherah** and **MAACAH [also spelled MAACHAH], wife of Rehoboam**)]

**ASHERIM** – see **ASHERAH**

**ASHIMA (also called ASHIMAH)** – an unidentified deity, perhaps Ashima was the Canaanite goddess of love and fertility, Astarte; or the Canaanite mother goddess Asherah; or Anath, the Canaanite goddess of war; Ashima was worshipped by the people of Hamath who were among the pagan peoples resettled in Samaria by the king of Assyria after the deportation of the Israelites; responding to the wrath of the Lord God Who sent lions to devour these pagans, the king recalled a deported priest of the Lord God to teach them all how to worship Him; they added worship of the Lord God to their own rites rather than worshipping Him alone [**2 Kings 17:** 30–34; **Amos 8:** 14 (see also **ANATH, ASHERAH** and **ASTARTE**)]

**ASHTAROTH** – plural of **ASHTART**, also spelled **ASHTEROTH** and **ASHTORETH**; see **ASTARTE**

**ASHTEROTH** – alternate spelling of **ASHTAROTH**, plural of **ASHTART**; see **ASTARTE**

**ASHTORETH** – alternate spelling of **ASHTAROTH**, plural of **ASHTART;** see **ASTARTE**

*ASIA – the personification of Asia (probably meaning Syria) as a prostitute, she allied herself with "Babylon" (usually understood as Rome) and imitated her corruptions; because, said the Lord God, she killed His chosen people continually, she would suffer the same afflictions she had inflicted upon His chosen – famine, military conquest, death by the sword, destruction of her cities and of her forests and fruitful trees by fire, the seizure of all her wealth and the carrying off of her children into slavery; Asia appears only in 2 Esdras, in the portion known as 6 Esdras, a section which may be either of Christian or of Jewish origin; the reference may be either to future events, or to the story of Odenathus, Prince of Palmyra and husband of Zenobia, who fought the Sassanian king, Shapur I (AD 240-273), allying himself and his country with Rome, and thus sharing in Rome's guilt, and punishment, for persecution of the Lord God's people, who may be either the Jews or the Christians* [**2 Esdras 15:** 46-63;**16:** 1-2]

**ASTARTE** (Greek form of **ASHTART**; plural **ASHTAROTH**, also spelled **ASHTEROTH** and **ASHTORETH**) – goddess of love and fertility, she was seen as consort of Baal and was sometimes associated with war or the stars; with Anath and Asherah, she was one of the three major Canaanite goddesses; in the Bible, she serves, with Baal, as a continuing occasion of idolatry for Israel from the death of Moses' successor, Joshua, onward; the pattern – idolatry, punishment (most often conquest), repentance with renunciation of idols, forgiveness and restoration to her place in the Covenant relationship – shaped Israel's history; Biblical references to Ashtaroth occur in place names indicating worship sites of foreigners; Biblical references to Astarte occur in descriptions of Israel's falls into idolatry, except for one

[1 Samuel 31: 10] where the Philistines honor Astarte by hanging the dead King Saul's armor in Astarte's temple in Beth-shan [called **ASHTAROTH (ASHTEROTH, ASHTORETH) in Genesis 14:** 5; **Deuteronomy 1:** 4; **Joshua 9:** 10; **12:** 4; **13:** 12, 31; **1 Chronicles 6:** 56; called **ASTARTE** in **Judges 2:** 13; **10:** 6; **1 Samuel 7:** 3-4; **12:** 10; **31:** 10; **1 Kings 11:** 5, 33; **2 Kings 23:** 13 (see also **ANATH, ASHERAH, QUEEN OF HEAVEN, King's DAUGHTERS, WIVES of the Remnant of Judah in Egypt**)]

**ATARAH** – she was the second wife of Jerahmeel, the eldest son of Hezron who was Judah's grandson through Perez; she was the mother of Onam; she became the grandmother of Shammai (who fathered Nadab and Abishur, husband of Abihail) and Jada [**1 Chronicles 2:** 26]

**ATARGATIS** – she was a Syrian fertility goddess, particularly of fish and grain; her name suggests she may be linked to the Canaanite goddesses of war (Anath) and fertility/sexual love (Astarte); at her shrine near the town of Carnaim in Gilead, the *Atergateion*, Judas Maccabaeus slaughtered twenty-five thousand men; the shrine may or may not be the *Ashteroth-karnaim* near which the four foreign kings conquered the Rephaim in a war which saw Abraham coming to the rescue of the abducted Lot, his women and children and all his possessions [**2 Maccabees 12:** 26; **Genesis 14:** 5 (see also **ANATH** and **ASTARTE**)]

**ATHALIAH** – she was the daughter (some scholars say granddaughter) of Omri, King of Israel (885-874 BC), and the sister (some scholars say daughter) of Ahab, King of Israel (874-853 BC); she married King Jehoram, or Joram of Judah (848-841 BC), the son of King Jehoshaphat (870-848 BC); she became the mother of Ahaziah, who became King of Judah on his father's death and ruled in Jerusalem for one year (841 BC); on Azariah's death at the hands of Jehu (anointed King of Israel by the Lord God's command; ruled 841-814 BC), she had all the males of royal stock killed and assumed the throne; she ruled Judah as Queen 841-835 BC; she was executed when Ahaziah's son, Jehoash, or Joash (rescued and hidden for six years in the Lord God's Temple by Jehosheba, Ahaziah's sister), supported by Jehoiada the priest and the royal guard, claimed the throne; Joash ruled Judah 835-796 BC and restored Israel to the Lord God [**2 Kings 8:** 18, 25-26; **11:** 1-20; **2 Chronicles 21:** 6; **22:** 2, 10-12; **23:** 1-15, 21; **24:** 7 (see also **JEHOSHEBA** and **Joash's**

NURSE); see *ATHALIAH and the Almost-Perfect Plan, JEHOSHEBA and the Vanishing King* and *JEZEBEL and the Stubborn Prophet*]

**AUGIA** – alternate spelling; see **AGIA**

**AZUBAH, first wife of Caleb** – either she or Jerioth bore three sons, Jesher, Shobab and Ardon, to Caleb, the son of Hezron, Judah's descendant through Perez; some consider her the mother of Jerioth; more often, she is thought of as another wife of Caleb [**1 Chronicles 2:** 18-19 (see also **JERIOTH**)]

**AZUBAH, wife of King Asa of Judah (911-870 BC)** – she was the daughter of Shilhi; she became the mother of King Jehoshaphat of Judah (870-848 BC) [**1 Kings 22:** 42; **2 Chronicles 20:** 31]

*AZUBAH* – *this was the name applied to Jerusalem/Zion, personified as female under various guises; the name, meaning "Abandoned"[JB], indicated her state before her redemption* [**Isaiah 62:**4 (see also *SHEMAMAH, BEULAH, HEPHZIBAH,* GOMER *and Jerusalem/Zion/Israel as Covenant BRIDE-TURNED-WHORE*)]

# B

**BAARA** – she was one wife of Shaharaim, the other being Hushim; they were dismissed by their husband after he went into exile on the plains of Moab and married Hodesh [**1 Chronicles 8:** 8-12 (see also **HUSHIM** and **HODESH**)]

*BABYLON* – *the quintessential enemy of Israel, used by the Lord God to punish His Bride for her idolatry/adultery, "Babylon," the voluptuous queen will, in her turn, suffer at His hands for her wickedness and cruelty, a total calamity from which nothing can save her; the Psalmist begs a blessing for any who will treat her as she has treated Israel, dashing her babies against a rock* [**Isaiah 47:** 1-15; **Psalm 137:** 8 (see also *Revelations' GREAT HARLOT*)]

**Babylonian Priests' WIVES** – these women conspired with their husbands, who took and resold offerings made to their gods; they took some of the meat offered in sacrifice and salted it down, but gave nothing to the poor and helpless; they were clothed by their husbands in the robes of their gods; in their monthly courses, they were not afraid to touch the sacrifices offered to their gods; they served food as an offering to their gods, a male function among the Israelites; these behaviors could be interpreted as indicating the impotence of these idols which the captive Israelites were, therefore, neither to fear nor to respect [**Baruch 6:** 27-29, 32]

**Babylonian SACRED PROSTITUTES** – these women sat in the streets, burning bran like incense, wearing cords around their waists; those chosen by partners mocked those not chosen; the women's actions can be interpreted as one more example of the spuriousness of false gods as measured in their worshippers' behavior [**Baruch 6:** 42-44]

**Barzillai's DAUGHTERS** – the girls born to Barzillai of Gilead; one (called Agia, or Augia, in 1 Esdras, but not named in the lists of returnees found in Ezra or Nehemiah) married an unnamed man (called Jaddus in 1 Esdras), who was then adopted into Barzillai's family and took his name; on Israel's return from the exile in Babylon, the adopted Barzillai's sons could not be found listed in the ancestral registers, and so were denied priestly status; nothing is known of any of Barzillai's other daughters [**Ezra 2:** 61-63; **Nehemiah 7:** 63-65; **1 Esdras 5:** 38-40 (see also **AGIA**)]

**BASEMACH (also spelled BASHEMATH), daughter of Elon the Hittite** – see **ADAH, daughter of Elon the Hittite**

**BASEMATH (also spelled BASHEMATH), daughter of Ishmael** – a sister of Nebaioth, she became the third wife of Esau; she was the mother of Reuel and the grandmother of Nahath, Zerah, Shammah, and Mizzah; Esau married her when he realized, from their instructions to Jacob, that his parents were distressed by his Canaanite wives; he hoped this marriage to a woman of their kin and a worshipper of the Lord God would please Isaac and Rebekah [**Genesis 36:** 3, 4, 6, 10, 13, 17; called **MAHALATH** in **Genesis 28:** 6-9 (see also **ADAH, daughter of Elon the Hittite; OHOLIBAMAH** and **Hittite and Canaanite women as WIVES)**]

**BASEMATH (also spelled BASMATH or BASEMETH), daughter of King Solomon** – she was the wife of Ahimaaz in Naphtali, one of the twelve administrators of King Solomon (ca. 970-931 BC); each provisioned the King's household for one month of the year [**1 Kings 4: 15**]

**BASEMETH** – alternate spelling; see **BASEMATH, daughter of King Solomon**

**BASHEMATH** – alternate spelling; see **BASEMATH, daughter of Ishmael**; also an alternate spelling for **BASEMACH**; see **ADAH, daughter of Elon the Hittite**

**BASMATH** – alternate spelling; see **BASEMATH, daughter of King Solomon**

**BATHSHEBA, wife of Uriah the Hittite** – she was the daughter of Ammiel (also spelled Eliam); she was impregnated by King David (ca. 1010-970 BC) while Uriah was away at war and, after Uriah's death (ordered by David), she was taken to wife by David; after the death of the child of their adultery, she bore David four sons in Jerusalem, Shimea (also spelled Shammua), Shobab, Nathan and Solomon, to whom David promised the kingship; when Adonijah, David's eldest living son by Haggith, was making a claim in action for the kingship, Bathsheba, warned by the prophet Nathan and following his instructions, reported the matter to the aged King David, who immediately made Solomon his successor; after David's death and Solomon's enthronement, she was approached by Adonijah and asked to request of Solomon the gift of Abishag, David's last concubine, for his bride; she made the request and was refused by Solomon who saw this as Adonijah's attempt at a coup; Solomon had Adonijah killed at once by Benaiah, captain of the Guard [**2 Samuel 11: 2-27; 12: 1-25; 1 Kings 1: 1-31; 2: 13-25; Psalm 51 superscription; Matthew 1: 6**; called **BATHSHUA** in **1 Chronicles 3: 5** where her four sons are listed; see *BATHSHEBA and the Rising of the Spring*]

**BATHSHUA** – see **BATHSHEBA, wife of Uriah the Hittite**

**BATHSHUA, wife of Judah** – this unnamed daughter of the Canaanite Shua is called Bathshua only in Chronicles; she married Judah, Jacob's son by Leah, and bore him three sons, Er, Onan and Shelah; at Bathshua's death, Tamar, widow first of Er and then of Onan, and having been denied Shelah by his fearful father, slept with Judah (who did not recognize her in her disguise) and bore him twins, Perez and Zerah, whom he acknowledged [**Genesis 38:** 1-5, 12-30; **1 Chronicles 2:** 3 (see also **TAMAR, mother of Perez and Zerah**)]

**Belshazzar's QUEEN** – she appeared in the King's throne room where he and his court were praising their own gods and drinking wine from the vessels Nebuchadnezzar had looted from the Temple of the Lord God; all were terrified by the hand writing mysterious words on the wall, and she told Belshazzar to summon Daniel, a reader of dreams and solver of puzzles, whom Nebuchadnezzar had renamed Belteshazzar and made head of the court magicians; Nebuchadnezzar summoned Daniel and Daniel explained the meaning of the words *Mene, Tekel* and *Parsin* [**Daniel 5:** 10-28]

**Belshazzar's WIVES and SINGING WOMEN** – these women joined Belshazzar in praising their own gods and drinking wine from the vessels Nebuchadnezzar had looted from the Temple of the Lord God [**Daniel 5:** 2-3, 23]

**Bel's Seventy Priests' WIVES** – these women, with their children, joined their husbands in slipping into the temple every night and eating all the food offered to their god; Daniel, to prove to the King, Cyrus of Persia (555-529 BC), that Bel was a powerless idol, had the floor sprinkled with ashes and the temple door sealed with the King's seal; given away by their footprints in the ashes, the priests, with their wives and children, were executed by the King the next morning, while Daniel destroyed the idol [**Daniel 14:** 10, 15, 20-22]

**(The) Benjaminites' Four Hundred Young WIVES (also called Jabesh-gilead's DAUGHTERS and Shiloh's DAUGHTERS)** – these four hundred virgins were allotted to the Benjaminites after their punishment for the rape and subsequent death of the concubine of the Levite of Ephraim; the other tribes of Israel, though they felt sorry for the Benjaminites (now reduced to a remnant, cut off from Israel, deprived of Israelite wives because of the oath the Israelites had sworn to the Lord God at Mizpah, and so doomed to extinction as a tribe), dared not openly give their daughters to the Benjaminites for wives; two accounts of the resolution of the difficulty follow; according to the first [vv.6-14], the remaining tribes decided to exterminate everyone but the marriageable virgins of the one group (settled at Jabesh-gilead) that had not come to the Lord God's presence at Mizpah, assisted in the punishment of the Benjaminites nor sworn the oath; the surviving Israelite virgins could then be given to the Benjaminites, saving the tribe from extinction without breaking the oath the rest had sworn to the Lord God; the slaughter was carried out and the four hundred girls were brought to the camp at Shiloh, in the land of Canaan; the Israelites then made peace with the remnant of Benjamin and gave them the virgins for wives, though, says the bridge between the accounts [end of v. 14], there were not enough women for all of them; the second account [vv. 15-23] makes no mention of Jabesh-gilead; in it, the Israelites told the Benjaminites to go to the Lord God's feast held every year at Shiloh, place themselves in ambush in the vineyards, and when the daughters of Shiloh had come out to dance in groups together, to emerge from the vineyards and each seize one as a wife; the Israelites further promised that, should the fathers and brothers of the girls complain, the Israelites would speak for them, asking forgiveness and explaining that their families could not have given the girls to the Benjaminites without breaking their oath to the Lord God; the plan was accomplished as outlined, and the Benjaminites returned to their inheritance with their Israelite brides, rebuilt their towns and settled there again [Judges 21: 6-23; (see also **Ephraimite Levite's CONCUBINE** and **Jabesh-gilead's WIVES and Children**); see *The Ephraimite Levite's CONCUBINE and the Price of Honor*]

**BERENICE, daughter of Ptolemy II Philadelphos** – see **King of the South's DAUGHTER**

**BERNICE (also spelled BERENICE), Herodian family member** – she was the daughter of Herod Agrippa I (37-44 AD; named to kingship by the Roman emperor Caligula, AD 37-41) and the sister of King Agrippa II (AD 48-53) and Drusilla; she became the wife of her uncle, Herod of Chalcis (AD 41-48); with Agrippa II, she heard Paul's testimony before Festus; later she became the mistress of Titus, the Roman general, later Emperor (AD 79-81) [**Acts 25: 13 – 26: 32**]

**Besieged MOTHERS who agreed to eat their sons** – threatened with starvation during the siege King Ben-hadad was maintaining around Samaria, these two mothers agreed with one another to eat their children; they killed and ate the child of the first woman, but the next day the woman whose son had not been eaten hid him; the first mother protested to the King of Israel who, on hearing the story, tore his garments (revealing that he wore sackcloth beneath them) as a sign of his horror; they were not punished for their deed; instead, the King of Israel swore vengeance on Elisha, as representative of the Lord God Who had sent this misery on the country [2 **Kings 6:** 26–33 (see also **WOMEN who eat their own children**)]

***BEULAH** – this was the name, applied to Jerusalem/Zion, personified as female under various guises; the name, meaning "Married," indicated the full restoration of the relationship of the marriage Covenant with the Lord God when her punishment for infidelity would be complete and the exile in Babylon ended* [**Isaiah 62:** 4 (see also ***AZUBAH, SHEMAMAH, HEPHZIBAH, GOMER** and Jerusalem/ Zion/Israel as Covenant **BRIDE RESTORED**)]

**BILHAH** – she was the slave-girl of Laban, given to Rachel at her marriage to Jacob to be her handmaid; at the then-barren Rachel's insistence, she became the mother of two sons by Jacob, Dan and Naphtali; the boys were considered Rachel's sons and so legitimate heirs of their father; Bilhah became the grandmother of Dan's son Hushim, and Naphtali's sons Jahzeel, Guni, Jezer and Shillem; after Rachel's death, Jacob's firstborn son Reuben slept with Bilhah, the incest causing him to lose his birthright to Joseph [**Genesis 29:** 29; **30:** 3-7; **32:** 12, 23-24; **33:** 1-7; **35:** 22, 25; **37:** 2; **46:** 25; **49:** 4; 1 **Chronicles 5:** 1; **7:** 13 (see also **RACHEL, LEAH** and **ZILPAH**); see *RACHEL, LEAH and the Duping of the Bridegroom*)]

**BITHIAH** – she was the daughter of a Pharaoh (not named); she became the wife (perhaps one of two, the other being Jehudijah, the "Judean wife") of Mered, son of Ezrah, a descendant of Judah; she was the mother of Miriam, Shammai, and Ishbah, Eshtemoa's father [1 **Chronicles 4:** 17-19 (see also **HODIAH** and **JEHUDIJAH**)]

**BRIDE at the wedding in Cana** – she is not mentioned, except with her new husband as half the couple, referred to as "they"; she was rescued, with her husband, from the embarrassment of running out of wine at the wedding feast by the intervention of Mary, who told her Son Jesus of their plight; though Jesus considered it none of His business, He changed water into wine because His mother had asked [**John 2:** 1-11]

# C

**Cain's WIFE** – an otherwise unidentified woman, Cain met her during his exile by the Lord God which followed Cain's murder of his brother Abel; she was probably a native of the unidentified land of Nod where Cain settled; she bore Cain a son, Enoch; nothing further is known of her [**Genesis 4:** 17]

**Cainan's DAUGHTERS** – alternate spelling; see **Kenan's DAUGHTERS**

**Canaanite WOMAN and her DAUGHTER** – see **Syro-Phoenician WOMAN and her DAUGHTER**

**Canaanite Woman's DAUGHTER** – see **Syro-Phoenician WOMAN and her DAUGHTER**

**CANDACE** – a title meaning Queen, this was probably not the personal name of this ruler of the Ethiopians; her chief treasurer, an unnamed eunuch, was converted to Christianity and baptized by the deacon Philip upon returning from a pilgrimage to Jerusalem [**Acts 8:** 27]

*Canticle of Canticles' BRIDE* – see *Song of Songs' BRIDE*

**CHLOE** – members of her household reported the development of factions in the church at Corinth (based on adherence to different Christian leaders) to the Apostle Paul; he took the members of the church to task for these divisions and urged them to the reconciliation and unity of belief and practice that befit them as believers in the one Redeemer, Christ [**1 Corinthians 1:** 11]

*Church as CHASTE BRIDE of Christ* – *Paul introduced the analogy in his letter to the Corinthians, telling his converts that he had arranged for them, the Church, to "marry Christ" and to be a chaste virgin given to this One Husband; he developed the analogy in his letter to the Ephesians as he instructed husbands and wives in the proper relationship they should strive to develop in marriage; as Christ was head of His Church, so the husband was to be head of his wife; he must therefore love his wife as Christ loved the Church and sacrificed Himself to make Her holy, cleansing Her with* *the water of Baptism so that She would be glorious and without fault; the husband must cherish his wife as he cherished his own body, feeding and looking after her, as Christ cared for His Church; the wife must regard her husband as she regarded the Lord and must submit to him in everything, as the Church submitted to Christ; Christ and His Church were one Body, as the husband and his wife joined in marriage as one new being; the analogy is a development of the marriage covenant imagery for the relationship between the Lord God and His Chosen People* [2 **Corinthians 11:** 2; **Ephesians 5:** 21-33 (see also *Jerusalem/Zion/Israel as CHOSEN BRIDE of the Covenant, Jerusalem/Zion/Israel as Covenant BRIDE RESTORED, Song of Songs' BRIDE,* and *Revelation's BRIDE of the Lamb*)]*

**Church as MOTHER and WETNURSE** – *following the initial transfer of the Lord God's designation "My People" from Jerusalem and the Israelites to the Church founded by Jesus on the Apostles, the Church was addressed as Mother and instructed to strengthen and instruct her children; the Lord God would provide her with help to accomplish her tasks; she was to care for widows, orphans and the helpless, nourish her children and rejoice that they, for whom she was to be held responsible, would share in the resurrection of the dead; twelve trees loaded with fruit, twelve springs flowing milk and honey and seven mountains growing roses and lilies were to be given to her to delight her children; she was not to lose hope in the face of tribulations for none should prevail against her, His servants, her children, would not perish and the Lord God's grace would not fail* [2 **Esdras 2:** 10-32]

**CLAUDIA** – she was a member of the Christian community at Rome who, with Eubulus, Pudens, Linus and the rest of the brethren, sent her greetings to Timothy through Paul [2 **Timothy 4:** 21]

**CLEOPATRA I** – see **DAUGHTER given in marriage**

**"CLEOPATRA, wife of Ptolemy"** – she was named, with her husband, in the Colophon as reigning when the Greek version of the Book of Esther (based on the Hebrew Bible Book of Esther) was produced; the identity of this pair of rulers is problematic; some scholars favor Cleopatra II and Ptolemy VI Philometor (ruled 180-145 BC); other candidates include Cleopatra V Tryphaenes and Ptolemy XII Auletes (ruled 80-58 BC and 55-47 BC) or Cleopatra VI (?) and Ptolemy XIV (ruled ca. 48bc); a more likely date for the Colophon and so this version of Esther, according to modern scholars, is 114 BC; favored candidates for rulers are, thus, either Cleopatra

III and Ptolemy VIII, Soter II (ruled 117-108 BC) or Ptolemy IX (ruled 116-107 BC), who first ruled with Cleopatra III, his mother, then married Cleopatra IV, divorced her and married Cleopatra Selene, with the last two women named seeming likelier candidates for the Cleopatra of the Colophon [**Esther 10:** 31 (or **Add. Esther 11:**1)]

**CLEOPATRA THEA** – she was the daughter of Ptolemy VI Philometor, ruler of Egypt 180-145 BC, and Cleopatra II, his wife, and the granddaughter of Ptolemy V Epiphanes (205-180 BC) and Cleopatra I; she was given by her father in marriage (150 BC) to Alexander Balas (150-145 BC), who had claimed Seleucid ruler Antiochus IV Epiphanes (175-164/3 BC) as his father and had taken his name to seal the alliance between Egypt and Alexander's Kingdom of the Greeks (newly taken in battle from King Demetrius I Soter, 162-150 BC, who was killed); within five years, Cleopatra Thea was taken from Alexander by her father Ptolemy and given as wife to Demetrius II Nicator, as an inducement to this son of Demetrius I to join Ptolemy in an attack on Alexander which would give Demetrius the kingdom of his father and Ptolemy the kingdom of Alexander; in the event, Ptolemy's army defeated Alexander (who was killed in Arabia, where he sought refuge, by Zabdiel the Arab); Ptolemy died three days later and Demetrius became king, ruling 145-138 BC and 129-125 BC; when the Parthians he was invading (139-138 BC) took Demetrius prisoner, Cleopatra Thea took his younger brother Antiochus VII Sidetes (138-129 BC) as husband, and on his death (129 BC), became Queen in her own right, then acted as regent for Antiochus VIII Grypus (129-121 BC), her son with Antiochus; she was caught plotting Antiochus' death by poison and was condemned to die by drinking the poison meant for him [**1 Maccabees 10:** 50-58; **11:** 1-12 (see also **DAUGHTER given in marriage**)]

**COZBI** – a Midianite, she was the daughter of Zur, a prince and clan chief of Midian; she became the wife of an Israelite, Zimri son of Salu, a leader of one of the patriarchal Houses of Simeon; she was a worshipper of Baal of Peor; when the people of Israel committed themselves by sacrifice and worship to Baal, the Lord God sent a plague on them (which killed twenty-four thousand) and demanded public execution of all the leaders of the people who were responsible for the defection; brought by her husband into his clan in full view of Moses and the whole mourning Israelite community gathered at the Tent of Meeting, Cozbi and her husband were slain with a spear by an outraged Phinehas the priest, son of Eleazer; at their death, the Lord God ended the plague and praised the zeal of Phinehas [**Numbers 25:** 6–18]

# D

**DAMARIS** – woman of Athens, she was converted to Christianity by the Apostle Paul after his speech before the Council of the Areopagus, identifying the "Unknown God" of the Athenians as the God of Israel, and offering the Resurrection of Jesus as proof of his argument; she followed Paul, as did Dionysius the Areopagite and several others; most other listeners ridiculed and rejected Paul [**Acts 17:** 34]

**Dathan's and Abiram's WIVES** – by the power of the Lord God and before the whole community, these women were swallowed up by the earth, with their whole families and all their possessions, because of their husbands' rebellion against Moses [**Numbers 16:** 25-35]

**DAUGHTER given in marriage (also called (A) Woman's DAUGH-TER, Women's DAUGHTER)** – she is identified by scholars as the first Cleopatra; the text indicates she was the daughter of Antiochus III (223-187 BC), second son of Seleucus II and King of the northern Seleucid empire (centered in Antioch), after the death of his elder brother, Seleucus III Ceraunus (227-223 BC); she was given in marriage (197 BC, betrothal; 193 BC, marriage, according to St. Jerome) by Antiochus to the infant King of Egypt, Ptolemy V Epiphanes (203-181 BC), ostensibly to seal the peace treaty Antiochus offered Egypt (to prevent Roman intervention on Egypt's behalf), but really in order that she might manipulate her spouse and destroy his kingdom, an intention which, as the prophet foresaw, did not succeed; she became the mother of Ptolemy VI Philometor (180-145 BC), for whom she served as regent of Egypt, and the grandmother of the Cleopatra who would be given in marriage to Alexander Balas; some scholars believe she was the daughter of Ptolemy V Epiphanes (203-181 BC) and was given in marriage to Antiochus III, Ruler of the Seleucid empire (223-187 BC), as part of the peace treaty, but this seems unlikely [**Daniel 11:** 17-18 (see also **CLEOPATRA THEA**)]

**"DAUGHTER of Abraham"** – see **WOMAN Who Suffered Eighteen Years**

*DAUGHTERS as Corner Stones* – *this image for the women of Israel appears in the prayer portion of Psalm 144; the Psalmist begged God that all Israel, rescued from their enemies, might dwell in prosperity of every kind; the women were pictured here symbolically as pillars, or possibly caryatids, to suggest strength, support of the home and the fullness of beauty and ideals of womanhood for the Israelites* [**Psalm 144:** 12]

**"DAUGHTERS of Jerusalem"** – see **"Jerusalem's DAUGHTERS"**

*DAUGHTERS of Kings* – *seen in Psalm 45 as part of the retinue of the Messianic King, these women gathered around him to do him honor and to celebrate his wedding with Israel, the bride; they were identified in Jewish tradition as the pagan nations converted to the worship and service of the Lord God and following Israel's example; in Christian tradition, they were seen as all the nations of the earth paying honor to Christ the King and Bridegroom of the Church (as of the individual soul) at their Marriage, which would be completed and perfected when the Kingdom of God came in glory after Christ had judged the world at its end; the psalm itself may have begun life as a secular wedding song for Solomon (970-931 BC), Jeroboam II (783-743 BC), or Ahab (874-853 BC), who married a Tyrian princess* [**Psalm 45:** 9 (see also **Revelations' BRIDE of the Lamb, King's DAUGHTER, QUEEN arrayed in gold, Song of Songs' BRIDE, Song of Songs' QUEENS, CONCUBINES, and Other MAIDENS** and **Jerusalem / Zion / Israel as Covenant BRIDE RESTORED**)]

**DAUGHTERS of Men** – these were human women, pictured here as being taken to wife by the "sons of God" who each took "as many as he wanted"; to them the women bore Nephilim, the "giants" and/or "famous men," the "heroes of days gone by"; all scholars agree this is a problematic passage; the "sons of God" were, at first, thought of as fallen angels, but from the fourth century of the Christian era onward, the "sons of God" were identified as the descendants of Seth, Adam's virtuous third son, while the "Daughters of Men" were seen as children of Cain; modern scholarship has identified this passage as a fragment of Hurrian myth which seems to have spread, by way of a Hittite translation, to the Phoenicians and Greeks; all interpreters agree that the licentious conduct reflected in this section was used to set the scene of increasing moral decay which would draw down on the human race the wrath of the Lord God and the Flood He would send to destroy all the wicked [**Genesis 6:** 1-4]

**David's Other CONCUBINES and WIVES** – these were the other women whom King David (ca. 1010-970 BC) married after he came from Hebron to Jerusalem; along with his other wives, they bore him Shammua, Shobab, Nathan, Solomon, Ibhar, Elishua, Nepheg, Japhia, Elishama, Eliada and Eliphelet; no indication is given here of which of all David's woman bore him which of these sons [**2 Samuel 5:** 13-16; **1 Chronicles 3:** 9; **14:** 3]

**David's SERVING GIRLS** – these women were referred to by Michal in her scornful upbraiding of her husband, King David (ca. 1010-970 BC), for dancing before the Ark of the Lord clad as a priest in just a loincloth and displaying himself before his serving girls; in reply, he told Michal that though she might think less of him, he had been dancing before the Lord God, and the very serving girls she had spoken of would honor him for it [**2 Samuel 6:** 20-23 (see also **MICHAL**)]

**David's Ten CONCUBINES** – these ten women were left in Jerusalem to care for the city when King David (ca. 1010-970 BC), with his officers, fled to the wilderness to escape Absalom, who had set himself up as king in Hebron, and to prevent Absalom from putting Jerusalem to the sword; they were taken as concubines by Absalom in a tent pitched, by the advice of Ahithophel, David's renegade counselor, on a housetop, so that all Israel could see that he had incurred David's wrath; the move was intended to strengthen the hearts of Absalom's supporters; the move also fulfilled Nathan's oracle that, for David's adultery with Bathsheba, another man would sleep "in the sight of all Israel" with the wives the Lord God had given him; when David returned in triumph to Jerusalem, these ten were put under guard and provided upkeep by David, but he never again went in to them as wives [**2 Samuel 12:** 8-12; **15:** 16; **16:** 20-23; **19:** 6; **20:** 3]

**DEBORAH, grandmother of Tobit** – she was the wife of Aduel and the mother of Ananiel who was Tobit's father; after the death of Ananiel left Tobit an orphan, she might have raised him; in any case, she taught Tobit proper ways of living which he observed along with the Law of Moses, offering sacrifice in Jerusalem, though the rest of the family and tribe of Naphtali (including his brothers) offered sacrifice to the calf King Jeroboam of Israel (931-910 BC) had raised at Dan [**Tobit 1: 4-8**]

**DEBORAH, judge and prophet** – the wife of Lappidoth, she sat under Deborah's Palm between Ramah and Bethel in the highlands of Ephraim and decided disputes the Israelites brought to her; she gave Barak (the son of Abinoam of Kedesh) the Lord God's command to march with ten thousand men to Mount Tabor, the place to which He would entice Sisera (the army commander of the Canaanite oppressor, Jabin), putting them all in Barak's power; when Barak demanded Deborah's presence, she agreed, but warned him that, in that case, the Lord God would deliver Sisera into the hands of a woman; Barak won the battle, Jael destroyed Sisera, and Deborah, Barak and Jael were celebrated with a hymn [**Judges 4: 4-14; 5: 1-31** (see also **JAEL**); see *DEBORAH and the Cautious Commander* and *JAEL and the Desperate General*]

**DEBORAH, nurse of Rebekah** – she accompanied Rebekah when Rebekah left her father Bethuel's house to marry Isaac; she died near Bethel and was buried under the oak tree which was then named the Oak of Tears [**Genesis 24: 59; 35: 8** (see also **REBEKAH**)]

**DELILAH** – woman of the Philistines, living in the Vale of Sorek, she was the lover of Samson (the son of Manoah and his formerly barren wife), sent by the Lord God to begin to rescue Israel from Philistine power; for eleven hundred silver shekels, she agreed with the Philistine chiefs to discover and betray to them the secret of Samson's strength so they could render Samson helpless and end his depredations among the Philistines; after suffering three of Samson's deceptions, she did some concentrated nagging and learned his nazarite vow was Samson's secret; she sent for the chiefs, lulled Samson to sleep in her lap and had a man cut the seven locks of his hair, stripping him of his strength and putting him in the Philistines' power [**Judges 16: 4-21** (see also **Samson's WIFE**); see *DELILAH and the Deadly Lure* and *Samson's WIFE and the Coils of Betrayal*]

**Devout Jewish WOMEN** – these women were influential members of the upper class of Antioch in Pisidia; when the Apostle Paul and Barnabas were preaching about Jesus and drawing many Jewish listeners and converts to follow Him, these women were successfully used, with some of the city's leading men, to turn the people against Paul and Barnabas and cause them to be expelled from the city [**Acts 13:** 44-50]

**DIANA of the EPHESIANS** – see **ARTEMIS**

**DINAH** – Jacob's daughter by Leah, his first wife; she was raped by Shechem, son of Hamor the Hivite ruler, when she went to visit the women of the town; Shechem fell in love with Dinah and his father agreed to make the match; Jacob accepted the offer, but Jacob's sons were outraged by the dishonoring of their sister; Dinah's brothers used the occasion of the circumcision of all the men of Hamor's city (a condition the sons had set for the marriage) to massacre the male population, enslaving the females; Dinah's story was referred to by Judith in her prayer to the Lord God asking for strength to be His instrument in destroying the Assyrians who threatened to conquer Jerusalem and destroy the Temple, a prayer which was answered [**Genesis 30:** 21; **34:** 1-31;46:15; **Judith 9:** 2-4 (see **JUDITH**); see *DINAH and the Impetuous Brothers*]

**DORCAS** – see **TABITHA**

**Drowned WIVES of Joppa** – violating agreements made by their overlords to allow the Jews to live in peace among them, the citizens of Joppa voted to ask these women, with their husbands and children, to board ships in the harbor; they did so, and the ships were taken out to sea and deliberately sunk; the women, with their families, drowned; their deaths were avenged by Judas Maccabaeus who set fire to the harbor, burned the boats and massacred those who had hidden there [**2 Maccabees 12:** 3-6]

**DRUSILLA** – she was the younger daughter of Herod Agrippa and the sister of Bernice; she left her first husband, Aziz, the King of Emesa, to marry Antoninus Felix (a freedman and a brother of Pallas, a favorite of the Emperor Claudius' wife Agrippina), who was Procurator of Judea (AD 52-59 or 60); she heard at least one of Paul's talks to Felix on the subject of faith in Christ Jesus, righteousness, self-control and the coming judgment [**Acts 24:** 24-26]

*EARTH* – *personified as female, Earth brought forth life and produced everything that came from her, but she herself was created by the Lord God, Who gave her His power, and she returned to Him her fruits, humankind* [**2 Esdras 5:** 41-49; **7:** 54-55, 62; **10:** 9-10, 14]

**Eber's DAUGHTERS** – the girls born to Eber, a fourth generation descendant of Noah and the son of Shelah (also spelled Salah), during the four hundred thirty years Eber lived after the birth (when he was thirty-four years old) of Peleg; nothing more is known of them than this mention in the list of patriarchs after the Flood [**Genesis 11:** 17]

*Ecclesiastes' WOMEN* – *as pictured by the speaker, Qoheleth (the Teacher, or Preacher), these women appear incidentally, illustrating the facets of the Teacher's thought but having neither life nor individual identity; in the voice of Solomon, the speaker mentions women as slaves or singing women together with their male counterparts, as part of the great wealth he had amassed which turned out to be vanity, chasing the wind [2:7, 8; JB]; woman is seen as the origin of each man who, in spite of his efforts, will depart from life as naked as he came from her womb [5: 14; JB]; even a hundred daughters, with a hundred sons, are vanity for a man who must die [6:3; JB]; treated as a universal, woman is seen negatively as leading men into sin which is the essence of folly, and so as more bitter than death, as a snare, "her heart a net, her arms chains," [7: 26; JB] and as captor of the sinner, while the man who eludes her pleases God [7: 26-28; JB]; seen positively, again treated as a universal, woman is seen as a gift of God and the lot in life of the husband who spends his life with the woman he loves [9: 9; JB]; as her ways with a child are a mystery which cannot be comprehended, so is the work of God behind everything [11: 5; JB]; women ceasing to grind at the mill, seeing only dimly through the window because the day is darkening and the sound of their song stilling are used as images for old age and the coming of death, when it will be too late to return to the Lord God [12:3-4; JB]* [**Ecclesiastes 2:** 7, 8; **5:** 14; **6:** 3; **7:** 26-28; **9:** 9; **11:** 5; **12:** 3-4 (see also **WISDOM**, **FOLLY**/the **Adulterous SEDUCTRESS**/the **ALIEN WOMAN**, *Proverbs' WOMEN*, *Sirach's WOMEN* and *Valiant WOMAN*)]

**EDNA** – she was the wife of Raguel and the mother of Sarah who married Tobias; she prepared her daughter for the wedding with Tobias and rejoiced with her husband when he survived the bridal-night [**Tobit 7:** 1-8, 13, 15-20; **8:** 4, 11-12, 19-21; **10:** 12-13; **14:** 13 (see **ANNA, wife of Tobit**, **SARAH, wife of Tobias** and **Raguel's MAIDSERVANTS**); see *SARAH and the Bridal Night Demon*]

**EGLAH** – she was the wife of King David (ca. 1010-970 BC); she bore to David his sixth son, Ithream, at Hebron [**2 Samuel 3: 5; 1 Chronicles 3: 3**]

**Eleazar's DAUGHTERS** – the girls born to the grandson of Merari who was head of the third order of Levites which was established by King David (1010-970 BC) in his old age; Eleazar had no sons, only these daughters who married their kinsmen, the sons of Kish [**1 Chronicles 23: 21-22**]

*Elect LADY* – *with her children, she was the recipient of the Second Letter of John; probably a rhetorical device rather than a person, Elect Lady stands for one of the churches under the jurisdiction of John the Apostle; she was praised for the "life of truth" [2 John v. 4; JB] her children (the members of the church community) had been living; she was not given a new commandment but urged to keep the one given at the beginning, "let us love one another" [2 John v. 5; JB]; she was reminded that "to love is to live according to His commandments" [2 John v. 6; JB], which meant "to live a life of love" [ 2 John v. 6]; she was warned about the deceivers, identified as the Antichrist, who denied that Jesus Christ had come in mortal flesh, and she was instructed to have nothing to do with such theological speculators who try to pass of their inventions as the true doctrine of Christ; she was told she would receive further instruction when John made the visit he proposed* [**Second Letter of John**]

*Elect Lady's SISTER* – *probably a rhetorical device rather than a person, this woman was described as the "chosen one"; she represented the church from which John was writing, perhaps that at Ephesus* [**2 John 1: 13**]

**ELISABETH** – alternate spelling; see **ELIZABETH**

**Elisha's MOTHER** – the wife of Shaphat of Abel Meholah, this unnamed woman bore him a son, Elisha, whom the Lord God designated to be Elijah's successor as prophet to Israel; when Elijah threw his cloak over Elisha (who was plowing in the fields), he asked to go back to kiss his father and mother before he followed the prophet; Elijah's response, "Have I done anything to you?" reminded Elisha that this was the Lord God's summons, and he promptly sacrificed his oxen, burnt the plough to cook them with, gave the meat to his men and followed Elijah, not returning to bid his mother and father farewell [**1 Kings 19: 16, 20-21**]

**ELISHEBA** – she was the daughter of Amminadab and the sister of Nahshon; she became the wife of Aaron, the brother of Moses, and bore Aaron four sons, Nadab, Abihu, Eleazar and Ithamar [**Exodus 6: 23**]

**ELIZABETH (also spelled ELISABETH)** – she was a descendant of Aaron; she became the wife of Zechariah, a member of the Abijah section of the priesthood; she was pleasing to God, but barren and very old; then, she was impregnated by Zechariah, through the intervention of the Lord God; she recognized in her cousin Mary (who had been told of Elizabeth's pregnancy and had come to visit and help her) the Child she was carrying, and called her "the mother of my Lord"; after her son's birth, Elizabeth insisted that the infant was to be named John, as the angel (who predicted his birth) had commanded Zechariah; the neighbors insisted on consulting Zechariah, who confirmed the name choice in writing and thereby regained his speech; working with Zechariah, she presumably instructed John in the nazarite practices the angel had said he was to follow and told him of the destiny the angel had indicated, that he would go before the Messiah *"with the spirit and power of Elijah"* [Luke 1:17; JB] to make Israel fit for the Lord God and bring the nation back to Him [**Luke 1: 5-25; 39-80 (see also MARY, mother of Jesus, Son of God)**; see *ELIZABETH and the Longed-For Child* and *MARY and the Mothering of God*]

**Enoch's DAUGHTERS** – the girls born to Enoch, the son of Jared and a sixth generation descendant of Adam, during the three hundred years Enoch lived after the birth (when he was sixty-five years old) of Methuselah; of Enoch, it is twice noted that he walked with God; instead of the formula "and then he died," Enoch's entry reads, *"Then he vanished because God took him"* [Genesis 5: 24]; of his daughters nothing more is known than this mention in the list of Adam's descendants before the Flood [**Genesis 5: 22**]

**Enos' DAUGHTERS** – alternate spelling; see **Enosh's DAUGHTERS**

**Enosh's (also spelled Enos') DAUGHTERS** – the girls born to Enosh, the son of Seth and Adam's grandson, during the eight hundred fifteen years that Enosh lived after the birth (when he was ninety years old) of Kenan (also spelled Cainan); nothing more is known of them than this mention in the list of Adam's descendants before the Flood [**Genesis 5: 10**]

**EPHAH** – one of Hezron's son Caleb's two concubines, Ephah bore him three sons, Haran, Moza and Gazez, who, through their father, were descendants of Judah through Perez; she was the grandmother of Haran's son, Gazez [**1 Chronicles 2: 46** (see also **MAACAH, concubine of Caleb**)]

**(The) Ephraimite Levite's CONCUBINE** – she was a woman from Bethlehem of Judah, taken as concubine (secondary wife) by a Levite living in the highlands of Ephraim; in a fit of anger, she returned to her father's house in Bethlehem; her husband, following her to reason with her and bring her back to his home, was welcomed by her father; after her father had given her husband five days of warm hospitality, she left with her husband, his servant and their two donkeys; she traveled with them to the Israelite town of Gibeah, in the land of Benjamin, where they were first refused hospitality, though they had their own provisions, then were taken in by an old man; when the townsmen demanded the Ephraimite from his host, that they might abuse him, and refused the host's offer of his own virgin daughter in place of his guest, she was brought out to the mob by her husband and turned over to them for their pleasure; she suffered numerous, successive rapes all night long and returned to their host's house at daybreak, dying with her hands clutching the threshold; she was found at full day when the Ephraimite stepped out the door to continue his journey; her body was cut into twelve pieces by her husband, who sent the pieces throughout the land of Israel, asking them to take vengeance against the Benjaminites; to avenge her mistreatment and death, Israel gathered an army, marched against Benjamin and, on the third day of battle, with the aid of the Lord God, defeated Benjamin, killed all the males (except for six hundred who escaped into the wilderness to the Rock of Rimmon), set fire to all the towns they came to in Benjamin, and swore an oath at Mizpah that not one of them would give a daughter in marriage to the tribe of Benjamin [**Judges 19: 1-30; 20: 1-48; 21: 1** (see also **Old Man of Gibeah's VIRGIN DAUGHTER, (The) Benjaminites' Four Hundred YOUNG WIVES** and **Jabesh-gilead's WIVES and Children**); see *The Ephraimite Levite's CONCUBINE and the Price of Honor*]

**Ephraim's WIFE** – when her sons launched a cattle-raid on the men of Gath and were all killed, she bore Ephraim (Joseph's son by his Egyptian wife, Asenath) another son whom she called Beriah, because, she said, *"in my house one is in misfortune"* [1 Chronicles 7: 23; JB]; she also bore him a daughter, Sheerah [**1 Chronicles 7:** 20-23 (see also **SHEERAH** and **ASENATH**)]

**EPHRATAH (also spelled EPHRATHAH)** – see **EPHRATH, mother of Hur**

**EPHRATH, mother of Hur** – the wife of Caleb, Hezron's son, she was a descendant of Judah through Perez; she bore a son, Hur, and became the grandmother of Hur's son Uri, who fathered Bezalel; she was called **EPHRATHAH (also spelled EPHRATAH)** in 1 Chronicles 2: 50; 4: 4, where her grandsons, Hur's sons, are listed as Shobal, father of Kiriath-jearim, Salma, father of Bethlehem and Hareph, father of Beth gader; the name **EPHRATHAH** or, more commonly, **EPHRATH**, became an alternate name for the district containing Bethlehem [**1 Chronicles 2:** 19, 50; **4:** 4; **Psalm 132:** 6; **Genesis 35:** 16, 19; **48:** 7]

**EPHRATHAH (also called ABIAH or ABIJAH), daughter of Machir** – she was the sister of Gilead; she became the second wife of Hezron, a descendant of Judah through Perez; she bore the sixty-year-old Hezron a son, Segub; she became the grandmother of Jair; after Hezron's death, she was taken in marriage by Hezron's son Caleb, to whom she bore Ashur, father of Tekoa [**1 Chronicles 2:** 21-24]

**EPHRATHAH (also spelled EPHRATAH), mother of Hur** – see **EPHRATH, mother of Hur**

**ESTHER (in Hebrew, HADASSAH)** – the name Hadassah is used only once [Esther 2: 7] and is translated immediately as Esther; she was the daughter of Abihail, whose nephew, Mordecai, was an official in the court of King Xerxes (probably Xerxes I, the Great (486-465 BC), called Ahasuerus in Hebrew and Artaxerxes in Greek); on her parents' death, Esther was adopted by Mordecai and raised as his own daughter; she was chosen for the royal harem after the banishment of Queen Vashti, and she became the favorite; Esther passed on Mordecai's report to her of an attempted assassination of the King, thus saving his life; when Haman determined to exterminate the Jews, Mordecai told Esther who, with the Lord God's help, foiled the plot, saved the Jewish people and accomplished the death of Haman, their enemy [**Book of Esther** (see also **Esther's MOTHER,**

Esther's **MAIDSERVANTS, VASHTI, ZERESH**); see *Esther and the Balance of Power*]

Esther's **MAIDSERVANTS** – the seven young women chosen by Hegai, who was in charge of the harem, and given to Esther to wait on her alone; they joined her in the three days' fast with which she preceded her attempt to visit her husband, the King, without his summons; two of them accompanied her to the King's throne room, one supporting Esther and one carrying her train [**Esther 2:** 9; **4:** 4, 16; **5:** 1a, b (see also **ESTHER**); see *ESTHER and the Balance of Power*]

Esther's **MOTHER** – her death, together with her husband's, occasioned the adoption and raising of their only child, Esther, or Hadassah, by her husband's nephew, Mordecai, a devout Jew living in Susa with the captives taken from Jerusalem by King Nebuchadnezzar of Babylon (604–562 BC) [**Esther 2:** 7 (see also **ESTHER**)]

**EUNICE** – she was the mother of Timothy, a protégé of the Apostle Paul; probably she was the daughter of Lois; she was converted from Judaism to Christianity, and she brought up her son as a Christian, though his father was Greek and was not converted; she lived in Lystra [**Acts 16:** 1; **2 Timothy 1:** 5 (see also **LOIS**)]

**EUODIAS or EUODIA** – alternate spelling; see **EVODIA**

**EVE** – she was the first woman, given as wife to Adam and created from his rib; she was the mother of Cain, Abel and later Seth; she became the mother of all the living; she chose to believe the serpent and, with Adam, to disobey the Lord God by eating the fruit of the Tree of the Knowledge of Good and Evil, thereby bringing death to them and all our race, among other consequences; her creation for marriage to Adam is referred to by Tobias in his prayer with Sarah for safety in their own marriage; she is seen in Sirach, though not named, as the source of sin in the world and as the final destiny of all people who return to the mother of the living after their life on earth; there is an indirect allusion to Eve in 4 Maccabees in the speech of the woman defending her purity by declaring that she had not been seduced by the serpent; she was used in the New Testament as a warning symbol, for the ease with which evil can seduce the unwary [**Genesis 1:** 26-31; **2:**18,

21-25; **3:** 1-14, 20; **4:**1-2, 25-26; **5:** 1-2; **Tobit 8:** 6; **Sirach 25:** 24; **40:** 1; **4 Maccabees 18:** 7; **2 Corinthians 11:** 3; **1 Timothy 2:** 13-14; see *Eve and the Charms of the Plausible Stranger* and *EVE and the First Fruits*]

**EVODIA (also spelled EUODIAS or EUODIA)** – she was a member of the Christian community at Philippi; with Syntyche, she was a helper of the Apostle Paul in his defense of the Good News; Paul urged her to be reconciled with Syntyche in the Lord [**Philippians 4:** 2-3 (see also **SYNTYCHE**)]

**Ezekiel's USED WOMEN** – the women who were defiled by men who broke the Law with them, betraying the Lord God and His Covenant; among other offenses, the men are castigated by the prophet for their treatment of these women, namely, for seducing their neighbors' wives, sleeping with women having their menstrual periods, using their daughters-in-law and sisters to satisfy their lusts, thus bringing the Lord God's wrath on Israel [**Ezekiel 18:** 6, 11, 15; **22:** 10-11; **23:** 26]

**Ezekiel's WIFE** – she was married to Buzi's son Ezekiel, the priest and prophet of the Lord God whose ministry (593-571 BC) covered the latter part of the Babylonian captivity, including the siege of Jerusalem, the successive deportations of King, nobility and skilled people, and the destruction of the Temple; she was the delight of her husband's eyes; the Lord God told the prophet of her death in advance, instructing him in his behavior in response to his loss, so that the whole event became a prophetic action, showing the House of Israel the coming destruction of His Temple and their own [**Ezekiel 24:** 16-27]

# F

**False PROPHETESSES (also called WOMEN who sew pillows to armholes)** – according to the indictment by the Lord God, uttered here through Ezekiel, these women encouraged the wicked to go on in their wickedness and discouraged the just from continuing to please the Lord God; they made up their "prophecies" in their own imaginations, dishonoring the Lord God and ensnaring the Lord God's people with lies; they caused the death of the just and the rescue of the unjust; for their own benefit, they tricked the people, chaining them with the *"frills"* [Ezekiel 13: 18; JB] (unidentified) around their wrists and using their "veils" (unidentified) to blind and trap them; these women distressed the just by telling them lies and supported the wicked in their refusal to change their lives (and so be saved); thus, they falsified the word of the Lord God, damaged His people and betrayed their own calling as prophets; as a result, the Lord God declared they would have no more lying visions and would make no more false prophecies; He would rescue His people from their power and they would learn that He was the Lord God [**Ezekiel 13:** 17-23]

*Five Wise and Five Foolish VIRGINS – these women appear in Jesus' parable to illustrate the truth that just belonging to Jesus' party is not enough to guarantee entrance to the Heavenly Feast of life after death, and to make the point unifying this group of stories, that the coming of the Lord, either at the end of the world or at one's own death, happens without prior warning; all ten virgins were gathered in the right place and had their lamps lighted, but only the wise five (who had made the additional preparation of bringing extra oil for their lamps, in case the Bridegroom – Jesus – was delayed and their lamps went out) were ready to go in with Him to the feast when, at last, He arrived; the foolish got locked out, for when the wedding party went in to the feast, they were trying to buy lamp oil, and by the time they got back, the doors were locked and the Bridegroom denied them entry, saying, "I do not know you!" a chilling response without possibility of appeal* [**Matthew 25:** 1-13]

*FOLLY/the Adulterous SEDUCTRESS/the ALIEN WOMAN – passages in Proverbs describing her serve as both a warning against adultery and a warning against betrayal of the Covenant with the Lord God by worshipping false gods and taking part in their sometimes sexual rites; Folly is the adulterous seductress who has forgotten the covenant of God, left Him, her first husband, and become the "alien woman" [2: 16-17; JB]; her ways lead to death, and those who follow her will never regain the paths of life [2: 18-19; JB]; she seeks to draw away from God men whom Wisdom, her opposite and enemy, will protect, if they so choose [2: 10-16; JB]; those who follow her apparent sweetness will experience bitterness and death [5: 1-6; JB]; even approaching her will endanger a man, causing him to desert Wisdom and her disciplines and leaving him in public misery [5: 7-14; JB]; leaving the wife of one's youth to fondle her will destroy one, because the Lord God sees him [5: 20-23; JB]; if the beauty of the "alien woman" captivates one, she will take the whole of his life, not just the wage of a harlot, and he will gain only disgrace and be the subject of her husband's revenge [6: 23-35; JB]; active in pursuit of everyone she can ensnare, she* catches the young man who has not laid hold of Wisdom and destroys his life [7: 5-27; JB]; she is identified as Dame Folly, the opposite of Wisdom, who makes the same invitation to all who pass by, but with opposite effect on those whom she seduces [9: 13-18; JB]; where Wisdom builds herself a house, Folly tears hers down with her own hands [14: 1; JB]; she is seen as a deep pit into which fall those the Lord God detests; in Wisdom, a foolish wife, along with depraved children and an accursed posterity, is seen as a punishment to be suffered by those who scorn wisdom and its discipline; the wisdom of purity and fidelity in marriage make even barrenness a blessing, while adultery never brings a profit; in 2 Esdras, Wisdom/Righteousness is pictured abhorring Folly/Iniquity as the righteous woman abhors the prostitute (an undeveloped image) when she dresses up, and will accuse her to God when He comes [**Proverbs 2:** 10-19; **5:** 1-14; 20-23; **6:** 23-35; **7:** 5-27; **9:** 13-18; **14:** 1; **Wisdom 3:** 12, 13; **2 Esdras 16:** 49-52 (see also *WISDOM, VALIANT WOMAN, Proverbs' WOMEN, Sirach's WOMEN* and *Ecclesiastes' WOMEN*)]

**Foreign WIVES** – the non-Israelite women whom many Israelites, priests, Levites and laity brought with them on their return from the Babylonian Exile; such marriages were forbidden in Deuteronomy because pagan wives tended to bring idolatry with them into the marriage and family; Ezra, with some of the leaders of the returned exiles, believed their presence jeopardized the entire restoration of Israel, because it was a defiance of the Lord God; after a day of formal mourning, Ezra confessed the sin of the exiles publicly, prostrate and weeping before the Temple, at the evening sacrifice; Shecaniah, a descendant of Elam, responded for the people, confessing their betrayal, and swore to the Lord God that they would put away their foreign wives and any children they had borne; the vow was kept; there is no record of what happened to these women or to their children [**Ezra 9:** 1-15; **10:** 1-44]

# G

**Gideon's CONCUBINE** – sometimes referred to as Abimelech's concubine mother, she was a woman who lived in Shechem; she bore to Gideon (also called Jerubbaal) a son whom he named Abimelech; Abimelech succeeded Gideon by gaining the support of his mother's family and exterminating sixty-nine of Gideon's seventy sons; Jotham, the youngest son, alone escaping, cursed both Abimelech and the men of Shechem and went into hiding [**Judges 8:** 31; **9:** 1-21 (see also **Gideon's WIVES**)]

**Gideon's WIVES** – an unspecified number of women whom Gideon (also called Jerubbaal) took to wife, these women bore him seventy sons, none of whom succeeded him as leader in Israel, for sixty-nine of them (Jotham, the youngest, escaping) were killed by Abimelech, Gideon's son by his concubine from Shechem, with the support of his mother's family [**Judges 8: 30; 9: 1-21** (see also **Gideon's CONCUBINE**)]

**Gilead's WIFE** – she bore legitimate sons to Gilead (considered by many modern scholars to refer to the geographical area; the name can also refer to a single person) who, when they grew up, exiled Jephthah, Gilead's son by a harlot and later one of the upright Judges of Israel [**Judges 11: 2**]

**GOMER** – daughter of Diblaim, she became a prostitute; Hosea married her and had children with her, as the Lord God had commanded him to do; Gomer was to be a symbol of the faithlessness of Israel to the Covenant; she became the mother of two sons and one daughter, each named by the Lord God to indicate the consequences of Israel's continued infidelity and rejection of Him, and each renamed to indicate His mercy when Israel should repent; she left Hosea for another lover; sent by the Lord God, Hosea, who continued to love her, bought her back and restored her to her position as his wife, symbolizing the Lord God's treatment of Israel, should Israel repent and return wholeheartedly to Him in fidelity to their Covenant [**Hosea 1: 2-9; 2: 21-25 3: 1-5; 2: 1-3** (see also **AZUBAH, BEULAH, HEPHZIBAH, SHEMAMAH, LO-RUHAMAH, RUHAMAH,** *House of ISRAEL, House of JUDAH, Jerusalem/Zion/Israel* as Covenant **BRIDE-TURNED-WHORE** and **Jerusalem/Zion/Israel** as Covenant **BRIDE RESTORED**)]

# H

**Hadad's WIFE** – see **Tahpenes' SISTER**

**HADASSAH** – Hebrew form of a Greek name; see **ESTHER**

**HAGAR (also spelled Agar)** – she was the Egyptian maidservant of Sarah, the then-barren wife of Abraham; at Sarah's insistence, Hagar conceived, by Abraham, a son whom an angel named Ishmael; driven out of Abraham's encampment at Sarah's insistence, Hagar settled with Ishmael in the wilderness of Paran and there chose him an Egyptian wife; descendants of Ishmael's twelve sons are sometimes called the sons of Hagar, and are seen in Psalm 83 as enemies of God plotting the overthrow of His people, Israel, and, in Baruch, as searchers for worldly wisdom and so unable to attain true Wisdom; allegorically in New Testament writings, Hagar stands for "enslavement" to the Law of the Old Covenant [**Genesis 16:** 1-16; **21:** 9-21; **25:** 12-16; **Psalm 83:** 6; **Baruch 3:** 23; **Galatians 4:** 21-31 (see also **Abraham's CONCUBINES** and **SARAH, wife of Abraham**); see *HAGAR and the Impatient Wife* and *SARAH and the End of Patience*]

**HAGGITH** – she was the wife of King David (ca.1010-970 BC) and bore him a son, Adonijah, in Hebron [**2 Samuel 3:** 4; **1 Kings 1:** 5, 11; **2:** 13; **1 Chronicles 3:** 2]

**HAMITAL** – see **HAMUTAL**

**HAMMOLECHETH (also spelled HAMMOLEKETH; alternate forms MALCHATH and MOLECHETH)** – she was the daughter of Manasseh's son, Machir, and the sister of Gilead; she became the mother of Ishod, Abiezer and Mahlah [**1 Chronicles 7:** 18]

**HAMMOLEKETH** – alternate spelling; see **HAMMOLECHETH**

**HAMUTAL, also called HAMITAL** – she was the daughter of Jeremiah from Libnah; she became the wife of King Josiah of Judah (640-609 BC); she was the mother of Jehoahaz who succeeded Josiah as King, ruled three months (609 BC), displeased the Lord God and was imprisoned by Pharaoh Neco, who replaced him with Jehoiahkim (609-598 BC); she was also the mother of Mattaniah, another of Josiah's sons (renamed Zedekiah by Pharaoh Neco), who succeeded Jehoiakim's son, Jehoiachin, after a reign of three months (598 BC), ruled eleven years (598-587 BC), and displeased the Lord God [**2 Kings 23:** 31; called **HAMITAL** in **2 Kings 24:** 18; **Jeremiah 13:** 18; **52:** 1; mentioned by allegory in **Ezekiel 19**]

**HANNAH** – she was the favored one of the two wives of Elkanah of Ramah, son of Jeroham, a Zuphite from the highlands of Ephraim; she was taunted for childlessness by Peninnah, the other wife, who had children;

she prayed in misery to the Lord God and promised that if He gave her a son she would give him to the Lord God's service for all his life, and that his hair would never be cut, a sign of his dedication; she was charged with drunkenness by Eli the priest who misread her silent praying, but he prayed with her when she explained; on her return home, she conceived of Elkanah and bore Samuel; she brought Samuel to the Temple when he was weaned and gave him to Eli for the Lord God's service; she brought a new tunic for Samuel each year when they came to offer sacrifice; she bore three more sons and two daughters, the Lord God's answer to Eli's yearly prayer that she would be given children to replace the one she had given to His service [**1 Samuel 1:** 2-28; **2:** 1-21 (see also **PENINNAH** and **Hannah's DAUGHTERS**); see *HANNAH and the Excellent Bargain*]

**Hannah's DAUGHTERS** – the two girls born to Elkanah by Hannah, his favorite wife, when her barrenness had been removed by the Lord God; the girls and three boys were born to Hannah in response to the prayer of Eli the priest, who asked the Lord God to give her children to be heirs to Elkanah; these were to replace his first son by Hannah, Samuel, who had been given to the Lord God to serve him, and who now lived at the shrine in Shiloh with Eli [**1 Samuel 2:** 19-21 (see also **HANNAH**)]

**HARLOT of Gaza** – see **Samson's HARLOT**

**HASSOPHERETH (also called SOPHERETH)** – the name means "female scribe" and appears listed with those of Solomon's slaves whose sons were among those returning to Jerusalem from Babylonian exile; some scholars suggest that Hassophereth could have been the founder and head of a guild of female scribes, for women scribes are known to have worked in Babylon; the name, however, is the only indication that Hassophereth was a woman [**Ezra 2:** 55; **Nehemiah 7:** 57]

**HAZELELPONI** – alternate spelling; see **HAZZELELPONI**

**HAZZELELPONI (also spelled HAZELELPONI)** – she was the daughter of Hur in Judah's line, and the sister of three brothers, Abi-etam, Jezreel, Ishma and Idbash [**1 Chronicles 4:** 3]

**HELAH** – she was one of two wives of Judah's descendant, Ashur, father of

Tekoa; she became the mother of Zereth, Zohar and Ethnan [**1 Chronicles 4: 5, 7** (see also **NAARAH**)]

**Heman's DAUGHTERS** – the three girls, along with fourteen sons, born to Heman, seer for King David (ca. 1010-970 BC); Heman directed all his children in the singing of the liturgy in the Lord God's Temple as King David instructed; they were accompanied by music on the cymbal, harp and lyre; these are the only women mentioned as having a role in the liturgical celebrations of the Temple under David [**1 Chronicles 25: 4-6**]

**HEPHZIBAH, wife of Hezekiah, King of Judah (716-687 BC)** – she was the mother of Manasseh who came to the throne at twelve, reigned fifty-five years (scholars say 687-642 BC), and displeased the Lord God [**2 Kings 21: 1**]

*HEPHZIBAH* – *this was the name applied to Jerusalem/Zion, personified as female under various guises; the name, meaning "My Delight is in her," indicated the love of the Lord God for His chosen Bride and His eagerness to restore her to the fullness of their Covenant relationship when her punishment for infidelity was complete and the exile in Babylon was ended* [**Isaiah 62:4** *(see also* ***AZUBAH, SHEMAMAH, BEULAH, GOMER*** *and* ***Jerusalem/Zion/Israel as Covenant BRIDE RESTORED***)]

**HERODIAS** – in one identification, she was the wife of Philip, who was the son of Herod the Great (43-4 BC) and a half-brother to Herod Antipas; in another identification, she was the daughter of Herod the Great's son Aristobulus (who was half brother to Philip and Herod Antipas), and so was a niece to Antipas, and wife of Philip, her uncle; she was the mother of a daughter, traditionally named Salome; she went to live (ca. AD 27) with her husband's half-brother, Herod Antipas (4 BC- AD 39), who was rebuked for living with her by John the Baptizer; she hated John and finally, with the aid of Salome, succeeded in having him executed [**Matthew 14: 3-12; Mark 6: 17-28; Luke 3: 19-20** (see also **SALOME, daughter of Herodias**); see ***HERODIAS and the Inconvenient Prophet*** and ***SALOME and the Silken Snare***]

**Herodias' DAUGHTER** – see **SALOME, daughter of Herodias**

**High Priest's HOUSE SERVANTS** – two girls who worked in the establishment of the High Priest Caiaphas; one of them (whom John calls the gatekeeper), saw Peter among those in the courtyard, warming himself by the fire; she identified him as being with Jesus the Galilean; Peter, in his first prophesied denial of Jesus, said aloud that he was not with man, did not know what she was talking about and then moved from the fire to the gateway; at the gateway, the second girl (Luke and John suggest the person is male) announced to the people standing around that Peter was with Jesus the Nazarene; Peter made his second denial of Jesus by saying, with an oath, that he did not know the man; it was not until his third denial, made at the challenge of a man who declared that Peter must be one of Jesus' followers, for his speech betrayed him as a Galilean, and the second crowing of the cock, that Peter realized what he had done in his fear, repented and went forth weeping bitterly [**Matthew 26:** 69-72; **Mark 14:** 66-72; **Luke 22:** 56-62; **John 18:** 15-27]

**Hiram's (Huram-abi's) MOTHER** – she belonged to the tribe of Naphtali (or Dan, according to Chronicles) and was the widow of a Tyrian worker in bronze, a highly skilled, intelligent craftsman, to whom she bore a son, Hiram (also called Huram-abi); her son was sent to Solomon to assist in the building of the Temple of the Lord God and of the rest of the royal buildings and, according to the letter of recommendation the King of Tyre sent with him, was *"skilled in the use of gold, silver, bronze, iron, stone, wood, scarlet, violet, fine linen, crimson, in engraving of all kinds and in the execution of any design suggested to him,"* [2 Chronicles 2: 13; JB], a description he fully lived up to; nothing further is heard of her [**1 Kings 7:** 13-14; **2 Chronicles 2:** 13; **4:** 16]

**Hittite and Canaanite women as WIVES** – Esau chose these women as his first two wives, distressing his parents, Rebekah and Isaac; as a result, Rebekah and Isaac sent Esau's brother, Jacob, to the family of Rebekah's brother, Laban, for a bride; hoping to please his parents, Esau then took a third wife from the family of Abraham's son, Ishmael [**Genesis 26:** 34-35; **27:** 46; **28:** 1, 6-9 (see also **ADAH, daughter of Elon the Hittite; OHOLIBAMAH** and **BASEMATH, Daughter of Ishmael**)]

**Hobab, the Midian Priest's DAUGHTERS** – see **Jethro, the Midian Priest's DAUGHTERS**

**HODESH** – she became the wife of Shaharaim after his dismissal of his first wives, Baara and Hushim; she bore him seven sons, Jobab, Zibia, Mesha, Malcam, Jeuz, Sachia and Mirmah [**1 Chronicles 8:** 8-12; see also **BAARA** and **HUSHIM**]

**HODIAH** – confusion surrounds the name; considered as male, he was the father of unknown sons upon an unnamed wife who was sister to Naham, the father of Keilah the Garmite and Eshtemoa the Maacathite; considered as female, she is sometimes seen as the sister to Naham the father of Keilah the Garmite and Eshtemoa the Maacathite (with unnamed sons), and also as identical with Jehudijah, as "Judean wife" of Mered, (with Bithiah as "Egyptian wife") and so as mother of Jered the father of Gedor, Heber the father of Soco and Jekuthiel the father of Zanoah; infrequently she is seen as female, sister to Naham the father of Keilah, and mother of Shimon the Garmite and Ishi the Maacathite [**1 Chronicles 4:** 17-19 (see also **JEHUDIJAH** and **BITHIAH**)]

**HOGLAH** – **third of the five daughters of Zelophehad** – see **MAHLAH, eldest daughter of Zelophehad**

**Hosea's Priest's WOMEN RELATIVES** – these, modern scholars say, were the mother, daughters and daughters-in-law of an important priest, probably in the northern kingdom; because the priest had led the people into sin, the Lord God would punish his family, destroying his mother, and punishing his daughters and daughters-in-law for their whoring and adultery, though, (some scholars read) not as severely (some scholars say not at all) as He would the men, and particularly the priest, who had led them astray [**Hosea 4:** 5, 13-14]

*House of ISRAEL – this female personification in Jeremiah shows the idol-worshipping Northern Kingdom (Kingdom of Israel), with Samaria as its capital, as a disloyal spouse-turned-whore; seen as betraying the Lord God by following other gods, like a woman betraying her lover, she was divorced by the Lord God; she was sister to the equally disloyal Judah, another female personification; she was now being called home to the Lord God to repent, with a promise that she would be reunited with Judah; in Hosea, the prophet's second and third children are given prophetic names to indicate the Lord God's rejection of the House of Israel and her idolatry, while He promises to save the House of Judah [Jeremiah 3: 1-20; Hosea 1: 3-7 (see LO-RU-*

*HAMAH, RUHAMAH,* **GOMER,** *OHOLAH, Jerusalem/Zion/Israel as Covenant BRIDE-TURNED-WHORE* and *Jerusalem/Zion/Israel as Covenant BRIDE RESTORED)]*

*House of JUDAH* – *this female personification in Jeremiah shows the Southern Kingdom (Kingdom of Judah) with Jerusalem, also called Zion, as its capital, as a faithless sister of the disloyal Israel, another female personification; undeterred by the Lord God's punishment of Israel, she continued worshipping idols; her whoring made her sister Israel's behavior look virtuous; she only pretended repentance, while continuing to follow other gods; now she was being invited to repent and return to the Covenant, worshipping the Lord God alone, and so, to be reunited with Israel; in Hosea, though the Lord God rejects the House of Israel for idolatry, He promises to save the House of Judah to whom He will give His love* **[Jeremiah 3: 1-20; Hosea 1:** 6-7 (see *LO-RUHAMAH, RUHAMAH,* **GOMER,** *JERUSALEM, OHOLIBAH, Jerusalem/Zion/Israel as Covenant BRIDE-TURNED-WHORE* and **Jerusalem/Zion/Israel** *as Covenant BRIDE RESTORED)]*

**HULDAH** – she was the prophetess who lived in the new town in Jerusalem; she was the wife of Shallum who was the son of Tikvah (or Tokhath), and grandson of Harhas, keeper of the wardrobe; she was consulted by King Josiah (640-609 BC) when those repairing the Temple found in it the Book of the Law; she prophesied the destruction of Jerusalem because of the idolatry of Israel, but said that Josiah, because of his recognition of the evil and his repentance, would have the mercy of dying before the punishment took place [**2 Kings 22:** 11-20; **2 Chronicles 34:** 14-28]

**Huram-abi's MOTHER** – see **Hiram's MOTHER**

**HUSHIM** – with Baara, she was the wife of Shaharaim; they were dismissed by their husband after he went into exile on the plains of Moab and married Hodesh; Hushim bore Shaharaim two sons, Abitub and Elpaal; she became the grandmother of Elpaal's sons, Eber, Misham and Shemed [**1 Chronicles 8:** 8-12 (see also **BAARA** and **HODESH**)]

# I

**Ibzan's DAUGHTERS** – the thirty girls born to Ibzan of Bethlehem in Zebulon (near Nazareth), for seven years one of the upright Judges of Israel; they were given in marriage to men outside his clan by their father, who brought in thirty foreign brides for his thirty sons; nothing further is known of them; many modern scholars believe the "sons" refer to political, rather than personal, realities **[Judges 12:** 8-9]

**Ibzan's DAUGHTERS-IN-LAW** – the thirty girls brought in to serve as bride for the thirty sons of Ibzan; nothing further is known of them; many modern scholars believe the "sons" refer to political, rather than personal, realities **[JUDGES 12:** 8-9]

**Ichabod's MOTHER** – she was the pregnant wife of Phinehas, who was the faithless son of Eli, the Priest of the Lord God at Shiloh; Ichabod's elder brother, Ahitub (probably her elder son), would father Ahijah, who would wear the ephod and serve King Saul (ca. 1030-1010 BC) as a contact with the Lord God; when she heard the news that the Ark of God had been captured by the Philistines and that Eli and Phinehas were both dead, she went into labor, bringing forth her second son when she was at the point of death; she named the boy Ichabod (meaning *"Gone is the glory from Israel!"*) [1 Samuel 4: 21; NAB], thinking of her father-in-law, her husband and the captured Ark; she died in bearing Ichabod **[1 Samuel 4:** 19-22; **14:** 3]

**Ichabod's Mother's ATTENDANTS** – the women assisting Phinehas' wife as she labored to give birth to Ichabod; they encouraged her, assuring her she had given birth to a boy; she paid no attention to them [1 **Samuel 4:** 20 (see also **Ichabod's MOTHER**)]

**Isaiah's CARELESS WOMEN at ease** – see **Isaiah's DAUGHTERS of Zion, Idle Women**

**Isaiah's DAUGHTERS of Zion, idle women** – the women of Israel, portrayed satirically here, spent their lives and resources seeking and flaunting external beauty and adornment, ignoring the beauty of spirit that would come from loving the Lord God, and failing to care properly for their families; their conduct served as an emblem of the infidelity of all Israel; in the days to come, when Israel would be turned over to her enemies by the Lord God, the adornments would become chains of slavery; because so many men of Israel would be destroyed in the war, the remaining women would join in groups to share a spouse; when the filth of the women, and of all Israel, had been cleansed, a faithful remnant would remain, and the Lord God would dwell with them; the women were told to repent in the face of the disaster coming to Israel in a little more than a year; the prophet urged them to don sackcloth, and in fear and trembling, mourn the loss of their fields, crops and city; scholars think the warning was issued in 702 BC, before the invasion of Sennacherib, when King Hezekiah (716-687 BC) ruled Judah [**Isaiah 3: 16-26; 4: 1-6; 32: 9-14**]

**Isaiah's TYRE and SIDON** – *these twin cities, female personification, were the centers of Mediterranean commerce (pictured here as whoredom);they were to be destroyed by the Lord God when Jerusalem/Zion/Israel was restored; Sidon was the ravished virgin seeking in vain for a safe place to live;Tyre, after a disappearance of "seventy years," would once again play the whore, courting her customers successfully, thanks to the Lord God's intervention, and her profits would go to buy food and clothing for those who lived in His presence* [**Isaiah 23: 1-18**]

**Isaiah's WIFE** – she was married to Isaiah, son of Amoz and a prophet of the Lord God; Isaiah was born about 765 BC, received his call in 740 BC, the year of the death of King Uzziah of Judah (781-740 BC), and lived and prophesied during the reigns of Uzziah's successors, Jotham (740-736 BC), Ahaz (736-716 BC), and Hezekiah (716-687 BC); Isaiah's wife was called "prophetess," perhaps because of her marriage to Isaiah; she bore him Shear-jashub (a prophetic name meaning "a remnant will return," referring to the conversion-return of some in Jerusalem to the Lord God), and Maher-shalal-hash-baz (another prophetic name meaning *"speedy-spoil-quick-booty,"* [Isaiah 8: 1; JB note] referring to the defeat of Judah's current enemies, the allied kings of Aramaea (capital Damascus) and Israel (capital Samaria); nothing further is known of her [**Isaiah 7: 3; 8: 3-4**]

**Isaiah's WOMEN RULERS** – these women exercising power were seen as a punishment by the Lord God; modern scholarship concludes the word should be "creditors" or "usurers" rather than "women"; those who read "women" see this as a possible allusion to the start of the reign of King Ahaz (736-716 BC) and the ladies of the court [**Isaiah 3: 12**]

**ISCAH** – she was the daughter of Terah's third son, Haran, and so the niece of Abraham and Nahor; she was the sister of Lot and of Milcah who married Nahor after Haran's death [**Genesis 11:** 29]

**ISRAEL** – *this is a shifting female personification of the People Israel; she appears as daughter, bride, whore, queen, mother with children, widow with children living or dead – the whole range of a woman's living experience; the particular identity chosen depends on the writer's message; see all **Jerusalem/Zion/Israel** entries.*

# J

**Jabesh-gilead's DAUGHTERS** – see **(The) Benjaminites' four hundred WIVES**

**Jabesh-gilead's WIVES and Children** – all the married women and all the women who were not virgins, together with all the children, who belonged to the group living at Jabesh-gilead; this settlement had *not* joined the rest of Israel in the punishment of the Benjaminites for their rape, with the subsequent death of the concubine of the Levite from Ephraim, and so were not bound by the avengers' oath; with their menfolk, they were slaughtered by the Israelites, who then took the four hundred maidens remaining to become the wives of the remnant of Benjamin [**Judges 21:** 8-14 (see **(The) Benjaminites' Four Hundred YOUNG WIVES, Old Man of Gibeah's VIRGIN DAUGHTER** and **Ephraimite Levite's CONCUBINE**); see *The Ephraimite Levite's CONCUBINE and the Price of Honor*]

**Jabez' MOTHER** – she appears among the descendents of Ashur, though no direct connection to that family is mentioned for her; she named her son Jabez (pain or distress) *"because I bore him in pain,"* [1 Chronicles 4: 9; NRSV-HC], but Jabez himself prayed that the significance of his name might be changed by the Lord God, saying, *"Oh, that You may truly bless me and extend my boundaries! Help me and make me free of misfortune, without pain!"* [1 Chronicles 4: 10; NAB], and the Lord God answered his prayer [**1 Chronicles 4:** 8-9]

**Jacob's DAUGHTERS and GRANDDAUGHTERS** – the women in Jacob's extended family who went with him when he left Canaan for Egypt;

this is a generic grouping which, with "sons and grandsons" is equivalent, the passage says, to "all his children"; nothing further is known of them [**Genesis 46:** 7, 15]

**Jacob's Sons' WIVES** – these women traveled with Jacob and their husbands and children to Egypt, riding in the wagons which the Pharaoh, at Joseph's request, had sent to convey them; they were not counted among the sixty-six people of Jacob's own blood who went with him into Egypt; nothing further is known of them [**Genesis 46:** 5, 26]

**JAEL** – she was the wife of Heber the Kenite who had cut himself off from the tribe of Kain and the clan of the sons of Hobab, the father-in-law of Moses; she was personally loyal to Israel, though her husband had made peace with Jabin, the Canaanite king who had oppressed Israel for twenty years; when Israel, instructed by the Lord God through Deborah the Judge and led by Barak, attacked and destroyed Jabin's army (ca. 1125 BC), Jael received its fleeing, suppliant commander, Sisera; while Sisera slept, Jael hammered a tent-peg through his temple and into the ground, killing him; she was praised for this deed, which completed the freeing of Israel, at least for the moment, in a hymn sung by Barak and Deborah [**Judges 4:** 12-22; **5:** 6, 24-31 (see also **DEBORAH, judge and prophet, Sisera's MOTHER** and **Sisera's Mother's PRINCESSES**); see *JAEL and the Desperate General* and *DEBORAH and the Cautious Commander*]

**Jairus' DAUGHTER** – she was the twelve year-old child of the head of the synagogue near Capernaum; seriously ill, she died before Jesus arrived at the house with her father who had asked Him to heal her; she was raised from the dead by Jesus in the presence of Peter, James, John, and her parents; she was given back to her parents, alive, by Jesus, who reminded them to give her something to eat and told them not to tell anyone what had happened [**Matthew 9:** 18-26; **Mark 5:** 21-43; **Luke 8:** 40-56 (see also **Jairus' WIFE** and **WOMAN with a Chronic Hemorrhage**)]

**Jairus' WIFE** – with her husband, she received their twelve year-old daughter from the hands of Jesus, Who had raised her back to life after her death from a serious illness; Jesus told them to give their daughter something to eat and warned them not to tell anyone what had happened [**Mark 5:** 40-43; **Luke 8:** 51-56 (see also **Jairus' DAUGHTER**)]

**Jared's DAUGHTERS** – the girls born to Jared, a fifth generation descendant of Adam and the son of Mahalalel (also spelled Mahalaleel) during the eight hundred years Jared lived after the birth (when he was one hundred sixty-two years old) of Enoch; nothing more is known of them than this mention in the list of Adam's descendants before the Flood [**Genesis 5:** 19]

**JECHOLIAH** – she came from Jerusalem; she was the wife of King Amaziah of Judah (796-781 BC); she became the mother of Uzziah (or Azariah) who, after his father's assassination, became King of Judah at sixteen, *"and he reigned for fifty-two years in Jerusalem"*[2 Kings 15: 2; JB], (781-740 BC, nineteen years, modern scholars say); he pleased the Lord God and prospered, until pride caused him to take the role of the priests in the Temple, causing the Lord God to strike him with leprosy; nothing more is heard of Jecoliah [**2 Kings 15:** 2; **2 Chronicles 26:** 3]

**JEDIDAH** – daughter of Adaiah of Bozkath, she became the wife of King Amon of Judah (642-640 BC); she was the mother of King Josiah of Judah, who came to the throne at eight and ruled thirty-one years in Jerusalem (640-609 BC), bringing the people back to the worship of the Lord God as laid down in the Law and pleasing the Lord God all the days of his life [**2 Kings 22:** 1]

**JEHOADDAN** – alternate spelling; see **JEHOADDIN**

**JEHOADDIN** – she came from Jerusalem; she was the wife of King Joash (Jehoash) of Judah (835-796 BC); she became the mother of Amaziah, who succeeded his father as King at twenty-five, *"reigned for twenty-nine years in Jerusalem"* [2 Kings 14: 2; JB], (796-781 BC, fifteen years, modern scholars say), pleased the Lord God, but did not abolish idolatry among the people and lost the Kingdom of Judah to Israel in a war which he started [**2 Kings 14:** 2; called **JEHOADDAN** in **2 Chronicles 24:** 3; **25:** 1]

**Jehohanan's WIFE** – she was the daughter of Berechiah's son, Meshullam, who was the leader of a repair team working under Nehemiah's direction on rebuilding the wall of Jerusalem (455-443 BC), near the Fish Gate, on the return of the Israelites from Babylonian captivity; she married Jehohanan, son of Tobiah the Ammonite official who was bitterly opposed to Nehemiah's work; neither she nor her husband had any effect on Tobiah's hostility

[Nehemiah 3: 4; 6: 18 (see also **Tobiah, the Ammonite Official's WIFE**)]

**JEHOSHABEATH** – alternate spelling; see **JEHOSHEBA**

**Jehoshaphat's Israelite WIFE** – she was a daughter of King Ahab of Israel (874–853 BC); she married King Jehoshaphat of Judah (870–848 BC) to seal an alliance between Judah and Israel; there is no indication which, if any, of Jehoshaphat's seven sons she bore [**2 Chronicles 18:** 1; **21:** 2]

**JEHOSHEBA** – she was the daughter of King Jehoram of Judah (848–841 BC) and the sister of King Ahaziah (841 BC), Athaliah's son; she became the wife of Jehoiada the priest; she rescued Joash (Jehoash), Ahaziah's son, from Athaliah's massacre of the royal family's males and heirs to the throne; Jehosheba hid this sole survivor for six years in the Temple, until he could be proclaimed King of Judah (835–796 BC) and his grandmother deposed and destroyed [**2 Kings 11:** 2–3; **2 Chronicles 22:** 11 (see also **ATHALIAH** and **Joash's NURSE**); see *JEHOSHEBA and the Vanishing King* and *ATHALIAH and the Almost-Perfect Plan*]

**JEHUDIJAH** – this name presents an unresolved tangle; it is not usually a proper name, though it has sometimes been treated so; it has been translated, variously, as "Judean wife" (of Bithiah and Mered's son, Eshtemoa) and "Judean wife" of Mered (where Bithiah is the "Egyptian wife"); in either case, she was the mother of three sons, Jered father of Gedor, Heber father of Soco and Jekuthiel father of Zanoah; sometimes Jehudijah is also considered identical to Hodiah, when Hodiah is considered as female rather than male [**1 Chronicles 4:** 17–19 (see also **HODIAH** and **BITHIAH**)]

**JEMIMA** – alternate spelling; see **JEMIMAH**

**JEMIMAH (also spelled JEMIMA)** – this name, meaning dove or turtle-dove, was given by Job to the first of the three daughters born to him after his trials; the three inherited equally with their seven brothers [**Job 42:** 14–15 (see also **Job's WIFE, KEZIAH** and **KEREN-HAPPUCH**)]

**Jephthah's DAUGHTER** – girl born of an unnamed mother to Jephthah, the formerly-exiled Israelite warrior who was recalled to be military leader of besieged Israelites of Gilead and later served six years as one of the upright Judges of Israel; she came dancing out of the house to the music of timbrels to greet her father on his victorious return from war against the Ammonites; told by her father that she had to be sacrificed because of the unbreakable vow he had made to the Lord God in asking for victory, she agreed without complaint that her father's vow had to be kept; she asked, and was granted, two months' freedom to go to the hills with her companions to mourn her coming death while still a virgin and so childless; she returned at the appointed time and was sacrificed as a holocaust to the Lord God, as Jephthah had vowed; a no-longer existing memorial of her fidelity was kept in Israel by the women, who left home every year to lament the daughter of Jephthah for four days [**Judges 11:** 34-40 (see also **Jephthah's Daughter's COMPANIONS** and **Jephthah's MOTHER**); see *Jephthah's DAUGHTER and the Cost of Victory*]

**Jephthah's Daughter's COMPANIONS** – girls who accompanied Jephthah's daughter on her two-months' retreat in the hills before her father sacrificed her, carrying out the vow to the Lord God which had brought him victory over the Ammonites [**Judges 11:** 37-38 (see also **Jephthah's DAUGHTER** and **Jephthah's MOTHER**); see *Jephthah's DAUGHTER and the Cost of Victory*]

**Jephthah's MOTHER** – she was a harlot who bore Jephthah to Gilead (considered by many modern scholars to refer to the geographical area; the name can also refer to a single person); on her account, Jephthah was exiled from Gilead by his brothers, legitimate sons of Gilead, and established himself as a warrior chief in Tob, later becoming one of the upright Judges of Israel [**Judges 11:** 1-4 (see also **Jephthah's DAUGHTER** and **Jephthah's Daughter's COMPANIONS**)]

**Jeremiah's MOTHER** – she was the wife of Hilkiah, a member of a priestly family living at Anathoth, in Benjaminite territory; she appears as part of her son's lament, declaring his misery that she had borne him *"to be a man of strife and of dissension for all the land"* [Isaiah 15: 10; JB], and to experience the rejection by Israel both of the Lord God's message, and of himself as messenger [**Jeremiah 1:** 1, 5; **15:** 10; **20:** 14, 17, 18]

**JERIOTH** – she is more usually considered, with Azubah, a wife of Caleb,

Hezron's son (a descendant of Judah), and possibly the mother of Caleb's three sons, Jesher, Shobab and Ardon; less frequently, she is seen as a daughter of Azubah and Caleb [**1 Chronicles 2:** 18-19 (see **AZUBAH first wife of Caleb**)]

**Jeroboam's WIFE** – she was married to King Jeroboam of Israel (931-910 BC); Jeroboam ruled the ten tribes which had rejected Rehoboam, the son and heir of King Solomon (970-931 BC), for his harshness; King Rehoboam ruled the remaining two tribes (931-913 BC); she bore Jeroboam a son, Abijah; when their son became ill, she went to Shiloh disguised as a common woman, as Jeroboam had commanded, to visit the Lord God's prophet Ahijah (who had prophesied to Jeroboam his kingship); the blind prophet, instructed by the Lord God, greeted her as Queen, gave her a message for Jeroboam indicating the punishments he had incurred for himself and his household from the Lord God for leading his kingdom, the Lord God's people, into idolatry; then the prophet told her that the boy would die the moment she set foot in the town, but would be mourned by all of Israel and, alone of all Jeroboam's household, would be buried in a tomb, for he had pleased the Lord God; she returned to Tirzah, where all Ahijah had prophesied happened precisely as he had said [**1 Kings 14:** 2-18]

**JERUSA** – alternate spelling; see **JERUSHA**

*JERUSALEM* – *this is a female personification of the capital of the Southern Kingdom (Kingdom of Judah); Micah describes her as the "sin of the House of Judah," and says that since the idolatry of the House of Israel was found also in her, her sons would be driven into exile in Babylon, leaving her to mourn; however, the Lord God would raise her up and she would defeat her captors and give the spoils to honor Him; in Ezekiel, she appears as the middle sister, between Samaria and Sodom; Jerusalem had committed worse crimes of idolatry than either of her sisters; she would be restored with Sodom and Samaria, whom the Lord God would make her daughters, and her shame would comfort them* [**Micah 1:** 5, 9-16; **4:** 9-13; **Ezekiel 16:** 44-63 (see also *OHOLAH, House of JUDAH,* and *OHOLIBAH*)]

**"Jerusalem's DAUGHTERS"** – these women were part of a large crowd of people who followed Jesus on the way to His crucifixion, mourning and lamenting over Him; He addressed them by this title and told them not to weep over Him but for themselves and their own children, for if He Who was innocent had to suffer this, they and their children who were guilty would have to suffer far more [**Luke 23:** 27-31]

*JERUSALEM/ZION – this is a female personification for the whole people of Israel as daughter, bride, whore, queen, mother with children, widow – the whole range of a woman's living experience; for particular identities, see all Jerusalem/Zion/Israel entries; see also ZION.*

*Jerusalem/Zion/Israel as CHOSEN BRIDE of the Covenant – in Ezekiel, the Bride is seen as rejected at birth and exposed to die by her parents, an Amorite father and Hittite mother; the Lord God saw her and willed her to grow; at puberty, she was chosen to be His Bride by the Lord God, Who bound Himself by oath in a Covenant with her, cleansed her, dressed and adorned her, fed her and made her a Queen, now famous for her beauty; in Jeremiah, the Lord God remembered her early affection and fidelity [**Ezekiel 16:** 1- 14; **Jeremiah 2:** 1-4 (see also Church as CHASTE BRIDE of Christ, Revelation's BRIDE of the Lamb, Song of Songs' BRIDE, ISRAEL, ZION and other Jerusalem/Zion/Israel entries)]*

*Jerusalem/Zion/Israel as Covenant BRIDE-TURNED-WHORE – in Ezekiel, the Covenant Bride is seen as having failed to keep Covenant with the Lord God; instead, she used His gifts to her, including her children's lives, to worship idols; she would be repaid by His returning her to the misery from which He had rescued her; in Isaiah, her abandonment of the Lord God for idols left Jerusalem like a shanty in a vineyard, a shed in a melon patch, and her whoredom corrupted the whole of her social fabric; her children, born of adultery, worshipped all the false gods and sacrificed children to them;, while she herself set up shop as a whore, disowned the Lord God, and refused Him a place in her heart; for this He would leave her to the mercy of the idols she had put in His place; Hosea was instructed by the Lord God to marry a whore, an action symbolic of His judgment that the whole of His people Israel had become a whore by breaking Covenant with Him and abandoning Him for idols; His consequent rejection of her, symbolized in the name of Hosea's third child, Lo-Ammi, meaning No-People-of-Mine would be effected by the withdrawal of all His gifts in crop failures; in Jeremiah, she is seen as a harlot for her unrepentant idolatry, driven by lust like a she-camel in heat, a failed bride, a hypocrite in Temple worship and a bold prostitute who would not cry to Him for mercy; though she was the beloved of His heart, she became His enemy; consequently, she (city and country) would be destroyed for her betrayal, her lovers (allies, idols) would desert her; her enemies, an army from the north, would conquer and enslave her, as His punishment [**Ezekiel 16:** 15-58;*

**Isaiah 1:** 8, 21-26; **57:** 3-13; **Hosea 1:** 2, 8, 9; **2:** 4-15; **Jeremiah 2:** 2, 20-25, 32; **3:** 1-5, 6-10, 20; **4:** 30-31; **5:** 7-11; **6:** 2-3, 6-7, 23-26; **11:** 15; **12:** 7; **13:** 20-27; **18:** 13, **30:** 14 (see also *AZUBAH*, **GOMER**, *House of ISRAEL, House of JUDAH, JERUSALEM, LO-RUHAMAH, OHOLAH, OHOLIBAH, SAMARIA, SHEMAMAH, SODOM, ISRAEL, ZION* and other *Jerusalem/Zion/Israel* entries)]

*Jerusalem/Zion/Israel as Forsaken, WIDOWED MOTHER* – *in Lamentations, the failed Covenant Bride, punished by the Lord God through the agency of men, was reduced from Princess to vassal; she spoke her sorrow and acknowledged her guilt; in Isaiah, she is pictured as having drunk the cup of the Lord God's wrath to the dregs, suffering the loss of her children, devastation, famine, and the sword; in Jeremiah, she is seen as Rachel, bewailing her dead children; in Baruch, she mourned because her children had chosen to sin, and so had been taken into captivity (in Babylon); Ezekiel was forewarned by the Lord God of the death of his beloved wife, instructed to show no signs of grief or mourning, and told that his actions would prefigure the response of Israel at the coming destruction of the Temple and the death of the people remaining in Jerusalem; Amos describes her as a virgin who died before marriage; in 1 Maccabees, devastated (by Antiochus IV Epiphanes in 167 AD) and deserted by her surviving children, she had become a place of mourning inhabited by strangers, her sanctuary was despoiled and desecrated (by the worship of Olympian Zeus ordained by Antiochus), her liturgy was made mourning and a mockery, her babies and young men were slaughtered, she herself was stripped of ornament and her freedom became slavery; in the fourth vision of 2 Esdras, the woman, Jerusalem, sent her children away, saying that though she had brought them up in gladness, she had lost them, could do nothing for them and mourned because they had offended the Lord God; she wept for the destruction of her city, her people, the Temple, rites and priesthood by the Romans in 70 AD; no reason was offered by the speaker, Ezra, but he encouraged her to bear her troubles bravely and trust in God that He might restore her* [**Lamentations 1:** 1-2, 7-22; **Isaiah 49:** 21; **51:** 17-20; **Jeremiah 31:** 15; **Baruch 4:** 5-29; **Ezekiel 24:** 15-27; **Amos 5:** 2; **1 Maccabees 1:** 36-40; **2:** 7-11; **3:** 45; **2 Esdras 2:** 2-4; **9:** 38 – **10:** 24 (see also *ISRAEL, ZION* and other *Jerusalem/Zion/Israel* entries)]

*Jerusalem/Zion/Israel as Covenant BRIDE RESTORED* – *the failed Covenant Bride, having repented, would be restored by the Lord God to all her former glory, while her persecutors would suffer as they had made her suffer; in Baruch, she is seen as wearing the crown of God's glory, with all her sons restored and the earth itself giving her safe passage; in Isaiah, the focus is on the suffering that would cleanse her for restoration; she would give birth to a new people, and all who loved her would be suckled and filled at her breasts; peace, like a river, would flow toward her; she would be adorned by all those coming back to her, once her conquerors had left, and kings and queens would support her and aid in her rebuilding, all because the Lord God had not deserted her; the Lord God would take away the curse of her widowhood by becoming her husband Himself; Hosea reports the Lord God's efforts in leading her to repentance and a return to Him, where He would purify her and again make a marriage covenant with her, a process the prophet was instructed to repeat in his own life with Gomer; Jeremiah repeats the Lord God's promise to rebuild her and restore her children, with His invitation to her to return to Him; in Ezekiel, the promised restoration seems to be part of the process of getting her to feel shame for her idolatry, and hence to return fully to Him; in 2 Kings, Isaiah reports the Lord God's words, promising Israel's enemy Assyria destruction; Micah predicted her exile in Babylon but said she would conquer her conquerors and dedicate the plunder to the Lord God; Zephaniah assured her that in the day of the Lord God all evil would be removed from her, and He would dwell in her and would renew her by His love; Zechariah identified the source of her restoration as the coming of the Lord God to dwell in her midst; though victorious, He would come humbly, riding on a donkey, a passage quoted in Matthew and John; in 2 Esdras, the speaker, Ezra, saw the weeping woman disappear and a city being built in her place, interpreted by the angel Uriel as the restoration of Jerusalem/Zion by the Lord God, following her destruction in AD 70 by the Romans* [**Baruch 4:** 30 – **5:** 9; **Isaiah 1:** 26-28; **4:** 4; **49:** 13 – **50:** 3; **51:** 21 – **52:** 10; **54:** 1-17; **66:** 7-13; **Hosea 2:** 8-23; **3:** 1-5; **Jeremiah 30:** 17a; **31:** 4, 16, 21-22; **Ezekiel 16:** 62-63; **2 Kings 19:** 21-28; **Micah 4:** 8-13; **Zephaniah 3:** 11-18; **Zechariah 2:** 14; **9:** 9-12; **2 Esdras 10:** 25-59; **Matthew 21:** 1-11; **John 12:** 12-16; (see also *BEULAH, DAUGHTERS of Kings, King's DAUGHTER, GOMER, HEPHZIBAH, House of ISRAEL, House of JUDAH, SAMARIA, SODOM, QUEEN arrayed in gold, RUHAMAH, Revelation's BRIDE of the Lamb, Church as CHASTE BRIDE of Christ, ISRAEL, ZION* and other *Jerusalem/Zion/Israel* entries)]

**JERUSHA (also spelled JERUSA and JERUSHAH)** – she was the daughter of Zadok; she became the wife of King Uzziah (Azariah), who ruled Judah 781-740 BC and was made a leper for his infidelity; she became the mother of King Jotham (740-736 BC), who served as Uzziah's regent and ruled Judah at his death, pleasing the Lord God [**2 Kings 15:** 33; **2 Chronicles 27:** 1]

**JERUSHAH** – alternate spelling; see **JERUSHA**

**Jesus' SISTER(S)** – the terms "sisters" and "brothers" can refer to female kindred as well as to siblings; with His mother and brothers, these women relatives came seeking to speak to Jesus while He was teaching (in Matthew and Luke, no mention is made of sisters arriving with the family group); in response, Jesus claimed that anyone who did the will of His Father *"is My brother and sister and mother"* [Mark 3: 35; JB]; in His preaching visit to Nazareth, sisters were mentioned (though not in Luke's account) as living in town and known to the Nazarenes who scorned Jesus because they had known Him all their lives and could not see Him as a miracle worker or a spiritual authority [**Mark 3:** 32-35; **6:** 1-6; **Matthew 12:** 46-50; **13:** 56; **Luke 8:** 19-21; **4:** 16-24]

**Jethro (also called Reuel and Hobab), the Midian Priest's DAUGH-TERS** – the seven shepherdesses whom Moses rescued from the male shepherds who had driven them away from the well when they had come to water their father's sheep; their rescue by Moses, who drove off their attackers and watered their sheep, earned him a place in the priest's household and one of his daughters, Zipporah, as his wife [**Exodus 2:** 16-21 (see also **ZIPPORAH**)]

**JEZEBEL, queen of Israel** – she was the daughter of Ethbaal, usurper-king of the Sidonians and priest of Astarte; she married Ahab, King of Israel (874-853 BC), and bore him Ahaziah (ruled 853-852 BC) and Jehoram (ruled 852-841 BC); when Ahab joined her in worshipping Baal, he built a temple to Baal in Samaria, drawing a drought from the Lord God on all the land; Jezebel butchered all the prophets of the Lord God, except for the hundred Obadiah had hidden; she vowed (unsuccessfully) vengeance on the prophet Elijah for his slaughter of the four hundred fifty prophets of Baal on Mt. Carmel after the Lord God had won the trial of strength to which Elijah had challenged them; she had Naboth murdered in Ahab's name to get Naboth's vineyard for Ahab, drawing a curse on Ahab and herself from the Lord God; she survived the repentant Ahab; unrepentant, she died by order of Jehu, chosen by the Lord God to be Israel's new king (841-814 BC), in Jezreel, where dogs ate her flesh, as both Elijah and his successor Elisha had prophesied [**1 Kings 16:** 31; **18:** 4, 13; **19:** 1, 2; **21:** 1-29; **22:** 53-53; **2 Kings 3:** 1-2, 13; **9:** 4-10, 22, 30-37; **10:** 13 (see also

ATHALIAH); see *JEZEBEL and the Stubborn Prophet* and *ATHALIAH and the Almost-Perfect Plan*]

**"JEZEBEL," self-styled prophetess** – this name is symbolic (recalling Israel's faithless queen); it was assigned to this woman by Jesus speaking through John; probably, she was a member of the Nicolaitan sect; she operated in Thyatira, with the encouragement, Jesus charges through John, of the church; among other errors, she had taught Christians to eat food sacrificed to idols, thereby dishonoring the Lord God, and, so far, had refused to repent; if repentance did not follow this warning, she and her followers would be destroyed [**Revelation 2:** 20-24]

**JOANNA** – she was the wife of Herod's steward, Chuza, and a follower of Jesus, listed with women who had been cured by Jesus of evil spirits and ailments; the group traveled with Jesus and the Twelve as they spread the Good News of the Kingdom of God; the women used their own resources to supply the needs of the group; on the third day after His death, Joanna went to Jesus' tomb with Mary Magdalene and Mary the mother of James, bringing spices for a proper burial of His body; on the angels' instructions, she and Mary the mother of James reported the resurrection of Jesus to the Apostles, and reminded them of His prediction of His death and rising; they were not believed; probably, Joanna was among those who stayed with the disciples after the Ascension of Jesus, awaiting the coming of the Spirit [**Matthew 27:** 55-56; **Mark 15:** 40-41; **Luke 8:** 2-3; **23:** 49, 55-56; **24:** 1-11; 22-24; **Acts 1:** 14 (see also **MARY wife of Clopas, MARY MAGDALENE, SUSANNA, SALOME, wife of Zebedee** and **MINISTERING WOMEN** of Jesus and the Apostles); see *MARY and the Questing Heart*]

**Joash (Jehoash)'s NURSE** – she served her charge, Joash, the son of King Ahaziah of Judah (841 BC); she and Joash were successfully hidden by the dead king's sister, Jehosheba, when the dead king's wife, Athaliah, had all the males of the royal family eligible for the kingship killed, took the throne for herself and ruled (841-835 BC); this nurse cared for Joash in hiding, until he took the throne to rule (835-796 BC)[ **2 Kings 11:** 2; **2 Chronicles 22:** 11-12 (see also **ATHALIAH** and **JEHOSHEBA**); see *JEHOSHEBA and the Vanishing King*]

**Job's FIRST DAUGHTERS** – three girls who were born to Job of Uz by his wife, along with seven brothers, before Job was tested by Satan; they used to feast with their seven brothers, traveling from house to house as each brother, in turn, served as host; with their brothers, they returned to Job's house after each series of seven banquets so that they could be purified and Job could offer a holocaust to the Lord God for each of them; they were killed, with their brothers, as they feasted in the home of their eldest brother, when a gale battered the walls and the house fell in on them; their deaths were a part of the first set of calamities Satan brought upon Job, testing his fidelity to the Lord God with His permission [**Job 1:** 2-19 (see also **Job's WIFE**)]

**Job's SERVING MAIDS** – these women joined the rest of Job's household in withdrawing from him during his trial by Satan; they now looked on Job as a foreigner; by Job's own testimony, they had never had their rights infringed by him, nor had any slave [**Job 19:** 15; **31:** 13 (see also **Job's WIFE**)]

**Job's SISTERS** – when the Lord God had restored Job's fortunes and given him double what he had had before (because he had prayed for the friends who had tried, and failed, to comfort him), these women returned, with Job's brothers and friends, to celebrate with him; they gave Job sympathy and comfort; each of the visitors gave Job a silver coin and a gold ring; they were not reproached by Job for their desertion of him [**Job 42:** 11 (see also **Job's WIFE**)]

**Job's WIFE** – she bore to Job of the land of Uz seven sons and three daughters before his trial by Satan; she did not complain at their deaths, nor at the loss of all their wealth; however, when Satan, in the second test, struck Job with malignant ulcers from head to toe, she reproached him as he sat in the ash pit scraping his boils with a piece of broken pottery, for continuing to claim innocence, saying *"Curse God and die!"* [Job 2: 9; JB]; she did not leave him, though Job claimed she could not bear even his breath; she was still loved by Job, who declared that he had never loved any other woman and offered as proof his prayer that if he had, she should be taken from him and given to another man; after his restoration, she bore him seven more sons and three more daughters [**Job 2:** 9; **19:** 17; **31:** 10; **42:** 10-17 (see also **JEMIMAH, KEZIAH** and **KEREN-HAPPUCH, Job's FIRST DAUGHTERS, Job's SERVING MAIDS** and **Job's SISTERS**)]

**JOCHEBED** – she was the daughter of Levi, born to him in Egypt; she was the wife of Amram, her great-nephew; she became the mother of Aaron, Miriam and Moses; she saved Moses from the death the Pharaoh had decreed for all male Israelites by concealing him at home for three months after his birth, then hiding him in a water-proofed basket in the reeds by the river; she nursed the child at the command of Pharaoh's daughter who had rescued him from the reeds and named him Moses; when he was weaned, Jochebed gave him to Pharaoh's daughter, who adopted him and had him educated [**Exodus 2:** 1-10; **6:** 20; **Numbers 26:** 59 (see also **PUAH, Pharaoh's DAUGHTER** and **MIRIAM**); see *MIRIAM and the Younger Brothers*]

**Judah's WIFE** – see **BATHSHUA, wife of Judah**

**JUDITH, daughter of Beeri the Hittite** – see **OHOLIBAMAH**

**JUDITH, widow of Manasseh** – she was the daughter of Merari, a descendant of Simeon; she was living as a widow in Bethulia when the forces of Holofernes, chief general of the armies of "King Nebuchadnezzar," captured the town's water sources; when the people forced King Uzziah of Judah (781-740 BC), to promise to surrender to the Assyrians, she called on the Lord God and went with an attendant to the camp of Holofernes; she deceived Holofernes and cut off his head with his own scimitar; demoralized, the Assyrians fled and were attacked and routed all along their escape route by Israelites; Judith lived out her life in peace; she never remarried, freeing her slave and dying at one hundred five; according to modern scholars, historical liberties have been taken with the details of her story, as the real King Nebuchadnezzar ruled 604-562 BC [**Judith 8:** 1 – **16:** 25 (see also **Judith's MAIDSERVANT, Judith's WOMEN of Israel**); see *JUDITH and the Edge of the Blade*]

**Judith's MAIDSERVANT** – this woman served the widowed Judith as both business agent and body servant; she summoned King Uzziah of Judah (781-740 BC) and the elders of Bethulia to hear Judith's censure and promise; carrying food and wine in a basket, she accompanied Judith as Judith made her way to Holofernes' camp; she stayed with Judith for the three days Judith lived in the camp; she accompanied Judith to the feast on the fourth night; she put Holofernes' severed head into the empty food bag and carried it back to Bethulia, accompanying Judith; she was freed by Judith before the latter's death [**Judith 8:** 10, 33; **10:** 2, 5, 10, 17; **12:** 15, 19; **13:** 3, 9; **16:** 23 (see also **JUDITH** and **Judith's WOMEN of Israel**); see *JUDITH and the Edge of the Blade*]

**Judith's WOMEN of Israel** – following Judith's beheading of Holofernes and saving of Israel, these women gathered to her and formed choirs of dancers; Judith gave them branches and joined them; wearing olive wreaths, singing and dancing, they processed, with Judith in the lead, and met the men, who were armed and garlanded; the two groups joined in hymns [**Judith 15:** 12-13 (see also **JUDITH** and **Judith's MAIDSERVANT**); see *JUDITH and the Edge of the Blade*]

**JULIA** – she was a member of the Roman Christian community to whom the Apostle Paul sent personal greetings at the end of his letter to the community as a whole [**Romans 16:** 15]

**JUNIA** – he or she was one of the Apostle Paul's compatriots and fellow-prisoners to whom Paul sent special greetings, with Andronicus, as an outstanding apostle; usually Junia is assumed to be male, with the name spelled Junias, an irregular form; some modern scholars see this person as female and spell the name Junia [**Romans 16:** 7]

# *K*

**Kenan's (also spelled Cainan's) DAUGHTERS** – the girls born to Kenan, Adam's great-grandson who was the son of Enosh (also spelled Enos), during the eight hundred forty years that Kenan lived after the birth (when he was seventy years old) of Mahalalel (also spelled Mahalaleel); nothing more is known of them than this mention in the list of Adam's descendants before the Flood [**Genesis 5:** 13]

**KEREN-HAPPUCH** – this name, meaning mascara or a cosmetics jar often used for mascara, was given by Job to the third of the three daughters born to him after his trials; the three inherited equally with their seven brothers [**Job 42:** 14-15 (see also **Job's FIRST DAUGHTERS, Job's WIFE, KEZIAH** and **JEMIMAH**)]

**KETURAH** – she was the wife of Abraham, most probably after Sarah's death; she became the mother of Zimram, Jokshan, Medan, Midian, Ishbak and Shuah; she was the grandmother of Jokshan's sons Sheba and Dedan (whose sons fathered the Asshurites, the Letushim and the Leummim), and of Midian's sons Ephah, Epher, Hanoch, Abida and Eldaah; she was also called Abraham's concubine [**Genesis 25:** 1-4; **1 Chronicles 1:** 32-33 (see also **Abraham's CONCUBINES**)]

**KEZIA** – alternate spelling; see **KEZIAH**

**KEZIAH (also spelled KEZIA)** – this name, meaning precious perfume, or cassia, was given by Job to the second of the three daughters born to him after his trials; the three inherited equally with their seven brothers [**Job 42:** 14-15 (see also **Job's FIRST DAUGHTERS, Job's WIFE, JEMIMAH** and **KEREN-HAPPUCH**)]

**King David's MOTHER** – she was the wife of Jesse of Bethlehem and bore him eight sons, of whom King David (ca. 1010-970 BC) was the youngest, and possibly two daughters; with her husband, she was given refuge at Mizpah with the King of Moab at David's request, when he and his followers fled the armed enmity of King Saul (ca. 1030-1010 BC), becoming wandering outlaws; nothing further is heard of her [**1 Samuel 16:** 10-13; **22:** 1-4 (see also **ABIGAIL, daughter of Jesse, NAHASH** and **ZERUIAH**)]

**King Lemuel of Massa's MOTHER** – to her are attributed the instructions which open Proverbs 31; she warned Lemuel against wasting his energy on pleasuring women, and against drinking liquor as a destroyer of kingly duty; she instructed him to give liquor only to the person about to die, or suffering bitterness or grave misfortune, as a way to forget his miseries; she urged him to speak for the powerless and unwanted, to give just judgments and to uphold the rights of the poor and the needy; nothing is known of King Lemuel, nor of his mother, though the meaning of Lemuel, *"acting foolishly"* [Proverbs 31: 1; ANC], suggests a general application may be intended [**Proverbs 31:** 1-9]

**King of the South's DAUGHTER** – she has been identified by scholars as Berenice, daughter of Ptolemy II Philadelphos (285-247 BC), second King of the Hellenistic dynasty in Egypt that began with Ptolemy I Soter (306-285 BC); her father gave her in marriage (ca. 252 BC) to Antiochus II Theos

(261-246 BC), King of the northern Seleucid empire (centered in Antioch), as a symbol and seal of their alliance; she died, with her son by Ptolemy and her attendants, by poison, at the hand of Laodice, wife and half-sister of Antiochus (who had put Laodice aside to marry Berenice); she was avenged by Ptolemy III Euergentes (247-221 BC), who successfully invaded the north, now held by Laodice's son, Seleucus II Callinicus (246-226 BC), bringing much booty back to Egypt [**Daniel 11:** 5-8]

*King's DAUGHTER* – *she was seen in Psalm 45, by Jewish tradition, as the bride, Israel, who would be taken to wife by the Messianic King; in Christian tradition, she was seen as the Bride espoused by God – the Church in general terms, the individual soul in particular terms; in any case, as bride, she was urged to detach herself from every relationship and value except the love of her Spouse if she would please Him, and so be happy; she would be given sons to replace the family she had left behind for His sake; the psalm itself may have begun life as a secular wedding song for Solomon (970-931 BC), Jeroboam II (783-743 BC), or Ahab (874-853 BC), who married a Tyrian princess* [**Psalm 45:**10-17 (see also ***Revelation's BRIDE of the Lamb, DAUGHTERS of Kings, QUEEN arrayed in gold, Song of Songs' BRIDE, Song of Songs' QUEENS, CONCUBINES, and Other MAIDENS*** and ***Jerusalem/Zion/Israel as Covenant BRIDE RESTORED***)]

**King's DAUGHTERS** – presumably these were the daughters of King Zedekiah of Judah (598-587 BC), who was blinded, loaded with chains and taken to Babylon with the remainder of the population of Jerusalem, except for a remnant of humbler people; they were entrusted by King Nebuchadnezzar (604-562 BC) to the care of Ahikam's son Gedaliah, whom the King had appointed his governor for the vanquished towns of Judah; they were captured by Nethaniah's son, Ishmael, when Ishmael assassinated Gedaliah; they were taken, with the remnant of Judah, from Mizpah, then rescued with the remnant by Kareah's son, Johanan; Johanan rallied all the men of Judah, with Ishmael, and drove away the assassin (who with eight men fled to the Ammonites); the women were taken with the remnant to Egypt by Johanan, in spite of contrary orders by the Lord God, transmitted by Jeremiah; they died with almost all of the remnant in Egypt as the Lord God had threatened [**Jeremiah 38:** 22-23; **41:** 1-16; **43:** 1-7 (see also **ASTARTE, WIVES of the Remnant in Judah in Egypt** and **QUEEN of Heaven**)]

# L

*LADY of Nineveh* — *she was either the Queen, or more likely, the statue of the goddess Ishtar, patron of the city; she would be carried off from the city into exile in the destruction of the city* [**Nahum 2:** 8 (see also **NINEVEH** and *Lady of Nineveh's ATTENDANTS*)]

*Lady of Nineveh's ATTENDANTS* — *these women would accompany the Lady into exile; they were either the entourage of the Queen or, more likely, the sacred prostitutes who attended the goddess in her shrine* [**Nahum 2:** 8 (see also **NINEVEH** and *Lady of NINEVEH*)]

**Lamech's DAUGHTERS** — the girls born to Lamech, the son of Methuselah and an eighth generation descendant of Adam, during the five hundred ninety-five years Lamech lived after the birth (when he was one hundred eighty-two years old) of the son he called Noah (because, he said, *"Here is one who will give us, in the midst of our toil and the laboring of our hands, a consolation derived from the ground that the Lord God cursed"* [Genesis 5: 29; JB]); of Noah's sisters, Lamech's daughters, nothing is known beyond this mention in the list of Adam's descendants before the Flood [**Genesis 5:** 29-30]

**LEAH** — she was the daughter of Rebekah's brother, Laban, and the granddaughter of Bethuel, the son of Abraham's brother Nahor and his wife Milcah; she was the sister of Rachel; through a ruse, she became first wife of Jacob; she was the mother of six sons, Reuben, Simeon, Levi, Judah, Issachar and Zebulon, and one daughter, Dinah, of her own body, and of two more sons, Gad and Asher, born to Jacob by her handmaid Zilpah; she was later seen, with Rachel, as the symbol of a fruitful marriage, building up Israel [**Genesis 28:** 2; **29:** 16-35; **30:** 1, 9-21; **31:** 4, 14-16, 27, 29, 31, 41, 43, 50; **32:** 1, 12, 23; **33:** 1-7; **34:** 1; **35:** 23, 26; **46:** 5, 15, 18; **49:** 31; **Ruth 4:** 11; **Hosea 12:** 12 (see also **ZILPAH, RACHEL** and **BILHAH**); see *RACHEL, LEAH and the Duping of the Bridegroom* and *DINAH and the Importunate Brothers*]

*Levi's MOTHER and Father* — *Levi personified the whole tribe of the servants of the Lord God in a blessing pronounced by Moses on his deathbed; in their single-minded loyalty, the Levites even killed their own families when, at Moses' command, they slaughtered all who had worshipped the golden calf; this loyalty is praised by Moses, who says that "Levi" had not made an exception in favor of these, his own relatives, in his zealous fidelity to the Lord God* [**Deuteronomy 33:** 9; see **Exodus 32:** 25-29]

**LILITH** – night hag, demon, succuba with wings; she appears without details or description and only in the prophetic oracle of the destruction of Edom with its transformation into a desert wasteland; in later, non-Biblical Jewish tales, she was seen as the first wife of Adam, who rejected his authority over her and fled; later she was seen as a demon who threatens childbearing women and men sleeping by themselves [**Isaiah 34:** 14]

**LOIS** – she was probably the mother of Timothy's mother, Eunice, and so the grandmother of Timothy who was a helper of the Apostle Paul in his mission to the Gentiles, and then became a Bishop; Lois was converted from Judaism to Christianity [**2 Timothy 1:** 5 (see also **EUNICE**)]

*LO-RUHAMAH – this name, meaning "Unloved" [JB], was given by the Lord God to the second child of Hosea's wife, Gomer, to signify the effect of Israel's infidelity on the relationship of the Lord God with His people; the name was changed by the Lord God to Ruhamah, "Beloved," [JB], to signify the effect Israel's repentance would have on that relationship through the Lord God's mercy* [**Hosea 1:** 6, 8; **2:** 3, 25 (see also *RUHAMAH, GOMER, House of ISRAEL, House of JUDAH* and *Jerusalem/Zion/Israel as Covenant BRIDE-TURNED-WHORE*)]

**Lot's DAUGHTERS** – two girls who were probably born to Lot, son of Haran and grandson of Nahor, after his separation from his uncle Abraham and removal to the fertile Jordan plain where he lived on the outskirts of Sodom; they were virgins, betrothed to local men; they were offered by their father to the men of Sodom as replacements, when these reprobates demanded Lot's two angelic guests for their sport; they were rescued by the angels; with Lot and their mother (but without their fiancés), they fled to Zoar, escaping the Lord God's destruction of Sodom and Gomorrah; left motherless and husbandless, they decided to carry on the family line by getting their father drunk and sleeping with him; they did so; the elder bore a son she named Moab, ancestor of the Moabites; the younger bore a son she named Ben-ammi, ancestor of the Ammonites [**Genesis 19:** 8, 12-26, 30-38 (see also **Lot's WIFE**); see *Lot's DAUGHTERS and the Wasted Life*]

**Lot's WIFE** – this unnamed woman was probably from Sodom or Gomorrah, where Lot had settled after parting from Abraham, his uncle; she bore Lot two daughters; she fled with Lot and her daughters (whose fiancés had refused to leave), warned and protected by the angels of the Lord God; the angels then destroyed these cities at His command; Lot's wife perished because she disobeyed the command of the angels not to stop nor look back in flight; she was turned to a pillar of salt; her death set the stage for her daughters' incest with Lot; she is seen in Wisdom as a monument to unbelief; her act and fate were used by Jesus to warn the disciples that, on the Day of His coming in glory at the end of the world, they were not to stop to pick up possessions nor to turn back for what they had left behind, but rather they were to be alert and prepared ahead of time for His coming [**Genesis 19:** 15-26; **Wisdom 10:** 7; **Luke 17:** 26-32 (see also **Lot's DAUGHTERS**)]

**LYDIA** – this able woman was a merchant of Philippi in Macedonia, dealing in purple goods; she was converted to Christianity by the Apostle Paul; after she and her household had been baptized, she successfully insisted that Paul and his party stay at her house; later, her house was the place where the Christians gathered to receive Paul's final encouragement before leaving the area [**Acts 16:** 11-15, 40 (see also **Philippi's WOMEN gathered for prayer**)]

# M

**MAACAH (also spelled MAACHAH), child of Abraham's brother Nahor** – this man or woman was child of Nahor's concubine Reumah; modern scholarship concludes this is a son [**Genesis 22:** 24]

**MAACAH (also spelled MAACHAH), concubine of Caleb** – she was the mother of Sheber and Tirhanah, and Shaaph who fathered Madmannah, and Sheva who fathered Machbenah and Gibea; through their father, her children were descendants of Judah [**1 Chronicles 2:** 48-49 (see also **EPHAH**)]

**MAACAH (also spelled MAACHAH), mother of Absalom** – she was the daughter of Talmai, king of Geshur; she bore Absalom, the third son of

King David (ca. 1010-970 BC), at Hebron [**2 Samuel 3:** 3; **1 Chronicles 3: 2**]

**MAACAH (also spelled MAACHAH), wife of Benjamin's descendant, Jeiel, the founder of Gibeon** – she was the mother of ten sons, Abdon, Zur, Kish, Baal, Ner, Nadab, Gedor, Ahio, Zecher and Mikloth who fathered Shimeah; through her son Ner, she became an ancestress of King Saul (ca. 1030-1010 BC) [**1 Chronicles 8: 29-31; 9: 35-37**]

**MAACAH (also spelled MAACHAH), wife of Manasseh's firstborn Machir who fathered Gilead** – this woman is first called Machir's sister (v. 15), then his wife (v. 16), an unresolved identification; she was the mother of two sons, Peresh, and Sheresh, and the grandmother of Sheresh's sons, Rakem and Ulam who was Bedan's father [**1 Chronicles 7: 15-16**]

**MAACAH (also spelled MAACHAH), wife of Rehoboam** – this woman is seen variously as daughter of Abishalom [1 Kings], of Absalom [2 Chronicles 11], or of Uriel from Gibeah [2 Chronicles 13], where her name is spelled **MICAIAH** or **MICHAIAH**; she worshipped idols instead of the Lord God; she was the most cherished of the eighteen wives of Solomon's son, King Rehoboam of Judah (931-913 BC); she bore him four sons, Abijah (ruled 913-911 BC), Attai, Ziza and Shelomith; she was the grandmother of Abijah's son, Asa (ruled 911-870 BC), who, unlike his father, his grandmother and his grandfather, stayed faithful to the Lord God; because of her worship of Asherah, Maacah was deprived of her title and position of Queen Mother by her grandson King Asa, who cut down the object she had made for the goddess and burnt it [**1 Kings: 15:** 2, 10, 13; **2 Chronicles 11: 20-22; 15: 16; 2 Chronicles 13: 2** (see also **MAHALATH, daughter of David's son Jerimoth and Eliab's daughter Abihail, Rehoboam's Other WIVES, CONCUBINES and DAUGHTERS, ASHERAH and WEAVERS of Clothes for Asherah**)]

**MAACHAH** – alternate spelling; see **MAACAH**

**Maccabees' MOTHER of seven martyred sons** – this brave woman was arrested with her seven sons by order of Antiochus IV Epiphanes (175-164/163 BC) in his attempts to Hellenize Jerusalem and Israel; they were all commanded to violate the Law of the Lord God by eating pork; she supported her sons in their refusal to obey the king and disobey the Law; she encouraged them as, one by one, they suffered and died, horribly tortured, in her presence; she herself died only after the last of her sons was killed; she served as an example of fidelity held up to all Israelites [**2 Maccabees 7:** 1-42; **4 Maccabees 1:** 8, 10; **8:** 3-4, 20; **10:** 2; **12:** 6-7; **13:** 19; **14:** 11 – **18:** 24]

**Maccabees' supplicant WOMEN** – the women who responded, in two cases, to a threat to the Temple in Jerusalem with prayer, supplication and public signs of mourning; they took to the streets in sackcloth and ashes, leaving their customary seclusion in the urgency of their plea; they were joined by the rest of Israel in prayer; they rejoiced at the punishment of their enemies, Heliodorus (called Apollonius in the 4 Maccabees account), agent of King Seleucus IV Philopator (187-175 BC), who wanted to take the Temple treasury, and King Ptolemy IV Philopator of Egypt (221-205 BC), who wanted to enter its Sanctuary; in the fourth chapter of 3 Maccabees, the women, with their families are gathered up to be deported to Schedia for an execution which the Lord God averts; brides were torn from their bridal celebrations, dragged unveiled in bonds, ashes in their hair, mourning and lamenting, through the streets to the docks and put on board ships as captives [**2 Maccabees 3:** 19-20; **3 Maccabees 1:** 18-20; **4:** 6-7; **4 Maccabees 4:** 1-14]

**Machir's DAUGHTER** – see **EPHRATHAH (also called ABIAH), daughter of Machir**

**Machir's WIFE** – she bore a son, Gilead, for her husband Machir, son of Manasseh; she could have been a Benjaminite, as Machir *"took a wife for Huppim and Shuppim"* [1 Chronicles 7: 15; JB], names which appear in the line of Benjamin; nothing further is known of her; nothing indicates that two wives are involved, as has been suggested [**1 Chronicles 7:** 15; **Numbers 26:** 29]

**MAHALAH** – alternate spelling; see **also MAHLAH, child of HAMMOLECHETH**

**Mahalaleel's DAUGHTERS** – alternate spelling; see **Mahalalel's DAUGHTERS**

**Mahalalel's (also spelled Mahalaleel's) DAUGHTERS** – the girls born to Mahalalel, a fourth generation descendant of Adam and the son of Kenan (also spelled Cainan), during the eight hundred thirty years Mahalalel lived after the birth (when he was sixty-five years old) of Jared; nothing more is known of them than this mention in the list of Adam's descendants before the Flood [**Genesis 5:** 16]

**MAHALATH, daughter of David's son Jerimoth and Eliab's daughter Abihail** – this woman was Jesse's double great-granddaughter, as both David and Eliab were Jesse's sons; she became one of the eighteen wives of King Rehoboam of Judah (931-913 BC), the son of King Solomon (ca. 970-931 BC); she was the mother of Jeush, Shemariah and Zaham [**2 Chronicles 11:** 18-19 (see also **Rehoboam's Other WIVES, CONCUBINES and DAUGHTERS** and **MAACAH, wife of Rehoboam**)]

**MAHALATH, daughter of Ishmael** – see **BASEMATH, daughter of Ishmael**

**Maher-shalal-hash-baz' Mother** – see **Isaiah's WIFE**

**MAHLAH, child of HAMMOLECHETH** – this may be a son or a daughter; name may indicate a female; see **HAMMOLECHETH** [**1 Chronicles 7:** 18]

**MAHLAH, eldest daughter of Zelophehad** – this was the eldest of five sisters (Mahlah, Noah, Hoglah, Milcah and Tirzah); they were the only children of Zelophehad, and the granddaughters of Hepher who was a descendant of Manasseh, Joseph's son by his Egyptian wife Asenath; when the land of Israel was being apportioned, the girls went to the priest Eleazar and to Joshua, the son of Nun, and the leaders, and reminded them that the Lord God had ordered Moses to give them the same inheritance which they would have had if they had been male; the Lord God's order given through Moses was obeyed [**Numbers 26:** 33; **27:** 1-11; **36:** 2-12; **Joshua 17:** 3-6; see *MAHLAH and the Challenged Inheritance*]

**MALCHATH** – see **HAMMOLECHETH**

**Manasseh's Aramaean CONCUBINE** – sometimes called *the Aramitess,* this woman is mentioned only in 1 Chronicles (in a list that, scholars have noted, is not clear), as having borne to Joseph's son Manasseh two sons, Asriel and the Machir who fathered Gilead; the genealogical list in Joshua names Machir as Manasseh's firstborn and includes Asriel among Manasseh's sons, but the corresponding list in Numbers places Asriel among Gilead's descendants, which would make Asriel, with Gilead's son Hepher, this woman's great-grandson rather than her son; further (as indicated in both passages in Numbers and in Joshua), Zelophehad was not her son (as suggested in 1 Chronicles), but the son of Gilead's son, Hepher, and so her great-great-grandson; these confusions have not been resolved [**1 Chronicles 7: 14; Numbers 26:** 29-33; **27:**1; **Joshua 17:** 1-3]

**(The) Man Born Blind's MOTHER** – this woman is mentioned only with her husband as the parents of the man born blind, whom Jesus cured on the Sabbath; the Pharisees, alerted by the man's neighbors, questioned the healed man who told them everything, then sent for his parents in order to disprove the miracle; with her husband, she attested both to the identity of the cured man as her son and to his blindness from birth, but denied knowledge of how he had come to see; the parents feared the Jewish leaders, who had already agreed that anyone acknowledging Jesus as the Messiah would be expelled from the synagogue and so from the whole life of the Israelite community [**John 9:** 2-23]

**Manoah's WIFE** – this woman married Manoah of Zorah, of the tribe of Dan, but she proved barren; she was visited by an angel of the Lord God, who told her she would bear a son; the angel instructed her to abstain from strong drink, wine and ritually unclean food during her pregnancy and, after his birth, not ever to cut the boy's hair, signs of the child's dedication to the Lord God; she was told that the boy had been chosen by the Lord God to start the work of releasing Israel from Philistine domination; Manoah's wife observed all the angel's commands; with Manoah, she objected when Samson desired the daughter of one of the Philistines in Timnah and demanded that they get her for his wife; also with Manoah, she ate of the honey from the carcass of the lion Samson had killed on his way to arrange the marriage; no further mention is made of her [**Judges 13:** 2-25; **14:** 1-9; **16:** 17 (see also **Samson's WIFE**); see *Manoah's WIFE and the Wonder-Son* and *Samson's WIFE and the Coils of Betrayal*]

**MARA** – symbolic name; see **NAOMI**

**MARTHA** – she lived in Bethany with her sister, Mary, and their brother, Lazarus, whom Jesus raised from the dead; she offered hospitality to Jesus when He was near Jerusalem; with Mary, she sent word to Jesus when Lazarus fell sick; when her brother died in Jesus' absence, Martha reproached Him, but declared her faith that He was the Messiah, the Son of God; Martha sent word to Mary, grieving at the house, that Jesus wanted to see her (though He had not said so); she waited on the guests at the banquet given for Lazarus after Jesus raised him from the dead [**Luke 10:** 38-42; **John 11:** 1-44; **12:** 2 (see also **MARY, sister of Martha**); see *MARTHA and the War for Order* and *MARY and the Costly Nard*]

**MARY MAGDALENE** – she was freed from seven devils by the power of Jesus, and joined the women who accompanied the disciples, caring for their needs; scholars believe she was neither the sister of Martha and Lazarus, nor the woman who wept over the feet of Jesus, dried them with her hair and anointed them with precious ointment in the house of Simon the Pharisee; she stood with Mary, the mother of Jesus, at the foot of His cross; she went with Mary, wife of Clopas and Salome and mother of James and John, to the tomb of Jesus, bringing spices; at the tomb, probably later, she failed to recognize the two angels in Jesus' open tomb, and mistook the risen Jesus for a gardener; she asked this "gardener" where he had taken the body of Jesus, saying that she would take it away; she recognized Jesus when He called her by name; at His instruction, she reported to the Apostles that she had seen Him and gave them His message [**Matthew 27:** 55-56, 61; **28:** 1-10; **Mark 15:** 40-41, 47; **16:** 1-11; **Luke 8:** 2-3; **23:** 49, 55-56; **24:** 1-11; **John 19:** 25; **20:** 1-18 (see also **MARY, wife of Clopas, SALOME, wife of Zebedee, JOANNA, SUSANNA, MARY, sister of Martha, Sinful WOMAN who anointed Jesus' feet, MINISTERING WOMEN of Jesus and the Apostles**); see *MARY and the Questing Heart*]

**MARY, mother of Jesus, Son of God** – by tradition, Mary was the daughter of Anna and Joachim; from earliest times, Christians have believed she was conceived free from Original Sin (her Immaculate Conception) because of the coming redemptive death and rising of Jesus, her divine Son; she was a virgin living in Nazareth and betrothed to Joseph, a descendant of David; she was invited through God's angel, Gabriel, to become the mother of God; she gave her consent; she conceived a son of the Holy Spirit, though still a virgin; she retained her virginity during and after the birth of the Child (the Virgin birth prophesied of the Messiah) and, many Christians believe, perpetually; she assisted her aged kinswoman Elizabeth with the birth of Elizabeth's son, John the Baptist; while in Bethlehem, she bore the Son of God; with Joseph, she named Him Jesus, as Gabriel had commanded; she welcomed angel-directed shepherds and later, star-led wise men who came to honor the Child; obeying the angelic warning given to Joseph in a dream, that Herod sought to kill the child, she fled with Joseph and Jesus to Egypt; they remained there until the angel told Joseph Herod was dead, then returned to Nazareth and raised Jesus according to the Law of Moses which she and Joseph observed faithfully; with Joseph, she suffered a three-day loss of the twelve-year-old Jesus in the Temple in Jerusalem; she supported Jesus in His public ministry and prompted His first miracle; she stood at the foot of His cross at His death; she joined the Apostles as they awaited the coming of the Holy Spirit; many Christian churches hold to the tradition that she was taken to heaven, body and soul at her death, a privilege called her Assumption [**Matthew 1**: 16, 18-25; **2**: 10-11; **12**: 46-50; **13**: 53-58; **Mark 3**: 31-35; **6**: 1-6; **Luke 1**: 26-56; **2**: 1-52; **4**: 16-30; **8**: 19-21; **11**: 27-28; **John 2**: 1-12; **6**: 42; **19**: 25-27; **Acts 1**: 14; **Galatians 4**; 4 (see also **ANNA** and **ELIZABETH**); see *MARY and the Mothering of God, MARY and the Sword of Sorrow* and *ELIZABETH and the Longed-for Child*]

**MARY, mother of John Mark** – it was to her house, where a number of the brethren were assembled in prayer, that Peter came upon his angelic release from the dungeon of Herod; her son was a companion of the Apostle Paul and Barnabas, his cousin, on their missionary journey, though he returned to Jerusalem, leaving the mission party at Pamphylia; John Mark is also traditionally identified as the disciple of Peter and author of the second gospel [**Acts 12**: 12, 25; **13**: 5, 13; **Colossians 4**: 10; **1 Peter 5**: 13; see *RHODA and the Knock at the Door*]

**MARY, Roman community member** – she was greeted by name by the Apostle Paul at the end of his letter to the Christian community in Rome; she was praised for her hard work for them [**Romans 16**: 6]

**MARY, sister of Martha** – she lived in Bethany with Martha and their brother Lazarus; she was a devoted listener to Jesus' teachings; she reproached Jesus for His absence when her brother died; in response to her grief, among other things, Jesus raised Lazarus from the tomb in which he had been buried for four days; in John's account of the feast that followed, given some days later in Bethany by an unnamed host, Mary is identified as the woman who anointed the feet of Jesus with costly nard and dried them with her hair; she was defended in this action when Judas Iscariot rebuked her for it; in Matthew and Mark, the banquet was given by Simon the Leper, the nard was poured over Jesus' head, the one pouring it was an unnamed woman, and in rebuking unnamed objecting disciples, Jesus promised that the woman's deed would be told wherever the Gospel was preached; in Luke's account, it is an unnamed sinful woman who pours nard over Jesus' feet, having previously washed them with her tears and dried them with her hair, the feast is given by Simon the Pharisee, and Jesus' rebuke is directed to Simon the Pharisee for scorning the woman because of her sins and not seeing her act as love and repentance; scholars who see in these accounts two, or even three, separate incidents (Matthew/Mark, Luke and John) agree that Mary of Bethany, Mary Magdalene and the sinful woman are three different people [**John 11: 1-20, 28-45; 12: 1-8; Matthew 26: 6-13; Mark 14: 3-9; Luke 10: 38-42** (see also **MARTHA, MARY MAGDALENE, Sinful WOMAN who anointed Jesus' feet**); see *MARY and the Costly Nard, MARTHA and the War for Order* and *The WOMAN and the Shattered Jar*]

**MARY, wife of Clopas** – this woman is commonly identified with the mother of James and Joseph; she is probably not, modern scholars think, the otherwise unnamed sister of Jesus' mother, Mary; she was one of the women who had followed Jesus from Galilee and looked after Him; with these women, she watched the crucifixion and death of Jesus from a distance; she went to Jesus' tomb on the first day of the week with Mary Magdalene and Salome, mother of Zebedee's sons James and John, where they received the news of the resurrection; though frightened, the women went to tell the disciples as the angel ordered; all embraced the feet of the risen Jesus Who met them on their way and repeated the angel's injunction; she was probably among those who stayed with the disciples after the Ascension of Jesus, awaiting the coming of the Spirit [**Matthew 27: 55-56, 61; 28: 1-10 Mark 15: 40-41, 47; 16: 1-8, 12-13; Luke 8: 2-3; 23: 49, 55-56; 24: 1-11; 22-24; John 19: 25; Acts 1: 14** (see also **MARY MAGDALENE, JOANNA, SUSANNA, SALOME, wife of Zebedee** and **MINISTER-**

ING WOMEN of Jesus and the Apostles); see *MARY MAGDALENE and the Questing Heart*]

**MATRED** – this man or woman was the parent of Mehetabel and either came from Mezahab, or was the son of Mezahab; modern scholarship generally concludes Matred was Mehetabel's father [**Genesis 36:** 39; **1 Chronicles 1:** 50]

**MEHETABEL** – she was the daughter of Matred from Mezahab; she became the wife of Hadad of Pau in Edom [**Genesis 36:** 39; **1 Chronicles 1:** 50]

**Menstruous WOMEN bearing monsters** – these women appear among the unnatural signs of the end time which the angel Uriel lists for Ezra in his apocalyptic vision [**2 Esdras 5:** 8]

**MERAB (also spelled MEROB)** – she was the elder daughter of King Saul (ca. 1030-1010 BC) and Ahinoam; she was the sister of Michal; she was promised as wife to David, if he would fight the Philistines, by King Saul (ca. 1030-1070 BC), for Saul hoped David would be killed in the battle; Merab was given instead as wife to Adriel, son of Barzillai, of Meholah; she bore to Adriel five sons (credited to Michal in some versions – incorrectly, scholars agree), who were later, with the two sons of Rizpah, handed over by King David (ca. 1010-970 BC) to the Gibeonites to be sacrificed before the Lord God in reparation for the lives Saul had taken [**1 Samuel 14:** 49; **18:** 17-19; **2 Samuel 21:** 8-9]

**MEROB** – alternate spelling; see **MERAB**

**MESHULLEMETH** – she was the daughter of Haruz of Jotbah and became the wife of King Manasseh of Judah (687-642 BC); she was the mother of King Amon of Judah (642-640 BC), who succeeded his father at twenty-two and ruled for two years; Amon displeased the Lord God by worshipping idols and was assassinated in his palace by his officers [**2 Kings 21:** 19]

**Methuselah's DAUGHTERS** – the girls born to Methuselah, the longest-lived of the patriarchs who lived before the Flood; he was the son of Enoch and a seventh generation descendant of Adam; his daughters were born during the seven hundred eighty-two years Methuselah lived after the birth (when he was one hundred eighty-seven years old) of Lamech; nothing more is known of them than this mention in the list of Adam's descendants before the Flood [**Genesis 5:** 26]

**Micah's MOTHER** – she bore a son, Micayehu (the name means "Who is like the Lord God?"; except for verses 1 and 3a, the name is shortened to Micah), a man of the highlands of Ephraim; having had eleven hundred silver shekels taken from her, she uttered a curse and further, solemnly dedicated the silver to the Lord God to make a carved image and an idol cast of metal, an erroneous form of worship undertaken innocently, it seems; her son returned the shekels confessing that he had taken them; at that she rejoiced and called down a blessing of the Lord God on her son; she took two hundred of the silver shekels to have the promised image made and placed it in a shrine Micah had built for it; nothing further is learned of her, but the image [see Judges 18: 1-31] ended in a sanctuary in the city of Dan [**Judges 17:** 2-13]

**MICAIAH (also spelled MICHAIAH)** – see **MAACAH, wife of Rehoboam**

**MICHAIAH (also spelled MICAIAH)** – see **MAACAH, wife of Rehoboam**

**MICHAL** – she was the daughter of King Saul (ca. 1030-1010 BC) and his wife Ahinoam, Ahimaaz' daughter; she was the younger sister of Merab (Merob) and her brothers, Jonathan, Ishvi and Malchishua; she fell in love with David (who would later succeed her father and rule (ca. 1010-970 BC)); Saul gave her to David as his wife; Michal saved David's life, helping him to escape from their house by letting him down through the window when Saul had ordered him killed in the morning; in David's absence, she was given as wife to Paltiel, son of Laish; after Saul's death, she was returned to David, on his demand, by Ishbaal, Saul's son and would-be successor; Michal despised David as he danced before the Ark of the Lord God and upbraided him for it; she was rendered barren on that account [**1 Samuel 14:** 49; **18:** 20-29; **19:** 10-17; **25:** 44; **2 Samuel 3:** 13-16; **6:** 16-23; **1 Chronicles 15:** 29 (see also **David's SERVING GIRLS**); see *MICHAL and the Dancing King*]

**Midian's WOMEN** – the women captured in the campaign Israel waged against Midian; after all the male warriors had been killed, they were brought with their children and the rest of the spoils to Moses; many of them were executed at Moses' order, for they were the ones who had drawn the sons of Israel to renounce the Lord God at Peor, and so were the cause of the plague which had struck Israel; all of these women who had slept with men and all the male children were killed; the virgins among them, the text says 32,000, were given to the Israelites for wives, except for the thirty-two who were the Lord God's portion and so were given by Moses to Eleazar the priest, as the Lord God had instructed [**Numbers 31:** 9-18, 35, 40-41]

**MILCAH, fourth of the five daughters of Zelophehad** – see **MAHLAH, eldest daughter of Zelophehad**

**MILCAH, wife of Abraham's brother Nahor** – she was the daughter of Haran and the sister of Iscah; she became the mother of eight sons, Uz, Buz, Kemuel (Aram's father), Chesed, Hazo, Pildash, Jidlaph and Bethuel (the father of Rebekah and Laban) [**Genesis 11:** 29-30; **22:** 20-24; **24:** 15, 24, 47]

**MINISTERING WOMEN of Jesus and the Apostles** – having traveled with Jesus and His followers, ministering to the group from their own means, these women stayed with Jesus until His death on the cross, watching from a distance; probably they were among those who stayed with the disciples after the Ascension of Jesus, awaiting the coming of the Spirit [**Matthew 27:** 55-56; **Mark 15:** 40-41; **Luke 8:** 2-3; **23:** 49, 55-56; **24:** 1-11; 22-24; **Acts 1:** 14 (see also **MARY MAGDALENE, MARY, wife of Clopas, JOANNA, SUSANNA, SALOME, wife of Zebedee** see *MARY and the Questing Heart*]

**MIRIAM, child of Mered and Bithiah** – the name of this child may be male or female; there is no other indication of gender provided; nothing else is known of this person [**1 Chronicles 4:** 17]

**MIRIAM, sister of Aaron and Moses** – she was the daughter of Jochebed and Amram, a descendant of Levi; as a child, she kept watch over the infant Moses when her mother had laid the boy in a basket in the reeds; she got Pharaoh's daughter, who had found the child, to send for the child's own mother to be his wet nurse; after the crossing of the Red Sea, Miriam led the women in the refrain of the triumphal hymn; she was considered a prophet, with Aaron and Moses; with Aaron, she challenged Moses for marrying a Cushite woman and was made a leper by the Lord God Who was enraged at the pair; at Moses' prayer, Miriam was healed after seven days isolation outside the camp; she died and was buried in the desert of Zin at Kadesh [**Exodus 2:** 4-10; **15: 20**-21; **Numbers 12:** 1-16; **20:** 1; **26: 59; Deuteronomy 24: 9; 1 Chronicles 5: 29; Micah 6:** 4 (see also **JOCHEBED, Pharaoh's DAUGHTER**); see *MIRIAM and theYounger Brothers*]

**MOLECHETH** – see **HAMMOLECHETH**

**Moses' Ethiopian (Cushite) WIFE** – see **ZIPPORAH**

**MOTHERS who had sons circumcised** – under the persecution by Antiochus IV Epiphanes (175-164/163 BC), at least two women whose sons had been circumcised were forced to parade around the square with their babies hung around their necks and were executed by being thrown over the wall of Jerusalem [**1 Maccabees 1:** 60-61; **2 Maccabees 6:** 10; **4 Maccabees 4:** 25]

# N

**NAAMAH, daughter of Lamech** – the daughter of Lamech's second wife Zillah, Naamah was the sister of Tubal-cain, the ancestor of metalworkers; she was the half-sister of Jabal, the ancestor of tent-dwellers and owners of livestock, and of Jubal, ancestor of all who play the lyre and flute [**Genesis 4:** 22 (see also **ADAH, first wife of Lamech** and **ZILLAH**)]

**NAAMAH, one of the wives of King Solomon (ca. 970-931 BC)** – this woman was an Ammonite; she became the mother of King Rehoboam of Judah (931-913 BC); it was Rehoboam who, by his harshness after the death of Solomon, caused the schism at Shechem (which split Israel and the north from Judah and the south); Rehoboam became king in Judah at forty-one, ruled seventeen years in Jerusalem and displeased the Lord God [**1 Kings 14:** 21; **2 Chronicles 12:** 13]

**Naaman's WIFE** — she was married to Naaman, a Syrian, a leper and the army commander favored by the king of Aram because he had led the Aramaeans to victory by the Lord God's favor; apparently, she repeated to her husband what her Israelite servant girl had told her about the prophet in Samaria (Elisha) who would cure Naaman of his leprosy if Naaman would go to him - information which proved to be true [**2 Kings 5:**2 (see also **Naaman's Wife's Israelite SERVANT GIRL**)]

**Naaman's Wife's Israelite SERVANT GIRL** — she was captured by the Aramaeans in a raid on the land of Israel; the girl told her mistress, Naaman's wife, that if Naaman would only go to the prophet in Samaria (Elisha), he would cure Naaman of his leprosy; Naaman's wife apparently reported this information to her husband, and it proved true [**2 Kings 5:** 2-4 (see also **Naaman's WIFE**)]

**NAARAH** — she was one of two wives of Judah's descendant Ashur, the father of Tekoa; she became the mother of Ahuzzam, Hepher, the Temeni or Timnites, and Haahashtari [**1 Chronicles 4:** 5-6 (see also **HELAH**)]

**NAHASH** — he or she was the parent of Abigail and Zeruiah, the sisters of King David (ca. 1010-970 BC) and his seven older brothers; if female, she would be the (elsewhere unnamed) wife of Jesse; most scholars take the name as male, suggesting it is either a textual error, or that Nahash was a deceased first husband of Jesse's wife and father of the two girls; no textual resolution is available [**1 Samuel 22:** 1-4; **2 Samuel 17:** 25 (see **ABIGAIL, daughter of Jesse, ZERUIAH** and **King David's MOTHER**)]

**Nahor's DAUGHTERS** — the girls born to Nahor, Serug's son and an eighth generation descendant of Noah, during the one hundred nineteen years Nahor lived after the birth (when he was twenty-nine years old) of Terah, father of Abram (later Abraham), Nahor and Haran; of Nahor's daughters nothing is known beyond this mention in the list of patriarchs after the Flood [**Genesis 11:** 25]

**NANAEA (also spelled NANEA)** — she was the goddess of the Persian city, Susa; she governed love and war and was also associated with the sun and moon; she was closely associated with the Ephesian goddess Artemis; attempting to plunder her temple in Elymais, Antiochus IV Epiphanes,

(175-164/3 BC) Seleucid ruler, was stoned by a ruse of the priests, who trapped him in an inner room of the shrine where its treasures, including the armor of Alexander the Great, were on display; 1 Maccabees 6: 1-13 offers a different version of his death but affirms the wealth of the temple, though without naming its deity [**2 Maccabees 1:** 13-17 (see also **1 Maccabees 6:** 1-13 and **ARTEMIS**)]

**NANEA** – alternate spelling; see **NANAEA**

**NAOMI** – she was the wife of Elimelech from Bethlehem of Judah; she became the mother of two sons, Mahlon and Chilion; after Elimelech's death, Mahlon and Chilion married the Moabite women, Orpah and Ruth; after about ten years, Naomi's sons died; on her return to Bethlehem with Ruth, she declared that she was no longer to be called Naomi, meaning fair one or pleasant, but Mara, bitter; she sent Ruth to glean in the fields and, when Ruth worked in the fields of Boaz, Naomi told her that Boaz was their kinsman and had the right and duty to marry Ruth; Ruth and Boaz married; their son, Obed, was counted as the son of Elimelech and Naomi [**Ruth 1:** 1-22; **2:** 1, 2, 18-23; **3:** 1-5, 16-18; **4:** 3-9, 14-17 (see **RUTH** and **ORPAH**); see *RUTH and the Unexpected Gleaning*]

**NECROMANCER of Endor** – she was consulted by King Saul (ca. 1030-1010 BC) in disguise; the king asked her to tell him the future by means of a ghost; she refused because Saul had cleared the country of necromancers and wizards and she feared a trap; then, believing the disguised Saul's oath, sworn by the Lord God, that she would suffer no blame for doing so, the necromancer conjured up Samuel as Saul had requested; the necromancer recognized Saul and was terrified; reassured by Saul, she described what she saw, and Saul, recognizing Samuel in the description, did the deceased prophet homage; after Saul had received Samuel's message of his coming defeat and death, the necromancer found him lying at full length, overcome by terror; with the aid of Saul's servant, she persuaded him to eat before returning to the army; she prepared for him and his servant a fatted calf and unleavened bread [**1 Samuel 28:** 3-25]

**NEHUSHTA** – she was the daughter of Elnathan of Jerusalem and the daughter-in-law of King Josiah (640-609 BC); she became the wife of Jehoiakim, King of Judah (609-598 BC); she was the sister-in-law of Kings

Jehoahaz (609 BC) and Zedekiah (598–587 BC); she became the mother of Jehoiachin or Jeconiah (598 BC), who came to the throne of Judah at eighteen, ruled for three months in Jerusalem and displeased the Lord God; with her son, she experienced the Babylonian exile prophesied by Jeremiah [2 **Kings 24:** 8, 12, 15; **Jeremiah 13:** 18; **22:** 26–27; **29:** 2]

**Nereus' SISTER** – she and her brother were members of the Roman Christian community to whom the Apostle Paul sent personal greetings at the end of his letter to the community as a whole [**Romans 16:** 15]

*NINEVEH* – *personified as female, Nineveh was seen as a whore who had enslaved nations with her spells and debauchery; she would be shamed before all by the Lord God for her crimes and left in ruins* [**Nahum 3:** 4-7 (see also **LADY of Nineveh** and **Lady of Nineveh's ATTENDANTS**)]

**NOADIAH** – she was a prophetess who joined Sanballat, Tobiah, Geshem the Arab and other enemies to threaten Nehemiah and make him break off rebuilding the wall of Jerusalem (ca. 445 BC), which he was doing with the assistance of the remnant of Israel, rescued by the Lord God from captivity in Babylon [**Nehemiah 6:** 14]

**NOAH – second of the five daughters of Zelophehad –** see **MAHLAH, eldest daughter of Zelophehad**

**Noah's sons' WIVES** – the women married to Noah's three sons, Shem, Ham and Japheth; they went on the Ark with their husbands, their parents-in-law and the animals the Lord God had commanded Noah to bring with him; they survived the Flood; no direct mention was made of them once they left the Ark; since no other wives were mentioned, we may assume that these three bore all the children Noah's sons had; Shem's wife bore him five sons, Elam, Asshur, Arpachshad, Lud and Aram; Ham's wife bore him four sons, Cush, Misraim, Put and Canaan; Japheth's wife bore him seven sons, Gomer, Magog, Madai, Javan, Tubal, Meshech and Tiras [**Genesis 6:** 18; **7:** 7, 13; **8:** 16, 18; **10:** 1-2, 6, 22]

**Noah's WIFE** – no mention is made of her origin or parents; she bore Noah three sons, Shem, Ham and Japheth; she went with Noah, his sons and their wives, along with the animals the Lord God commanded they bring, into the Ark; she survived the Flood; no mention is made of her once Noah and she left the Ark with their family and all the animals [**Genesis 6:** 10, 18; **7:** 7, 13; **8:** 16, 18]

**Noble of Canaan's DAUGHTER** – she was traveling with the sons of Jambri from Medeba and a large retinue to her wedding; when her party had met the celebrating bridegroom, coming with his groomsmen and family to welcome her, the whole group was ambushed by Jonathan (160-142 BC; High Priest and leader of the Jewish resistance against the Greeks after the death of his brother, Judas Maccabaeus) and his brother Simon; the attack was made in vengeance for the death of Jonathan and Simon's brother John and the capture of the resistance baggage wagons by the sons of Jambri; the ambush succeeded, and the survivors of the wedding group fled to the mountains, leaving their baggage train in the hands of Jonathan and Simon [**1 Maccabees 9:** 32-42]

**NURSE who let child fall** – this woman cared for Meribbaal (also called Meribosheth), the son of Jonathan (son of King Saul, ca. 1030-1010 BC); when news came to them of the deaths of Saul and Jonathan, she picked up the five year old (whose feet were crippled) and fled the royal household; she dropped the child in her flight, perhaps doing him further injury; nothing more is known of her, though Meribbaal, her charge, found a refuge with the household of Machir son of Ammiel at Lo-debar; Meribbaal was later brought back to Jerusalem by King David (ca. 1010-970 BC), for Jonathan's sake; he was given a place in the royal household and finally was given back half of Saul's kingdom, the other half going to Ziba, Saul's servant who had been loyal to David during the rebellion of Absalom [**2 Samuel 4:** 4]

**NYMPHA** – he or she was a Christian of Colossae at whose home a local church community met; he or she received personal greetings from Paul the Apostle at the end of his Letter to the Christian community at Colossae; many scholars see the name as masculine [**Colossians 4:** 15]

# O

*OHOLAH (also spelled Aholah)* – *in Ezekiel's allegory, she was the girl who stood for Samaria, capital of the Northern Kingdom of Israel; with her younger sister, Oholibah (standing for Jerusalem), she belonged to the Lord God; she betrayed her Covenant with Him by the prostitution and adultery of idolatry, both in Egypt in her youth and later in Assyria where she defiled herself with Assyrian idols; the Lord God turned Samaria over to the Assyrians who conquered her; the prophet was commanded to charge her with her crimes against the Lord God; in His process of purging the land of idolatry, the sisters would be destroyed, with the approval of good men who recognized the evil the sisters had done* [**Ezekiel 23:** 1-49 (see also **OHOLIBAH, SAMARIA, House of ISRAEL, JERUSALEM** and *Jerusalem/Zion/Israel as BRIDE-TURNED-WHORE*)]

*OHOLIBAH (also spelled Aholibah)* – *in Ezekiel's allegory, she was the girl who stood for Jerusalem, capital of the Southern Kingdom of Israel; with her older sister, Oholah (standing for Samaria), she belonged to the Lord God; she betrayed her Covenant with Him by the prostitution and adultery of idolatry more flagrantly even than her sister; after her youthful shame in Egypt, she followed the idols of Assyria, then of Chaldea, Babylon, Pekod, Shoa and Koa successively; she would be handed over by the Lord God to all these peoples who would strip her of all she had; in recent days she had welcomed new, idolatrous alliances; the prophet was commanded to charge her with her crimes against the Lord God; He would purge the land (with the approval of good men who recognize the evil the sisters have done), turning it over to those who would slaughter the people and burn the city* [***Ezekiel 23: 1-49*** (see also **OHOLAH, JERUSALEM, House of JUDAH, SAMARIA** and *Jerusalem/Zion/Israel as BRIDE-TURNED-WHORE*)]

**OHOLIBAMAH (also spelled Aholibamah)** – she was the daughter of Anah the Horite, the son of Zibeon; she became the first Canaanite wife of Esau, mother of Jeush, Jalam, and Korah [**Genesis 36:** 2, 5, 6, 14, 18, 25; she is also called **JUDITH, daughter of Beeri the Hittite** in **Genesis 26:34** (see also, **ADAH, daughter of Elon the Hittite, BASEMATH, daughter of Ishmael** and **Hittite and Canaanite women as WIVES**)]

**Old Man of Gibeah's VIRGIN DAUGHTER** – she was offered to the lustful Benjaminites in place of his guest, the Ephraimite Levite, whom they wished, presumably, to sodomize; no harm came to her as the offer was refused by the Benjaminites [**Judges 19:** 24; (see also **Ephraimite Levite's CONCUBINE, (The) Benjaminites' Four Hundred YOUNG WIVES** and **Jabesh-gilead's WIVES and Children**); see *The Ephraimite Levite's CONCUBINE and the Price of Honor*]

**ORPAH** – she was the woman of Moab who married Chilion, the son of Naomi and Elimelech; when Naomi's husband and both sons died, Orpah offered to return to Bethlehem with Naomi, but she listened to Naomi's disclaimer and request and returned to her own people and gods [**Ruth 1:** 4, 14 (see also **NAOMI** and **RUTH**); see *RUTH and the Unexpected Gleaning*]

# P

**PATRIOT WOMAN of Thebez** – she joined her townsmen on the roof of the fortified tower in the city of Thebez when Abimelech (Gideon's Shechemite concubine's son) besieged the town (ca. 1150 BC) as part of his finally unsuccessful war to put down the rebellion of Shechem against him; she threw down a millstone on Abimelech's head, crushing his skull; Abimelech commanded his armor-bearer to run him through with a sword, lest he die at the hands of a woman; the armor-bearer obeyed and the Israelite army returned home; as predicted by his commander Joab, King David (1010-970 BC) cited the incident in questioning the army's close approach to the battlements in besieging Rabbah [**Judges 9:** 50-57; **2 Samuel 11:** 18-24; see *The PATRIOT WOMAN of Thebez and the Grasping General*]

**Paul's SISTER** – she does not appear in her own person but only through her son, the Apostle Paul's nephew; he had heard of the ambush planned by more than forty Jews, who promised to kill the Apostle Paul when he was on his way down to a spurious reexamination by the Sanhedrin; the conspirators had told the chief priests to apply to the Governor to obtain an order for such a reexamination; her son reported this to Paul who sent him to report it to the Tribune; the Tribune, in response, had Paul spirited out of the fortress and delivered unharmed to Felix the governor at Caesarea with a covering letter [**Acts 23:** 12-22]

**Peleg's DAUGHTERS** – the girls born to Peleg, Eber's son and a fifth generation descendant of Noah, during the two hundred nine years Peleg lived after the birth (when he was thirty years old) of Reu; nothing more is known of them than this mention in the list of patriarchs after the Flood [**Genesis 11:**19]

**PENINNAH** – she was the less-favored of the two wives of Elkanah; she was a Zuphite from Ephraim; she bore Elkanah many children; she was envious of Hannah, Elkanah's other wife, because, though Hannah was barren, Elkanah loved her better than he did Peninnah; of the yearly sacrifice offered to the Lord God in Shiloh, Elkanah gave Hannah a single portion equal to the total of the portions given to Peninnah and each of her children; Peninnah taunted Hannah for her barrenness yearly at the sacrifice, just to make her miserable [**1 Samuel:** 1-8 (see also **HANNAH** and **Peninnah's DAUGHTERS**); see *HANNAH and the Excellent Bargain*]

**Peninnah's DAUGHTERS** – the girls born by Peninnah to Elkanah; with their brothers, they were a source of pride for Peninnah, who used their existence to taunt her rival Hannah, Elkanah's favorite wife, for her barrenness; with their mother and brothers, each girl received a portion of the sacrifice Elkanah offered to the Lord God yearly in Shiloh at the Feast of Tabernacles [**1 Samuel 1:** 2-6 (see also **PENINNAH**)]

**PERSIS** – she was one of the women of the Christian community at Rome whom Paul greeted by name at the end of his letter; she was identified as a friend who had done much for the Lord [**Romans 16:** 12]

**Peter's MOTHER-IN-LAW** – lying ill in bed with fever, she was cured when Peter and his brother Andrew, with their fishing partners James and John, came back to the house on the Sabbath with Jesus (Whom they had seen cure a demoniac); they asked Him to do something for her; when He rebuked the fever and took her hand and helped her up, she rose, cured, and at once began to wait on them [**Matthew 8:** 14-15; **Mark 1:** 30-31; **Luke 4:** 38-39]

**Peter's WIFE** – there is no mention of her being present, or even alive, at the healing of her mother, who seems to have been the household's only housekeeper, a role she would probably not have had if her daughter had been living; she is seen by some as the "Christian woman" accompanying Cephas, a possible reading, some scholars say [**1 Corinthians 9:** 5]

**PHANUEL** – he or she was the parent of Anna the prophetess, and belonged to the tribe of Asher; modern scholarship concludes this is Anna's father [**Luke 2:** 36]

**Pharaoh's DAUGHTER** – she was born to the new ruler of Egypt, perhaps Ramses II (1301-1234 BC), who did not know the history of the coming of the Israelites to Egypt and the service that Joseph, Jacob's son, had done the country; the Pharaoh feared this growing population of foreigners and so enslaved them; his daughter disobeyed her father's decree that all male Israelite babies should be killed, by rescuing the son of Amram whom his mother, Jochebed, had hidden in a basket in the reeds at the river's edge; at the suggestion of a small girl (Miriam, Moses' sister) standing near, she gave the child to an Israelite wet-nurse (Jochebed herself) until he should be weaned; when Jochebed turned the boy over to her after his weaning, the Pharaoh's daughter treated him as her son and saw to it that he was given a thorough Egyptian education; she named the child Moses (from Hebrew *mosheh,* to draw out) because she had drawn him out of the water [**Exodus 2:** 5-10; **Acts 7:** 21; **Hebrews 11:** 24-26 (see also **MIRIAM** and **JOCHEBED**); see *MIRIAM and the Younger Brothers*]

**Pharaoh's daughter's SLAVE-GIRLS** – they accompanied the Pharaoh's daughter when she went to bathe in the river; one of them, obeying her mistress, brought to her the basket that had been floating among the reeds; the basket held the infant Moses [**Exodus 2:** 5 (see also **Pharaoh's DAUGHTER**); see [*MIRIAM and the Younger Brothers*]

**PHEBE** – alternate spelling; see **PHOEBE**

**Philippi's WOMEN gathered for prayer** – these women customarily gathered for prayer at a place by the river outside the city gates; they met the Apostle Paul and Luke there and listened to Paul's preaching about Jesus; at least one of their number, Lydia, a merchant selling purple dye, was converted [**Acts 16:** 11-13 (see also **LYDIA**)]

**Philip's DAUGHTERS** – the four virgin daughters of Philip, called the evangelist, one of the original seven deacons; they were prophets and lived with their father in Caesarea; the Apostle Paul, Luke and their companions stayed with the family, arriving from Tyre, by way of Ptolemais, on their way to Jerusalem; nothing further is known of the girls or of their prophetic gifts [**Acts 6:** 5; **21:** 7-9]

**PHOEBE (also spelled PHEBE)** – she was a deaconess of the church at Cenchreae; she was probably the bearer of the letter in Romans 16 to the Christian community at Rome; she was commended to the Roman community by the Apostle Paul, who asked the community to welcome her and assist her with anything she needed; she was praised by Paul as one who had looked after a great many people, himself included [**Romans 16:** 1-2]

**Pilate's WIFE** – she was married to Pontius Pilate, Procurator of Judea; when Jesus of Nazareth had been brought to her husband by the religious leaders of the Jewish people, she warned Pilate to have nothing to do with Him, because he was a holy man about whom she had had an upsetting dream; her message did not save Jesus from death; she is mentioned only here [**Matthew 27:** 19]

**Potiphar's WIFE** – she was the unnamed spouse of the Egyptian official who had bought Joseph, son of Jacob and Rachel, from Ishmaelite traders and made him steward of his household; she lusted after Joseph who refused her; she trapped him, but he fled the house, leaving his tunic in her hands; then she summoned the servants and claimed to them, and to her husband, that Joseph had tried to rape her; the official had Joseph arrested and put into the jail where the King's prisoners were kept; nothing further is heard of her nor of her deceived husband [**Genesis 39:** 7-21; **41:** 44-45 (see also **ASENATH**); see *Potiphar's WIFE and the Respectful Slave*]

**PREGNANT WOMEN ripped open by conquerors** – the fate of these women was a deed foreseen by Elisha the prophet (fl. 849-785 BC); Elisha prophesied that Hazael of Damascus would do this deed when he became King of Aram, though no Biblical mention is made of his having done so; the usurping King Menahem of Israel (743-738 BC), in his sack of Tappush, did commit the atrocity, a way of eliminating the coming generation of the conquered city, in addition to its present destruction; the women's fate appears as a curse against Babylon in Psalm 137; it is also cited by Isaiah,

Nahum, Hosea and Amos [**2 Kings 8:** 12-13; **15:** 13-16; **Psalm 137:** 9; **Isaiah 13:** 16; **Nahum 3:** 10; **Hosea 10:** 14; **13:** 16 (**14:** 1); **Amos 1:** 13-14]

## PRISCA – see PRISCILLA

**PRISCILLA** – she was the wife of Aquila, a Jew from Pontus and a tent-maker; she and her husband were devout Christians; the couple traveled to Corinth when the edict of Claudius expelled all Jews from Rome; they were visited in Corinth by the Apostle Paul who lodged with them and worked as a tentmaker with Aquila to support himself; they left Corinth with Paul and stayed in Ephesus; the couple gave further instruction to Apollos, an Alexandrian Jew; Apollos preached accurately about Jesus but had only experienced the baptism of John; Priscilla and Aquila met Timothy at Ephesus; the couple returned to Rome, where a Christian community met at their house; they were greeted by Paul directly in his letter to the Roman community and, through Timothy, in his second letter to Timothy; they were remembered to the community at Corinth by Paul; Priscilla is not mentioned apart from her husband Aquila [**Acts 18:** 2-3, 18-19, 24-26; called **PRISCA** in **Romans 16:** 3-5; **1 Corinthians 16:** 19; **2 Timothy 4:** 19]

**Prophet's WIDOW** – this woman had been married to a member of the Prophetic Brotherhood and had borne her husband two sons; with her husband's death, his creditors had come to sell her and her two children into slavery to pay his debts; as she had no way to pay them and only had a pot of oil in the house, she appealed to Elisha the prophet; Elisha told her to borrow as many empty jars from all her neighbors as she could, close the door with her children in the house, and pour the oil into each jar until it was full; she followed his instructions; when she ran out of jars, the flow of oil stopped; she reported this result to Elisha who instructed her to sell the oil, pay off her husband's debts and live on the remainder [**2 Kings 4:** 1-7]

**PROSTITUTES bathing in Ahab's blood** – when King Ahab of Israel (874-853 BC), wounded in battle, finally died, his servants buried his body in Samaria; then they washed his chariot, with his blood pooled in the bottom, at the Pool of Samaria; there dogs licked it up and prostitutes washed in it, fulfilling Elijah's prophecy [1 Kings 21: 19]; Elijah had said that this would happen in the same place where dogs had licked the blood of Naboth (whom Jezebel had had executed on false charges so Ahab could take his vineyard); see **JEZEBEL [1 Kings 22: 35-38]**

*Proverbs' WOMEN* – *in Proverbs, the universal, or generic, "woman," appears in individual, unconnected aphorisms, many of which are common assumptions treated as truisms; the effects of her actions and choices have great impact on those associated with her, though she herself has no apparent power; she delights in her children and sees them as unique [4: 3; JB];she is seen, with her husband, as teacher of her sons [1:8; 6: 20; 31:1; JB]; coupled with her husband, she suffers for the folly of her son [10: 1; 15: 20; 17: 25; 29: 15; JB]; she can bring her husband honor or dishonor, depending on her conduct [11: 16; 12: 4; 18: 22; JB]; as a scold, she can make the entire household miserable and is impossible to control [19: 13; 21: 9, 19; 25: 24; 27: 15-16; JB]; if good, she is a gift of the Lord God and makes her household happy [18: 22; 19: 14; JB]; with her husband, she should be honored (in her old age especially), by her sons [19: 26; 20: 20; 23: 22, 25; 28: 24; 30: 11, 17; 31: 28; JB]; her beauty, without discretion, is like a gold ring in a pig's snout [11:22; JB]; as a widow, she is protected by the Lord God Who pulls down the houses of the proud [15: 25; JB]; as a harlot, she destroys what she touches, and resorting to her is the height of folly [22: 14; 23: 27-28; 29: 3; 30: 20; 31: 3; JB]; the leech's two daughters, named Give and Give [30: 15a; JB], are a metaphor for his all-consuming greed; among things that defy understanding is the way of a man with a maid [30: 19; JB]; among unendurable things are the rejected wife who keeps her place with her husband [30: 23a; JB], and the serving girl who supplants her mistress, perhaps by bearing a child while her mistress is barren [30: 23b; JB]* **[Proverbs 1:** 8; **4:** 3; **6:** 20; **10:** 1; **11:** 16, 22; **12:** 4; **15:** 20, 25; **17:** 25; **18:** 22; **19:** 13, 14, 26; **20:** 20; **21:** 9, 19; **22:** 14; **23:** 22, 25, 27-28; **25:** 24; **27:** 15-16; **28:** 24; **29:** 3, 15; **30:** 11, 15, 17, 19, 20, 23; **31:** 1, 3, 28 (see also *WISDOM, FOLLY/ Adulterous SEDUCTRESS/ALIEN WOMAN, VALIANT WOMAN, Sirach's WOMEN* and *Ecclesiastes' WOMEN*)]

**PUAH** – she was one of two crucial Hebrew midwives in Egypt at the time of Moses; with her partner Shiphrah, she refused to obey the Pharaoh's direct order to kill the boy babies of the Hebrew women while letting the girl children live; questioned by Pharaoh later, the midwives claimed that the Hebrew women were very strong and gave birth before the midwives were summoned; God rewarded the midwives for honoring Him and gave them descendants; the Hebrew people continued to increase and Pharaoh, giving up on the midwives, ordered all male children born to the Hebrews to be thrown into the river [**Exodus 1:** 15-21 (see also **SHIPHRAH** and **JOCHEBED**); see *PUAH and the Thwarting of the Pharaoh*]

**Putiel's DAUGHTERS** – one of the girls became the wife of Eleazar, son of Moses' and Miriam's brother Aaron, and bore him Phinehas; nothing, beyond this mention in the genealogy of Moses and Aaron, is known of her or of her sisters [**Exodus 6:** 25]

# Q

**QUEEN** *arrayed in gold* – *this female personification was seen in Psalm 45, by Jewish tradition, as the chief of those attending upon the Messianic King at his espousal of Israel, his chosen bride; in Christian tradition, the Queen was seen as the Virgin Mary, Mother of God, attending upon the Triune God and supporting the long-sought Bride, each individual soul, as well as the Church; the psalm itself may have begun life as a secular wedding song for Solomon (970-931 BC), Jeroboam II (783-743 BC), or Ahab (874-853 BC), who married a Tyrian princess* [**Psalm 45:9** (see also **Revelations' BRIDE of the Lamb, King's DAUGHTER, DAUGHTERS of Kings, Song of Songs' BRIDE, Song of Songs' QUEENS, CONCUBINES, and Other MAIDENS** and **Jerusalem/Zion/Israel as Covenant BRIDE RESTORED**)]

**QUEEN of Heaven** – probably she was either the Assyrian-Babylonian Ishtar, or the Canaanite goddess, Astarte; in Jerusalem and the towns of Judah, she was given credit for their previous prosperity and safety by the remnant of Judah, who saw their current miseries (famine, the loss of everything, war) as the result of their neglect of her; this remnant had been spared captivity in Babylon by the Lord God, but were now living in Egypt, in spite of His prohibition delivered through Jeremiah, and the women, particularly, had resumed the idolatrous cult; all refused to repent despite Jeremiah's report of the Lord God's warming that this would mean their deaths [**Jeremiah 7:** 18-20; **44:** 9, 15-30 (see also **ASTARTE, King's DAUGHTERS,** and **WIVES of the Remnant of Judah in Egypt**)]

**QUEEN of Sheba, also called QUEEN of the South** – she ruled on the Arabian peninsula, some scholars believe in one of the Sabaean settlements of north Arabia, rather than in the southwest where Sheba is located;

having heard of Solomon, she came to Jerusalem to test him; she had all her questions answered to her satisfaction; she observed the Kingdom and its people, saw all that Solomon had built and was doing, noted the manner of his hospitality, and declared that what she saw there surpassed all she had heard of his wisdom and prosperity; she praised the Lord God Who had set Solomon on the throne of Israel to administer law and do justice; she gave Solomon much gold and great quantities of spices and precious stones and received magnificent gifts in return from him; then she returned to her own country [**1 Kings 10:** 1-13; **2 Chronicles 9:** 1-12; **Matthew 12:** 42; **Luke 11:** 31]

**QUEEN of the South** – see **QUEEN of Sheba**

**Quick-witted WOMAN from Abel** – she confronted Joab, David's army commander, when he was besieging Abel, and demanded to know why he was destroying this old and respected city, and so damaging Israel; she accepted Joab's bargain, that if they would turn the rebel Sheba over to him he would raise the siege against the city; she explained the situation to the townsfolk; they chopped off Sheba's head and tossed it over the wall to Joab, who promptly lifted the siege and returned to David in Jerusalem [**2 Samuel 20:** 14-22; see *The WISE WOMAN from Abel and the Obvious Solution*]

**Quick-Witted WOMAN from Tekoa** – she was summoned by Zeruiah's son Joab, the army commander of King David (ca. 1010-970 BC), when he understood that David's wrath against his banished favorite son, Absalom, had cooled; instructed by Joab, the woman went to King David and posed as a widow with two sons, one of whom had killed the other; her townsfolk had demanded the killer, she said, so that they could execute him, an act which would leave her without hope and her deceased husband without name or survivor; David took an oath that her son would be spared and she herself protected, whereupon, still acting on Joab's instructions, she challenged him for the harm he was doing Israel by leaving Absalom in exile; questioned about Joab's involvement in making the story she had told him, she admitted that Joab was its source; she suffered no punishment for her deception, and saw the King tell Joab to bring Absalom back (though on his return, Absalom was confined to his own house) [**2 Samuel 14:** 1-24; see *TAMAR and the Broken Bread*)]

# R

**RACHAB** – alternate spelling; see **RAHAB**

**RACHEL** – she was the daughter of Rebekah's brother, Laban, and the granddaughter of Bethuel, who was the son of Abraham's brother Nahor and his wife Milcah; she was the sister of Leah; she became the second and favored wife of Jacob after a trick of her father and sister made Leah his first wife; she was the mother of two sons, Joseph and Benjamin, of her own body, and of two more sons, Dan and Naphtali, born to Jacob by her hand-maid Bilhah; Rachel died giving birth to her second son, whom she named Ben-oni (*son of my sorrow*; JB); Jacob named the boy Benjamin (*son of happy omen*; JB); she was buried on the road to Ephrath, at Bethlehem, where Jacob raised a monument which became a landmark; later, with Leah, she was seen as symbol of a fruitful marriage building up Israel; she was also seen, in her mourning of Joseph whom she and Jacob thought dead, as symbolic of the absolute bereavement of Israel in her loss of the Lord God's favor and of her own children; this mourning would find joy beyond words when the Lord God forgave His people, freed her captive children and restored Israel to her lands, finally sending her His Messiah; Rachel was seen as also symbolic of the mourning caused by Herod the Great's massacre of the baby boys in Bethlehem and the surrounding area in his attempt to kill the new King the Magi had asked him about [**Genesis 28:** 2; **29:** 6-14, 16-22, 25-31; **30:** 1-8, 14-15, 22-25; **31:** 4, 14-16, 19, 26, 28, 31, 32-35, 41, 43, 50; **32:** 1, 12, 23; **33:** 1-7; **35:** 16-21, 24-25; **37:** 10; **43:** 29; **44:** 20, 27; **46:** 19, 22, 25; **48:** 7; **Ruth 4:** 11; **1 Samuel 10:** 2; **Jeremiah 31:** 15; **Hosea 12:** 12; **Matthew 2:** 18 (see also **BILHAH, LEAH, ZILPAH** and **Rachel's MIDWIFE**); see *RACHEL, LEAH and the Duping of the Bridegroom*]

**Rachel's MIDWIFE** – this woman encouraged Rachel in her difficult labor bringing forth Benjamin and told Rachel that she had a son; she was unable to save Rachel's life [**Genesis 35:** 16-18 (see also **RACHEL**)]

**Raguel's MAIDSERVANTS** – one of these girls taunts Sarah for her ill-fortune in losing seven husbands, each on her wedding night; the one sent to check on Sarah and Tobias on their wedding night found both asleep and all well; a number of these maidservants were sent with Sarah when she went home with Tobias as his wife [**Tobit 3:** 7-9; **8:** 12-14; **10:** 10

(see **EDNA, SARAH, wife of Tobias** and **ANNA, wife of Tobit**); see *SARAH and the Bridal-Night Devil*]

**RAHAB** – she was a harlot of Jericho who concealed the spies sent by Joshua and bargained with them for the lives of her family; she was rescued with her family when the Israelites captured Jericho; she married Salmon and bore him a son, Boaz, who became an ancestor of Jesus through the House of King David (ca. 1010-970 BC), his great-grandson [**Joshua 2:** 1-21; **6:** 16-25; **Matthew 1:** 5; **Hebrews 11:** 31; **James 2:** 25 (see also **Rahab's MOTHER and SISTERS**); see *RAHAB and the Scarlet Cord*]

**Rahab's MOTHER and SISTERS** – with the rest of her family, these women were spared when Joshua took their town, Jericho, because Rahab had hidden Joshua's spies and helped them escape, bargaining with them to spare her family members' lives in exchange for her help [**Joshua 2:** 13, 18; **6:** 17, 22-25 (see also **RAHAB**)]

**REBECCA** – alternate spelling; see **REBEKAH**

**REBEKAH (also spelled REBECCA)** – she was the daughter of Bethuel, the son of Abraham's brother Nahor and his wife Milcah; she was the sister of Laban; she became the wife of Isaac; she was the mother of twin sons, Esau and Jacob; she became the grandmother of Esau's sons Eliphaz (by Adah), Reuel (by Basemath) and Jeush, Jalam and Korah (by Oholibamah), and of Jacob's sons Reuben, Simeon, Levi, Judah, Issachar and Zebulon (by Leah), Gad and Asher (by Leah's handmaid, Zilpah), Joseph and Benjamin (by Rachel) and Dan and Naphtali (by Rachel's handmaid, Bilhah); she favored her son Jacob, second-born of the twins, and conspired with him to accomplish the transfer to him of the blessing of the firstborn, a deed later seen as the Lord God's choosing of Jacob as His own; Rebekah did not live to see Jacob's return and reconciliation with Esau; she and Isaac were buried in the cave in the field at Machpelah, opposite Mamre, in the land of Canaan, which Abraham had bought from Ephron the Hittite as a burial plot and where he and Sarah were buried [**Genesis 22:** 23; **24:** 15-67; **25:** 20-28; **26:**7-11, 35; **27:** 5-17, 29, 42-46; **28:** 2, 3, 5; **29:** 12; **35:** 8; **49:** 31; **Romans 9:** 10-13 (see also **DEBORAH, nurse of Rebekah, Rebekah's MOTHER, Rebekah's MAIDS**); see *REBEKAH and the Camels of Courtship* and *REBEKAH and the Golden Opportunity*]

**Rebekah's MAIDS** – girls who accompanied Rebekah as she traveled with Isaac's servant to become Isaac's bride; they rode camels the servant had brought, as did Rebekah [**Genesis 24:** 61(see also **REBEKAH** and **Rebekah's MOTHER**)]

**Rebekah's MOTHER** – she received rich gifts from Abraham's servant as he asked, for Isaac, for Rebekah's hand in marriage; she joined her son Laban, Rebekah's brother, first in suggesting that Rebekah remain with the family a while longer, before she departed with Isaac's servant to become Isaac's wife, and then in asking Rebekah her choice; she agreed to let Rebekah go with Isaac's servant when Rebekah said this was her choice [**Genesis 24:** 53-60; (see also **REBEKAH** and **Rebekah's MAIDS**)]

**Rehoboam's OTHER WIVES, CONCUBINES and DAUGHTERS** – these women were remarkable only for their number; in addition to Mahalath and Maacah, King Rehoboam of Judah (931-913 BC) had sixteen wives, sixty concubines and sixty daughters, along with twenty-eight sons [**2 Chronicles 11:** 21(see also **MAHALATH, daughter of David's son Jerimoth and Eliab's daughter Abihail** and **MAACAH, wife of Rehoboam**)]

**Reuel, the Midian Priest's DAUGHTERS** – see **Jethro, the Midian Priest's DAUGHTERS**

**REUMAH** – she was the concubine of Abraham's brother, Nahor; she became the mother of Tebah, Gaham, Tahash and Maacah [**Genesis 22:** 24]

**Reu's DAUGHTERS** – girls born to Reu, Peleg's son and a sixth generation descendant of Noah, during the two hundred seven years Reu lived after the birth (when he was thirty-two years old) of Serug; nothing more is known of them than this mention in the list of patriarchs after the Flood [**Genesis 11:** 21]

*Revelation's BRIDE of the Lamb* – *this female personification appears the narrator's vision of things to come, first in the praise of the multitudes in heaven who rejoiced that, with the victory of God over His enemies accomplished and the reign of God begun, the time for the marriage of the Lamb to the Bride had come; she was dressed in shining white linen, "made of the good deeds of the saints" [Revelation 19: 8; JB]; following the double battle of the End and the Last Judgment, she would come down out of heaven as a Bride adorned for her Husband and would be named the New Jerusalem, the holy city; the Bride would join the Spirit in praying for the consummation of the Revelation in the final coming of the Lord Jesus in glory and the beginning of God's eternal reign; here, scholars interpret the Bride as the Church, the community of all who have died faithful to the Lamb and to God; she is seen as the New Jerusalem, and as keeping the new marriage Covenant Jesus brought to replace the First Covenant between the Lord God and Israel, and paid for with His blood; more broadly, this Bride includes all whom God recognizes as His own, who have responded to His love and remained faithful to Him through death* [**Revelation 19:** 7-8; **21:** 2, 9-11; **22:** 17 (see also ***Jerusalem/Zion/Israel* as CHOSEN BRIDE of the Covenant, *Jerusalem/Zion/Israel* as Covenant BRIDE RESTORED, *Song of Songs'* BRIDE, DAUGHTERS of Kings, King's DAUGHTER, Church as CHASTE BRIDE of Christ** and **QUEEN *arrayed in gold*)**]

***Revelation's GREAT HARLOT*** — *this female personification appears in the first vision of her punishment as one with whom all the kings of the earth have committed fornication; she would rule enthroned beside abundant waters and would ride a scarlet beast with seven heads and ten crowned horns, with blasphemous titles written all over it; she would be dressed in purple and scarlet, adorned with gold, jewels and pearls, and would carry a gold wine cup filled with the filth of her fornications; she would have "Babylon the Great, mother of all prostitutes and all filth practices on the earth" [17: 5; JB], written on her forehead; she would be drunk with the blood of the saints and of the martyrs of Jesus as the angel explained; the beast and its ten allies would turn against her and strip her naked; then they would "eat her flesh and burn the remains in the fire," [17: 16; JB] the Lord God's punishment; in a second vision she was identified as the fallen Babylon the Great, "haunt of devils and lodging for every foul spirit and dirty, loathsome bird" [18: 2; JB]; by the Lord God's condemnation, she is to be paid back double the miseries she has caused; plague, disease, mourning and famine would destroy her and all her wealth; the kings, merchants, traders ship captains and their employees, who made their living serving her needs, would mourn her destruction, though from a safe distance, while heaven would celebrate her downfall as God's just punishment; in a third vision, all heaven would rejoice at the just and eternal punishment of the Harlot, as God's vengeance; though one interpretation sees the Harlot as Jerusalem, unfaithful to God by rejecting Jesus as Israel's Messiah, most commonly, scholars identify her as pagan Rome; more broadly, the Harlot is seen as any place/institution where self-idolatry (under any guise) and active or passive* *enmity to God prevails; scholars differ in their identification of the individual details, particularly as to whether the prophecies have already been fulfilled (and how), or await completion with the end of the world* [**Revelation 17:** 1-18; **18:** 1-24; **19:** 1-4 (see also *BABYLON*)]

*Revelation's WOMAN CLOTHED WITH THE SUN – this female personification appears as a sign in the heavens; she was wearing the sun for a garment, was standing on the moon, and had a crown of twelve stars on her head; she was pregnant and in labor, her delivery immanent; she was screaming with the pain of birthing her child, as a dragon crouched in front of her, ready to eat the child as soon as she gave birth to it; the son she bore, who would rule the nations, was snatched up to God's throne; the woman escaped to the desert sanctuary God had prepared for her, while the dragon went to make war on the children of men; liturgically the image is associated with Mary, the Mother of God* [*Revelation 12: 1-6; 13-17*]

**RHODA –** she was the maidservant who answered the door at the home of Mary, John Mark's mother, the night Peter was released by the angel from captivity in Herod's dungeon; she recognized Peter's voice and, in her joy, left Peter standing outside while she ran in to tell the assembled brethren; despite the skepticism of the brethren, she continued to insist that it was Peter himself and not his angel, while Peter continued to knock until they opened the door and saw the truth [**Acts 12:** 13-17; see *RHODA and the Knock at the Door*]

**RIZPAH –** she was the daughter of Aiah; she became the concubine of King Saul (ca. 1030-1010 BC); Abner, Saul's army commander, slept with her and, rebuked by Ishbaal, Saul's son (whom Abner had made king over all Israel), switched his allegiance to David; Rizpah bore Saul two sons, Armoni and Meribbaal; when her two sons by Saul were handed over, with Saul's five grandsons (the sons of Merab and Adriel), to the Gibeonites to be impaled (as reparation for the deaths Saul had caused), she kept watch over their bones, protecting them from the birds and the wild beasts; Rizpah performed this service from the beginning of the barley harvest until the rain ending the three-year famine came; her action prompted David to reclaim the bones of Saul and Jonathan from Gilboa and bury them honorably together with the bones she had protected [**2 Samuel 3:** 7; **21:** 8-11 (see also **MERAB**); see *RIZPAH and the Bones*]

**Rufus' MOTHER** – she, with her son Rufus, received the Apostle Paul's personal greetings at the end of his letter to the Roman community; she had apparently treated Paul as another son; some scholars think this Rufus may be the brother of Alexander and the son of Simon of Cyrene who helped Jesus carry his cross, though the only connection seems to be the name [**Roman 16:** 13; **Mark 15:** 22]

*RUHAMAH* – *this name, meaning "Beloved" [JB], replaced Lo-Ruhamah, "Unloved" [JB], the first name given to the second child of Gomer, the prostitute-made-wife of Hosea; the new name was given by the Lord God, to indicate the mercy and love He would show a repentant Israel* [**Hosea 2:** *3, 25* (see also **LO-RUHAMAH, GOMER,** *House of* **ISRAEL,** *House of* **JUDAH** *and* **Jerusalem/Zion/Israel as Covenant BRIDE RESTORED**)]

**RUTH** – she was a woman of Moab who married Mahlon, the elder son of Naomi and Elimelech; Elimelech and his family had come to Moab from Bethlehem of Judah because of a famine; when Naomi's husband and two sons died, Ruth insisted that Naomi's God and people would be her God and people and that she would stay with Naomi; on arrival in Bethlehem, Ruth went by chance to the fields of Naomi's kinsman, Boaz, to glean; at Naomi's instruction, Ruth slept at Boaz' feet that night; Boaz then took her to wife and she bore him Obed, who would be the grandfather of King David (ca. 1010-970 BC) and ancestor of Jesus; legally the child was credited to Naomi and Elimelech, though the genealogy of Jesus quoted from the Book of Ruth by Matthew does not mention Elimelech's name, but credits Boaz [**Book of Ruth; Matthew 1:** 5 (see also **NAOMI** and **ORPAH**); see *RUTH and the Unexpected Gleaning*]

# S

**Salah's DAUGHTERS** – alternate spelling; see **Shelah's DAUGHTERS**

**SALOME, daughter of Herodias** – though it is never mentioned in Scripture, this is the name traditionally given to the daughter of Herodias and, presumably Philip, Herod's half-brother; she danced for King Herod (with whom Herodias was living) at his birthday dinner, and so pleased the

King that he offered her whatever she wanted; prompted by Herodias, she requested, and got, the head of John the Baptizer on a plate; John had made an enemy of Herodias by his blunt denial of the validity of her union with Herod; Salome turned the head over to Herodias [**Matthew 14:** 6-11; **Mark 6:** 17-28 (see also **HERODIAS**); see *SALOME and the Silken Snare* and *HERODIAS and the Inconvenient Prophet*]

**SALOME, wife of Zebedee** – she was the mother of the Apostles James and John and, perhaps, a sister of Mary, the mother of Jesus; she was one of the women who followed Jesus and assisted Him and the disciples; she was present at the crucifixion; she joined Mary, wife of Clopas and Mary Magdalene in bringing spices to the tomb of Jesus; with her companions, she received news of the resurrection from the angel and brought it to the Apostles who did not believe them; she was probably among those who stayed with the disciples after the Ascension of Jesus, awaiting the coming of the Spirit [**Matthew 20:** 20-23; **27:** 55-56; **Mark 15:** 40-41; **16:** 1-8; **Luke 8:** 2-3; **23:** 49, 55-56; **24:** 1-11; 22-24; **John 19:** 25; **Acts 1:** 14 (see also **MARY, wife of Clopas; JOANNA, MARY MAGDALENE, SUSANNA** and **MINISTERING WOMEN** of Jesus and the Apostles); see *MARY and the Questing Heart*]

*SAMARIA* – *this is a female personification of the capital of the Northern Kingdom (Kingdom of Israel); Micah, describing her as the "sin of the House of Israel," [JB], said she would be destroyed for the Kingdom's idolatry; her punishment would be repeated in the Kingdom of Judah; she was seen by Ezekiel as the faithless elder sister of Jerusalem/Zion; her crimes of idolatry were suggested, not specified; she and Sodom, her youngest sister, would be restored to their former condition, and would be made daughters of the repentant and restored Jerusalem/Zion in the new Covenant the Lord God promised to establish* [**Micah 1:** 5-7; **Ezekiel 16:** 46, 61 (see also **OHOLAH, House of ISRAEL, SODOM,** *Jerusalem/Zion/Israel as Covenant BRIDE-TURNED-WHORE, Jerusalem/Zion/Israel as Covenant BRIDE RESTORED* and **OHOLIBAH**)]

**Samaritan WOMAN at the Well** – see **WOMAN at the Well**

**Samson's HARLOT, also called HARLOT of Gaza** – she was a prostitute who lived in Gaza; she welcomed Samson into her house; he remained until midnight, then left, tearing out the posts, doors and bar of the town gates, and leaving them at the top of the hill facing Hebron; his early departure frustrated the townsmen who, on Samson's arrival at the prostitute's house, had set up an ambush, planning to kill him at daybreak; nothing further is said of this woman [Judges 16: 1-3]

**Samson's MOTHER** – see **Manoah's WIFE**

**Samson's SISTER-IN-LAW** – she was the younger sister of Samson's Philistine wife from Timnah; she was offered as a replacement bride to Samson by her father, after he had given Samson's abandoned wife to another; nothing came of the offer; she died with the rest of the family when the Philistines set fire to the house to punish Samson's wife and her family for the damage Samson had done to their cornfields, vines and olives [Judges 15: 2 (see also **Samson's WIFE**)]

**Samson's WIFE** – she was the daughter of a Philistine living at Timnah; she married Samson, whom she and all her people feared; at the seven-day wedding feast, in a riddle-game, she betrayed Samson to the thirty Philistines assigned as a guard of honor to stay with (and contain) Samson; she was abandoned by Samson, who left, enraged, for his father's house; she was then given in marriage to the companion who had been best man at the wedding; on Samson's return, bearing a small goat as a present for her, she was protected by her father who refused Samson entry, explained his daughter's remarriage and offered Samson his bride's younger sister in her place; she was burned to death with her family by the Philistines, as the cause of Samson's having burned their cornfields (sheaves and standing corn), vines and olive trees; her destruction caused Samson to take vengeance on the Philistines [Judges 14: 1-20; 15: 1-8 (see also **DELILAH, Manoah's WIFE** and **Samson's SISTER-IN-LAW**); see *Samson's WIFE and the Coils of Betrayal, DELILAH and the Deadly Lure* and *Manoah's WIFE and the Wonder-Son*]

**Sanballat's DAUGHTER** – she was born to Sanballat the Horonite, who was displeased at the return of the exiles from Babylon to Jerusalem and ridiculed Nehemiah and his party for attempting to rebuild the walls of Jerusalem, accusing him of planning a revolt against the King; she was married to one of the sons of Jehoiada, son of the high priest Eliashib; on her account, the son of Jehoiada was expelled from the presence of Nehemiah, from the restored Jerusalem and from the community of Israel as one who, as son of the high priest, had betrayed the Covenant of Israel with the Lord God, had degraded the priesthood and had polluted the city by marrying a woman who was not an Israelite; nothing further is said of her [**Nehemiah 2:** 10, 19; **13:** 28-29]

**SAPPHIRA** – she was the wife of Ananias; with her husband, she belonged to the early Christian community; she persuaded her husband to hold back part of the purchase price received for a property they had sold and turn the rest in to the Apostles for the community, while claiming that what he turned in was all they had received; challenged by Peter, Ananias, who lied as planned, dropped dead at his feet and was buried, all in her absence; questioned by Peter some three hours later, Sapphira affirmed that the amount turned in was the whole of the purchase price; when Peter revealed their perfidy, she dropped dead at his feet, and was buried beside Ananias, to the awe of the whole Church [**Acts 5:** 1-11; see *SAPPHIRA and the Better Bargain*]

**SARAH, daughter of Asher** – alternate spelling; see **SERAH**

**SARAH, wife of Abraham (Abram, earlier)** – she was barren until the age of ninety; at seventy-six, she tried to bring to fulfillment the Lord God's promise to Abraham that he would be the father of *"a multitude of nations"* [Genesis 17: 3; JB] by having Abraham beget Ishmael on Hagar, her handmaid; after God had changed her name Sarai to Sarah and Abram's to Abraham, by His power, Sarah, at ninety, conceived Isaac by Abraham, who was then one hundred years old; Sarah died at one hundred twenty-seven and was buried in a cave at Machpelah, opposite Mamre, which Abraham had purchased from Ephron the Hittite, Zohar's son for a family burial plot; later Sarah was seen as a symbol of persevering faith and absolute trust in the Lord God and His promises, and of wifely obedience; allegorically Sarah became the new Covenant established by Jesus' death and rising, and the new Jerusalem [called **SARAI** in **Genesis 11:** 29, 30, 31; **12:** 5, 11-20; **13:** 1; **16:** 1-9; called **SARAH** in **Genesis 17:** 15-22; **18:** 1-15; **20:** 1-18; **21:** 1-12; **23:**1-2, 5-20; **24:** 36, 67; **25:** 10, 12; **49:** 31; **Isaiah 51:** 2; **Romans 4:** 19; **9:** 9; **Galatians 4:** 21-31; **Hebrews 11:** 11; **1 Peter 3:** 6 (see also **Abraham's CONCUBINES, HAGAR**); see *SARAH and the End of Patience* and *HAGAR and the Impatient Wife*]

**SARAH, wife of Tobias,** – she was the daughter of Raguel and Edna; the demon Asmodeus killed seven successive bridegrooms before any could consummate a marriage with her; she was given as wife by Raguel to Tobias, his kinsman; Tobias, acting on instructions from his companion, the archangel Raphael (disguised as Azarias, a kinsman), defeated Asmodeus and freed her; they consummated the marriage, and Sarah went home with Tobias [**Tobit 3:** 7-17, 25; **6:** 11-18; **7:** 8-20; **8:** 1-8, 20-21; **10:** 7-13; **11:** 3, 15-18; **12:** 3, 12-15 (see also **EDNA, ANNA, wife of Tobit, Raguel's MAIDSERVANTS** and *WIFE of Seven Brothers*); see *Sarah and the Bridal-Night Demon* and *ANNA and the Homecoming*]

**SARAI** – see **SARAH, wife of Abraham (Abram, earlier)**

**SERAH (also spelled Sarah), daughter of Asher** – she was the daughter of Asher who was Jacob's son by Leah's handmaid Zilpah; she was the sister of Imnah, Ishvah, Ishvi, and Beriah [**Genesis 46:** 17; **Numbers 26:** 46; **1 Chronicles 7:** 30]

**Serug's DAUGHTERS** – girls born to Serug, Reu's son and a seventh generation descendant of Noah, during the two hundred years Serug lived after the birth (when he was thirty years old) of Nahor; Nahor became the father of Terah and grandfather of Abram (later Abraham) and his brothers Nahor and Haran; of Serug's daughters nothing is known beyond this mention in the list of patriarchs after the Flood [**Genesis 11:** 23]

**SERVANT GIRL who was to be a messenger** – serving as the High Priest Zadok's messenger, she was supposed to report to Abiathar's son Jonathan and Zadok's son Ahimaaz, stationed at the Fuller's Spring, the plans and actions of Absalom and his party in Jerusalem; the men were to relay the information to King David (ca. 1010-970 BC), waiting in the wilderness; in the event, her services were not used, as Jonathan and Ahimaaz were seen and their presence reported to Absalom [**2 Samuel 17:** 17-18 (see also **WOMAN of Bahurim's household**)]

**Seth's DAUGHTERS** – girls born to Seth, the third son of Adam and Eve during the eight hundred seven years that Seth lived after the birth (when he was one hundred five years old) of Enosh (also spelled Enos); nothing more is known of them than this mention in the list of Adam's descendants before the Flood [**Genesis 5:** 7]

**Shallum's DAUGHTERS** — the children of Shallum, son of Hallohesh and ruler of half the district of Jerusalem; they are called *daughters* in the Hebrew text but that reading has been corrected to *sons* by some modern scholars; they assisted their father in repairing the section of the walls of Jerusalem next to Malchijah (son of Harim) and Hasshub (son of Pahath-moab), whose work stopped at the Tower of the Furnaces [**Nehemiah 3:** 12]

**Shaul's Canaanite MOTHER** — she was the concubine of Simeon, the second son of Jacob; she bore him Shaul; nothing further is known of her [**Genesis 46:** 10; **Exodus 6:** 15]

**SHEERAH (also spelled SHERAH)** — she was the daughter of Ephraim, Joseph's son by his Egyptian wife Asenath; her brother was named Beriah; these two children were born after the death of their brothers in a cattle raid; Sheerah is here identified as the builder of both Lower and Upper Beth-horon on the southern border with Ephraim, and of the otherwise unidentified Uzzen-sheerah [**1 Chronicles 7:** 24 (see also **ASENATH** and **Ephraim's WIFE**)]

**Shelah's (also spelled Salah) DAUGHTERS** — the girls born to Shelah, Arpachshad's son and Noah's great-grandson, during the four hundred three years Shelah lived after the birth (when he was thirty years old) of Eber; nothing more is known of them than this mention in the list of patriarchs after the Flood [**Genesis 11:** 15]

**SHELOMITH, daughter of Dibri** — she was an Israelite woman of the tribe of Dan in the days of Moses; married to an Egyptian, she became the mother of a man who quarreled with an Israelite in the camp, surrounded by the sons of Israel, and blasphemed and cursed the Name of the Lord God; this deed defiled the whole community, and resulted in the man's being stoned by the whole community at the Lord God's command, and in new law's being given by the Lord God for Israel; Shelomith was not harmed in the punishment of her son [**Leviticus 24:** 10-16]

**SHELOMITH, daughter of Zerubbabel** — she was the sister of Meshullam and Hananiah; recent archaeological evidence indicates she may have been spouse to Elnathan, who succeeded Zerubbabel as ruler of

Judah, and may have served as co-ruler with him; her father Zerubbabel (who, with the high priest, ruled Judah after the exile) was a descendant of Jehoiachin, a descendant of King David (ca. 1010-970 BC) in the royal line, and so an ancestor in the human genealogy of Jesus which ends with Joseph, His foster-father and the husband of Mary His mother [1 **Chronicles 3:** 19 (see also **Matthew 1:** 12-13)]

**SHELOMITH, child of Absalom's daughter, Maacah** – he or she was fathered by King Rehoboam of Judah (931-913 BC), the son and successor of King Solomon (ca. 970-931 BC); Rehoboam precipitated the split of Israel into two kingdoms and married Maacah after he married Mahalath; this child is probably a son, not a daughter, as the name is more often used for males and, when it is given to a woman, the fact is noted [2 **Chronicles 11:** 20]

**SHELOMITH, descendant of Bani** – this boy or girl was the child of Josiphiah; he or she returned from the Exile with one hundred sixty males; most scholars see this child as male though some see the child as both the parent of Josiphiah and female [**Ezra 8:** 10]

*SHEMAMAH* – *this was the name applied to Jerusalem/Zion, personified as female under various guises; the name, meaning "Forsaken" [JB], indicated her condition before her redemption* [**Isaiah 62:** 4 (see also *AZUBAH, GOMER, BEULAH, HEPHZIBAH and Jerusalem/Zion/Israel as Covenant BRIDE-TURNED-WHORE*)]

**Shem's DAUGHTERS** – the girls born to Shem, Noah's firstborn son, during the five hundred years Shem lived after the birth (when he was one hundred years old, two years after the Flood) of Arpachshad; nothing more is known of them than this mention in the list of patriarchs after the Flood [**Genesis 11:** 11]

**SHERAH** – alternate spelling; see **SHEERAH**

**Sheshan's DAUGHTER** – he or she was the child of Jerahmeel's son, Sheshan, who was a descendant of Judah through Perez and his son Hezron; Sheshan had no sons; she was given to Sheshan's slave, Jarha, as wife, and carried on the family line by bearing to Jarha a son, Attai [1 **Chronicles 2:** 34-35]

**Shiloh's DAUGHTERS** – see **(The) Benjaminites' four hundred WIVES**

**SHIMEATH (also called SHOMER, SHIMRITH)** – she was an Ammonite woman; she became the mother of Zabad, also called Jozacar; Zabad, with Jehozabad, killed King Joash (Jehoash) of Judah, in a death seen as the vengeance of the Lord God for his leading Judah into idolatry and his ordering the murder of Zechariah the high priest; Zechariah was the son of Jehoiada, the high priest who had saved Joash's life and placed him on the throne; possessed by the Spirit of God, Zechariah had rebuked Joash for this infidelity [**2 Chronicles 24:** 17-26; **2 Kings 12:** 21 (see also **ATHALIAH** and **JEHOSHEBA**); see *ATHALIAH and the Almost-Perfect Plan* and *JEHOSHEBA and the Vanishing King*]

**Shimei's DAUGHTERS** – the six girls born, along with sixteen sons, to Shimei, a descendant of Jacob's son, Simeon, one of the original twelve patriarchs of Israel; nothing more is known of them [**1 Chronicles 4:** 24-27]

**SHIMRITH** – see **SHIMEATH**

**SHIPHRAH** – she was one of two crucial Hebrew midwives in Egypt at the time of Moses; see **PUAH**

**SHOMER** – see **SHIMEATH**

**SHUA** – she was the daughter of Heber, a descendant of Jacob's son Asher (by Zilpah, Leah's handmaid); she was the sister of three brothers, Japhlet, Shomer and Hotham [**1 Chronicles 7:** 32]

**Shua's DAUGHTER** – see **BATHSHUA, wife of Judah**

*(The)* **SHULAMITE** – see *Song of Songs' BRIDE*

**(The) SHUNAMMITE MOTHER** – a childless woman of rank, she was married to an old man; she pressed Elisha to stay for a meal with her and her husband whenever he was visiting Shunem; then she had a small room built on the roof for Elisha to stay in whenever he came to their town; she answered Elisha's promise (made at his servant Gehazi's suggestion) that she would hold a son in her arms at that time in the following year, by asking him not to deceive her; she bore a son when and as Elisha had promised; when her son died, she ran for Elisha, who raised her son to life; on Elisha's instruction, she fled Shunem for the land of the Philistines for the seven years of the famine; on her return, she petitioned the king for the return of her house and lands; Gehazi attested to her identity, and she received back all her property, together with all the revenue that had come from her land during the whole time of her absence [**2 Kings 4:** 8-37; **8:** 1-6; see *The SHUNAMMITE MOTHER and the Promise Kept*]

**SIDONIAN WIDOW from Zarephath** – she was selected (though not so informed) by the Lord God to provide sustenance for the prophet Elijah the Tishbite during His famine in the Kingdom of Israel under King Ahab (874-853 BC); she used all her remaining flour and oil to make a cake for the prophet at his command, believing his promise from the Lord God that the jar of meal and the jug of oil would not be emptied while the famine lasted; she rejoiced that the prophet's words proved true; when her son fell sick and died, Elijah obtained the return of the child's life from the Lord God; she received her son alive again, from the prophet, and professed belief in him and in the Lord God; she was used as an example by Jesus to remind His audience that pagans often believed in the Lord God and in the words of His prophets when they experienced His favors, where they, themselves, though children of Israel and His chosen ones, did not accept Him, in spite of the wonders He had shown them [**1 Kings 17:** 7-24; **Luke 4:** 25-26; see *The SIDONIAN WIDOW and the Last Meal-Cake*]

**Silly WOMEN** – these women were the prey of hypocritical men (roundly condemned by the Apostle Paul), who wormed their way into family groups; the men worked on the scrupulosity of the women so they could control them; the women were fixated on their own sins; they followed popular religious fads, one after another, looking for truth and failing to find it; Paul seems to think that these men's machinations are doomed because, sooner or later, everyone will see through them [**2 Timothy 3:** 6-7]

**Simon (Thassi)'s MOTHER** – she was the wife of Mattathias; she became the mother of five sons, John (Gaddi), Simon (Thassi), Judas (Maccabaeus), Eleazar (Avaran) and Jonathan (Apphus); Simon, High Priest and ruler of the Jews (142–134 BC), raised a monument to her, one to his father and one for each of his four deceased brothers at Modein; nothing further is known of her [**1 Maccabees 13:** 28]

**Sinful WOMAN who anointed Jesus' feet** – in the four accounts of this incident (which may have described two or three separate occurrences), Matthew and Mark agree on the place, Bethany, the host, Simon the Leper, and the act as the pouring of the expensive ointment over Jesus' head by an unnamed woman; they report that some objected to the waste, saying the money could have been used for the poor, and that the woman's deed was praised by Jesus Who identified it as a good work, a preparation for His burial and a thing that would be remembered about her *"wherever in all the world this Good News is proclaimed"* [Matthew 26: 13; JB]; Luke alone identifies the woman as a sinful woman, interprets her act of pouring the ointment over Jesus' feet after her tears have washed and her hair dried them, as repentance and records Jesus' rebuke to Simon the Pharisee, the host, for his neglect of the hospitality the woman offered; according to Luke, Jesus declared that the woman must have had many sins forgiven her because she had loved this much, and then forgave the woman's sins, told her that her faith had saved her and bade her to go in peace; John alone names the Bethany feast a celebration (given by an unnamed host), as one of gratitude for Jesus' having raised Lazarus (present) from the dead; John attributes the pouring of the ointment over Jesus' feet to Mary, the sister of Martha (serving at the meal) and identifies the complainer of waste as Judas Iscariot (whom he names thief, stealing from the common purse entrusted to him) [**Luke 7:** 36-50 (see also **Matthew 26:** 6-13; **Mark 14:** 3-9; **John 12:** 1-11; **MARY, sister of Martha** and **MARY MAGDALENE**); see *The WOMAN and the Shattered Jar* and *MARY and the Costly Nard*]

*Sirach's WOMEN* – *in Sirach, a book of instructions for men on gaining an education in wisdom (seen as fulfillment of the Law of the Lord God), the universal or "generic" woman appears in all her life-roles, and serves both as illustration and as subject matter; in general, a woman, by her beauty, was dangerous to men, even to one as wise as Solomon, for she could lead them to lust, adultery, fornication and incest and the loss of both strength and honor, particularly when wine is added to the mix [9: 3-9; 19:2-3; 23: 5-6, 16-27; 25: 21; 41:20-24; 47: 19; JB]; a woman, whose wickedness is worst of all, gave rise to shame and reproach now, just as a woman's sin had caused death for all [25: 19, 24; 42: 14b; JB], and a man's spite was preferable* to a woman's kindness [42: 14a; JB]; woman's vices of spite, jealousy, wantonness, garrulousness, foolishness and willfulness gave rise to other miseries which made her a bad wife who should be gotten rid of ( if she would not improve), lest she weaken and depress her husband [25: 8b, 13, 16-18, 20, 23, 25, 26; 26: 6-9, 23a, 24a, 25a, 26b, 27; 37: 11; 42: 13-14; JB]; if she were not guarded, properly taught and controlled, she would chase other men, bear children to them and shame her husband and family [9: 1-2; 23: 22-27; 36: 25; 42: 12-13; JB]; she was not to be trusted, nor allowed to rule, lest she destroy her husband, particularly if she was disliked [7: 26; 25: 22; 33: 20; 42: 6a; JB]; a good wife, one who was sensible, graceful, accomplished, modest, silent, diffident even with her husband, gentle of tongue, God-fearing, respectful of her husband, well-trained, chaste of character and beautiful of face and body, kept her home well, obeyed her husband and pleased him [7:26; 25: 8a; 26: 13-18, 23b, 24b, 25b, 26a; 36: 22-23; JB], was a blessing, a joy who would double his lifespan, a helper, a pillar to lean on, the start of his fortune, of more worth than cattle and vineyards, one to whom he should not teach evil ways, of whom he ought not be jealous, and whom he should not cast off, for without her he would be aimless, querulous and not to be trusted [7: 19; 9:1; 26: 1-4, 26 c, d; 36: 24, 26-27; 40: 19; JB]; in his turn, since a whore was not worth spitting on, a husband ought to have children only with his lawful wife, who would be strong as a tower for him, and he should not turn against her nor believe a slander against her that could drive this virtuous wife out of her home, for the union of a husband with a good wife was better than that between friends or comrades, and was the delight of God and men [7: 19, 26; 25: 1; 26: 19-22; 28: 15; 40: 23; JB]; a daughter was a loss at birth and a father's serious worry, for she had to be brought up without self-indulgence and, if headstrong, strictly controlled, so that she would not become a wanton who would disgrace her family by bearing children out of wedlock, but would be accepted in marriage by a sensible husband and become his treasure [7: 24-25; 22: 3-5; 26: 10-12; JB]; her father was aware that, though a woman must accept any husband, some daughters are better than others, and the man had the choice, so he worried lest she not marry, or be cast off when she had married, or if headstrong, lost her virginity before marriage and bore a child while unmarried, thus shaming him publicly [36: 21; 42: 9-12; JB]; widows existed in Sirach as needing protection, with their prayers and tears over the men who had harmed them being heard by God [4: 10; 35: 14-15; JB]; with widows, mothers were the only women with whom Sirach had no fault to find; pairing them always with fathers and seeing the parents together as the source of life which cannot be repaid and of instruction and good example that would sharpen both conscience and social behavior, he declared them worthy of honor and comfort, not to be forgotten, dishonored by a shameless daughter, nor angered, nor to *have their rights denied, for that would displease the Lord God [3: 2-16; 7: 27-28; 22: 4-5; 23: 14; 1: 17; JB]* [**Sirach 3:** 2-16; **4:** 10; **7:** 19, 24-28; **9:** 1-9; **19:** 2-3; **22:** 3-5; **23:** 5-6, 14, 16-27; **25:** 1, 8, 13, 16-26; **26:** 1-27; **28:** 15; **33:** 20; **35:** 14-15; **36:** 21-27; **37:** 11; **40:** 19, 23; **41:** 17, 20-24; **42:** 6, 9-14; **47:** 19 (see also *WISDOM, FOLLY/the Adulterous SEDUCTRESS/the ALIEN WOMAN, Valiant WOMAN, Proverbs' WOMEN* and *Ecclesiastes' WOMEN*)]

**Sisera's MOTHER** – she appears in Deborah's Song of Victory; the Song was sung after the Lord God had destroyed King Jabin's Canaanite army (led by Sisera), using the Israelite army led by Abinoam's son Barak from Kedesh in Naphtali; in a passage that follows immediately upon the graphic description of Sisera's murder at Jael's hands, Sisera's mother is pictured as waiting by the window with her princesses for her son's return and being comforted by them with thoughts of his victory and the spoils of war he and his men were sharing; the irony of that placement is made explicit in the last verse; nothing further is known of Sisera's mother [**Judges 5:** 24-31 (see also **JAEL** and **Sisera's mother's PRINCESSES**)]

**Sisera's mother's PRINCESSES** – these women appear in Deborah's Song of Victory; the Song was sung after the Lord God destroyed King Jabin's Canaanite army (led by Sisera), using the Israelite army led by Abinoam's son Barak from Kedesh in Naphtali; they comfort Sisera's mother with images of her victorious son sharing out the spoils of battle with his men, an ironic passage which immediately follows the graphic description of Sisera by Jael; nothing else is known of them [**Judges 5:** 25-31 (see also **JAEL** and **Sisera's MOTHER**)]

**Skilled WOMEN** – see **WOMEN Contributing Wealth, Skill to the Building of the Sanctuary**

*SODOM* – *a female personification of Sodom, a city proverbially the absolute in corruption, as the younger sister of the failed Covenant Bride, Jerusalem/Zion/Israel and of Samaria; her notorious crimes are used as a foil for the far worse infidelity of the faithless Bride; with Samaria, Sodom will be restored by the Lord God as part of the combined punishment/restoration of Jerusalem/Zion/Israel* [**Ezekiel 16:** 46-61 (see also **SAMARIA, Jerusalem/Zion/Israel as Covenant BRIDE-TURNED-WHORE** and **Jerusalem/Zion/Israel as Covenant BRIDE RESTORED**)]

**Solomon's FIRST WIFE** – she was the daughter of a Pharaoh whom scholars tentatively identify as Psusennis, last king of the Twenty-First Dynasty; she was taken to wife by King Solomon (ca. 970-931 BC) and brought to the Citadel of David, pending completion of the royal palace, the Temple of the Lord God and the wall around Jerusalem; her father conquered the city of Gezer, burnt it down, massacred the Canaanites living there, and gave her the city, as a dowry; Solomon later rebuilt Gezer; she had a special house, paneled in cedar from floor to rafters like the Hall of the Throne, built for her by King Solomon; when she moved from the Citadel of David to this house, Solomon built the Millo, making a flat surface of the steep hillside on which the palace and Temple were built, scholars explain [**1 Kings 3:** 1; **7:** 8; **9:** 16-17, 24; **11:** 1; **2 Chronicles 8:** 11]

**Solomon's Later WIVES and CONCUBINES** – the seven hundred wives and three hundred concubines (secondary wives) of King Solomon (ca. 970-931 BC), taken from the surrounding pagan peoples (Moabites, Edomites, Sidonians and Hittites), in spite of the Lord God's forbidding such marriages to all the Israelites as certain to lead them into idolatry; in his old age, Solomon's heart was drawn to the false gods worshipped by his wives, and he built altars on the high places at which they could worship, himself offering worship to Astarte (god of the Sidonians) and Milcom (god of the Ammonites); this defection earned him the displeasure of the Lord God and the loss of his kingdom, except for one tribe, to his son and heir [**1 Kings 10:** 8; **11:** 1- 13; **Nehemiah 13:** 26]

*Song of Solomon's BRIDE – see Song of Songs' BRIDE*

*Song of Songs' BRIDE (also called Song of Solomon's BRIDE, Canticle of Canticles' BRIDE and (The) SHULAMITE) – "black but beautiful" [JB], the Bride longed for her bridegroom who was beloved of all maidens, and sought him; she was praised by her Bridegroom as loveliest of women; their love progresses through a dialogue of mutual praise and desire, a first consummation, her loss of him through hesitation, her painful quest to find him again, their reunion in the garden, and the ultimate consummation of their love in permanent union; most commonly, the Song is seen as originally tracing the Covenant relationship between the Lord God (as Bridegroom) and Israel (as His chosen Bride), which would end with their joyous, fully committed union, the Messianic Kingdom; Christian interpreters have seen the relationship as the New Covenant between the Lord God and His Church established by Jesus Christ Who became the Bridegroom, or as the relationship between God and the individual soul; in any case, the longing of Bridegroom and Bride for one another is mutual, when they are apart they search for one another, and in their consummation both are equally ravished and satisfied, a stunning picture when one considers that the Bridegroom is God and the Bride is (whatever the interpretation), His creature* [**Song of Songs** (see also *Jerusalem/Zion/Israel as* **CHOSEN BRIDE** *of the Covenant, Revelation's* **BRIDE** *of the Lamb,* **King's DAUGHTER, DAUGHTERS** *of Kings, Church as* **CHASTE BRIDE** *of Christ,* **QUEEN** *arrayed in gold* and other *Song of Songs'* entries)]

*Song of Songs' Bride's* **MOTHER** – *she bore one girl, who was her favorite child, and several boys; she had no part in the anger of the brothers with their sister, nor in its consequences for her daughter; her house and room were seen by her daughter as a safe refuge to which she could bring her Bridegroom, and where He could teach her; the Bride regretted that her mother was not also the Bridegroom's mother, for then the Bride could greet the Bridegroom in public with a kiss without garnering the neighbors' scorn; scholars' readings of her identity and role vary according to the overall interpretation given the entire Song of Songs* [**Song of Songs 1:** 6; **3:** 4c, d, e, f; **6:** 9c, d; **8:** 1-2a, b; 5c, d, e (see also other *Song of Songs'* entries)]

*Song of Songs'* **CHORUS** *(also called Song of Songs'* **DAUGHTERS** *of Jerusalem, Song of Songs'* **DAUGHTERS** *of Zion)* – *these women were addressed by both Bride and Bridegroom as Daughters of Jerusalem, and by themselves as Daughters of Zion; in the structure of the poem, the group gives the Bride and the Bridegroom someone else to speak to, serves as the Bride's counselor and support, and moves the action of the Song forward; scholars' readings of the identity and role of the Chorus vary according to the overall interpretation given the entire Song of Songs* [**Song of Songs 1:** 4d, e; 5a, b, c, d, e; 6, 8; **2:** 7; **3:** 5, 6-11; **5:** 8, 9, 16; **6:** 1; **7:** 1; **8:** 4, 5a, b; 8-9, 13 (see also other *Song of Songs'* entries)]

*Song of Songs'* **DAUGHTERS** *of Jerusalem* – (see *Song of Songs'* **CHORUS**)

*Song of Songs'* **DAUGHTERS** *of Zion* – (see *Song of Songs'* **CHORUS**)

*Song of Songs' King's Mother* – *she crowned the King ("Solomon," the Messianic King; here the Bridegroom) on his wedding day with a diadem which he wore on his progress to meet his Bride; scholars' readings of her identity and role vary according to the overall interpretation given the entire Song of Songs* [**Song of Songs 3:** 11(see also other *Song of Songs'* entries)]

***Song of Songs' QUEENS, CONCUBINES, and Other MAIDENS*** – *the "sixty queens, eighty concubines and countless maidens" [JB], who appeared and were quoted in the Bridegroom's song of praise of His Bride as superior and unique; the maidens proclaimed her blessed; the queens and concubines sang her praises saying, 'Who is this arising like the dawn, / fair as the moon, / resplendent as the sun, / terrible as an army with banners?' [JB], a paean applied in Church liturgy to the Blessed Mother Mary; scholars' readings of their identity and role vary according to the overall interpretation given the entire Song of Songs* [**Song of Songs 6: 8–10** (see also ***DAUGHTERS of Kings, QUEEN arrayed in gold*** and other ***Song of Songs'*** entries)]

**SOOTHSAYER slave-girl** – this woman lived in Philippi, a Roman colony and principal city of Macedonia; she made much money for her masters by telling fortunes; when the Apostle Paul and his party arrived and began to preach, she met them one day on their way to prayer; thereafter, followed them daily, proclaiming, *"Here are the servants of the Most High God; they have come to tell you how to be saved!"* [Acts 16: 17; JB]; she had her demon driven out by Paul (who lost his temper one day and commanded it to leave her in the Name of Jesus Christ); her cure infuriated her masters (who could make no further money from her fortune-telling), and they seized Paul and Silas, charged them as Jews who were making a public disturbance and teaching things unlawful for Romans to accept or follow; the charge was upheld by the hostile crowd and earned the missioners a flogging and jailing; the girl's fate is unknown [**Acts 16: 16-24**]

**SOPHERETH** – see **HASSOPHERETH**

**SUSANNA, daughter of Hilkiah** – she was a very beautiful, God-fearing descendant of Judah, who lived in Babylon during the period of exile; she had been well-instructed in the Law of Moses by her faithful parents; she became the wife of Joakim, to whom she bore children; she thwarted the lust of the two wicked old men serving as elected judges of the people for the year by refusing to submit to their desires; she was rescued by the young Daniel, who remarked that the elders' wiles had worked on daughters of Israel but not on this daughter of Judah, a contrast between the faithful remnant of Judah and the unfaithful of Israel [**Daniel 13:** 1–64 or Apocrypha **Susanna** 1–64 (see also **Susanna, daughter of Hilkiah's MOTHER** and **Susanna, daughter of Hilkiah's MAIDSERVANTS**); see *SUSANNA and the Weighty Word*]

**Susanna, daughter of Hilkiah's MAIDSERVANTS** – the two young girls who accompanied Susanna into the garden, fetched oil and balsam so she could bathe and, at her instruction, shut the garden door, unknowingly leaving the hidden evil elders locked in with her; they were used by the elders as "proof" that Susanna wanted the garden empty so she could entertain a lover [**Daniel 13:** 15, 17, 19, 21 (see also **SUSANNA, daughter of Hilkiah**); see *SUSANNA and the Weighty Word*]

**Susanna, daughter of Hilkiah's MOTHER** – she bore Susanna to Hilkiah and raised her in the Law of Moses; with her husband, weeping, she accompanied her daughter to her trial on the false charge of adultery raised by the thwarted, evil elders; she rejoiced with her husband, Susanna and her husband and all their relations when Daniel had acquitted her of the false charges and the elders had been punished [**Daniel 13:** 3, 30, 33, 63 (see also **SUSANNA, daughter of Hilkiah**); *SUSANNA and the Weighty Word*]

**SUSANNA, follower of Jesus** – this woman was one of a group of women who had been healed by Jesus of evil spirits and ailments, traveled with the group of disciples and Jesus and ministered to them, using their own means; she was probably among those who stayed with the disciples after the Ascension of Jesus, awaiting the coming of the Spirit [**Matthew 27:** 55–56; **Mark 15:** 40–41; **Luke 8:** 2–3; **23:** 49, 55–56; **24:** 1–11; 22–24; **Acts 1:** 14 (see also **MINISTERING WOMEN of Jesus and the Apostles, MARY MAGDALENE, MARY, wife of Clopas, JOANNA** and **SALOME, wife of Zebedee**); see *MARY MAGDALENE and the Questing Heart*]

**SYNTYCHE** – she was a member of the Christian community at Philippi; with Evodia, she was a helper of the Apostle Paul in his defense of the Good News; she was urged by Paul to be reconciled with Evodia in the Lord [**Philippians 4:** 2–3 (see also **EVODIA**)]

**Syro-Phoenician (Canaanite) WOMAN and her DAUGHTER** – she met Jesus with His disciples in the Tyre-Sidon area and begged Him to heal her daughter who was tormented by an evil spirit; she persisted in pleading for the girl's restoration in spite of the impatience of His disciples, a brush-off and then an insult from Jesus Himself (which she countered brilliantly); the daughter, though not on the scene, was healed at the very moment Jesus finally spoke the word her mother had been begging for [**Matthew 15: 21-28; Mark 7: 24-30**]

# T

**TABITHA (in Greek, DORCAS)** – she was a disciple living in Jaffa who worked tirelessly, helping the poor and serving others; she died and was laid out in an upstairs room; the other disciples sent for the Apostle Peter who was visiting the community in nearby Lydda; he came, prayed, raised her from the dead and restored her to the community [**Acts 9: 36-42**; see *TABITHA and the Other Side of the Journey*]

**TAHPENES** – she was the chief wife of the Pharaoh, perhaps Siamun (975-955 BC); her sister was given as wife to Hadad the Edomite prince, who, as a boy, had escaped the soldiers of King David (ca. 1010-970 BC); with some of his fathers retainers, Hadad had fled to Egypt, becoming the enemy raised up by the Lord God against the aged and now idolatrous King Solomon (ca. 970-931 BC); Tahpenes raised her nephew Genubath, son of her sister and Hadad, with the Pharaoh's children [**1 Kings 11: 19-20** (see also **Tahpenes' SISTER**)]

**Tahpenes' SISTER** – she was the sister of the Great Lady Tahpenes, wife of the Pharaoh, perhaps Siamun (975-955 BC); she was given in marriage by the Pharaoh to Hadad, refugee son of the King of Edom; the King of Edom had been killed, with all the males of Edom, by Joab in the conquest by King David (ca. 1010-970 BC); Hadad, with a few of his late father's retainers in Egypt, lived in the Pharaoh's household; Tahpenes' sister bore to Hadad a son, Genubath, whom Tahpenes brought up and educated in the Pharaoh's palace with the Pharaoh's children [**1 Kings 11: 19-20** (see also **TAHPENES**)]

**TAMAR, daughter of Absalom** – she was a beautiful woman; she was the sister of three brothers; in some ancient versions, she was called Maacah and identified as wife to King Rehoboam (931-913 BC), her uncle [**2 Samuel 14:** 27]

**TAMAR, daughter of King David** – she was the daughter of King David (ca. 1010-970 BC) and Maacah; she was the sister of Absalom; she was deceived by Amnon, her half-brother and David's firstborn son by Ahinoam; though he could have asked David for her in marriage, Amnon raped Tamar, then rejected her and had her put out of the house; Tamar was found mourning in the street by her full brother, Absalom; Absalom took her in, tried to comfort her and, two years later, arranged for the death of Amnon, in vengeance for Amnon's treatment of Tamar; Absalom then fled his father's wrath, taking refuge with Talmai son of Ammihud, king of Geshur, for three years [**2 Samuel 13:** 1-32; **1 Chronicles 3:** 9; see *TAMAR and the Broken Bread*]

**TAMAR, mother of Perez and Zerah (also spelled THAMAR)** – she was the wife of Judah's firstborn, Er, who offended the Lord God and so died; on Er's death, she was given to his brother Onan who refused to beget children for Er on her and for this offense also died at the Lord God's hand; she was then sent back to her father as a widow by Judah, to await the maturity of Judah's youngest son, Shelah; she was refused Shelah as a husband by Judah, who was afraid he would lose his third and last son as he had the other two; she disguised herself as a harlot, seduced Judah and bore him twin sons, Perez and Zerah, whom he acknowledged; she became the grandmother of the sons of Perez, Hezron and Hamul, and of the sons of Zerah, Zimri, Ethan, Heman, Calcol and Dara; through her son Perez, she became an ancestress of Joseph, husband of Mary and foster-father of Jesus, Son of God and Messiah [**Genesis 38:** 6-11, 13-30; **Ruth 4:** 12; **1 Chronicles 2:** 4; **Matthew 1:** 3 (see also **BATHSHUA**); see *TAMAR and the Long Way Around*]

**Tamar, mother of Perez and Zerah 's MIDWIFE** – this woman assisted the daughter-in-law of Judah as she gave birth to Judah's twin offspring; she identified the first child to arrive by tying a scarlet thread to his hand; when he withdrew and his brother was born she said, *"What a breach you have opened for yourself!"* [Genesis 38: 29; JB] prompting the name Perez for the child; the son marked with the scarlet thread was called Zerah [**Genesis**

**38:** 27-30 (see **TAMAR, mother of Perez and Zerah**); see *TAMAR and the Long Way Around*]

**Tammuz' MOURNERS** – women shown to the prophet in his vision as examples of the sins of Jerusalem; they sat at the entrance of the north gate of the Temple of the Lord God in Jerusalem and performed the yearly mourning rites for the Sumerian-Assyrian-Babylonian god Tammuz (Adonis in the west; he was the bringer of spring growth and the spouse of Ishtar), in memory of his death and following stay in the underworld; their act, performed before the Lord God's Temple, was considered blatant idolatry and was one of the reasons for the Lord God's anger with His people [**Ezekiel 8:** 14-15]

**TAPHATH** – she was the daughter of King Solomon (ca. 970-931 BC); she was married to the son of Abinadab, one of Solomon's twelve administrators, caring for the whole region of Dor [**1 Kings 4:** 11]

**THAMAR, mother of Perez and Zerah** – alternate spelling; see **TAMAR, mother of Perez and Zerah**

**THEBES** – *in this female personification, Thebes is pictured going into exile, her little ones dashed to pieces at every crossroad; if she did not escape this fate, the prophets asks, how can Nineveh expect to?* [**Nahum 3:** 8-10]

**TIMNA** – she was the daughter of Seir and the sister of Lotan; she became the concubine of Esau and Adah's son, Eliphaz; she was the mother of Amalek; some scholars see the daughter of Seir, Lotan's sister, as different from Eliphaz' concubine [**Genesis 36:** 12, 22; **1 Chronicles 1:** 39]

**TIRZAH** – she was the youngest of the five daughters of Zelophehad; see **MAHLAH, eldest daughter of Zelophehad**

**Tobiah, the Ammonite official's WIFE** – she was the daughter of Arah's son Shecaniah, keeper of the East Gate of Jerusalem; she tied her husband in to the authorities in Judah, particularly those who opposed Nehemiah's work of rebuilding the city's wall (455-443 BC); she bore two sons, Shemaimah and Jehohanan; Shemaimah worked on the wall near the Horse Gate; Jehohanan married the daughter of

Berechiah's son, Meshullam, who was the leader of a repair team working on the wall near the Fish Gate; neither his wife nor her sons lessened Tobiah's hostility to Nehemiah's work [**Nehemiah 2:** 10; **3:** 4, 29; **6:** 18 (see also **Jehohanan's WIFE**)]

**TRYPHAENA (also spelled TRYPHENA)** – together with Tryphosa, she was greeted by name as one who worked hard for the Lord, by the Apostle Paul as he concluded his letter to the Christian community at Rome [**Romans 16:** 12]

**TRYPHENA** – alternate spelling; see **TRYPHAENA**

**TRYPHOSA** – together with Tryphaena, she was greeted by name as one who worked hard for the Lord, by the Apostle Paul as he concluded his letter to the Christian community at Rome [**Romans 16:** 12]

**Two QUARRELING MOTHERS of Solomon's time** – two prostitutes living alone in the same house who had given birth to children on successive days; each woman kept her baby in bed with her while she slept; one woman rolled over on her child and killed it, then placed her dead child in bed with the other, and took the other's living child to her own bed; the mother whose living child had been removed discovered the substitution in the morning and challenged her housemate; the two came to King Solomon (ca. 970–931 BC) for a judgment; having heard their story, Solomon sent for a sword and commanded that the living child be split in two, half being given to each claimant; the child's true mother begged that the child's life be spared, telling the King to give the child to the other woman, while the false claimant expressed satisfaction that now neither of them would have the living child; Solomon awarded the living child to its true mother [**1 Kings 3:** 16-28]

*Two WINGED WOMEN – these female figures appear in the seventh vision of the prophet Zechariah; they picked up the lead-sealed bushel containing the woman, Wickedness, and, as the wind filled their stork-like wings, they raised it midway between earth and heaven; the angel explained to the prophet that the women would take the bushel to the land of Shinar, where they would build a temple for it and make a stand on which to put it [**Zechariah 5:** 9-11 (see also WOMAN Sitting in a Bushel)]*

***Two WOMEN grinding grain at the mill*** – *doing the same common work, one woman will die and the other will not, for no apparent reason; Jesus cites this example of the suddenness of His coming and its effects on the world, warning everyone to be alert for a death that is both definitely coming and unpredictable in time and place, and so to be prepared to die at any moment, that is, always to live the life God asks* [**Matthew 24:** 41; **Luke 17:** 35]

# U

***Unjust steward's WIFE*** – *she appears in Jesus' parable of the unjust steward as an adjunct; she was to be sold into slavery, together with her children and all the rest of the steward's possessions, to repay his debt of ten thousand talents to his master; she was not included in the steward's final punishment (of being turned over to the torturers until he repaid the debt), incurred when he refused his fellow-servant the mercy the master had shown him by forgiving the debt upon the steward's plea for more time* [**Matthew 18:** 23-35]

# V

***VALIANT WOMAN*** – *she appears as the subject of the alphabetic poem that ends the final chapter on the Book of Proverbs; her virtues were wisdom, obedient respect for the Lord God and fidelity to the Covenant; she is first defined as a perfect wife whose price is beyond pearls; she displayed superior competence in every area of domestic living and made a place for herself in business; she brought her husband, who trusted her completely, satisfaction and renown in the city; she worked effectively, spinning and weaving both wool and flax, clothing her servants warmly, making her own clothing and quilts for the household, and weaving sheets and sashes for sale to the merchants; she was a good businesswoman, buying property and planting a vineyard with the profit she had earned from her work; she provided food for her household and for the poor, and she ran her household properly; she worked day and night; she spoke wisely and had no fear of the future; she was praised by her husband and sons as the wise woman who had earned her praise at the city gates* [**Proverbs 31:** 10-31 (see also **FOLLY/*Adulterous* SEDUCTRESS/ALIEN WOMAN, WISDOM,** ***Ecclesiastes' WOMEN, Sirach's WOMEN*** and *Proverbs' WOMEN*)]

**VASHTI** – she was the principal wife of King Ahasuerus of Persia (probably indicates Xerxes I, the Great, ca. 486-465 BC; he was called Ahasuerus in Hebrew, Artaxerxes in Greek); she refused to appear before the King who had sent his seven eunuchs to bring her to his banquet; her refusal was seen as contempt for the King, wronging him, the administrators and all the nations in the King's domain, and as a dangerous precedent (encouraging all women to disobey their husbands); for those reasons, Vashti was permanently banished from the presence of the King by a royal edict, irrevocably incorporated into the laws of the Persians and Medes; her fate was intended to make all women respect and obey their husbands; after a time, she was replaced by Esther [**Esther 1:** 9-20; **2:** 1-4, 17 (see also **ESTHER**)]

**VIRGIN MOTHER prophesied** – this was the sign given by the Lord God to King Ahaz of Judah (736-716 BC) that His promise (that the plans of the kings of Aram and Israel to conquer Judah would be thwarted), made through His prophet Isaiah, would be kept; Ahaz had refused to ask the Lord God for this sign, despite the prophet's instruction; the sign was that a virgin would bear a son and would call him Emmanuel (*"God-is-with-us"* [Isaiah 7: 14; JB]); though many see this sign as referring immediately to the birth of Ahaz' son Hezekiah, it was early understood to refer to the direct intervention of the Lord God in sending His Messiah; Christians have always seen it as a hidden prophecy of the birth of Jesus of Nazareth, the Christ, the Son of God together with the virginity of Mary, his mother at His birth; Micah prophesies that the birth will be the signal for the return and restoration of the remnant of Isaiah [**Isaiah 7:** 14; **Micah 5:** 2; **Matthew 1:** 23 (see also **MARY, the mother of Jesus, Son of God**); see *MARY and the Mothering of God*]

# W

**WEAVERS of clothes for Asherah** – the women who worked in the house of male prostitutes set up in the Temple of the Lord God in Jerusalem in the earlier part of the reign of King Josiah of Judah (640-609 BC); they wove cloth there for the image of Asherah, used either as garments for the image or as curtains for the shrine; they were probably dispersed when King Josiah tore the house down (ca. 622 BC), ending the worship of false gods in the Lord God's Temple and in the Kingdom of Judah [**2 Kings 23:** 7 (see also **ASHERAH** and **MAACAH, wife of Rehoboam**)]

**WIDOW of Nain's son** – weeping, accompanied by many of her towns-men, she followed the body of her only son being carried out through the town gates of Nain for burial; seeing her, Jesus felt sorry for her, stopped the bearers and commanded the dead man to rise; he did so, sitting up on the bier and beginning to talk; she received her son alive from Jesus as everyone, awed, praised God and proclaimed Jesus as a prophet through whom God was visiting His people [**Luke 7:** 11-19]

*WIDOW seeking justice* – *she appears in a parable designed by Jesus to teach His hearers to pray continually and never give up hope; in the story, she had been begging an unjust judge "who feared neither God nor man"* [Luke 18: 2; JB], *to give her rights to her against her enemy; though he refused to listen, she persisted until finally, because, he said, she was exhausting him and might attack him physically, he found in her favor* [**Luke 18:** 1-5]

**WIDOW with two mites** – though she was a very poor woman, she contributed two small coins to the Temple treasury; her action was observed by Jesus, Who declared that her gift, the smallest in monetary worth, was more valuable than all the others had put in, because she had given, not from abundance but from poverty, and had given everything she had [**Mark 12:** 41-44; **Luke 21:** 1-4]

**WIDOWS of Uz** – by Job's own testimony, these women had never failed to receive his help [**Job 24:** 3, 21; **29:** 14; **31:** 16]

**WIDOWS speaking Greek** – the widows of Christians from outside Palestine who, in the synagogues of Jerusalem, had the Scriptures read in Greek; they had no families to support them, and consequently, became the charge of the Christian community, the custom for such widows in Israel; they lived in common with the rest of the Christian community; they received their daily food from the community; a complaint lodged with the Apostles on their behalf, saying that they were being neglected in favor of the Hebrew-speaking widows in the daily food distribution, led to the Apostles' ordering the community to choose seven deacons to see to the physical aspects of running the community; when this was done, the Apostles were freed to concentrate on their spiritual responsibilities [**Acts 6:** 1-6 (see also **WIDOWS speaking Hebrew**]

**WIDOWS speaking Hebrew** – the widows of Christians native to Palestine who, in the synagogues of Jerusalem, had the Scriptures read in Hebrew; they had no families to support them, and consequently, became the charge of the Christian community, the custom for such widows in Israel; they lived in common with the rest of the Christian community; they received their daily food from the community; a complaint lodged with the Apostles, charging that they were being favored over the Greek-speaking widows in the daily food distribution, led to the Apostles' ordering the community to choose seven deacons to see to the physical aspects of running the community; when this was done, the Apostles were freed to concentrate on their spiritual responsibilities [**Acts 6:** 1-6 (see also **WIDOWS Speaking Greek**)]

*WIFE of seven brothers – this woman appears in a test case bearing a distinct resemblance to the life of Sarah, the wife of Tobias; the case was posed to Jesus by Sadducees who disbelieved in resurrection of the dead and wished to force Him to discredit this belief; in this case, there was no rescue for the woman, and the Sadducees asked whose wife she would be in the resurrection since she had married all seven brothers and died without issue; Jesus answered by saying that they had misunderstood both the Scriptures and the power of God, that in the Resurrection there would be no marriage (so their question was moot); Jesus extended the lesson, saying that the dead had to rise, for God had said of Himself "I am the God of Abraham, the God of Isaac and the God of Jacob!"* [Exodus 3: 6; JB] *(all of whom had died), and He is the God of the living, not of the dead; the argument silenced His critics and impressed His listeners* [**Matthew 22:** 23-33; **Mark 12:** 18-25; **Luke 20:** 27-40; see ***SARAH and the Bridal-Night Demon***]

*WISDOM – this quality was personified as female; in contrast with Folly, the adulterous seductress, she led men always to God and goodness; her essence was the loving respect for the Lord God Who had made Covenant with Israel; in Proverbs, she stood at the crossroads calling out, urging Israel to follow her ways and warning them that if they refused they would suffer calamity and be unable to find her, but if they followed her ways they would have quiet, secure lives [1: 20-33; JB]; she was more valuable than silver, gold or pearls, and her paths led to contentment and length of days [3: 14-19; JB]; commitment to her would bring life, safety and protection [4: 4-9, 13; JB]; she was the wife of Israel's youth, to whom fidelity is urged [5: 15-19; JB]; was to be called sister and dearest friend [7:4; JB]; she was the source of discretion, lucidity of thought, the source of the rule of kings and of just laws, of riches, honor, justice, and virtue [8: 12-21; JB]; she was present at the Creation in every act of the Creator, serving as the "master craftsman" at His side, delighting in His presence and "at play everywhere in His world, delighting to be with the sons of men" [8: 22-31; JB], a passage applied by Christian liturgy to the Virgin Mary; she built herself a house and invited the foolish to abandon their folly by coming to feast with her [9: 1-6; JB]; she built herself a house with her own hands [14: 1; JB]; she was to be found in the hearts of the discerning, but had no place in the fool [14: 33; JB]; in Baruch, God, the only One Who can grasp her fully, had given her to Israel as His Law; God was her origin and the loss of her, in the failures of observance of that Law, was seen as the cause of Israel's exile; in Sirach, she was identified as the first of all created things, whose ways were fully known only to God and whose beginning is the fear (respect) of the Lord [1: 1-20; JB]; she was seen as mother and teacher, bringing up her own sons who, if they trusted her and learned her lessons, would be happy, gain honor, judge rightly and dwell secure; if they followed her faithfully through difficulties, they would be brought back to the straight path [4: 11-19; JB]; she would give rest, joy, a strong defense and honor to those who accepted her discipline, while those who resisted would suffer [6: 18-37; JB]; whoever feared (that is, respected) the Lord God, and grasped the Law, would cling to wisdom, and she would meet him like a mother and greet him like a virgin bride, giving him happiness, honor before people and an everlasting name, while she would reject the proud, liars and sinners [14: 20-27 − 15: 1-10; JB]; she would be recognized by any sensible man, who respected anyone who had found her [18: 20; JB]; she described herself as created by the Lord God, seeking a place in His universe, being told by Him to settle in Israel, doing so and flourishing there, and she invited all who desired her to come and take their fill [24: 1-22; JB]; the book of the Covenant of the Lord God and keeping the Law of Moses were identified as her source, and no man could grasp the whole of her [24: 23-27; JB]; faithful pursuit of Wisdom would bring her seeker to delight and to what the soul most thirsted for [51: 13-30; JB]; in 2 Esdras, Wisdom, with understanding, was called a mother; and seeking her had brought the speaker a vision which God interpreted[13: 54-55; NRSV-HC]; she is also pictured as Righteousness, abhorring Folly/Iniquity when she dressed up, and accusing her to God when He came [16: 49-50; NRSV-HC]; in Wisdom, Solomon described her as having every kind of intelligence and power [7: 22-24; JB], as being a breath of the power of God and a reflection of His light, and so, totally pure [7: 25-26; JB], as making people friends of God, and as outshining the sun [7:27-30; JB]; she ordered all things in the universe to good, and so, said Solomon, he chose her for his bride, for her closeness to God Who loved her, and for her superiority to any other desire (wealth, virtue, experience), because she contained them all [8: 1-8; JB]; she was indispensable* to the ruler, and Solomon determined to ask the Lord God for her, as no man could master her himself [8: 9-21; JB]; in his prayer, Solomon identified her as consort of the Lord God's throne, as present at the creation, and as understanding what pleased Him and accorded with His commandment; he asked that God might send her to teach him what would please Him, thus ensuring that all Solomon did would please the Lord God, and that he would govern the Lord God's people justly, for without Wisdom this would be impossible [9: 4, 9-18; JB]; surveying history, Solomon noted that Wisdom had protected and brought to the Lord God all who followed her, drawing Adam to repentance, directing Noah through the flood, strengthening Abraham to obey God and sacrifice Isaac, saving Lot, rescuing Jacob fleeing Esau and making him rich, keeping Joseph free from sin and bringing him to power in Egypt, delivering Israel from the Egyptians, leading them through the Red Sea, and working through Moses, while those who abandoned her (Cain, the Egyptians) perished [10: 1-21; 11: 1; JB]; in Matthew and Luke, Jesus remarked that Wisdom was proved right by her children, that is, her deeds [**Proverbs 1:** 20-33; **3:** 14-19; **4:** 4-9, 13; **5:** 15-19; **7:** 4-5; **8:** 1-36; **9:** 1-6; **14:** 1, 33; **Baruch 3:** 9 – **4:** 4; **Sirach 1:** 6-10, 14-17, 19-20; **4:** 11-19; **6:** 18-37; **14:** 20 – **15:** 8; **18:** 20; **24:** 1-27; **51:**13-30; **2 Esdras 13:** 54-55; **16:** 49-50; **Wisdom 6:** 12-25; **7:** 7-14, 22 – **8:** 21; **9:** 4, 9-18; **10:** 1-21; **11:** 1; **Matthew 11:** 19; **Luke 7:** 35 (see also *Wisdom's FEAR OF THE LORD, Wisdom's MAIDSERVANTS, FOLLY/ Adulterous SEDUCTRESS/ALIEN WOMAN, VALIANT WOMAN, Sirach's WOMEN, Ecclesiastes' WOMEN* and *Proverbs' WOMEN*)]

*Wisdom's FEAR OF THE LORD* – *personified as female, she was the beginning of Wisdom, created in the womb with faithful people, clinging faithfully to men with whom she had been from the beginning [1: 14-15; JB]; she was the perfection of wisdom, which intoxicated people with her fruits, gave them their heart's desire and filled their storerooms [1:16-17; JB]; she was assessed by the Lord who gave her learning and good judgment, giving fame to those who clung to her [1: 19; JB]; she was the root of wisdom and her branches were long life [1; 20; JB]* [**Sirach 1:** 14-17, 19-20 (see also *WISDOM*)]

*Wisdom's MAIDSERVANTS* – *they were sent out by Wisdom to summon all who were not wise to come to eat at her table of their own accord, and so leave their folly* [**Proverbs 9:** 3-6 (see also *WISDOM*)]

**Wise-hearted WOMEN** – see **WOMEN contributing wealth, skill to the building of the Sanctuary**

**(The) WISE WOMAN of Abel** – see **Quick-witted WOMAN from Abel**

**(The) WISE WOMAN of Tekoah** – see **Quick-Witted WOMAN from Tekoa**

**WIVES of the remnant of Judah in Egypt** – the women left in Judah with the remnant of the people, after King Nebuchadnezzar (604–562 BC) had destroyed Jerusalem and deported most of the people to Babylon, under the care of the King's governor Gedaliah, Ahikam's son; they were captured and taken from Mizpah with the remnant by Ishmael, Nethaniah's son; they were rescued by Johanan, Kareah's son, and brought by him with the remnant to Egypt, in spite of the Lord God's disapproval; with the approval and support of their husbands, they continued the cultic rituals they had practiced in Jerusalem and Judah, honoring the Queen of Heaven (probably Ishtar, or Astarte), defying the Lord God's prohibition conveyed to them by Jeremiah; they died in Egypt with their husbands when the Lord God made good His threats to destroy all of this remnant, except for a very few who would be saved and would return to the land of Judah [**Jeremiah 39:** 1-10; **40:** 5; **41:** 1-16; **42:** 1-22; **43:** 1-7; **44:** 9-30 (see also **ASTARTE, King's DAUGHTERS** and **QUEEN of Heaven**)]

**WOMAN at the well** – she came, at noon, to Joseph's well in her town, Sychar in Samaria, to draw water; there, she encountered Jesus Who had stopped there to rest and had sent His disciples to get some food; she responded to Jesus' request for a drink of water with the ironic comment on the fact that He, a Jew, was asking a Samaritan for water, the Jews having forbidden communication between themselves and the Samaritans (whom they considered heretics and so unclean); in the ensuing dialog, Jesus laid bare her past (she had had five husbands and was not married to the man she was currently living with) and revealed His identity as Messiah; she ran back to town to tell everyone that the Messiah was there, offering in proof His recounting of her past; coming to Jesus, the townsfolk listened to His preaching, kept Him there for two more days and believed Him because of His own words, not just on her testimony [**John 4:** 5-42; see *The Samaritan WOMAN and the Meeting at the Well*]

***WOMAN baking bread*** – *in this parable told by Jesus, she was making bread,* *kneading the dough so that the yeast would be fully worked into the whole three measures of flour and all the bread would rise; this action is an image for the formation of the Kingship of God over and within us – the work of God within the soul, or within His Church, or within the whole world of humans, transforming each, little by little, from human-centered to God-centered by means of initial hard work on some faithful person's part* [**Matthew 13:** 33; **Luke 13:** 20-21]

**WOMAN of Bahurim's household** – she welcomed David's men, Abiathar's son Jonathan and his companion, Zadok's son Ahimaaz, when they were spotted at the Fuller's Spring by one of Absalom's men; she hid them in a cistern, putting a covering over the mouth of the cistern and scattering crushed grain on it so that no opening was visible; when they arrived, she told Absalom's servants that Jonathan and Ahimaaz had gone further on, toward the water; when Absalom's men had gone on, searched, found nothing, and returned to Jerusalem, Jonathan and Ahimaaz climbed out of the cistern, went to King David and warned him to cross the Jordan at once, reporting the plan of Ahithophel and Absalom's rejection of it, for a plan offered by the apparent turncoat, Hushai the Archite, who was actually still working for David [**2 Samuel 17:** 15-22 (see also **SERVANT GIRL Who Was To Be a Messenger**)]

**WOMAN of Endor** – see **NECROMANCER of Endor**

**(A) Woman's DAUGHTER** – see **DAUGHTER Given in Marriage**

*WOMAN sitting in a bushel* – *she appeared in the seventh vision of the prophet Zechariah; the angel directed the prophet's attention to a bushel measure moving forward; as the angel identified the contents as the iniquity of the remnant, a lead disc was raised and a woman was revealed, sitting in the bushel; naming the woman Wickedness, the angel forced her back into the bushel and resealed its mouth with the lead disc; two winged women took up the bushel, removing it from the land* [*Zechariah 5:* 5-11 (see also *Two **WINGED WOMEN***)]

**WOMAN taken in adultery** – she was caught in the act of adultery by the scribes and Pharisees, who brought her, without her partner, to Jesus, allegedly for judgment; she was supposed to be punished for this crime by being stoned to death, according to the Law of Moses; she stood before Jesus, waiting with her captors, who had brought her as a challenge to Jesus, to see if He would spare her (and thus break the Law of Moses), or agree to the stoning (and nullify all His own teachings about the mercy of God and the possibilities of repentance); Jesus responded by writing in the dust, then saying that the person without sin should be the first to cast a stone; Jesus went back to writing in the dust and she remained standing before Him as all her accusers left; asked by Jesus where her accusers were and whether anyone was left who condemned her, she replied that there was no one; Jesus said He wouldn't condemn her either and dismissed her, telling her to stop sinning [**John 8:** 3-11; see *The WOMAN and the Stone Unthrown*]

**WOMAN who praised His mother** – as Jesus was speaking, this woman called out from the crowd; she praised Him by praising His mother, saying, *"Blessed is the womb that carried You and the breasts at which You nursed."* [Luke 11: 27; NAB]; Jesus used her praise of His speaking to redirect the attention of all His hearers to the essential, saying that those who practiced the word of God they had heard were the ones who were really blessed [**Luke 11:** 27-28]

**WOMAN who suffered eighteen years** – she suffered from an infirmity which had kept her bent double for eighteen years; she was healed by Jesus on the Sabbath; she was called "daughter of Abraham" by Jesus in response to the complaint of the indignant synagogue official (directed to the woman but addressed to all the people present) that cures should be sought during the week and not on the Sabbath; Jesus asked why, if it was acceptable to untie the bonds of an ox or an ass to water it on the Sabbath, it was not acceptable to untie the bonds of "this daughter of Abraham" on the Sabbath, a response that silenced His adversaries and pleased everyone else [**Luke 13:** 10-17]

*(The) WOMAN whose hour has come* – *this general example was used by Jesus as an analogy for the feelings of His disciples facing His coming death; as the mother in labor wept and wailed in pain, but forgot her suffering once her child was born and rejoiced in this new life, so they would mourn now but would rejoice when they saw Him again; at this point, the disciples did not understand that He would die, but that He would rise from the dead* [**John 16:** 20-22]

**WOMAN with a chronic hemorrhage** – she had suffered from an incurable hemorrhage for twelve years; she had spent all her money on doctors who had been unable to help her; believing she would be healed, she touched Jesus' clothing as He was on His way to the home of Jairus to cure Jairus' daughter; at once she knew herself to be healed; when Jesus, having felt power go out of Him, asked who had touched Him, she acknowledged what she had done; she was told by Jesus that her faith had wrought her cure and was dismissed to go in peace [**Matthew 9:** 20-22; **Mark 5:** 25-34; **Luke 8:** 43-48 (see also **Jairus' DAUGHTER**)]

*WOMAN with leaven* – *see WOMAN baking bread*

*WOMAN with a lost piece of silver* – *she appeared in Jesus' parable about the mercy of God and His delight in the repentance and return of the lost sinner; having lost one of her ten coins, she lit a lamp and swept the house, searching until she found it, then called her neighbors together to celebrate with her the finding of her lost treasure; Jesus said that heaven, and therefore God, rejoiced with that relief and delight over the return to Him of the repentant sinner* [**Luke 15:** 8-10]

*WOMAN with seven husbands* – *see WIFE of seven brothers*

**WOMEN assembling at Tabernacle** – see **WOMEN who served at the entrance of the Tent of Meeting**

**WOMEN contributing wealth, skill to the building of the Sanctuary** – these women answered the call of Moses for wealth and workers to contribute to the beautification of the Sanctuary being built for the Lord God at His command; they brought gold jewelry if they had promised gold to the Lord God; they also brought rich materials; skilled women spun purple material of violet and red, crimson material and fine linen; some spun goats' hair as well; all contributed as their hearts prompted them [**Exodus 35:** 25-29; **36:** 3-7]

**WOMEN dancing and singing** – on David's vanquishing of Goliath (with a single stone thrown from a sling), these women came out with cries of joy to meet him as he was returning to King Saul (ca. 1030-1010 BC); they danced to the sound of the tambourine and lyre, singing, *"Saul has killed his thousands, and David his tens of thousands!"* [1 Samuel 18: 7; JB]; their song ignited Saul's jealousy, causing Saul's war against David which ended only with Saul's death, when David became King (ca. 1010-970 BC) [**1 Samuel 18:** 6-9]

**Women's DAUGHTER** – see **DAUGHTER Given in Marriage**

**WOMEN weeping for Tammuz** – see **Tammuz' MOURNERS**

**WOMEN who eat their own children** – some of the mothers who had no food to give to their starving children, when the children died, boiled and ate their bodies; this occurred in the extremity of the famine which came on Jerusalem under the successful siege conducted by Nebuchadnezzar's Captain of the Guard, Nebuzaradan (587 BC); with the conquest of Jerusalem, their deed was seeas the Lord God's punishment for the sin of His people, Israel, for idoltry and not keeping His Law, a traditional view [**Lamentations 2:** 12, 20; **4:** 3-5, 10; see **Leviticus 26:** 27-29; **Deuteronomy 28:** 53-57; **Jeremiah 19:** 4, 9; **Baruch 2:** 3 and **2 Kings 25:** 8-12 (see also **Besieged MOTHERS who agreed to eat their sons**)]

**WOMEN who served at the entrance to the Tent of Meeting** – they gave their bronze mirrors to be used to make the basin of bronze and its bronze support; their service at the Entrance to the Tent of Meeting has not been determined; using them as prostitutes, as Eli's sons did, was identified by Eli a sin against the Lord God, and brought about the sons' deaths and the end of Eli's house [**Exodus 38:** 8; **1 Samuel 2:** 22]

**WOMEN who sew pillows to armholes** – see **False PROPHET-ESSES**

**WOMEN with tabrets** – see **WOMEN dancing and singing**

**WOMEN worshipping the Queen of Heaven** – see **QUEEN of Heaven**

# Y

**Young MAIDENS going out to draw water** – they met Kish's son, Saul, as he sought his father's she-asses in the Land of Zuph; they assured Saul that the seer (whom his servant had suggested they consult), was ahead of him; the seer had come into the town to bless the sacrifice the people were going to offer at the hilltop shrine near the town; they told Saul and his servant that they would meet the seer just as soon as they entered the town, before he had gone up to the place of sacrifice, if they went at once; Saul and his servant followed the girls' directions and found Samuel, an encounter which would end with Samuel's anointing of Saul as the future first King of Israel (ca. 1030-1010 BC) [**1 Samuel 9:** 9-27; **10:** 1]

# Z

**ZEBIDAH (also spelled ZEBUDAH)** – she was the daughter of Pedaiah from Rumah; she became the wife of King Josiah of Judah (640-609 BC); she was the mother of Eliakim, renamed Jehoiakim by Pharaoh Neco who placed him on the throne of Judah where he ruled eleven years (609-598 BC) and displeased the Lord God [**2 Kings 23:** 36]

**ZEBUDAH** – alternate spelling; see **ZEBIDAH**

**ZERESH, also called ZOSARA** – she was the wife of Haman of Agag, highest-ranking of the ministers of King Xerxes (probably indicates Xerxes I, the Great (ca. 486-465 BC); called Ahasuerus in Hebrew, Artaxerxes in Greek); with his friends, Zeresh suggested to Haman that he build a gibbet fifty cubits high and have Mordecai hanged on it; when the King had him honor Mordecai, Zeresh joined his friends in telling Haman that Mordecai had caused this fall from favor and would finally ruin him [**Esther 5:** 10, 14; **6:** 13 (see **ESTHER**); see *ESTHER and the Balance of Power*]

**ZERUAH** – she was the widow of Nebat, an Ephraimite from Zeredah; she became the mother of Jeroboam, who served King Solomon (ca. 970-931 BC) but revolted against his heir, becoming King of Israel (931-910 BC), as the prophet Ahijah of Shiloh had promised; Solomon's firstborn and heir, King Rehoboam of Judah (931-913 BC), had alienated all but those who lived in Judah, effectively dividing the Kingdom; this was the Lord God's punishment of Solomon for his idolatry; Jeroboam led his kingdom into idolatry, displeasing the Lord God [**1 Kings 11:** 26]

**ZERUIAH** – she was the daughter of Jesse; she was the sister of Abigail, King David (ca. 1010-970 BC), and his seven older brothers; she was the aunt of Amasa; she became the mother of Abishai, Joab and Asahel; she is mentioned most frequently with her sons, both to distinguish them from others of similar name and to signal their relationship with their uncle, King David [**1 Chronicles 2:** 16; **11:** 6, 39; **18:** 12, 15; **26:** 28; **27:** 24; **1 Samuel 26:** 6; **2 Samuel 2:** 13, 18; **3:** 39; **8:** 16; **14:** 1; **16:** 9, 10; **17:** 25; **18:** 2; **19:** 22-23; **21:** 17; **23:** 18, 37; **1 Kings 1:** 7; **2:** 5, 22; (see also **ABIGAIL, daughter of Jesse, NAHASH** and **King David's MOTHER**)]

**ZIBIAH** – coming from Beersheba, she was the wife of the murdered King Ahaziah of Judah (841 BC); she became the mother of King Joash (or Jehoash) (835-796 BC), who came to the throne of Judah at seven, ruled forty years in Jerusalem and pleased the Lord God throughout the lifetime of Jehoiada, the priest who got him the throne; Joash later worshipped idols and was murdered in his bed [**2 Kings 12:** 2; **2 Chronicles 24:** 1]

**ZILLAH** – she was the second wife of Lamech, a descendant of Cain's son, Enoch; she became the mother of Tubal-Cain, ancestor of all metal workers in bronze or iron, and his sister, Naamah [**Genesis 4:** 19, 22, 23 (see also **ADAH, first wife of Lamech** and **NAAMAH, daughter of Lamech**)]

**ZILPAH** – she was the slave-girl of Laban, given to Leah on her marriage to Jacob; at Leah's insistence, she conceived Gad and Asher by Jacob; she became the grandmother of Gad's sons Ziphion, Haggi, Shuni, Ezbon, Eri, Arodi and Areli, and of Asher's sons Imnah, Ishvah, Ishvi, Beriah and their sister Serah [**Genesis 29:** 24; **30:** 9-13; **32:** 12, 23; **33:** 1-7; **35:** 26; **37:** 2; **46:**18 (see also **LEAH, RACHEL** and **BILHAH**); see *RACHEL, LEAH and the Duping of the Bridegroom* and *DINAH and the Importunate Brothers*]

*ZION* – see *JERUSALEM/ZION* and all *Jerusalem/Zion/Israel* entries

**ZIPPORAH** – she was one of seven daughters of Reuel (called Jethro in Exodus 3:1, 4:18, and Hobab in Judges 1:16), the priest of Midian; she helped her sisters draw water for their father's sheep; with her sisters, she was defended and assisted by Moses, who was fleeing from Pharaoh's court; she was given to Moses in marriage and bore him two sons, Gershom and Eliezer; she traveled with Moses and Gershom to Egypt to free the Israelites from bondage; on the journey, she circumcised Gershom, using a flint to cut off his foreskin and saved Moses from the Lord God's wrath by touching her son's foreskin to Moses' genitals and claiming him as *"bridegroom of blood"* [Exodus 4: 25]; she was dismissed by Moses (for reasons unknown), and returned, with her sons, to her father; later, brought by her father, she visited Moses, taking her sons with her; modern scholars identify her as the Cushite woman Moses married; for this marriage, Miriam and Aaron, jealous of Moses' superior position, upbraided him (as a basis for challenging his authority and the Lord God's choice of him); they were punished by the Lord God for their arrogance [**Exodus 2:** 16-22; **4:** 20-26; **18:** 2-12; **Numbers 12:** 1-2 (see also **Jethro, the Midian Priest's DAUGHTERS**)]

**ZOSARA** – see **ZERESH**

# THE BOOK
## OF STORIES

# ABIGAIL
## and the Sudden Smile

"He what?" Abigail, wife to Nabal of Carmel, a wealthy herder of sheep and goats, was horrified.

"He called David a runaway slave and refused him food for his men, though there was plenty prepared for the shearers," the servant, exclaimed. "And we owe David. His men have been protecting the shepherds and the beasts the whole time they've been in our hills. They've never taken a thing for themselves, not even a lamb, and so they reminded the master."

"Who having already insulted the man, lost his temper and wouldn't listen to anyone." Abigail finished the sentence with a sigh. "And I suppose...?"

Her servant nodded. "David will destroy us all for his ingratitude. See what you can do, or we're lost!"

Abigail paused. This wasn't the first time she had had to rescue them all from a dilemma into which her peasant-shrewd husband's stubborn short-sightedness and greed had thrust them. But it might be the last – and she had no time.

Summoning her steward and cook, she learned that there were five sheep already prepared, two skins of wine and a hundred bunches of raisins in the store room, five measures of roasted grain in the bin and two hundred cakes of figs in the cooling room.

"There are still three donkeys here," the steward reported.

"Excellent!" exclaimed Abigail. "Then, Jacob, will you see to it that the stores are packed on two and the third fitted with a saddle and bridle? I'll ride that. Just give me time to dress for the journey – no. On second thought, Jacob, you'd better go on ahead of me with the provisions. Take the spur trail as soon as the beasts are packed; I'll catch up. There's no time to lose!"

"But how will you find him?" asked the cook, who was also wondering where she would get more food for the feast Nabal was sure to order.

"I'll follow Jacob until I come to the promontory; I should be able to see David coming – all the dust his men will be raising will be visible for miles." Then, seeing her cook's worried frown, she suddenly smiled. "Don't worry about the feast, Miriam! Have Judah slaughter five more sheep now, and take my key for the reserve storeroom. There's a good supply of figs there, so you can make more cakes, and another five measures of grain ready for roasting. There are also more raisins. Can you manage with that Miriam?

Oh, yes – wine. I tucked three skins in there with the rest, just in case. The last time we had extra!"

"Don't worry! With all that we'll be fine. A little extra work never hurt any of us. But you – do take care! We need you back in one piece!"

"Not unless I can succeed in deflecting the furious David," said Abigail. "Well, nothing ventured, nothing gained."

Twenty minutes later, she was dressed for travel. As she went to the yard where the mule awaited her, saddled and bridled as she and the mule preferred, she spotted the puff of dust on the road. "Good man, Jacob," she smiled to herself. "We're underway already!" She mounted the mule, and turned to follow. "But whatever shall I say to him?" she wondered, then scolded herself, "Find him first, Abigail! Then the Lord God will help, unless we must suffer for Nabal's stupidity."

Riding behind the provisions, Abigail kept a sharp watch, and as they reached the promontory, she saw him coming toward them – David, armed, with an armed troop. She caught her breath, slid off the mule and prostrated herself before him, still not knowing what she was going to say. Then the words came.

"I'll take the blame," she began. "Pay no attention to Nabal – he really *is* as brutish as his name. No sense at all! *I* didn't see your soldiers. My prayer for you is that the Lord God, Who kept you from spilling blood with your own hands to avenge yourself, will give all your enemies Nabal's fate. Please, give the provisions I've brought to your soldiers, and please forgive our ingratitude. You're fighting the Lord God's battles! Surely He will give you a lasting dynasty, for you haven't an evil bone in you! And then, when the Lord God has saved your life, defeated your enemies, given you rule over Israel and kept all His promises to you, you'll be glad you took no vengeance on us! And – when the Lord God *has* rewarded you, remember us?"

And that seemed to be all. Abigail stopped and waited, holding her breath. Would he be angry? Would he kill her outright? Had she done any good at all?

"Blessed be the Lord, the God of Israel," David began, and she looked up, to see a sudden smile break the dusty warrior's concentrated seriousness...

"...and I have no idea what he said next!" she exclaimed to Miriam that night in the kitchen as the cook prepared a late supper for her. She had returned home as soon as David's men had accepted her provisions, checked at once on Nabal, deep in his harvest feast and in no condition for her news, and then made her way to the kitchen to report, the steward Jacob following her in. "I was so worried, to begin with, and then when he began with a blessing and I looked up, he smiled, and – ! Well! I've never seen a smile like that before! It was like the sun breaking through the end of a storm and chasing the last of the clouds away! But I don't know what he said! Jacob – ?"

"He said," supplied the steward with a smile of his own, "that your coming to him had, indeed, saved him from shedding blood to get vengeance on Nabal, and that he would have wiped us out, all the males anyway, if you hadn't! What did Nabal say when you told him?"

"I didn't. He, well, you know. Harvest feast." Steward and cook nodded, matching wry smiles with her. "Tomorrow I'll tell him."

When Abigail told him, Nabal dropped like a rock; his coma ended in his death. Under her management, the flocks prospered, but when she received a proposal of marriage from David, her yes flew to him, singing all the way. "That smile!" she would say in later years. "What a gift from the Lord God, to him *and* to me!"

[**1 Samuel 25:** 2-44; **27:** 3; **30:** 3, 5, 18; **2 Samuel 2:** 2; **3:** 3; **1 Chronicles 3:** 1; see **ABIGAIL, daughter of Jesse**]

# ANNA
## and the Homecoming

I'm watching the road, of course! What else would I be doing? That's the road by which my son Tobias will be coming home to me – God send it so! How I wish he'd never gone!

It's all Tobit's fault, of course. That man, good husband though he may be – and he is, though sometimes he's enough to make a donkey envious, he's that stubborn – he's obsessed. Money, all the time money! "I don't care about the money!" I told him. "We have enough! We three have each other. Why do you want the ten talents of silver you left in trust with Gabael in Media? We don't need it!"

But would he listen? No! He had to send my baby, my Tobias, off with some stranger "looking for work" that he picked up in town. I'll bet! But Tobit believed him when he said he was kin, and off they went. Simple as a baby, that one. He'd believe anything anyone wanted to tell him – unless, of course, it might make *my* life easier!

Did I tell you what happened when he first went blind? I must have. No? Well, then!

He was doing what he always did – obeying the Lord God's Law. Now, you know I have nothing against the Lord God. But there are times when my dear husband's idea of keeping His law is just beyond everything.

He's obsessed, I tell you! This time it was burying the dead. I don't think the Lord God would have minded, not much anyway, if Tobit had skipped this corpse. After all, that's what got him exiled, all our goods confiscated and a price on his head in the first place! He had just been restored – you know, change of kings and everything's up for grabs – and here he goes again. And I had *just* put the meal on the table, and not any old dinner! This was his homecoming feast *and* the feast of Pentecost, and let me tell you, I had cooked up a storm for that dinner.

Does he sit and eat? No! My son has to go out and find him a poor man to share the meal. Well, there was plenty, of course. I don't skimp. But Tobias came back without a guest and with the news that one of our countrymen had been murdered and left in the market place. Nothing would do but my dear husband has to rush out, snatch the body and bring it to my spare room! Filthy thing it was, too. And *then,* after sunset, he buries it.

You'd think the Lord God would have sent him a gift for his faithfulness – so why did that blamed sparrow land his stuff in Tobit's eyes? He was blind within the year, in spite of the doctors, and that's when it happened, the thing I haven't forgiven him for yet.

I had to go to work to support us. So I took in wool and spun it, and took in spun wool and wove it for anyone who wanted to pay. I must say I was very good at both. My mother had taught me well, and I have some gift for patterns – though I surely can't see the pattern here. It's just a snarl without an end.

Anyway, there I was, working day and night, but keeping us alive, putting bread on the table, and one day one of my customers gave me a kid for a meal as a special treat. She had paid the full price for the weaving, too. "I just love the design you've woven into the cloak," she said. It's beautiful!"

So I brought the kid home, and wouldn't you know? The poor little thing bleated, and that set off my dear husband. "Where did this creature come from?" he snaps at me. "Take it back, quick, or they'll think we stole it!"

"Relax," I said. "It was a present one of my customers gave me. And she paid me the full price for my work, too!"

"You stole it!" he declared. "Now take it back!"

Well! I was so angry I nearly spit! Mr. Pious Believer accusing me, his own wife, the one whose work was feeding him because *his* holiness had cost him his eyesight, of STEALING! You could have heard me scream in the market place! I don't remember all I shouted at him, but it was a lot. I guess I'd been saving it. I know I ended with something like, "and look at you now – for all your good works. Everyone knows what return *you've* had for them!"

And he doesn't fight fair. I'd have loved it if he'd given me a mouthful – I was ready to answer it with a barrel-full! But what does he do? Gets all sad and sings a song of sorrow to the Lord God. Does he apologize to *me?* Guess again!

I think that's when he started to brood about the money Gabael was holding for him in Rhages – in Media of all places! It wasn't long after that he hatched this scheme that sent my baby traveling. Oh, I fussed at him for that, I tell you! After all, Tobias is our only child! I told my Tobit that he was sending away his arms and legs as well as his eyes – and suppose Tobias never came back! Travel is dangerous, and frankly, I couldn't see that we needed the money that much. Even if we did, nothing, not even starving, was worth losing Tobias over.

Well, I might as well have been talking to the walls. Neither my Tobit nor my Tobias heard a word – and Tobias was as eager to go as Tobit was to send him. I tell you, I thought I'd lose my mind, at least until I met Azariah. He's a kinsman of ours, you know – just happened to be in the marketplace when Tobias went out to hire a guide – and he knew all the roads between here and Rhages. Said he'd be glad to go with Tobias, and he seemed so – I don't know - steady, maybe. And wise. Anyway, they were on the road before I caught my breath, with that dog Tobias is so mad about trailing along after them. I haven't seen him since.

I think it's my fault. If I hadn't been so furious about that kid, and flared out that I was earning our living now, not he, maybe he wouldn't have felt he had to get us money. I do know better, you know. I know women take reverses better than men! Somehow, we don't get as frightened. We know there's always *something* you can do. No, I should have taken his pride into account – having me be breadwinner can't have been easy; I didn't need to rub it in. Oh, if only I could see my baby walking down that road, I'd apologize to Tobit, and mean it, and never give him a cross word again!

Look! Look! Do you see that? It *is* a cloud of dust, isn't it? And – and that's Tobias' dog! He's home! Tobit! Tobit! Tobias is home! My baby is home!

It was a wonderful homecoming! Tobias – well, it was amazing! I wouldn't have believed it, except I saw it with my own eyes! He *cured* my Tobit's blindness! Azariah was a godsend – and he's the one who told my baby the cure!

What happened was, they camped by a river the first night they were traveling, and Tobias went for a swim, and this huge fish jumped at him and all but took off his foot! He screamed, of course, and Azariah hollered to him not to lose the fish but to drag it ashore. When he did, Azariah told him to take out the gall, liver and heart and pack them away, that they were medicines for body and spirit. It was the gall from that fish that Tobias used for an eye ointment for Tobit – smeared it on his eyes and peeled away this white film that it formed. Now Tobit can see as well as he ever could!

And guess what! My baby is married now! Yes, married – to a sweet little thing who simply adores him! Sarah is her name – only child of Raguel and Edna. Anyway, she thinks Tobias is ten feet tall and the Lord God's own gift to her. Tobias is her *eighth* husband! She was being haunted by Asmodeus, you see, a demon who killed off each of her husbands on the night of the wedding. Honestly! That's the Lord God's own truth!

Anyway, Azariah told Tobias to burn the heart and liver of that blessed fish on the wedding night, and it would drive any demon far away – for good. So he did, after they prayed together, of course, and – well, now they're home safely and happy as can be! And so am I – and relived too!

As for the silver, Azariah got that while Tobias was celebrating his wedding. And the feast we had – how I wish you could have been there! It was perfect! I've never been so happy. And guess what? Azariah is *really* the Lord God's angel Raphael, one of the seven who stands before His throne. Azariah told us himself when Tobias and Tobit offered him half of everything they brought back with them from Media, wedding gifts and all. He was so sweet – and so, shining. He refused the payment, of course, told us all about Sarah and Tobit praying at the same time and the Lord God sending him to answer both prayers. He made the Lord God present with us, it seemed – we could feel His love. Raphael told us to write down the whole story – Tobit will do that, I suppose – and we praised the Lord God as Raphael rose again to his place in Heaven!

And what about me? I'm fine. I apologized to Tobit – and would you believe it? He apologized for doubting me! Said I was the best wife a man could ever have. Said he'd find a way to tell the world the whole truth about himself and me, and how wonderful I am. Can you believe it! I'm the most blessed woman on this earth, I think!

[**Tobit 1:** 9, 20; **2:** 1, 11-14; **4:** 3-4; **5:** 17-22; **6:** 1; **10:** 4-7; **11:** 4-6, 9; **14:** 10, 12; see **ANNA, wife of Tobit** (see also **EDNA, SARAH, wife of Tobias, Raguel's MAIDSERVANTS**); see *SARAH and the Bridal-Night Demon*]

# ATHALIAH
## and the Almost-Perfect Plan

It had all been so smooth, almost easy, Queen Athaliah reflected, watching in the bronze mirror as her maid combed her lustrous black hair. "The jeweled combs, the ones with the ruby flowers, I think," she said to her reflection, and her maid nodded.

"Yes, mistress. The red gown with them, or the ivory?"

"The red, yes, the red will do very nicely," she said and smiled.

The smile was not a nice one. The maid shivered in spite of herself, and the Queen, watching her, felt her lips stretch a bit more. Yes, red would do very well indeed. Red was for blood, wasn't it? And blood was life. Her life – before, now and always. Odd how that kept coming back, that last day before…

"Before everything," she thought. "Before I was myself. When I was only someone's daughter, someone's wife, someone's mother – beholden, bidden, constrained. Weak."

It had not been a bad life, exactly, she reflected. Only – limited. Blocked. Powerless, really. As Ahab of Israel's baby sister, she had lived in the court he kept with Jezebel and had tasted their heady brew of absolute authority and worship of Baal and the Canaanite pantheon in defiance even of the Lord God's prophets. When she married, she wore her own crown and called a king husband, but found the power she had sought had no substance, only ceremony.

Then Jehoram had died – not in kingly fashion, but like a mis-killed beast, his bowels consumed in an agony of pain and stomach-turning stink she could still smell.

"And that was six years ago," she reminded herself, taking a deep breath of the unguents her maid was working into her hair as she dressed it.
That death had changed everything. "How blind I was until then," she mused. "And how quickly I had to learn how to see!"

With her son Ahaziah taking his father's place as King of Judah, she had far more responsibility, of course. Jehoram had been an able king, but this son of his, the youngest, had had no training. His rule had been an accident, she thought. If the Arabs and Philistines had not killed his older brothers, he would never have ruled.

So she took over his training, though subtly – Jezebel had taught her well.

Like his father, Ahaziah had been amenable to the worship of the Canaanite gods she favored. The priests of the Lord God she scorned, and taught him to do the same; Jehoram had not needed teaching, she remembered, and suppressed a sigh. She still missed him.

Then the unthinkable had happened. In the first year of his reign, Ahaziah had been killed by Jehu, sent by the Lord God *he* said as part of his program to wipe out the house of Ahab. Jehu had killed Ahab's son, Jehoram of Israel at the same time, and had followed it up with the elimination of Jezebel, whose own eunuchs had, at Jehu's challenge, tossed her out the window of her own palace in Jezreel to smash on the stones of the courtyard. Dogs had eaten her flesh after Jehu had ridden over it on horseback and left it there, unburied. A fate that still made her shiver at the man's cruelty, though he had piously declared that the whole thing was the Lord God's doing. "And if *that's* true," she said whenever she thought back on the grisly end of her model in queenship, "I'm certainly glad that he's no god of mine!"

But Ahaziah's death had been a blow that had almost finished her – would have, except that she had known what would happen if she gave way, and took action to prevent it. She still didn't much *like* what she had done but, as she asked herself in a well-worn dialogue of justification, "What else was I to do? There was no one left strong enough to rule. Jehu would have conquered the Kingdom and that would have ended everything – worship of our gods, autonomy of the throne, freedom – my own life! I *had* to secure the throne – to save us all – and I had to act instantly!"

Unconsciously, she shrugged and shook her head. Hastily her maid backed away, and she rose. "All that blood," she murmured, raising her arms as the maid slipped the red gown over her head, "all that blood. But it was worth it. And I *had* to. If I had left even a single heir of Jehoram's alive.... But I didn't. And now I'm safe. My plan worked! It was perfect! I am the Queen, and I shall hold this Kingdom no matter what. Jezebel would have been proud of me! I did it! "

Arranging the folds of the gown, she smiled again. "The crown?" Her maid handed it to her and, as she placed it carefully on her head, they both heard a roar coming from the Temple. They exchanged a single, startled glance. Then the queen, whipping up the modest train of her gown in one hand, ran for the door.

Pushing into the Temple, Athaliah saw a huge crowd – Temple Guards armed to the teeth, the heads of families, everyone who could squeeze a way in. And they were shouting something that sounded like, "Long live the King!"

Shocked, the queen caught her breath. How could this be happening? She had had all the heirs of Jehoram killed!

Her eyes found her enemy, the despised priest of the Lord God, Jehoiada, at once, but the seven-year old standing by the pillar in the King's place, surrounded by the armed circle of Temple guards, crowned and carrying a copy of the Lord God's Law she did not know. Who was this imposter?

And then she recognized Ahaziah's sister, Jehosheba, standing next to her husband Jehoiada with a smile of triumph, and remembered Joash, Ahaziah's son. "That – she must have hidden the brat! They'll never get away with it!" flashed through Queen Athaliah's mind.

"Treason! Treason!" she screamed with all her power, ripping her red gown from shoulder to hem. Her enraged voice cut through the shouts of rejoicing like a sword, creating the instant of silence she waited for her people to fill.

But it was Jehoiada who filled it.

"You can't kill her in the Temple of the Lord God," he said to the Captain of the Guard, "so take her outside the precincts, and put to the sword any who dares to follow her."

And as she felt her arms gripped by the guards and began to move, numb, unresisting, toward the palace and the entry to the Gate of the Horses, Queen Athaliah knew, with a chill that invaded her bones, that her perfect plan had failed utterly, and that she had, finally, lost. Everything. "All that blood," she murmured regretfully, "and it did no good at all."

[**2 Kings 8:** 18, 25-26; **11:** 1-20; **2 Chronicles 21:** 6; **22:** 2, 10-12; **23:** 1-15, 21; **24:** 7; see **ATHALIAH** (see also **JEHOSHEBA** and **Joash's NURSE**); see *JEHOSHEBA and the Vanishing King* and *JEZEBEL and the Stubborn Prophet*]

# BATHSHEBA
## and the Rising of the Spring

It was warm for a month into spring, Bathsheba reflected. She missed her husband. Uriah the Hittite had been with Joab, commander of David's forces since the equinox, raiding the Ammonites first, and then, having succeeded there, besieging Rabbah. She would not see him until the rains made fighting impossible, she supposed.

She sighed. "I *could* have married a baker, I guess!" she said aloud so she could hear the words. They made her smile. She and Uriah had made a running joke of them. Whenever the summons to war came, one or the other of them would make the remark, the other would reply, "But then who would guard the King and keep the bakers safe?" and they would both laugh. "And like as not head for bed, whatever the time of day!" she said, smiled, and sighed again.

"How I miss that man! And how I want to bear him a child!" She had so hoped they had conceived just before Uriah left with Joab for this year's warring, but her monthly courses, just now finished, had put rest to that. "Lord God, may I not prove barren!" she prayed.

Then she shook herself. "Come, my girl! No more nonsense!" she commanded herself. "Get on with the weaving, and you can have a nice bath on the rooftop this evening. You can watch the sun set, and the stars rise, and dream – well, whatever you like! But let's not waste the daylight!"

The sky was darkening now, and the stars had begun to show against the deepening dusk. The sunset had been spectacular, a wash of pink, gold, red, purple and gray that had lifted her heart. Bathsheba, sitting on the bench Uriah had had built for them, leaned against the parapet and smiled. How decadent she had felt, soaking in the warm, perfumed water and watching the flow of glory across the whole of the sky as she dreamed of her husband and the delights she had so often shared with him.

"Good thing no one could see me!" she thought idly, gazing at the puddle left behind after the servants had removed the tub. "I don't need that kind of trouble. But how I wish Uriah had been here, instead of sitting on a rock somewhere, facing the enemy and planning for tomorrow's battle. What a waste of a glorious night!"

Bathsheba shifted on the bench, flicking the skirt of her favorite robe so that its ivory folds poured down her leg like cream. It was lovely, one of Uriah's favorites, and she felt him nearer when she wore it. She smiled to herself. "Imagine! Me, a respectable married woman, desiring my own husband so much!" Then the smile faded, almost to bitterness. "But Uriah is a soldier born and bread. Take that away and what would he do? How would he even – be? He loves me, but I'm just not enough to make a life for him."

She shook her head. It was a familiar dilemma, and she had no more solution for it now than she had had when she first faced it. For him, it seemed not even to *be* a problem. When, tentatively, she had raised it, he simply looked blank, was silent for a moment, then shrugged. "You knew I was a soldier when you married me, and I still am," he offered doubtfully. "But I love you more now than ever I have, and that love keeps on growing...."

She had leaped to reassure him, and herself she now acknowledged, that she loved him as he did her, and as long as they loved each other everything would be fine.

"And it is," she insisted to herself. "But still...."

"Mistress," said a hesitant voice.

"Myra?" she asked. "What is it?"

"There are some messengers from the Palace, Mistress," her former nurse, now her maid answered, "and the Steward says to tell you that the King wants to see you."

"Not now, surely!"

"I'm afraid so, little one," said another voice from the doorway. It belonged to her steward, who had been her father Eliam's steward for all her childhood, and at his death, had joined her household.

"Jacob? What's going on?" Bathsheba was frightened.

"I don't know, mistress," he replied formally, and Bathsheba knew the messengers must have come up the stairs. "But you are summoned to attend King David now."

She drew in a deep breath and slowly released it, recapturing her calm. Whatever was happening, it would not do to show in less than full command of herself, her household and the situation – the penalty of being a woman alone in time of war. "Certainly," she replied with equal formality. "Myra, my cloak and sandals, and the black veil. Jacob, you may tell the messengers I shall be with them directly."

In King David's presence some minutes later, Bathsheba retained her calm. The king seemed awkward, trying to find a way to say something he found difficult, evidently, but she did not help him. Summon her at night, would he! Well, he could just deal with it! Let him squirm!

"Um – I wanted to tell you, Mistress, how very pleased I am with the great bravery of your husband, Uriah," he began. She nodded, one eyebrow rising in inquiry.

"He – he is an excellent soldier, resourceful and brave. Joab depends on him and so do his comrades." David caught his breath, then went on, "And so do I, of course. You must miss him! I am sorry for that; you are so lovely you should never – I should –" He stopped and blushed. "Don't look at me like that!" he exclaimed, and her other eyebrow rose. Still, she said nothing, though a small frown was beginning to form. This was the oddest encounter she had ever had.

"I – you –" He stopped. "There is no way to say this," he declared after a pause, "simply no way. Come with me!" and he extended his right hand and grasped her left. A shiver ran up her spine and she pulled back, but David did not seem to notice as he led her into the next room and sat her on the bed.

Home again, she could not have said how, Bathsheba began to shiver in reaction. Sitting on the end of the bed, she held herself tightly as the memory of the encounter replayed itself. David had been – he had not hurt her. Not at all. He had not demanded her, had not even asked her, in fact – just kept on looking at her that way, so sad, so very – into her eyes and into her heart, it seemed. Then he had touched her lips – only that one finger, on her mouth. And she had responded. Her body had risen in revolt and taken the gift he offered, so very gently, and then so very masterfully, and had gloried in the giving and the receiving.

"But not my heart!" she insisted. "Not my heart, beloved!"

Suddenly she heard Uriah's voice from, oh, years ago, saying to her one night after they had loved each other thoroughly, saying with a laugh that held a strange note of sorrow, "You know, my dearest one, the body has its own laws and its own will, quite apart from the spirit. I belong, by right and by my heart, to you, as you do to me, but given the chance, the flesh will seek loveliness and take it wherever it finds it! The flesh has no memory and no conscience – but I have both. And I swear to you, on my life, that whatever my body may desire, or even do, it will not take with it my heart. That is yours alone, and always will be."

"Oh!" she breathed. "So *that's* what you meant! Oh, beloved! Beloved!" And, oddly comforted, she wept.

Six weeks later, Bathsheba was certain. Courses two weeks overdue, morning nausea, tender breasts, backache – it had to be. Now what was she to do! "Myra," she called, and her nurse looked in the doorway.

"You finally need your rags? You're late, you know!" she said, and waited, her mouth firm as it had been when Bathsheba was a child and had gotten herself into trouble she could not find a way out of.

"I – I – " Bathsheba began, then stopped. "You know," she accused, halfway between mortification and relief.

"Of course I *know*," Myra returned shortly. "What do you take me for?" Then, seeing tears welling in Bathsheba's eyes, she said, "Oh, love! It wasn't your fault, you know. Kings are kings – and there's no saying no to them. But that one – shame on him, I say. And the wife of one of his own best men in the bargain! He should pay for that. But he won't. You're going to tell him, of course!"

"How?" she asked simply. "I can't just barge in there! Everyone will know – and I won't have Uriah go through that, having me the talk of the town. I'd rather – well, I don't know. Myra, I don't know what to do!"

"I do," said her nurse calmly. "You'll send me to him with a message. No letter – too risky. Just the words. He'll take care of it. He has to, or lose everything. And he will know that."

The next weeks passed in an eerie calm, it seemed to Bathsheba. She heard nothing from the Palace, though she noticed more messenger soldiers than usual leaving and returning from the place. One evening she even thought she recognized Uriah as one of them.

"But that can't be," Myra objected. "If he were in the city, even on the king's business, surely he would find the time to stop here, if only for a cup of wine and a kiss!"

"Maybe," said Bathsheba, "but somehow, I don't think he would, even if the King told him to – or even if he sent him home. Uriah would feel he was being disloyal to his men who are still in the field and want to be home as much as he does, and disloyal to the Ark of God – that's still in the field, too. No – much as he loves me and longs to be with me, he wouldn't do it."

"Funny kind of love, seems to me!" sniffed her nurse, "but if you say so! Too bad, though. Uriah in the house, even one night, would solve our problems."

"I wonder," said Bathsheba.

"Why?" Myra demanded. "He'd never think the child wasn't his, would he? Surely you wouldn't *tell* him what happened! That would get you both killed – you when you tell him, and him when he attacks the king. There's no sense in that, none at all!"

"Well," said Bathsheba, "maybe. But I don't know. Live a lie? Die, or have him die, for my truth? How can I choose?"

In the event, she never had to. Uriah, placed in the front lines of the battle and abandoned there by Joab, following David's secret orders, died in the fighting. The Palace messengers came to her to report his death and extend the King's sympathies. After her mourning time was over, they returned to bring her to David's house where he made her his wife, rejoiced with her at the birth of their child, and mourned with her at its death. She bore him four sons and was a patient, kind and faithful wife, receiving him always with a smile. But the radiance illumining her beauty vanished, and he never heard her when she whispered into night's void, "But not my heart, beloved. Never my heart."

[**2 Samuel 11:** 2-27; **12:** 1-25; **1 Kings 1:** 1-31; **2:** 13-25; **Psalm 51 superscription**; Matthew 1: 6; called **BATHSHUA** in **1 Chronicles 3:** 5 where her four sons are listed; see **BATHSHEBA, wife of Uriah the Hittite**]

# DEBORAH
# and the Cautious Commander

The day was hot, even in the highlands of Ephraim. There was a small breeze, but it was hot too. Under the tree, Deborah shifted position slightly as she scanned the crowd and then the horizon, and suppressed a groan. "This bench must have had rocks for ancestors!" she thought. "It gets harder and harder as the day wears on. I didn't think oak could grow angles with points in odd places, not once it was dead! Oh, well. The sun *has* to set eventually."

Aloud she snapped, "Barak!"

"Not here yet," her husband Lappidoth, serving as her herald and clerk, replied.

"I sent for him at dawn!" she hissed. "How dare he!"

Her husband looked at her calmly. "He'll come, eventually. He dare not refuse. You are the Lord God's judge and prophet! Put him out of your mind for the present. Do your work, even if he's not doing his!'

She glowered briefly, then nodded. "Next case, please!" he called out, and she straightened herself to deal with the two older men who presented themselves before her. Evidently, they were herders, quarreling over their beasts, or perhaps pasturage or water rights. At any rate, they had brought a goat with them and glared at each other over its back. The goat ignored them and checked around for something to chew on – preferably grass, but in a pinch, brambles might do.

Patiently Deborah extracted their story, which took a while, as they were both angry and neither wanted to let the other finish a sentence. Finally, she sat back. "Let's see," she said. "This goat is yours, Simon." The taller man nodded. "And you, Samuel, claim that Simon's goat ate a piece out of your cloak – "

"My *best* cloak," Samuel declared, hands balled into fists and planted on his hips. "And out of the very middle, too. Anna is furious with me!"

"With you?" Deborah asked in some surprise. "Why?"

"Because of *where* Samuel and the cloak and the goat *were* at the time!" Simon responded sardonically. Samuel squirmed but did not back down.

"And that was?" inquired Deborah.

Samuel mumbled something.

"Again, please? I didn't hear that," Deborah said, a chill in her voice.

Taking a deep breath, Samuel said clearly, "We were in the Amalekite's enclosure."

"Drinking, whoring or gambling?" inquired Deborah briskly.

Simon stared at her open-mouthed and Samuel blinked. "Gambling," he said simply. "I don't like to drink spirits, and I can't afford his girls!" Then he clapped his hand over his mouth. "Anna will kill me! Please – " He looked at Deborah, dropped his hand in discouragement, and sighed. "I know I shouldn't have, but I had to! I needed the money! Anna's being so – difficult, these days, always wanting things – I thought, maybe if I got her something pretty ... well, that was why."

"But Samuel, you always lose when you gamble!" Simon protested.

"Everyone who gambles with the Amalekite loses!" Deborah observed tartly. "You have children, Samuel?"

"Seven," he announced proudly, "and the eighth is on the way!"

"Ah!" said Deborah. "That would make me – difficult – too. But that doesn't tell me how the goat got involved. And how he ate a piece of your cloak! Go on."

Now Samuel blushed in earnest. "The goat was there because I brought him there," he began. He leaned over the goat and showed Deborah a lead he had fastened around the goat's neck. "I used my sash," he explained. "I thought if I brought the goat the Amalekite would think I had plenty of money and would let me bet my coins. I thought I could win enough on the first throw to be able to bet more on the next, and so on. I wanted to win enough to buy a length of crimson for Anna. At first I won. But then, on the third throw, I lost it all."

"The goat," Deborah reminded him.

Samuel hung his head. "The Amalekite made me an offer," he said softly. "He knew I had no more coins, so he offered to let me do best-two-of-three throws with his dice – double all the money I had lost against the goat."

"Simon's goat," Deborah repeated, and both men nodded. "What happened? Surely you didn't win! The sun rose in the east this morning!"

Samuel looked puzzled, but answered. "That's when the goat took the piece out of the center of my cloak. I was – that *goat* tiptoed over to me while I was concentrating, picked up a fold of my cloak and gnawed a piece out of it. And then – he *bit* me!" Reflexively, his hands sought his rear and he winced. "Really *hard!*" he added.

Simon, who had been struggling against a smile, gave up and laughed aloud.

Deborah was more successful at maintaining her decorum, though there was a suspicious twinkle in her eyes. "So," she summarized, "you *stole* Simon's goat, and were about to gamble it away to the Amalekite. The goat compensated its true owner for the theft by damaging your cloak. Then the goat very cleverly defended its life, as every creature has a right to do. It prevented the mortal injury you were about to perpetrate on its person by inflicting a much lesser injury on you. The goat is here, hale and hearty. Its owner is here – Simon, take your goat. But return Samuel's sash to him." Simon bent to undo the sash.

"And you are here," she went on, "in court under false pretenses. You are asking for damages from its *true* owner for the injuries the goat you *stole* has done you! There is a lie in there, as well as an intent to defraud – to say nothing of the original theft. You have a case, Simon!"

"I don't want it!" he exclaimed. "I mean, Lady, I've suffered no harm, thanks to you. And Samuel didn't really steal the goat – he couldn't! It's his!"

"How?" demanded the judge with a frown.

"Well, you see, we started the flock together, Samuel and me," Simon explained, "when we were youngsters. We felt like everything was both of ours. Then when we married, the wives felt – well, they wanted – well, it just seemed easier to say we had split the flock. So that's what we put in the marriage contracts. But really, day by day – well, they're still all ours. Both of ours. So Samuel didn't really *steal* the goat."

After a long moment, Deborah nodded.

"Then, Samuel," she said, "I think our business is concluded. And," she went on, her tone stopping Samuel in his tracks, "when next you want to please your wife, you might consider giving her what she *really* wants of you. I think that might be yourself. Notice when she's tired; show her that you value all she does for you and your children. Give her a hand, even! And STAY AWAY FROM THE AMALEKITE!" she thundered, "and I mean FOREVER! Is that clear?"

"Yes, Lady! Oh, yes!" Samuel gabbled, white-faced, and fled at her dismissal. Simon, leading the goat, turned to wink at her as he left.

"Well done, Lady," drawled a lazy voice. Its owner detached himself from the boulder he had been leaning against and approached. "You sent for me, I believe?"

"At dawn, Barak!" she snapped. Suddenly she grew very still. Slowly she rose, seeming to Barak's eyes to grow taller and broader as she stood gazing just above his head. Then her eyes fastened on his.

Despite himself, Barak caught his breath. He knew he was trapped, caught in a deadly mesh of events over which he could have no control. The Lord God had fixed on him, and there was no way he could escape this destiny, whatever it was. He felt an unexpected kinship with the luckless Samuel, who had only wanted to please his wife, and now, having lost their coins and his cloak ruined, helplessly faced her rage with whatever disasters that might bring.

Involuntarily, he smiled at his image of the hapless goat herder, but his smile died, and he felt his bowels go to water as Deborah began to speak.

"Barak, son of Abinoam from Kedesh in Naphtali," Deborah intoned, bronze weapons clashing and war drums thundering in her voice, "this is the order of the Lord God of Israel to you: *March to Mount Tabor and take with you ten thousand men from the sons of Naphtali and the sons of Zebulun. I will entice Sisera, the commander of Jabin's army, to encounter you at the wadi Kishon with his chariots and troops; and I will put him into your power.*"[Judges 4: 6-7; JB]

Barak was horrified. He knew he was caught between a hostile army outnumbering him and the wrath of the Lord God if he did not give battle. He felt ill. Visions of spectacular failure competed with visions of the Lord God's wrath and this lady-prophet's contempt to make his head spin and his heart pound at triple speed. Having missed two breaths, he snatched the third and opened his mouth to protest.

From a swiftly growing distance, he heard himself say, "You come with me, and I'll do it, but if you won't, neither will I!"

The shock of hearing his own voice calmly setting conditions for both the prophet and the Lord God brought him back to the hilltop with a thud. Pouring sudden sweat, he added hastily, "Look! I have no idea how to pick the right day! How am I supposed to know when the Lord God's angel is going to be there to guarantee success?" and his tone made the words an abject plea.

Apparently, it was enough. "All right," Deborah answered mildly, though with an edge, both amused and warning, "I'll go along with you. But re-member – that means Sisera will be beaten by a woman, not by you, and there goes your glory!"

Relief made Barak a bit giddy. "Suits me!" he said just under his breath, and turned to go. Deborah extended her hand and Lappidoth gave her the satchel she had packed after she had sent for Barak. "I'll close the court," he said. "Be well, my love, and be safe!" She smiled at him, kissed him, and followed Barak.

As the sun rose at over the river Kishon, bringing morning upon Sisera and his assembled troops and nine hundred ironclad chariots, Deborah and Barak waited, ready to put their plan into action. Anticipation made the time pass quickly.

"This is it! Let's go! The Lord God is handing Sisera over to you – and He's leading your troops!" Deborah finally commanded to a very tense Barak.

At once Barak sounded the charge, and the ten thousand men he had summoned from Zebulun and Naphtali followed him, pouring down from Mount Tabor upon Sisera's forces. At Barak's advance, the Lord God roused absolute terror in Sisera and his forces. Sisera himself leaped down from his chariot and fled on foot. Pursued by Barak and his forces, Sisera's chariots and troops fled as far as Harosheth-ha-goiim, where Barak had them slaughtered to a man.

Then Barak went after Sisera. Nearing the tent of Heber the Kenite, he saw Heber's wife, Jael, coming toward him. "Come in," she greeted him, "and I will show you the man you are looking for." He ducked his head and went into the tent. There at his feet lay the general Sisera, dead. A tent peg had been hammered through his temple and into the ground. The sight, and Jael's flat calm, shook him to the soul.

At that evening's celebration, as he joined Deborah in singing the victory song, Barak kept glancing from her to Jael. The vision of the enemy, Sisera, pegged through the tent floor by the docile Jael, was balanced by the memory of the unlucky Samuel, rescued by Deborah, and that goat. "Lord God!" he thought, "Lord God!" as he sang with a will: "*So perish all you enemies, Lord God! And let those who love You be like the sun when he arises in all his strength!*" [Judges 5: 31; JB]

Deborah smiled privately. Neither she nor the Lord God would have any further trouble from Barak! Of that she was certain.

[Judges 4: 4-14; 5: 1-3; see **DEBORAH, judge and prophet** (see also **JAEL**); see *JAEL and the Desperate General*]

# DELILAH
## and the Deadly Lure

"You want me to do what?" asked Delilah, a disbelieving smile turning to a laugh.

"Get your lover to share his secret," answered the spokesman for the Philistine chiefs curtly. "Convince him to tell you what makes him so much stronger than any other man that he can destroy anyone, any time he wants to. You *can* do that, I suppose?"

Delilah drew herself up, an imperious frown underlining her scorn. "Certainly I *can!* But why should I? Why do *you* interfere in the matter? What will *you* get out of it?"

"You find out where his strength comes from," he answered her matter-of-factly, "and tell us. Then we can take care of him – see to it that he's no longer a threat to us."

"Because?"

"Because he is our enemy!"

"Samson's not my enemy," she smiled lazily. "Not at *all!*" And she smoothed her skirts with her hands, a sensuous gesture that made the man blink in spite of himself. She caught the reaction and her smile broadened as he flushed.

"Well then," he said slowly, his voice like honey, "because, if you *do*, we shall give you eleven hundred silver shekels!" He paused significantly, his eyes narrowing as they met hers directly, and his lips smiled very slowly indeed.

The image of a hungry mountain cat toying with a plump rabbit came irresistibly to mind, and Delilah felt a shiver work its way up her spine. She understood. If she refused to entrap Samson, she would suffer, perhaps even die, and the chiefs would find some other way to destroy him. If she agreed – well, poor old Samson, handsome and strong as he was, excellent lover as he had proved to be, was doomed anyway. And eleven hundred silver shekels would buy a very, very nice marriage, afterward.

Pursing her lips, she nodded. "Done," she said quietly, and held out her hand.

Taking it, the spokesman bowed. "Done," he repeated. His lips brushed her palm, and he was gone.

It had not occurred to the lady of Sorek that she might have difficulty learning

Samson's secret. He was besotted with her, after all, "and with good reason!" she assured herself, checking the fit of her green gown. "I've *got* him, poor thing! Honey cakes from an infant!"

Delilah began her campaign that night with a direct question. "Tell me, lover," she purred, "where did you get your great strength from?" She smiled at him enticingly, then moved in for another kiss. When she caught her breath she murmured, "You're so strong! I wonder, what could one possibly do to take that strength away?"

She pressed against him in a way he found entirely distracting, and only rather later and after a suggestive "Hmmm?" from the lady did he answer.

"If anyone could tie me up using seven fresh bowstrings – you know, before they're dried – that would do it! My strength would drain away and I'd be just like anyone else!"

"Impossible!" she replied, breathlessly, continuing her seduction.

Several days later, supplied with seven new, undried bowstrings by the chiefs (whose men were concealed in her room), Delilah entertained Samson, to their mutual delight. She had feared the presence of observers might inhibit her but, in fact, forgot them entirely in the first deep kiss that seemed to her to mingle their souls as well as their bodies.

When their passion finally abated and Samson had fallen deeply asleep, Delilah felt herself beginning to drift, still swimming the sea of pleasure they had made. Somehow, though, she couldn't quite cast off from the shore; there was something nagging at the back of her mind. As though one of the watchers had upended the bedside pitcher over her, dousing her with chilled wine, she caught her breath and sat up with a bounce. The bowstrings! Scrabbling in the drapery surrounding the bed, she loosened the bowstrings, slipped them out of their hiding place and bound Samson with them, hand and foot. Yes, the knots were tight. They would hold an ordinary man.

Sliding back into the bed next to him, she pulled up the cover, then, as though startled, flung it back, shouting, "Beloved! Samson! It's the Philistines! Help!"

At the signal, the hidden soldiers sprang from their hiding places to launch themselves on Samson. Before they could touch him, he leaped up, broke the bowstrings as though they were spider webs, and took off after his attackers, who had wasted no time in racing out the door as fast as they could.

"You're lucky he didn't kill them!" Delilah said to the chiefs' spokesman the next morning. "Good thing they were all sprinters! They ran like the wind!"

"They'd better have!" he growled. "They know enough not to let Samson get anywhere near them! And mistress," he added in a wintry tone, "if they *hadn't* escaped that, that *monster*, it would have been your fault! Your information was wrong!"

"Not my fault," Delilah blazed. "That is exactly what Samson said!"

"*If* that's true," he said, "you're slipping. Even a penny-whore can tell when her mark's telling her tales – and you're top of the line. You say."

Delilah was livid. "How dare you!" she hissed. "I am *not* a whore of any description! I am a well-bred lady who enjoys the companionship of civilized men who *appreciate* my mind. And my charms. If they give me gifts, that is their business, and mine, not yours."

"Whatever," the spokesman returned without interest. "Try again. We *must* neutralize Samson, one way or another. Try – harder," he advised, gave her a long look, and left.

Delilah was shaken, both by her failure and by the unsubtle threat of the chiefs. She *did* know when a man was lying to her, she was sure, and Samson's successful deceit frightened her. "I'm not losing my touch!" she told herself. "I can't be!"

Several nights later, entertaining Samson with delight, for she really found him a marvelous lover, Delilah said, "You know, I'm really glad the bowstrings didn't take away your strength, beloved, even though you did play me for a fool with your lie. It was very clever of you – and it saved my life with yours. I'd just die if anything ever happened to you!"

She watched Samson smile and preen himself a bit. He was thinking, she knew, that everyone praised and feared him for his strength, except her. She was the only one who saw beyond her own delight in his physical being to his real strength, his brains. This was a delight he had never experienced before, and she knew he would want to experience it again. But this time, she was sure, he would tell her the truth, to impress her if nothing else, with how very clever he had been.

This then, was the time to ask. She began to tease him, again, to tell her the "real" secret of his strength. "Just in case," she said, "someone wants to harm you and I find out about it before you do. I can protect you!"

At that he laughed. "Not to worry, sweet thing," he said confidently. "That will never happen!"

"But suppose it does – and I don't know! That would be terrible! I'd never forgive myself if I weren't able to save you, just because I didn't know where the danger was." The non-verbal persuasions she added did the trick. Once he had begun breathing normally again, he told her that if somebody tied him up with seven brand-new ropes that no one had ever tied, his strength would vanish. "You wouldn't know me from any other man," he said and smiled sidelong at her.

"Now I know you're fibbing!" she laughed back. "I'll always know you from every man in the world!

It was several days later that she again allowed the chiefs' men to hide in her room. The new rope, seven strands of it, was laid out around the room on the floor, right next to the wall. The strands would look like part of the decoration of the room if anyone checked, but the room was dim, and Delilah had no intention of allowing Samson to concentrate on anything but her. Her success was, as usual, complete, and Samson slept like a rock afterwards. Nimbly she tied his limbs with the new rope, doubling the knots. She thought about dampening them with water, but decided the risk of wakening her lover was too great. "Besides," she reflected, "it's the new rope that will steal his strength, not the knots."

Sliding back into bed, she rested against him for a moment, regretting what she had done but realizing that, really, she had had no choice. Then, drawing a deep breath, she screamed, "Samson! Beloved! The Philistines have broken in! Help me!" And Samson surged to his feet, the ropes seeming to melt from his arms and legs as he took a swing at the nearest Philistine emerging from his hiding place. As they had done earlier, the attackers fled, Samson after them at top speed, and she was left to confront her second failure and to prepare for the chiefs.

They were not happy. For that matter, *she* was not happy. Had she fallen in love with her lover, instead of simply rendering him helpless in her toils, bound by his lust and her charms? It was a worrying thought, one she resolutely thrust aside. She would manage Samson, she told the chief who came to see her the next day. He could rely on her.

"You'd better," was all he said, but she got the message. Time was running out, and so was her credit. If she wanted to save her own life, let alone earn that eleven hundred silver shekels, it had to be soon. There could be no more mistakes. But what else could she do?

Pausing at her weaving, Delilah considered. Tears? No. Not to start with, anyway. Teasing? She'd done that. Sexual, um, experiments? There were a couple of those she hadn't used on him yet. Maybe. But she needed a – something, something to distract him, disarm him. She winced at the word, her failures lurid in her memory.

"I've got to find something!" she told herself intensely, punching the shuttle angrily between the web strands. "Something that will take his attention away from what he's telling me, so he doesn't realize what he's done. Something – wait! What about this?" She looked at the hanging she was weaving as though she had never seen it before, let alone designed and woven it up to this point. It was to be a lion at bay, surrounded by hunters and obviously doomed, but so valiant, so strong, so powerful that he looked as if he might very well eat those who had him trapped. She had gotten as far down as the lion's head with the weaving and there had found her design unsatisfactory. Suppose she asked Samson to take a look at the design and tell her what was wrong with it? That might work! "Then I'll get his secret out of him," she promised herself. "It will be easy!"

The weaving did catch Samson's attention, but oddly. He laughed heartily at it, then sighed, his mouth twisting in a fleeting bitterness she had not seen in him before. "Nothing, nothing," he answered when she asked, concerned, what was wrong. He studied her design. "Your lion will do very well," he said at last, "provided you give him really sharp teeth and claws! And keep his head up – defiant and proud. Make sure the eyes are open and that he's glaring at his tormentors. They may take his body, but they must never take his spirit. No. That would be wrong." She understood and with a few quick charcoal lines caught the spirit he was talking about. He was delighted. "Do that and you'll have the best lion in the world!" he boomed.

Later, in their lovemaking, he had said with an odd smile, answering her usual tease, "Weaving is dangerous, love! Catch my seven locks of hair in the web of your weaving and you'll reduce me to ordinary strength. I'll be just like any poor soul in your nets!"

"Nonsense!" she had returned. "If anyone is in the nets, I am! I'll never escape you, beloved, and I certainly don't want to!" Her heart pounded. She had the answer she had sought. She knew she did.

And that failed, too. The seven locks of hair she had so carefully woven into the web, into the lion, in fact, dogging the peg down as tightly as it would go, had simply melted out of the weaving the moment her screams roused him from his sleep in her arms, and he had roared in his pursuit of the unfortunate soldiers of the chiefs.

"That's it," their spokesman declared the day after her third failure.

"You're useless. We'll get him some other way. Kiss your shekels good-bye, mistress." He gazed stonily at her, and when he left, he shut her door with an exaggerated care more terrifying than a slam.

Galvanized, Delilah determined she *would* break Samson and learn his secret. Her determination rose, not just because her own life was at stake, nor because she wanted the eleven hundred shekels. Now, what she feared was that her own powers had vanished in the fires of their passionate and delightful couplings, "and that would be a *real* disaster," she thought.

So she began, skillfully and with no hint of annoyance, nor, indeed of anything but besotted adoration, to nag him, declaring each time they met that he could not possibly love her and withhold the insignificant truth she had asked of him. "I'm no Philistine!" she would laugh. "And you are, most certainly beloved, *not* my enemy!"

"Mmmhhh," he would answer, devouring her, but would give her no further reply.

Days later, yielding to her persistence as much as to his enchantment with her, now at its height, he gave in. "It's not much of a secret," he told her, smiling, his index finger wiggling the very tip of her nose as she giggled. "It's the hair! I was consecrated a nazarite by my mother when I was conceived."

"Nazarite?" she asked, puzzled. "What's that?"

He looked at her, startled, then nodded. "Right. You'd have no way of knowing that. Basically, it means no wine or spirits, no food our Law calls unclean, and no haircuts! The consecration is to the Lord God and those are its signs."

"So you've never had a haircut?" Delilah was intrigued. She had wondered at the luxuriousness of his hair, as thick and shining as her own.

"And if I do," he added quite matter-of-factly, "that would be the end of my strength."

"Why?" she asked, for the moment forgetting that this, at last, was the secret he had guarded so well.

"Because the consecration wasn't my mother's idea, but the Lord God's. And the strength I have is being given me for His purposes. If I break that consecration, it means I'm turning from Him, and His strength will leave me. Very simple. Now," and he smiled in the particular way Delilah had come to recognize, with a shiver of delight, as a prelude to passion. "Yes, beloved!" she whispered.

Afterwards, she had sent word to the chiefs, on the chance that their offer would still be open. She rather hoped it was not, for, more and more, she was coming to regret her involvement with them, and to see her prying as a kind of betrayal. But, if the eleven hundred silver shekels were still on offer, it seemed a shame to let them get away, if Samson were going to be destroyed anyway. "He'd want me to have that much," she told herself firmly, if illogically, "and anyway, they may really have given up on me and not do anything about my information."

They had not given up on her. A band of soldiers, one equipped with a shining sharp barber's razor, disposed themselves in their usual hiding places in her chamber. They'd brought chains with them, and one of them had a sack that clinked significantly, but no one mentioned either.

Delilah found loving Samson that day especially sweet, and tinged with bitter sorrow as well. Her "lion" was in excellent spirits, suspecting nothing, and he took them to heights beyond any they had scaled before, laughing in his joy. She joined him in the laughter, though hers had a touch of tears, and when, at last, they returned to earth and he fell asleep, trustingly, in her arms, she wanted nothing so much as to have her observers and "allies" vanish into smoke.

They had not. At her tentative gesture, the man with the razor emerged, carrying a basin of water, soap and a towel. Expertly, he shaved off the seven locks of hair and, as each one fell into the towel, Delilah felt her heart sink a little further. Finally, the "barber" nodded to her, scooped up the towel full of Samson's hair, dropped the razor into his basin, rose and slipped back, leaving the field of action clear for his fellow-soldiers.

Delilah cleared her throat, and around the lump of unshed, tears, called, "Samson! Samson! Wake up! The Philistines have broken in!"

At once he rose, meeting the emerging soldiers as he had before, but when he called upon his strength, he found none. His face white with shock, he raised both hands to his head and felt his shaved scalp. His howl of misery was met by the ferocity of the soldiers, no longer afraid of this enemy. They blinded him as he stood there, and his scream tore at Delilah's heart. Horrified at their cruelty, she made a gesture as if to stop them, but dropped her hand to her side, helpless. They loaded their blinded enemy with bronze chains, and as they huddled him out of her room, the chief who had first contacted her dropped the clinking sack on her bed with a contemptuous, "Your wage, mistress!"

A year later, Delilah learned the rest. They had taken him directly from her room to Gaza and set him to turning the mill there. Then, several months later at a festival of Dagon, they had had him brought in to the temple to entertain them with feats of strength. His hair had grown back, but his superhuman strength had not returned with it, though his commitment to the Lord God was stronger than it had ever been. He had asked the boy who led him around to bring him to the central pillars, the ones supporting the building, and to fix his chains to the ring there. The boy did so, and Samson, uttering his prayer to the Lord God for a final return of the strength He had given him to use against the Philistines, had pulled the building down and killed the thousands inside it, dying with them.

Hearing the news, Delilah felt her heart lift. "Good for you, my lion!" she thought. "You've beaten them all! You've won!" She swallowed the lump in her throat, closed her eyes briefly, then looked at her companion. "More wine, husband?" she smiled.

[Judges 16: 4-21; see **DELILAH** (see also **Samson's WIFE**); see *Samson's WIFE and the Coils of Betrayal*]

# DINAH
## and the Impetuous Brothers

There was a lot to be said for being the younger sister of ten brothers, Dinah knew, but just at the moment her mother Leah's sons were being really obnoxious, and she had had about enough of them. "They act as though they were each my father!" she stormed to Leah.

Leah simply sighed, then smiled gently. A lifetime of acting on her conviction that she *had* to be kind, diplomatic, gentle, practical, excellent in anything that gave comfort to others, and endlessly patient to be accepted at all, had made that smile, usually without the sigh, her response to aggravation. And, no question about it, Dinah was being extremely aggravating. "They're trying to protect you," she explained for what had to be the dozenth time. "You *know* that, Dinah! Why do you let it annoy you?"

"And you!" Dinah returned with a sudden smile. "I'm sorry, Mother. I know I'm being really annoying about this – "

"Then why don't you stop, instead of adding 'BUT' as you're about to do?" injected Zilpah, Leah's maid, closest friend and mother of two of Leah's sons, Gad and Asher. "Again."

Dinah opened her mouth, then closed it again. There was a pause. "You're right," the girl said at last. "I really don't object to their wanting to protect me. It's very good of them, and I appreciate it. It's just – no, Aunt Zilpah, this isn't just another 'but'; it's a real problem. I'm scared that they'll mess up Shechem and me!"

Leah frowned. "I still don't like the idea of your marrying a Canaanite, even if his father did sell us land to live on and build an altar to the Lord God."

"Bad business, mixing blood that way – to say nothing of mixing religions," Zilpah opined, kneading the meal, water and yeast for bread vigorously. "The way those people go on when they're worshipping – well! No decent woman would want anything to do with it!"

"But I've never – " Dinah interrupted indignantly.

"Hush child," soothed Leah. "Of course you haven't. Yet. But if you marry Shechem you might have to – to keep peace in the family. And that would be a disaster."

"I don't see why you ever let her go to visit those women in the first place," snorted Zilpah. "Nothing but trouble – what *were* you thinking?"

"That I wanted her to see some women her own age and have a little pleasure before she was married off to whoever Jacob thinks will do the family the most good!" said Leah, her placid tone at odds with her words.

Both women stared at her, shocked. This was Leah? Patient Leah? Goodness! In the silence, Leah said. "Now Dinah, it's time for you to tell me exactly what's happened between you and Shechem. This time what you *did,* not just what you and he said!"

Dinah suddenly blushed to the roots of her hair. She opened her mouth but nothing came out.

"I see," said Leah quietly. "But you must say it. Out loud. So you can hear the words."

The girl dropped her eyes. She was silent.

Seeing that Zilpah was about to challenge her, Leah made a sharp gesture. Zilpah subsided, though her expression was mutinous, her eyes knowing. "Dinah?" her mother asked.

Dinah's head came up proudly. "Mother? Aunt Zilpah? Shechem and I have slept together. And *oh,* how very special it was!"

"Told you so!" muttered Zilpah so softly only Leah, standing next to her, heard. Ignoring the comment, she asked quietly, "Has this happened more than once?"

"No, just the one time," said Dinah, a little sadly. "And yes, I have had my bleeding time since. Though it wouldn't matter if I hadn't," she added. "Because afterwards, he said he really wanted me to have his child. He said he was going to ask his father to ask my father for me as his bride!" She smiled at the memory, her flush settling to radiance. "Oh, mother! If my brothers interfere and ruin this match, I'll just die! Couldn't you talk to father first?"

Leah remembered her own desperation before she had become Jacob's wife. Her eyes met Zilpah's, and slowly the maid nodded. "Of course I'll speak to your father," Leah assured her. "I *do* understand. But Dinah, remember – if this doesn't work out, you need not fear. *You* are beautiful, truly beautiful! You will never lack for a husband if you want one."

Leah was as good as her word. She persuaded Jacob that this match would be a good one, establishing the family in this area. With Dinah married to Shechem, the son of Hamor, the Hivite who ruled the area, they would have no difficulties about water rights or lands for planting. But Jacob was troubled, for he assumed the union between Dinah and Shechem had been forced on her. He kept his silence, however, because his sons were away, scattered throughout the countryside.

In due course, Hamor approached Jacob and asked for the hand of Dinah in marriage. Shechem had persuaded his father that he simply had to have Dinah for his wife, and Hamor saw the advantages the union would bring to his people. He offered to give the women of his tribe to Jacob as brides for his sons, cementing an alliance that would be good for both families. He also offered as a marriage settlement any price Jacob wanted to ask, a sign of how eager he was for his son's marriage to Dinah.

Dinah's brothers soon returned home. Hearing the story, they, like their father, assumed that Shechem had taken their sister by force, and they wanted revenge. But given Hamor's enthusiasm for the match, the huge bridal price offered, the advantages of the alliance and Hamor's assumption that his offer would be gratefully agreed to, they were stymied. Marriage, after all, would save Dinah's honor, so they had no pretext for vengeance.

The brothers and Jacob agreed to the marriage, making only one condition. They could not, they said, give Dinah to an uncircumcised man, for that would dishonor her and them. If Hamor, Shechem and all the males of the tribe would undergo circumcision so that the two tribes could truly share life, then the marriage could go forward. If not, there would be no marriage.

Hamor and Shechem were delighted and quickly agreed. They knew that with the marriage all the property of the Israelites would be theirs as well, and all that cattle was a powerful inducement.

Leah reported the result of the meeting to Dinah, who simply glowed with joy. Even Zilpah seemed content. But Leah was not. She was terrified, though she could not have said why. "It was just too easy," she said to herself. "Something is bound to go wrong." But she kept her fears to herself and helped her daughter prepare for the wedding for which she longed.

Unfortunately, Leah's instincts were right. On the third day after the circumcision of Hamor, Shechem and all the males of their tribe, when they were all still weak with the pain, Simeon and Levi took their swords, walked into Hamor's town and, with cold efficiency, cut the throat of every man in the place, from Hamor down to the least significant boy.

When they had finished their slaughter of the helpless, Simeon and Levi snatched up everything of value in the town, gathered up all the cattle, flocks and donkeys and went back to Jacob. He berated them for their rashness and pointed out that they had made enemies that left them all in great danger.

"We couldn't let our sister be dishonored!" was all the brothers said in answer, and the discussion was terminated.

After the disaster, when the family had moved to Bethel, no one spoke of the aborted marriage. Indeed, Dinah did not speak at all, and grew thin and pale with grieving and with anger.

Leah and Zilpah tried for weeks to comfort her, without success, and they began to fear she would die. Finally, one late afternoon, they confronted her together.

"You've *got* to stop this nonsense!" Zilpah declared. "Silly girl! Nothing *happened* to you except that you didn't get to marry that foreigner, who was no better than he should be, if you ask me. You should be ashamed of yourself, drooping around this way! No, Leah," she added, "don't interrupt. You've been too soft on her, and look at the consequence. No more use than a dishrag! Shame on you, Dinah!"

Dinah sat down suddenly, her mouth open in shock. "Aunt Zilpah?" she said. "Aunt Zilpah, Simeon and Levi went and *murdered* my Shechem, his father and all the men of the town — when Hamor had already agreed with father for the marriage, *my* marriage, and they had all had themselves circumcised, as *my dear* brothers had demanded for the bridal price. And for what? They're the ones who ought to die — and I'm the one whose life has been cut off!"

"Cut off?" snorted her aunt. "You're still solid enough, my girl! You'll get another man to marry! You'll have your children! What's cut off about that?"

"They thought you had been raped by Shechem, Dinah, not that you had willingly slept with the man," said Leah, an unusual edge on her voice. "I didn't tell them different. Jacob didn't tell them different. Zilpah didn't tell them different. Did you?"

"Of course not!" said Dinah. "But why *didn't* you? I thought —"

"You did nothing of the kind," declared Zilpah. "You felt. Lusted. Maybe loved. But you didn't ever *think*, not through this whole thing. Now, do! What do you suppose would have happened to *you* if your mother, or your father, *had* told them that their favorite baby sister had slept with a Canaanite like a common whore?"

The color drained from Dinah's face.

"Right," Zilpah said. "They'd have killed you on the spot. And there's nothing anyone could have done to stop them."

Leah nodded. "So we didn't. And they accepted the marriage — seemed to think it was a good thing. Simon and Levi, though — "

"Didn't," Dinah finished. Then she sighed. "I think I've cried every tear

I'll ever cry," she said softly. "I loved Shechem. I really did. But it's over, isn't it? And there's nothing any of us can do about it, is there? Not even Simeon and Levi."

"Except go on," said Leah, remembering the morning after her wedding and the look on Jacob's face. "Simply go on. Will you, daughter?"

"Yes," said Dinah.

[**Genesis 30:** 21; **34:** 1-31; **46:** 15; **Judith 9:** 2-4; see **DINAH**; see *RACHEL, LEAH and the Duping of the Bridegroom*]

# ELIZABETH
# and the Longed-For Child

"I tell you, Mary," grunted Elizabeth as she shifted position on the bench and raised her swollen feet onto the stool again, "I am *ready* for this baby to be born!"

Mary jumped as though she had been poked with a sharp stick. Her eyes widened. "*Now*, Aunt? Shall I run for the midwife? Shall I send Uncle Zechariah? What should I do?"

"For a start," returned her aunt, laughing, "sit down again! Nothing's happening, I promise you. I have nine weeks to go, more or less. What I meant was, I'm really, really *tired* of carrying this child! My back aches all the time, my feet and legs swell, I'm hot, I can't get comfortable any place – and I simply *waddle* when I try to walk! Enough! I'm too old for this! Now you, when your time comes – it'll be much easier. You're only – what?"

"Fifteen," said Mary, flushing.

"Well, I'm sixty!" declared Elizabeth. "And trust me girl, this is *not* what sixty-year-old women were meant to be doing, angel or no! Yes, yes," she added, seeing Mary's horrified expression, "I know the Lord God knows His business, but why, if He meant to bless us with a child, He couldn't have seen fit to do it forty years ago, I do *not* see. And so I've told Him! Come, now, help me up. I've got to walk around or I'll cramp again."

"Of course," said Mary, helping her aunt to her feet. Then, curiously and somewhat fearfully, she asked, "You *really* said all that to the angel?"

"What angel?" snorted Elizabeth. "*You* got an angel, of course – had to. The Lord God was going to father your Child Himself – but no angel ever spoke to me, I promise you! Not that I don't understand. Since Zechariah had the duty of fathering the child, I guess it only fitting for him to get the news first. But still, the angel could have come to both of us, and so I said to the Lord God. I didn't *see* Him, of course. He didn't answer me, either, but I told Him just the same. I do think, you know, that *I* could have been consulted, especially since I'm going to have to do the suffering."

"But didn't Uncle Zechariah tell you what the angel said when he came home?" asked Mary, puzzled.

Elizabeth looked at her oddly. "Of course not, child! He couldn't remember! The angel struck him dumb when he didn't believe what the angel said. He couldn't speak a word!"

"Well then, how," began Mary, but Elizabeth interrupted.

"Simple," she said with a laugh. "He grabbed me, and things – went from there. That's what I mean! I certainly didn't mind – but it would have been nice to know. And what would one more angel have cost the Lord God?"

Mary decided not to touch that one. She cleared her throat instead. "Grabbed?" she asked faintly, Elizabeth's picture did not match her ideas of old age and a staid, religious couple doing God's will.

"Yes," her aunt replied. "Nicely, of course – Zechariah is always a gentleman. And, after all, he couldn't *tell* me what was going on, could he? And given the Lord God's command, and the promise of a baby at last, he really didn't want to wait to write the story out!"

"So," said Mary tentatively, "you didn't know, when you, er –"

"Not a thing!" Elizabeth laughed. "I all but fell over when your uncle finally wrote out for me the whole story of what had happened to him in the Temple! Imagine! A baby boy! I was so thrilled, and so was Zechariah. I'm not so sure now, but I've seen enough other women having babies born to know *that's* normal. It'll be all right once he's born!

"Aunt? You know how to read? Like the scribes?" Mary was wide-eyed.

"Certainly," Elizabeth answered, thumping down onto the cushioned bench again, puffing a bit. "That's one of the things Zechariah taught me when it was clear that we weren't going to have children for a while. 'Good for you!' he said. 'Keep your mind occupied – you can help me, too! And you never can tell when it'll come in handy.' So he taught me to read and write – Hebrew first, for the Scriptures, and then Aramaic. He taught me numbers, too, so I could keep the accounts. Arabic and Roman, would you believe! Zechariah is thorough, I'll say that for him!"

"So you didn't know what was going to happen until you read Uncle Zechariah's account?" she asked.

"Not a thing," her aunt assured her. "You can imagine how excited I was when I read that we were finally going to have a child *and* that his job would be to get Israel ready for the Messiah! Here," she said, and reached for the loose scroll on the shelf. "Read it for yourself."

Mary blushed. "I – can't read, Aunt."

"Heavens! Whatever was Joachim thinking of, not to teach you!" Elizabeth was indignant. "Men! They never *think!* Well, sit down here. We'll start you learning now. It'll take your mind off your morning sickness, for one thing," she added, and Mary flushed scarlet as Elizabeth hugged her. "And you never can tell. It might come in handy some day!"

Nine weeks later, Elizabeth suddenly caught her breath and went white. "What's wrong, Aunt?" demanded Mary, catching hold of her.

"Time," gasped Elizabeth. "Tell Zechariah and have him send David for the midwife. Go! I'll be all right for a bit."

Mary flew to the study rooms of the synagogue, had the attendant fetch Zechariah, gave him Elizabeth's message, and ran back, skidding in through the doorway. "Are you all right?" she demanded, breathless as her cousin.

"I will be," Elizabeth answered grimly. "Just help me to walk between the pains. It's the best thing to do," she added. "Let's the baby know he's not going to get any peace *inside,* so he might just as well come on out!" Mary laughed, shaking her head, and her aunt smiled. "It's true, though, so just you remember it. You might need to know that some day, if you're the only one around a woman about to birth a child. And when Judith comes, stay with me and watch everything. Ever seen a baby – born?" she gasped as the next pain caught her.

"No," Mary responded, rubbing Elizabeth's back as she bent over her middle. "Just the start, and then they put me out with the children."

"You must, then," Elizabeth declared. "You can't count on a child's coming when the midwife's there, you know. I think every woman should know what to do. Save lives that way – oh!" And she gasped again. "Pains are coming quicker," she said. "Won't be long now!"

"How often?" asked a new voice, and both women turned toward the speaker. "Judith!" exclaimed Elizabeth. "Am I glad to see you! About 200 slow heartbeats apart now."

"Good timing," said the midwife. "I'm glad you didn't wait longer. Child," she addressed Mary, "you don't need to stay if you don't want to. We can manage."

"She *does* have to stay," her aunt declared firmly. "She needs to learn this, and to see everything. Just in case she has to do it for someone and there's no one to help her – AAH!"

"All right Elizabeth. Breathe now, the way we practiced," said Judith calmly.

It was the eighth day after the birth – an easy one, all things considered, according to Judith. "Maybe so," said Elizabeth, "but if that was *easy,* I'd hate to have had a *hard* time! Never mind Mary, I'm all right. Just grouchy – no sleep! And I wish your uncle would get his voice back before they all get here for the *bris*. Once they've done the circumcision, Zechariah has to give the boy his name!"

"But you know the name! Couldn't you do it?" Mary asked. To her, it seemed that Zechariah was no nearer being able to speak than he had been three months ago.

"Not officially," her aunt answered. "Giving the name is the father's acknowledgement that the child is his, and that he accepts responsibility for the child's upbringing. And I *want* that for this baby. Don't forget when yours comes — it's important! Oh! Here they are!"

Greeting the guests, Mary missed the vigorous discussion among the relatives, only raising her head in alarm when she heard Elizabeth declare in a tone that brooked no argument, "His name is John!"

"But, my dear!" came a protest. "None of your relatives has that name! Zechariah is his father's name!" There was a murmur of agreement that died under Elizabeth's icy glare.

"Let's ask Zechariah!" someone suggested, turning to him with relief. Zechariah signaled impatiently for a writing tablet, and as all heads turned to stare at its surface, wrote, 'JOHN IS HIS NAME!' in very large letters. The murmur of dismay was drowned by Zechariah's *"Blessed be the Lord, the God of Israel, for He has visited His people…"* [Luke 1:68; JB], and by a healthy squall from the newly named John, whom Elizabeth had placed in his arms.

Over the heads of father and son, Mary met Elizabeth's triumphant smile with one of her own. The Lord God had done it again! Blessed His Name, indeed!

[**Luke 1:** 5-25; 39-80; see **ELIZABETH** (see also **MARY, mother of Jesus, Son of God**); see *MARY and the Mothering of God*]

# The Ephraimite Levite's CONCUBINE and the Price of Honor

"Whatever were you thinking!" her grandmother demanded. The girl shrugged and reached for another of the sweet grapes. "Don't just shrug! Explain! Unless, of course, you really *didn't* have a reason."

"*Didn't* have a reason!" the girl repeated, stung. "I most certainly *did* have a reason! The best! That Ephraimite you *sold* me to simply didn't love me! He insulted me! My honor was at stake!"

"Ah! Now we're getting somewhere," her grandmother said with satisfaction. "You're really angry with us, not your husband, and you're taking it out on him and shaming us at the same time. Very mature, dear! Just like your dear mother!"

"I'm *not* like Mother and you know it!" the girl answered, eyes flashing. "I never did a thing to distress the man you sold me to. I just – "

"Stop right there, missy!" her grandmother snapped, her tone icy. "You were not *sold* to that good Levite from Ephraim. He asked your father and me for your hand in marriage, as his second wife. He offered the customary bride-price. And *you* consented! You couldn't wait to get on that mule and ride out of here!"

The girl pursed her lips. What her grandmother said was a truth she could not deny nor, in truth, did she really want to. She nodded. "That's true, Grandmother," she said, her tone conciliatory. "But what happened after we got to Ephraim – *that* none of us foresaw. And that's why I came back to Bethlehem."

"So what happened?" her grandmother asked again. The girl was silent. "Tell me, Love. Maybe I can help you."

"Oh, grandmother," the girl said, tears forming in her eyes. "It was just so terrible! I've never been so humiliated in my life. He – he actually – he still loves his first wife! He – well. He went with her. He ignored me! I was dishonored!"

"Well child, what did you expect? That she'd vanish the second your sandal crossed the threshold? That he'd send her out to live in the orchard?" her grandmother asked her, not quite able to believe what she was hearing.

"I didn't *expect* him to go near her! I mean, there I was, his brand new bride. He was supposed to be finished with her. So what was she still doing there? And if he still loved her, why did he marry me? He greeted her with the biggest smile and warmest hug – as if I'd disappeared, or was some piece of furniture or something that he didn't even see. I tell you, my honor simply couldn't stand for it!"

"How a man, even a husband, deals with his own wife – and she *is* still his wife – is no concern of anyone else, not even of his second wife. And it certainly has nothing to do with her honor nor his," declared the old woman. "In fact, you ought to be down on your knees in gratitude for such a man!"

"What?" exclaimed her granddaughter. "Gratitude for being ignored?"

"You won't always be a brand new bride, dear one," her grandmother reminded her. "Some day you may be in the position of having to welcome a new wife to the household, and of wondering what will happen to you. His first wife must have been very worried when you stepped through the door – thinking, maybe, that she would be dismissed, or sent to live with the mules. They do that, some of these hillmen. Or so I've heard.

"Oh!" said the girl. "I never thought of that!"

"You need to," said the old woman. "But look what he did. He went out of his way to reassure her that her place was safe, that he still loved her, that she was still his wife and need fear no such ill-treatment. And I think he thought you'd understand that, would see the need. Certainly, it never crossed his mind that you would think yourself unloved. I'm sure he intended no insult to you."

"But," the girl began.

"No but, granddaughter," declared her grandmother briskly. "The way he treated her is the way he'll treat you, when it's your turn to step aside and make way for his new bride. Isn't that worth being grateful for? If anything, he *honored* you in letting you see how he still values her. He married you because you're beautiful and sweet-tempered, I think, and that's the girl he was trusting would understand. And you didn't, did you?" The girl shifted on her stool, her eyes on the straps of her right sandal. For a time she was silent. Then, as if her grandmother had said nothing at all, she continued her complaint. "You keep referring to our *household* grandmother, and being open to the new one crossing the *threshold*. What household? What threshold? The 'house' my husband brought me to was a tent!"

"Did it leak?" asked her grandmother interestedly. "I always wondered about that!"

"No, it didn't leak," said the girl through gritted teeth, "but it didn't have separate rooms or doors you could close either! No, there we all were, crammed in together. I had no privacy at all! Living like that is beneath my station. It dishonored me," she finished triumphantly, sure she had made an unbreakable case.

Her grandmother gave the exaggerated sigh of one whose patience is being severely tried. "Good thing you weren't born when your mother and father were," she said dryly. "You'd never have survived! Our family only moved up to a house with three separate rooms when you were born and most of the neighbors thought we were putting on airs. When I was a girl, moving into a house was a big step up. So honor has nothing to do with it. It's luck! Honor has to do with how you accept what comes to you – and on that standard, *you*, my girl, have dishonored your husband. Frankly, I'm ashamed of you."

"Grandmother!" sputtered the girl, now seriously upset.

"So now we know why you ran away and came home to us," said her grandmother briskly, "and have stayed here four months. But tell me, grand-daughter, what happens now? I mean, what did you *think* would happen?"

The girl's shoulders drooped and she suddenly looked like the little girl she had been a year ago. "I *thought* he'd come to get me," she said in a small voice. "I *thought* he'd understand why I was angry and would come to appease me – and would put that other woman aside, for good!"

"But he didn't," said her grandmother, "and I sincerely doubt he will, Love. I fear you've disillusioned him, shown him how spoiled you are and how unpleasant you can be. He may come – but that will be to demand back the bride-price he paid us, or I miss my guess! And just how do you think we'll be able to pay him? We used that money for the business, to keep it from failing, and we've had no return on it yet, at least not enough to pay back the Ephraimite."

"Then what *will* happen to me?" the girl wailed.

Her grandmother paused. "I don't know," she said finally. "Obviously, another marriage is impossible, and it looks as though you've ruined this one beyond repair. But, if by some miracle, he *should* come to make peace with you, and should actually *want* to take you back with him, I'd say *go* – and don't even turn your head toward Bethlehem, lest he send you back here, and you learn what a real loss of honor is! Make up your mind to show him nothing but gratitude and obedience from that moment on – or you will really be ruined."

"But his first wife," the girl began, a frown marring her beauty.

"Has her own problems!" rejoined her grandmother tartly. "Make it your business to reassure her. Be her friend. Learn from her what you've obviously not learned from us – how to be a real woman and a real wife! You'll not be sorry if you do, and if you don't, you won't last."

"But my honor!" she objected.

"That's not honor, dear girl," the old woman answered, "that's pride. Real honor means keeping your word, no matter what – and you gave yours to him when you married him. Real honor will keep you in one piece no matter what happens – even if you should die in the doing. But your *honor* – it's a fraud, Love. It will kill your soul and, no matter what you think it gives you, that price is too high for anyone to pay."

The girl did not answer. She suspected her grandmother was right, but not for the world would she have admitted aloud, nor even to herself. Instead she shrugged again, gathered her wounded sensibilities around her like a cloak and swept from the room. Her grandmother, watching her, sighed. "No good will come of this," she murmured. "No good at all."

To everyone's surprise, and the enormous relief of her father and grand-mother, the Levite from Ephraim appeared on their doorstep the next day, seeking to make peace with his wife, their daughter. Her father was effusive in his welcome. Her grandmother was determined that the girl should behave sensibly.

The girl herself was of two minds. She still wanted to punish the Levite for his "dishonoring" of her but, even more, she feared what would happen if she refused his overtures of peace. Her grandmother's warnings had impressed her, little as she liked to acknowledge it, and for once, she did as the old lady had so strongly suggested. Taking pains to present herself as hurt and bewildered, frightened but not, oh definitely not, angry, she managed to charm her husband thoroughly, and so they made their peace with one another.

On the fifth day after his arrival, surfeited with the feasting his rejoicing father-in-law had insisted upon, the Levite packed up his wife and her baggage on the mules and, with his servant, began the long ride back to Ephraim.

They had no trouble on the journey that first day – except for finding a place to stay the night. They had gotten as far as Gibeah, for the Levite had been unwilling to trust to the party's safety in the Jebusite-held settlement in eastern Jerusalem, but insisted on getting to an Israelite settlement. It looked as though they would have to camp in the town square, for no one stepped up to offer them hospitality, even though they had sufficient provisions for themselves and their beasts.

Then an old man, coming back into town from working in the fields, saw them. It developed that he, too, was from Ephraim. Though he had settled in Gibeah, the local people, all Benjaminites, considered him an interloper, so he was glad to have someone to talk to, and equally glad to offer hospitality to those who, if not kinsmen, were at least from his old home area.

The evening went well at first. The girl was accepted as part of the Levite's household and found their host's daughter, a charming girl somewhat younger than she, a delightful companion whom she went out of her way to charm. The Levite was pleased with her and she often smiled at him. Her resentment of his previous "dishonoring" of her was still simmering beneath the surface but, after her four days at her father's house with him, her insecurities had faded. She felt she could, in time, displace the first wife and so avenge her honor, but she was in no hurry to begin. "Time enough," she thought complacently, "when he has come to need me so much that *she* will be expendable. She's getting old! It won't be that long! And meanwhile, I'll see to it that he really gets to like me. A lot!"

Oddly enough, some of the conversation at the table turned on the question of honor. The man who had taken them in spoke of his doing so as a matter of honor. Hospitality was not optional, if one were a man of honor, nor were its obligations lightly to be disregarded. The host was obliged, it emerged, to protect anyone whom he had taken under his roof or fed at his table, even if it cost him his life, or what he held dearest in the world.

The Levite agreed. Indeed, the guest had similar obligations to his host. Never must he allow anyone to harm his host; certainly he himself, in accepting hospitality, had put the obligation of doing his host no harm on both himself and all his kin. And he, too, was obliged to come to his host's defense, even should he die for it, or lose what was closest to his heart.

The girl found herself becoming uncomfortable. With these standards, she had clearly had no business running away from her husband in the first place. And his congress with his first wife was an obligation of *his* honor – for he had taken her into his home as his own. In fact, any hope of his fidelity to herself rested on his fidelity to his first wife, for if he could lay aside his honor with his first wife, he could do the same to her. "And then where would I be?" she thought, shaken. Truly, her grandmother had been right. For some "honor" the price was just too high!

Her musing was shattered with the banging at the door and the shouts of the drunken ne'er-do-wells, so the host described them, of the town. "Bring'm out!" shouted one. "The tall, handsome one!"

"Yeah!" slurred another at the top of his voice. "We wan' getta know'm!"

"Hurry up!" urged another. "Send'm out! You c'n hav'm back after, if you're not done!"

Their host paled. Grimly, he rose and slipped out the door, closing it firmly behind him and placing his back solidly against it. "Gentlemen!" he remonstrated. "Brothers! No! Don't even think of such a thing! He's my guest! This is a crime!"

The crowd rumbled, growing more rowdy as the moments passed. The host's argument had not impressed them. "Now! Gi'm to us now!" one shouted, and the rest surged forward, echoing him.

"Wait!" commanded the host, the edge of desperation in his voice. "I'll tell you what! My daughter is a lovely virgin! I'll give her to you to do with what you please – but leave my guest unharmed!"

Inside, the host's daughter went white with shock. So did the Levite's concubine. "Honor!" she thought. "Honor! That's not honor – that's crazy! They'll kill her, the drunken louts!"

But before any of them could speak, the crowd had shouted, "NO! Give us the man! Give us the man!"

In the tumult, the host slipped back inside. He looked at the door. No, it would not withstand the assault of the mob outside. They would all die. He looked up and met the Levite's eyes, but before he could say anything the Levite spoke. "My brother," he said, "let me try to save us. My honor is involved here, too."

He put out his hand to his concubine and pulled her close to him with a smile. She caught her breath and felt a surge of triumph. Her honor had won and there hadn't been a price. Grandmother had been wrong! She was his wife, and she would confront this crowd as *his*. So much for her rival!

She smiled brilliantly at him and moved with him, slipping out the door as the host had done. Seeing him, the crowd grew silent, and the girl, still tucked in beside him, wondered what he had in mind but was not worried. She was his and that was enough. He would deal with these people and they would go home together, and she would see to it that her life went the way she wanted it to, whoever had to pay the price. He might have to offer them himself, of course, but she would be safe. And anyway, they'd never accept.

That would be dishonorable!

When he began to speak, the girl was transfixed with horror. It was not himself he was offering to the mob to save their host, but her! She heard again his voice saying, "what is closest to my heart," and understood, at last, that he had meant her, that she had held him honor-bound, heart to heart, as she had thought she desired to do — and that the price of this honor, real honor, was finally going to cost her everything she had and everything she was.

The crowd took the Levite's offer and snatched her from his grasp. After that it was all a wash of breathless terror and ceaseless, ever-changing pain.

Finally, it all stopped. The rising sun had begun to paint the sky red-gold. The dew had soaked through the girl's dress, now bloody rags, when she staggered to her feet. Stumbling to her knees from time to time, she made her way back to the door of their host. No one was awake, nor had the house been damaged, she saw, so the Levite's device had worked. He had kept their honor as guests, paying the price of his dearest love, herself — though not in the same coin in which she had paid it.

She fell at the door, collapsing, her hands extending over the threshold, the guest and the wife keeping honor to the end. "Grandmother was right," she murmured. "Real honor may cost you your life, but it does keep you in one piece with your soul alive. How I wish I'd never traded it for the other kind — the price to get it back was so high! But if I hadn't — that price would *really* have been too high! Oh, beloved!" she sighed.

Then she was still.

At full day, the Levite came to the door, opened it and saw her lying there. "Get up now," he said, though gently. "It's time for us to be on our way."

She answered him not a word.

He looked down at her compassionately, sorry for what she had suffered, but glad he, and she, had been able to save their host and his daughter. "Come on," he said again, and reached down to touch her.

His hand on her cold, tenantless flesh told him the truth. Subtly his face changed, from flesh to carven rock it seemed. She was dead — and they would pay, these sons of Benjamin, the honor price for him and for her. "Blood for blood," he thought, "life for life. And I will have it, to the very last man of that benighted tribe. Our honor demands no less a price."

He picked up her body, gently set it on the mule and headed for Ephraim and home.

[Judges 19: 1–30; 20: 1–48; 21: 1; see (The) Ephraimite Levite's CON-
CUBINE (see also Old Man of Gibeah's VIRGIN DAUGHTER, (The)
Benjaminites' Four Hundred YOUNG WIVES and Jabesh-gilead's
WIVES and Children)]

# ESTHER
# and the Balance of Power

I hate politics, you know. Really! And I've had nothing but politics since poor Queen Vashti, silly woman, got above herself. She actually *refused* the King's summons to attend him at a royal banquet! You just don't *do* that to Artaxerxes, King of the Medes and the Persians – Ahasuerus we call him. He is *King,* after all. I mean, it's just not right to refuse him, however annoyed you might be at having your own banquet interrupted, or however much you might hate being shown off before a drunken group of sycophantic royal administrators – talk about pearls before swine!

But refuse she did, and that was the end of her. No, of course he didn't kill her – it might have been kinder. He had her banished from his presence forever, by edict, and his court cheered. They were terrified that *their* wives might take a leaf out of Vashti's book and start disobeying *them!*

I wasn't at court then. I was living with Uncle Mordecai, who took me in when my parents died and raised me as his own daughter. I was called Hadassah then – our whole family is Jewish, you see; we were deported from Jerusalem under Nebuchadnezzar of Babylon and landed here in Susa.

Well, eventually, the King calmed down about Vashti and began to feel lonesome. So his courtiers suggested he replace her, and I won the – contest, really. They brought in pretty girls from all over the country and I was one. I went by Esther – didn't tell anyone I was Jewish; Uncle had warned me not to. Anyway, they put us in the harem and gave us a year's worth of beauty treatments and lessons in court etiquette. Hegai, the King's eunuch – he was custodian of the harem – thought I was wonderful, I guess. He gave me seven maids and moved us to the best part of the harem! I was really surprised. And then, at the end of the year, they dressed us up and sent us, one by one, in to the King to see who would please him and replace Vashti.

When it came my turn, I just went in wearing what Hegai gave me – no extra jewelry or anything – and, well, that seemed to be enough. I was named the favorite! That banquet was fantastic!

It was shortly after the banquet that I had my first conscious experience of politics. Really scary. It happened when Uncle, who worked at the Chancellery, discovered that Bigthan and Teresh, the King's own eunuchs, had planned to assassinate him! Uncle told me, I told the King, and the conspirators were hanged. The whole incident was written up in the Book of Chronicles in the King's presence, but Uncle got no reward. Then, the very same week, the King raised Haman to be chief officer of the state and ordered that all Chancellery people were to bow and prostrate themselves before him.

When I heard it, I was livid! The King owed Uncle Mordecai and me his life! Why hadn't he rewarded Uncle with this power and honor? I gave Uncle an earful the next time I saw him privately, and he taught me my first political lesson.

"Politics" he said, "is the art by which a ruler stays in power. Now, the first thing a King learns is that all his subordinates, *all* of them, want his power, or, failing that, as much power *over* him as they can get. Every one of them is always watching all the rest to make sure that no one has more power over the King that he does. To stay alive and in power, then, the King has to keep *all* the power he delegates *in balance*. To do that, he has to make sure that all his followers have equal, or equivalent, power over him, *and* that that power is more apparent than real. All the *real* power he keeps for himself. Clear so far?"

"Yes, but," I said, and he hushed me. "We have no time, my dove! Just listen! Now, when someone saves the King's life, his power over the King *looks*, to everyone else, all but absolute. The King is the First Man in the Kingdom, and he *owes* us – and what's the King's life worth? Anything we'd care to name!"

I couldn't keep still. "So what does he think he's doing raising that Haman to Second Man in the Kingdom, if he *owes* us his life? That makes no sense!"

"What he's doing, my pet, is saving my life," Uncle said, and it was clear he wasn't joking. "If he had given me that honor, it would have thrown delegated power in the Kingdom completely out of balance. Consequently, I would draw all the envy of the whole court – I wouldn't live out the month. By naming Haman, and making the whole Chancellery bow and prostrate before him, the King has *balanced* the delegated power again by setting up another apparent power base equal to the one we earned by saving his life. And since that saves *my* life, he doesn't *owe* us anymore! He's paid the debt in kind. Very wise man, our King, and clever as a basket of snakes! Don't *ever* cross him – or underestimate him!"

Uncle left then, and I thought about what he'd said. It made sense. It also explained why Vashti's refusal was so terrible, and why she *had* to be removed, *and* left alive. She was challenging him for his royal power, upsetting the crucial balance of power completely. If she were not punished, the King could lose the Kingdom. But she could not be killed, for with Vashti dead, the incident was over, but with her *alive,* her offense and its consequences were an active reminder to *everyone* of who was King and what that meant. As Uncle said, clever as a basket of snakes and a dangerous man to cross. "Takes one to know one!" I thought.

But a couple of days later, I really began to wonder. My wise and prudent Uncle, I learned through the harem grapevine, was defying Haman and scorning his power, and the King's orders, by refusing to bow and prostrate himself before that slug! Now that was unbalancing the power of the Kingdom spectacularly! Oh, I understood *why,* all right. I knew that we Jews only bow and prostrate ourselves before the Lord God, as He is the only God there is or can be. And that's that. Uncle couldn't bow. And so he told the Chancellery officials when they asked. But still – what he was doing was more than dangerous. It was suicidal.

In fact, it proved worse than that. When the Chancellery officials reported Uncle's refusal to Haman, he saw for himself that Uncle would not do him homage, so he asked Uncle's race. When he learned Uncle was a Jew, he declared war on us all.

Not openly, of course – he just reported to the King that there was this one race of people who consistently defied all the King's edicts, to the detriment of the Kingdom and the King's interests, and that if the King would decree their destruction, he, Haman, would put ten thousand talents of silver in the Royal Treasury. That is a *lot* of money!

Haman was being a barrelful of snakes at that point! He played on the King's fear of revolt, of usurpation and of destabilization of the Kingdom, and on his greed and the fact that the Treasury always needed more money – and it worked!

"Keep the money," said the King, giving Haman his signet ring, "and take the people; do as you please with them."

That's when Uncle came to me. Not directly, of course – that wasn't possible. The edict Haman had sent out, under the King's name, had put a death sentence on Uncle and every one of us Jews. We were to be slaughtered, men, women and children, on the fourteenth day of the twelfth month, and there was no appeal - not to the King or the government, that is.

For us, however, there was the Lord God. Weeping and tearing his garments, Uncle put on sackcloth and ashes, came to the gate of the Chancellery, and stayed there wailing loudly and bitterly.

It took about three minutes for news of *that* to get to me! I sent out some clothes for Uncle to put on instead of the sackcloth. He refused. So I sent Hathach, the eunuch the King had appointed to wait on me, and told him to find out what was going on. When he came back, he had the whole story, a copy of the edict of extermination that had been published in Susa, and a note from Uncle, reminding me of what I owed *him* for bringing me up – talk about politics! – and telling me to pray to the Lord God and then go to the King and plead for our people.

Well! I sent a message back explaining that I couldn't just barge into the King's inner court any time I wanted, that I had to wait to be summoned, and anyone who did go in without a summons would be killed instantly, unless the King extended his scepter to him. That was the law – still is, for that matter.

Uncle's answer was classic – the balance of power again, only this time the Lord God was at the heart of the equation.

"Don't think for a minute," he said, "that you're going to be the one Jew to escape, just because you live in the harem of the royal palace. I promise you, you're not! If you keep your mouth shut and think you can hide your race behind a Greek name, you'll perish, and your father's house will vanish with you – and the Lord God will deliver us through someone else's help!" Then, for good measure, he added, "Who can tell? Maybe this was the Lord God's reason for having you come so close to the throne in the first place!"

What could I do? There I was, caught at the balance point of the powers of earth and Heaven, standing between the King and my people, the Lord God's people, to speak His word and, maybe, save us all, or to be silent and certainly die. No contest! But I was terrified I tell you!

I sent word to Mordecai to start a strict fast with all the Jews in Susa – nothing to eat or drink, day or night, for three days. I promised my maids and I would keep the same fast, and then I would go to the King if I had to die for it.

And that's what we did. I put on sackcloth, put ashes and dung in my hair and spent the three days and nights in prayer to the Lord God for His people. I reminded Him that He was my only helper, and told Him that though His punishment of exile was all we deserved for sinning against Him, these enemies were planning to wipe us out entirely. I begged Him to save us, to save His power on earth. And then I asked Him for courage, and to transform the fires of the King's enmity toward His people, lit and fanned by Haman, into love and favor for us. There was more, I guess, but I can't remember it right now.

After the fast, I bathed, had my hair washed and dressed, put on my very best clothes and every single one of my jewels, all gifts of the King. Two of my maids walked with me – I couldn't have moved without them, I was so weak. I still didn't know what I was going to say, but as I didn't know whether I'd be alive to say anything once I put a foot inside the door of the inner court, that didn't seem a problem.

At the door, I took a very deep breath, then stepped over the threshold, raised my eyes and saw the King's face. Startled? Enraged? Something! I didn't stop to study it. I sank right down in a court obeisance as the room spun. I leaned on my maid and held my breath. The next several seconds lasted a century or so. Then I felt his arms around me and heard him asking frantically, "What's the matter, Esther?" He held me tight, assuring me that I would not die, that the order was meant only for ordinary people. "Come to me!" he finished, and laid the golden scepter on my neck.

I was overwhelmed – so grateful! I babbled something about his looking like an angel and being frightened on that account, and then, to my shame, I fainted completely. What a champion the Lord God chose in me! He saves my life and I pass out!

When they finally revived me, the King kept telling me I should ask for whatever I wanted and he would grant it. I guessed I should bring up Haman and the Jews, but when I opened my mouth I was as surprised as anyone in that room to hear myself inviting him and Haman to come to a banquet that very day! He laughed in relief, said of course they would come and sent for Haman to tell him, and I went back to the harem wondering how on earth we would get a royal banquet ready in four hours.

Bless Hegai! He set every slave in the palace to work on that meal and it was splendid! Haman arrived with the king, they feasted with pleasure, and the King asked me again what I wanted, that even if it were half his kingdom, it was mine.

Now that scared me. I was remembering that balance of power and Vashti's fate, you see, and glancing at Haman's face, I realized that I already had too much power to keep. Somehow, things had to shift back, but Uncle had never taught me how to do that. "Lord God, help me now!" I prayed, and opened my mouth. What came out was an invitation to both of them to another banquet the following day, and a promise that then I would make my request. They were delighted – Haman especially. He had never been so honored!

Let me tell you, I was shocked! What was the point of a second banquet? Then it occurred to me that the Lord God must have sent the words – I never would have said them on my own. So I got Hegai started on the next banquet.

Later on, of course, I learned what the Lord God was doing between that day and the next. Unable to sleep that night, the King had had the Book of Chronicles read to him, had heard the passage describing Mordecai's saving his life from the would-be assassins, Bigthan and Teresh, and, in asking, had learned that Mordecai had never been rewarded. He decided that *that* would never do, and as Haman had just arrived on his own business – to get the King's permission to execute Uncle for contempt, using the fifty-cubit gallows he had just had built – the King asked his advice about a reward for someone unnamed.

Assuming that someone was himself, Haman went all out! The King's clothes, his horse, a diadem, a street parade with proclamation by a high noble – all that was to be this person's reward!

"Hurry, then," the King said, "and do all that for Mordecai the Jew who works at the Chancellery. On no account leave anything out that you have mentioned!"

Shocked to the core, Haman opened his mouth but, fortunately for him, could say nothing. Instead, he smiled and set off, no doubt grinding his teeth once he was well away from the palace. He knew he had to carry out for his enemy, to the letter, the reward he had designed for himself! That's how the Lord God restores the true balance of power – and that was only the beginning.

Haman finished up, went home and told his wife Zeresh and the others what had happened. They were the ones who had advised him to build the gallows and execute Mordecai in the first place, but they gave him no comfort. Indeed, they reminded him that, if Mordecai, who had just risen above him so dramatically, happened to be a Jew, Haman would never be able to surpass him. And at that point, the servants from the palace arrived to bring him to my banquet.

I knew nothing of Haman's forced honoring of Mordecai that day, of course, and it was a good thing. I was frightened enough as it was of the man's hatred and envy, and of that decree hanging over us. The banquet passed for me in a blur, and we got to the last of the wine in what seemed like ten breaths, though I know it was three hours or more.

Once again the King asked me what I wanted of him and promised he would give me anything I asked. This time when I took my deep breath and opened my mouth, the words that came out were no shock to me, for they were the truth of my heart and my being. I asked him to grant me my life and the lives of my people, for we had all been condemned to die. I told him I wouldn't have asked if we were simply to be enslaved, but since we were to be killed, the one man who persecuted us could not possibly repair the damage that would be done to the kingdom, nor undo the King's own loss.

Don't look at me! That whole speech was the Lord God's doing, first to last! Remember, the King had to keep power in his realm in balance, but the Lord God holds the hearts of Kings in His hands, and can arrange matters as He wishes for His chosen ones.

"Who's the man?" the King demanded, breaking in. "Who would dare to do such a thing? Where is he?" He was white with rage and angrier than I've ever seen him. Angrier than I ever hope to see him again! That was the Lord God's wrath, I believe, burning through the King.

"Who is he?" I repeated. "The one who hates us and has condemned us to die? Why it's Haman – sitting right there!"

Well, Haman started to quake. The King flung himself from his couch and plunged out into the garden in his fury, and Haman, knowing his life was forfeit, threw himself across me, blubbering and begging for his life.

I never got a chance to answer him. The King stormed back in to the banqueting hall, saw Haman prostrate across my couch pinning me in, and froze, his mouth dropping open. Then, very softly, in a tone so deadly it made the hair stand up on the back of my neck, he said, "And now he's going to rape *my* Queen in *my* palace before my very *eyes?*"

And that was the end of Haman. They hanged him on the gibbet he had had built in front of his house, for Uncle Mordecai.

Happy ending? Well, yes. But that decree of extermination was still in place, remember. So back I went to the King, weeping and pleading with him to send a written decree to undo the decree Haman had issued. He just smiled and told Uncle to write out in the King's name whatever kind of decree he wanted for the Jews and to use the King's signet to seal it so it would be irrevocable.

And that's what Uncle did! The decree, which countermanded Haman's decree, took effect the same day Haman had hoped to slaughter us all.

So that's what happened, and that's how the Lord God takes care of His own. Men balance power. The Lord God IS power. Blessed is His Name!

[**Book of Esther**; see **ESTHER** (see also **Esther's MOTHER, Esther's MAIDSERVANTS, VASHTI** and **ZERESH**)]

# EVE and the Charms
# of the Plausible Stranger

The woman opened her eyes and looked around. She was intensely aware of warmth, though she had no name for the sensation, and of love, which cherished her to the depths of her being, though she had no names for any of these realities.

She turned and saw the One she would learn to call God, the Lord God, and He smiled at her extending His hand. She took it, returning the smile, and they moved together to a figure lying asleep in the green shade of what she would come to know as a tree.

As they drew near, the figure awoke, rubbed its eyes and rose. The woman waited, wide-eyed, lips parted on an indrawn breath, devouring this wonder that faced her. She knew, somehow, they belonged together, knew neither of them would be complete without the other, though why that should be, or how it could be, she had no idea.

The figure seemed to be having the same response as she - awe and delight. And then it spoke. *"This one, at last, is bone of my bones and flesh of my flesh; this one shall be called 'woman,' for out of 'her man' this one has been taken!'* [Genesis 2: 23; NAB]

His words, the first the woman had ever heard, made a chord of right- ness that surrounded them and fitted them exactly in to each other, and centered them, now joined, in the love of the Lord God surrounding them and penetrating them at the same time.

"Woman!" she repeated at last. "I am woman? And you are man?"

He nodded. "The Lord God made me Himself, out of the earth." She looked her puzzlement, and he continued, "When I opened my eyes, I felt this wonderful warmth, and I looked up. There He was, sitting back on His heels, His hands open on His thighs and muddy to the wrists, smiling. He had just breathed life into me, He said, and He was going to build me a Garden to live in. And He did!"

"So we are in a Garden?" the woman asked. "Why – um, how – um, what – Oh, dear!" She stopped. "All right. A Garden. We are to live here. How?"

He smiled. "We are to cultivate and take care of the Garden, He said."

"Which tells me nothing!" she exclaimed with some heat. "What *is* all this, anyway?" She gestured vigorously, pointing.

"That's grass, that stuff you're standing on," he answered, suppressing a smile as he followed her jabbing finger, "and that's a peach tree, that's a magnolia tree, that's a camellia bush, that's a pine tree, that's a hickory nut tree, that's the river that waters the Garden, and – sorry! I can't see what you're pointing at."

"That!" She repeated her jab at the ground. "It's moving, and not just with the – what's that stuff that's making the bush and the trees move?"

"Wind," he answered.

"Right," she said. "Not just moving with the wind, but by itself. That gray-brown thing. There! What's that?"

"An animal," he answered. "In this case, a squirrel. It's alive, as we are, but it can't speak as we do, or ask questions, or know itself."

"Are there any more of them?"

"Squirrels? Yes, I think so."

"No, animals. Are there any more animals?"

"Lots and lots!" the man said enthusiastically. "Horses, dogs and cats, rabbits and sheep, tigers, cows, snakes, chipmunks – I'll show you! And there are fish. They swim in the water of the river and breathe it! There are birds, too. They fly in the air," he pointed, as a creature swooped into view. "That's a crow. That tiny brown one is a sparrow, and that," he indicated a gray bird pecking the ground near their feet, "is a dove."

"What's it doing?" the woman asked.

"Eating. A seed, I think," he answered. "Some birds eat insects – the tiny bugs crawling right there? And some eat worms – long things that move by wriggling, like that one there, just working its way into the dirt. And some eat smaller animals."

"Yuck! That's disgusting!" The woman shuddered. "Why do they do that?"

"Eat? To stay alive. Or did you mean why do they have to eat small animals to stay alive?"

"Yes. It seems a waste!"

"Well, there's a balance in it, but why it should be that way I don't know. That's just how the Lord God made everything."

The woman was silent for a moment, thinking. "How do you know? I mean, what everything's name is and how everything lives? Who told you? Or did you make it all up?"

"Well," the man began, then stopped. He frowned. "When the Lord God settled me in the Garden, to take care of it, and gave me the Command, He said it wasn't a good thing for me to be all by myself, so He was going to make a fitting companion to be with me. Then He made all the animals and birds out of the mud, and brought each of them to me – to see if any of them would do, I guess – and as I looked at each one, somehow, I knew its name, so I spoke it. So, I guess I did, sort of, make up the names, but not really. I more *saw* the name with the animal."

"What about this 'fitting companion' business?" the woman asked with some asperity.

"What about it?" he returned. "Oh! Well, that turned out to be you, of course!"

"Then where did I come from? I know the Lord God was the first One I saw, but His hands were perfectly clean – no mud at all! I know because He took my hand to bring me to you. So He can't have made me the way He made you."

"He didn't," the man explained. "What He did was put me to sleep, and while I was asleep, I think He took one of my ribs – from here," he touched his side, rubbing it a little, "and wrapped it up in flesh – and then He brought you to me!"

"So that's what you meant by 'bone of my bone, flesh of my flesh'! That's why I feel I know you – you're the other half of me. Or, maybe, I'm the other half of you! We're meant to fit together, to be together. Too bad we're in separate bodies; we should be one!"

The man looked into her eyes smiling, and the woman felt her insides turn over, in a most peculiar but entirely pleasant way. She shivered. He said gently, "You're right. And we can be. Come." And he extended his hand. She took it, and together they walked into the green shadows.

Later, when the cresting flood of their joy had broken and floated them gently back to speech, the woman said, "Oh, I understand now! I see how we are one, body and soul, even when we are apart."

"That's because of the spirit," the man replied, "the breath the Lord God breathed into us when He made us. It lets us remember our joining, and live in the love that brought us together, no matter what we're doing. Are you hungry?" he added. "I'm starving!"

"Yes," his wife said, "but what are we to eat? Not those worms, I hope!"

"No, no," her husband laughed. "The Lord God said that we could eat the fruit of any tree in the Garden, except, of course, the Tree of the Command."

"What Command?" asked the woman.

"That the only tree that we may *not* eat of is the Tree of the Knowledge of Good and Evil. *'For,'* He said, *'on the day you eat of it, you shall most surely die.'* [Genesis 2: 17; JB] It's that tree in the middle of the Garden, next to the Tree of Life."

"I wonder why," she said thoughtfully.

"Because we'll die, of course! We won't be alive anymore! That's why!" he replied impatiently.

"No," said his wife. "That's not what I meant. Obviously, we're not going to eat it, if we're going to die. But why would a Tree of Knowledge kill us? Knowledge is good! And why would He put a Tree that could kill us in our Garden? Why would He make it at all?"

"I don't know," her husband answered. "But in the first place, it's not really our Garden. It's His. We're only caretakers. And then, I'm not the Lord God. I'm sure He has his reasons, and at least He warned us. The Tree evidently has to be where it is, and we have to care for it along with all the other plants, without touching it or eating its fruit. That really shouldn't be hard — wait till I show you all the other fruit trees there are, and the nuts we can gather, and all the vegetables that will feed us full! We won't ever be hungry! We don't need to eat the fruit of that Tree. Here! Try this plum!"

The woman accepted the golden fruit from her husband and bit into it. Juice ran down her chin and she squealed with delight, "Ooh!" she exclaimed when she had swallowed the fruit. "This is wonderful! Are there any more?"

"As many as you want," he assured her. "And there are grapes! Here, try them!"

They ate until they were full, and the subject of the Tree of the Knowledge of Good and Evil was not raised again. But the woman thought about it, off and on, wondering.

Days and nights in the Garden soon took on their own rhythm. The man and his wife woke early, tended the plants and trees in the Garden, swam in the river, and made friends with the animals, even the ones we call wild. They ate and slept and joined in love and knew all manner of delights. Best of all, the Lord God came to walk and talk with them in the Garden in the cool evenings, answering their questions and assuring them of His love just by His presence and His interest in their discoveries and their labors. The woman still thought about the Tree and wondered, but less often and with less urgency. She did not, however, speak of it, either to her husband or to the Lord God.

One day, when her husband was working across the Garden and she was working alone, the woman encountered a Serpent, who asked her "Is it true that the Lord God told you not to eat the fruit from the trees in the Garden?"

The woman laughed. "Of course not!" she said. "We're allowed to eat fruit from any tree in the Garden, except from that one, in the middle. The Lord God says if we do, we'll die."

The Serpent laughed. "Silly! You're not going to die! God told you that because He knows that if you do eat the fruit of that tree, you'll be like gods! You'll know good and evil!"

The silence was electric. The Serpent's words had opened a door in the woman's mind, through which enticing light flowed. Knowledge! Not just learning things – the *essence* of Knowing! To Know Good and Evil with *that* Knowledge would be to decide for herself what was good and what was evil, and to make that *be* reality. It would be to have Power. To become Power. She – no, they – would be like gods! Maybe, even *be* gods!

She caught her breath and looked, again, at the Tree. Her eyes were drawn by the Tree's fruit, which seemed to glow. Her hand reached toward it, until her fingers almost touched its ruby skin. It would taste wonderful, she knew, for everything in the Garden did, but more – it would give her and the man the one thing they lacked, the Knowledge/Power that would raise them beyond themselves.

Her fingers touched the fruit and plucked it, then took a second and a third. She raised the first piece to her lips and bit into it, just as the man appeared beside her. His eyes opened wide as he realized what she was doing. He opened his mouth to speak, but could find no words. "Here!" said the woman, giving her husband the dripping fruit from which she had just eaten a piece. "Eat this! It's the most wonderful thing I have ever eaten! And, see? I haven't died! The Serpent was right! He said we wouldn't! Oh, hurry! The fruit will give us Knowledge beyond anything we have ever imagined! Wait till I tell you! Hurry! Eat with me!"

Stunned by his wife's boldness and by the fact that she was very much alive, and drawn by the beauty of the fruit, the marvelous aroma from its bitten, dripping flesh, and the promise of this wondrous Knowledge, the man ate.

The light in the Garden changed subtly for them then. The sweetness of the fruit faded, the sunlight turned brassy, the birdsong grew shrill and discomfort announced itself. And then, looking at the man, the woman realized that she was naked. She began to blush, turning away from him and dropping the remaining pieces of fruit to hide herself with her hands. As she did so, the man gasped, awareness of his own nakedness flooding over him as shame, and he turned from her.

There was an uncomfortable silence.

"What do we do now?" she asked him at last.

"Cover ourselves," he replied. "It's getting late. The Lord God will be coming to the Garden soon. We'll have to hurry."

"Let's deal with the covering first," she said. "Then, you figure out what we can say to Him." Looking around, she saw the fig tree. "Here, help me gather some fig leaves. We can make loin cloths out of them if we each sew a couple of them together."

They had just finished when they heard the sound of the Lord God walking in the Garden in the cool of the evening. The man and his wife looked at each other, and without saying a word, hid from Him among the trees of the Garden.

The Lord God called to the man, "Where are you?"

"I heard You coming through the Garden," the man replied, "I got scared because I'm naked. I was hiding."

"Who told you that you were naked?" the Lord God demanded. "You've been eating the fruit of the tree I forbade you to touch, haven't you."

"It was the woman *You* put here with me!" he blustered. "*She's* the one who picked the fruit and gave me some. So I ate it," he finished lamely, pointing to his wife.

The Lord God turned to the woman. "What got into you to make you do a thing like that?" He asked, very quietly.

The woman took a deep breath and tightened her lips. The flood of attraction, rationalization and desire that had swept her, along with her husband, from the Garden's safety and order to the fruit and its now-unfolding disaster had ebbed, leaving only the consequences and, in plain sight, their cause, as she saw it. "The Serpent," she said. "It was the Serpent. He's the one who pushed me into it. So I ate the fruit." She nodded. That was right.

Then the Lord God said    to the Serpent, *"Because you have done this, be accursed beyond all cattle, all wild beasts. You shall crawl on your belly and eat dust every day of your life. I will make you enemies of each other — you and the woman, your offspring and her offspring. He will crush your head, and you will strike at his heel."* [Genesis 3: 14–15; JB]

The woman nodded her satisfaction. Served the Serpent right for deceiving them so. She became aware that the Lord God was looking at her, but she saw in His steady gaze no anger, only sadness and love. She dropped her eyes in shame and heard Him softly say, *"I will multiply your pains in childbearing; you shall give birth to your children in pain. Your yearning shall be for your husband, yet he will lord it over you."* [Genesis 3: 16; JB] And with these words, the woman felt her relationship with her husband changing, subtly and irrevocably. A weight settled on her spirit and the Garden seemed gray.

Then the Lord God turned to the man. *"Because you listened to the voice of your wife,"* He said, *"and ate from the Tree of which I had forbidden you to eat, accursed be the soil because of you. With suffering shall you get your food from it every day of your life. It shall yield you brambles and thistles, and you shall eat wild plants. With sweat on your brow shall you eat your bread, until you return to the soil, as you were taken from it. For dust you are, and to dust you shall return."* [Genesis 3: 17-19; JB]

The words dropped into the darkening silence one by one, quiet as drops of rain, inexorable as the death they promised. In them the man and the woman heard the end of the life they might have had, and began to taste the bitter rind of their coming reality. The man looked at his wife, and called her Eve because she would be the mother of everyone else who would ever live. His own name was Adam, because he had been made from the soil.

Everything seemed to be over. Adam and Eve looked at each other without hope, but the Lord God was still with them, and they felt His warm presence. Surprised, they looked at Him, questioning, hoping…? He smiled slightly, and shook His head with sympathy it seemed. Then He bent down, picked up some skins of animals and made clothing for them, for He was unwilling to send them away from the Garden with no protection against the cold.

As they dressed, they heard Him talking to Himself. *"See, the man has become like one of us, with his Knowledge of good and evil. He must not be allowed to stretch his hand out next and pick from the Tree of Life also, and eat some, and live for ever."* [Genesis 3: 22; JB]

Hearing the words, Eve nodded. The Serpent *had* been right, but not as she had understood him. Their eating of the fruit had really been, not just ascending to godly powers they could hold and use, but attempting to be God for themselves and the universe, and that they could never have done. They would have destroyed everything, she knew, and if they were to live forever, the destruction would never end.

She looked at Adam to tell him what she'd understood, but there was no time. The Lord God was leading them to the edge of the Garden. They turned to look at Him one last time in this form and then, at His nod, stepped out of the Garden hand in hand, and began to walk.

Behind them, the Lord God set His cherubim with a flaming sword, to guard the way to the Tree of Life and prevent their ever returning to the Garden of their beginning.

[**Genesis 1:** 26-31; **2:**18, 21-25; **3:** 1-14, 20; **4:**1-2, 25-26; **5:** 1-2; **Tobit 8:** 6; **Sirach 25:** 24; **40:** 1; **4 Maccabees 18:** 7; **2 Corinthians 11:** 3; **1 Timothy 2:** 13-14; see **EVE**; see *EVE and the First Fruits*]

# EVE and the First Fruits

She should have known, Eve reflected years later, as she tended her grandson Enosh, Seth's son. She should have realized it, when she and Adam had not died the death, as the Lord God had warned them they would. They had not garnered that promised first fruit of their deceived, foolish disobedience. Thinking to be as gods, they had lost everything. But they had not died. Instead, they had been sent from the Garden alive, to find a new place, to learn to live there as best they might, wresting a living from the now-hostile earth. She should have known, then, that the fruit of their disastrous choice, delayed, would be harvested little by little, and would entangle their children as well, and their children's children. "Forever," she breathed, almost aloud. "Forever and forever. This dying will never end."

She should have seen this particular horror coming though, she thought. She had recognized its elements from the beginning. She should have done something to stop it before it had a chance to start. It was a familiar thought, accompanied by a familiar stab of pain. There was nothing she could have said, nothing she could have done, that would have changed what happened, would have prevented the disaster.

Watching Enosh playing with flat stones by her bench, building something it seemed, she found her mind circling back to that disastrous day to live it again. This time she did not struggle against the familiar wash of memory but let it fill her, let it have its way.

The day had been hot. It was the end of summer. Proudly, she had watched Cain, her firstborn son, going out to his fields to choose some of his crop as an offering for the Lord God. She remembered how happy she had been on the day of his birth. She had named him Cain, this new little man she and Adam had gotten from the Lord God, and they had rejoiced together in every new thing he learned.

She had been equally pleased when Abel, their second son was born. The boys had made their marriage complete in a way neither she nor Adam had envisioned, and they delighted in both, though the two were very different in talents and temperament, and relations between them were uneasy. Nevertheless, they had loved each other deeply, and Eve had trusted that their affection would smooth out the difficulties in the relationship when they had come to manhood.

Abel was easygoing, accepting everyone cheerfully. As he was loving and uncomplicated, everyone loved him, so he found his paths smoothed and found joy in all he did. Everything seemed to prosper under his hands and to flourish in his care.

Cain was more edgy. He loved his brother, but he seemed to feel that he was in competition with Abel for their parents' love and attention, a competition Abel didn't even seem to notice, which hadn't helped at all, Eve thought. She'd tried, carefully, to intervene, but she was unable to convince Cain that he was as well loved as Abel, and Abel only laughed in disbelief when she mentioned the problem to him and continued to treat Cain as he always had, with warm, if casual, affection.

And so matters had stood, on the day the brothers were to offer sacrifices of thanksgiving, first fruits of their labors, to the Lord God. Eve remembered thinking, as she watched Cain disappear into his fields, that this might be the occasion when he and Abel, who had gone out the day before to choose lambs from his flocks for his offering, might finally enter fully into brother-hood, and Cain might find some peace.

The young men had both labored hard and prospered equally. Cain's harvests of grain, fruit and vegetables had been abundant. Abel's flocks of sheep and goats had multiplied and grown strong and fat. There was no ques-tion that the Lord God had loved and blessed them both, and their parents in them. Perhaps now Cain could believe that his parents, too, loved them both and valued each brother as himself and for his own gifts.

Eve remembered that she had even allowed herself, at that moment, to hope that this prosperity was a sign that the Lord God had forgiven them, that they might not have to die the death, maybe even that they might be allowed to return to the Garden! She smiled bitterly. How foolish she had been. And then she sighed. If only she could have frozen that moment, when both her beloved sons were gathering their offerings, and hope was alive that they would finally be able to love each other without the tension of Cain's fear and its bitterness! If only she could have stopped time there!

But at that point, she hadn't known, and even if she had, there was noth-ing she could have done. There was nothing she could do now, either, except to stop this remembering, drive out the pictures and the sounds and turn her mind to something else. But she wasn't sure she wanted to do that.

She felt a tug at her skirt and looked down. Enosh had finished his building project and wanted her to look at it. "It's lovely, baby," she said absently, and then looked more closely. "Enosh?" she asked, her eyes wide. "What have you built?"

"Altar!" he announced, proud to be able to get his tongue around the grown-up word. "Like Da-Da and Gampa's. Fire there! Sac — saccy -," he stopped, frowning impatiently at the words he could not say.

"Sacrifice," Eve said softly, feeling tears begin to gather behind her eyelids and in her throat.

"Saccy-fice!" the child repeated triumphantly. "Good? Altar saccy-fice good?"

"Very good!" whispered his grandmother. "It's a beautiful altar of sacrifice, Enosh. There's never been a better!"

The boy grinned at her praise. "I build house now, Gamma!" he announced and set to work.

"Yes, baby," Eve murmured, "you build the house. Good boy!" Her lips thinned as she pressed them together against the pain of the memories Enosh's altar had brought to vivid, present life.

They had returned, her boys, bearing their gifts. Cain's sheaf of grain had been perfect, the apples ripe and fragrant, the squash large and sound. Abel's lambs, the firstborn of his flocks, had been healthy creatures, their legs strong and their wool springy and clean, for he had washed them. The sacrifices had been offered with love and reverence, the brothers standing side by side. Adam and Eve stood behind them waiting to make their own offering from their labors, an offering to the Lord God of their two chief treasures, their sons, their real first fruits.

Then the unthinkable had happened. The Lord God had looked with favor on Abel and his offering, but He had rejected Cain and his offering. Adam was stunned. Abel was nonplussed, and reached out with dismay to touch and comfort his brother. Cain was devastated and absolutely furious. Eve closed her eyes feeling sick. This was going to be dreadful.

For a long moment, no one made a sound. Then the Lord God spoke. He addressed Cain, but His words penetrated each of them. *"Why are you angry and downcast? If you are well-disposed, ought you not to lift up your head? But if you are ill-disposed, is not sin at the door, like a crouching beast which you must master, hungering for you?"* [Genesis 4: 7; JB]

In the silence that followed, Eve began to breathe again. The Lord God had not rejected Cain; He was only testing him. Surely Cain would see that! They had all heard the words. Surely Cain would respond!

She had opened her eyes, her hand reaching out to touch her firstborn, but Cain was no longer standing in front of the altar. She spun around, but he had gone. Only a puff of dust showed the direction; he must have been running. "Probably crying, and ashamed to let us see it," she had thought. "Well, that's all right then. When he comes back, we'll talk to him and show him, make him see the Lord God has not abandoned him. It will be all right."

Eve breathed a sigh of relief that was also a prayer and gripped Adam's arm. He looked at her and said, "When he comes back, we'll have to make him see that the Lord God hasn't abandoned him, that this is a test – "

"Yes," she had agreed eagerly. "We will."

"I'll help," Abel offered. "Well," he went on, responding to their startled attention, "I need to. He probably thinks it's my fault, that I got the love and acceptance from the Lord God that should have been his. Like he does about your love." He looked at his parents. His mother's jaw had dropped in utter astonishment, and his father had gone very still as he did in extreme emergencies.

Gently, Abel went on, "He does, you know. He thinks you love me better than you love him, and that hurts him. I know that it's not true. You love us both, just as we are. But he can't see that. I'm sorry to tell you, because I know it didn't even occur to you that he might feel that way, but he does, and that's what we have to deal with when he comes back. I'm sorry, Mother. I'm sorry Father."

"We knew, son," said Adam softly.

"We've been trying and trying to show him he's wrong, that we do love him, do love you both, as our dearest, dearest treasures," Eve interrupted, "but we haven't succeeded. And now – "

"And now he thinks the Lord God has done the same thing," Abel went on. "But we all know that's not true. We know that He's asking Cain to trust Him and listen, and try again. So, I think we have to work on him together, to make him see what we do."

"And then," Eve said, looking at Adam, "maybe we can help him believe, *know* that we love him as we do Abel, as himself."

"Maybe," said Adam. He shook his head. "Somehow, I think it won't be that easy."

"But we have to be ready!" Abel looked at his parents. "I can't tell which of us he'll go to, but we all have to be ready. We have to listen to him, and then – "

"Bring him home," Eve had said, looking at her husband and her son. "Whatever happens, bring him home with you, so we can all help him. If he comes to me, I'll keep him home. It will work." Silently she had added, "It has to. It just has to."

"House! Gamma, look!" crowed Enosh at her feet. "I build house! House good?"

Eve blinked, disoriented at her sudden return to the present. She rubbed her eyes, still wet with memories, and examined the stones Enosh had arranged. It did look like a house, she noticed, surprised. "That's wonderful, baby!" she smiled. "That's a marvelous house!"

"Hungry!" he announced, fixing her woven bag with a stare that could have cut holes in it. "Enosh hungry! Cakes? Please, Gamma, cakes?"

His grandmother laughed and opened the bag. "Cakes!" she agreed, took one and broke it in half. She gave the half to the child, and he held it in both hands but did not eat it.

"You eat, Gamma!" he commanded, and fixed her with the same look he had given the bag, a look, she suddenly realized, that was pure Cain, though the boy had never seen his uncle. "You eat!" he said again, and she looked from him to the broken cake in her hand. Slowly she bit into it, and as Enosh, satisfied that she was being fed, began to eat himself, she allowed the end of that dreadful, dreadful time to live again in her memory.

Cain had not come back that night. Adam hadn't been particularly worried. Cain had often spent the night out of doors; the weather was fine, and he probably needed some time to compose himself. Abel agreed, so Eve kept still, though a sense of foreboding grew within her until she was ready to scream with the tension. Morning came at last, and Abel had said he'd look around for Cain. "I know a couple of places he likes to hole up," he told his parents, "and I can go to him without – with less – " He stopped. "You know what I mean," he finished with a half-shrug that might have meant anything.

They did. "Go on, then," Adam nodded, and Eve hastily shoved a couple of hearth cakes into a woven bag.

"Here," she said. "He'll be hungry. There's enough for both of you. Hurry!" she added, though she had not known why, and shook her head impatiently at herself. "Sorry," she said. "Sorry."

Abel had hugged her, hard, and left, meeting Adam's eyes and grasping his forearm as he hurried out the door. "Good man," Adam said, his pride in his younger son blazing like the morning sun. And she had agreed.

It had been a long day, stretched to the breaking point before noon, and then well past it as the shadows extended their lengths in the yard and the light began to fail. Adam had left shortly after Abel, saying something about the wheat, but she knew he had gone to search for Cain himself. After he left, she had been unable to settle to anything, though there was plenty that needed doing. Finally, she began to grind grain and make hearth cakes. These, as least, she could not spoil, and they would come in handy no matter what.

It was just before sunset when Eve heard the sounds she had been waiting for, two sets of footsteps approaching the door. She turned, her mouth open to speak her son's name, to ask if he had found his brother, and saw Cain silhouetted in the doorway, Adam behind him, grim and watchful, though she had not taken that in at that moment.

"Cain," she began, reaching for him, then stopped. Cain's clothing was splashed with something dark, and so were his hands. He was standing stiffly, as if he would collapse if he relaxed a single muscle. His whole being screamed pain. "Are you hurt?" she had cried. "Cain? What happened? Abel?"

Then, growing cold and still, she knew - knew what had happened as clearly as if she had been standing there watching, seeing what Cain, his voice lifeless, his face fixed in horror, was telling her.

She saw Abel hailing Cain, heard the older brother invite the younger to go with him, and watched them travel into the open country. She saw Cain's rage overmaster him. Saw him batter his brother to death, hitting him over and over until Abel's blood soaked into the ground and not a bone of him remained whole.

And she saw Cain running, running, collapsing in exhaustion under a tree. She heard with him the voice of the Lord God questioning him, asking him where his brother Abel was. Heard Cain answering with the sneer he used to mask his feelings, in this case terror, if he were supposed to be his brother's keeper. And she heard the Lord God's reply as if He were speaking it here, in their presence: *"What have you done? Listen to the sound of your brother's blood, crying out to Me from the ground! Now, be accursed and driven from the ground that has opened its mouth to receive your brother's blood at your hands. When you till the ground, it shall no longer yield you any of its produce. You shall be a fugitive and a wanderer over the earth."* [Genesis 4: 10-12; JB]

She had frozen at that. Time had seemed to stand still. It was over. Everything was over. Things could be no worse, and they could not be fixed. So why was Cain still talking?

Eve had to force herself to breathe, to attend, to hear the words, though she knew, even then, that she wasn't really taking them in. And it wasn't Cain, but Adam, she realized, who was speaking now. His voice was harsh, grating with emotions she could not untangle. Anger, certainly, and deep pain, and something else.

He had, it seemed, found Abel's body and, torn between horror and rage, had followed the trail of the killer's headlong flight. He had arrived at the tree in time to hear Cain's protest to the Lord God at the sentence He had passed. The punishment was too harsh, Cain had protested. Since he was no longer able to till the soil, and he would have to avoid the Lord God's presence, he would have to become one of the fugitives of the earth, and anyone who met him would consider him fair game. He would be hunted to his death!

Even in her stunned state, Eve marveled, horrified at her firstborn's audacity. Who would dare speak so to the Lord God! Yet, Cain was still standing, still alive — what on earth had happened?

His father's voice had gone on, "The Lord God said that if anyone killed him, he would be avenged sevenfold. And then the Lord God put His mark on him, to prevent anyone who might come across him from killing him." Adam paused. "He was going to go away right then, but I told him he had to tell you what he had done. Himself," he added.

Cain had met her eyes, his own dead, then dropped them. He shook his head slightly and was still.

That seemed to be all of the story. Eve waited. The silence was leaden.

Finally, Cain had cleared his throat, looked at her and said dully, "I have to go away. Now."

Eve had nodded and, blindly reaching for a woven bag, had begun, mechanically, to fill it with the hearth cakes she had made that interminable day. She felt nothing. Nothing at all.

Adam, his movements precise, his face expressionless, had filled another bag with Cain's clothing, a small sack of grain, some vegetables and a sharp knife with its sharpening stone. He had handed the bag to Cain with a stout walking staff, and a filled waterskin.

Cain shouldered his bag and hung the waterskin from its cord around his neck. He planted the staff in the dirt and leaned his weight on it. He sighed and opened his mouth, but seemed to think better of it. "Sorry," Eve thought she heard, but she had never been sure. She handed him the bag of hearth cakes and touched his cheek. "Cain," she began, but he dropped his eyes and the words died before she could even think them.

At the last moment, Adam had reached out and touched Cain's arm. "Son," he said, but nothing followed, and other than giving a slight shiver, Cain showed no sign of having heard. The light caught Cain's face as, at last, he turned to go, and his parents could see the protective mark of the Lord God on his forehead.

It was their last memory of him. Though they did learn, much later, that he had settled in the land of Nod, east of Eden, had married and fathered a son who founded a town and continued the family, they had never seen him again nor heard from him,

That night, with Abel now buried in the field behind the house, and Cain gone without hope of return, Adam and Eve found themselves alone as they had not been since the disaster in the Garden. They had begun to talk about what had happened, about why it had happened.

As they looked at it all, it had seemed to Eve that, somehow, Cain's deed was the same as their choice in the Garden, but a thousand times worse. Or maybe not. Maybe it was the same choice. They had made themselves God through greed and ambition by eating the fruit; Cain had made himself God by dealing death to his brother through fear and envy. And now, like them, he had to leave his home, the only one he had ever known.

"Die the death," she had said to Adam. "Death is the first fruit of the Tree. Now Cain has to die the death too, by living and suffering and realizing what he has done to Abel, and to us, and to himself, the way we did."

Adam had nodded. "And still do," he said. "Over and over again. Have you begun to die yet, with Abel? And with Cain? And die to rage at Abel for dying, and at Cain for killing him? It's coming, you know. We can't escape."

"No," Eve had answered slowly. "I haven't. I haven't even begun to feel. But I know I will. And that dying will not end, any more than the dying from the Garden has."

Adam had sighed then, much as Cain had done just before he left them. "No," he said, "it won't. But maybe, maybe..." His voice trailed off.

"While we live," she had said, finally, "we can hope. And the Lord God did show him mercy, in a way, protecting him from those who would kill him, as He protected us. So maybe Cain will learn. Maybe he will find his peace. Maybe we will, too."

They had joined then, in sorrow, and in a love deeper than any they had known, and in that joining, Eve had conceived Seth. When he was born, she had welcomed him as the child the Lord God had given her to fill Abel's place, and felt the first faint thread of healing begin.

Seth had been a joy to her and Adam, not a substitute for Abel nor a wiping out of Cain's deed, but entirely the Lord God's gift of comfort to them in himself, as himself, and they had loved him so.

His son, Enosh, was their delight, and Eve smiled to see him, curled up asleep on her old cloak, which he carried with him everywhere.

[**Genesis 1:** 26-31; **2:**18, 21-25; **3:** 1-14, 20; **4:**1-2, 25-26; **5:** 1-2; **Tobit 8:** 6; **Sirach 25:** 24; **40:** 1; **4 Maccabees 18:** 7; **2 Corinthians 11:** 3; **1 Timothy 2:** 13-14; see **EVE**; see *Eve and the Charms of the Plausible Stranger*]

# HAGAR
# and the Impatient Wife

I knew it was a bad idea from the moment Sarah – she was Sarai then – proposed it, but there was nothing I could do. I was her slave girl. I had to obey.

It was just like her though. Patience? She had none. The Lord God had promised her and Abraham – he was still Abram at that point – a child. The child they had both longed for all their lives. You'd think that would be enough. She had God's guarantee that her barrenness would end, and she would finally give Abram a son. It wasn't.

You see, the Lord god hadn't said *when* the child would come, and Sarai thought *will give* meant *instantly* where her desires were concerned. So, when she didn't get pregnant immediately, my mistress got impatient and made a plan. And I was right in the middle of it.

"Hagar," she said to me, the morning after her monthly courses had started, "I have an idea! I think I know what the Lord God wants us to do about that child He's promised us." She looked at me, and I could see the pain she was hiding under her brisk, no nonsense attitude. It was in her eyes. "It's plain that I can't conceive. Not myself, in my own body. So I'm going to send you in to Abram for me. You're young and healthy, and you'll be able to conceive a child and carry it to term. And because you're my slave, that child will count as mine! Isn't that brilliant!"

I tell you, I was in a panic! I wanted to shout, "That's not brilliant – it's insane! And it's dangerous! This is the Lord God's plan you're playing with, not just some business proposition! You really *do not* want to make Him angry; not if you mean to go on living very long."

But what I said was, "Yes, Mistress," as my heart dropped to my sandals.

She smiled at me. "Good! I knew you'd think so! I'll tell Abram tonight so you'd better bathe before supper. I don't want any delays!"

That gave me the day to worry, which I did. I was only twenty-two at the time, and I was about midway in my cycle, so I would probably get pregnant – if Abram were capable of giving any woman a child.

I wondered about that. I figured the Lord God *wanted* this child to be His miracle, so He might have wanted both Abram and Sarai to be physically beyond having children before He sent it. In that case, Sarai's decision to bypass her barrenness by using me as a surrogate, if it succeeded, would thwart His plans. Not a good idea. And if Abram and Sarai had been supposed to wait for His promised child until He lifted *Sarai's* barrenness, what would he do to me for being in the middle? And to my child?

Then, suppose Abram didn't get me pregnant. To me that would be a clear sign that Sarai had been wrong and that we should settle down and wait for the Lord God's time. Unfortunately, I didn't think my mistress would see it that way. Suppose she decided that Abram would have to get a surrogate too? As far as I was concerned personally, that mightn't have been too bad. But this was the Lord God's plan we were rearranging. Suppose this surrogate and I had a child? Would the child and I be cast out in the desert to die? Would we die?

Of course Sarai *might* also be right; this just might be what the Lord God wanted, but I strongly doubted that. In any case, the whole thing was risky, to say the least – and I was in the target area if Sarai were wrong. Oh, I tell you, the more I thought about it, the more I really hated this whole plan.

But I couldn't tell Sarai that. She'd have killed me. Literally! At least that's what I thought then; now, I think I might have been right.

In any case, evening arrived in what seemed like half an hour. Sarai sent me, bathed, perfumed and wearing her silk robe, to Abram. No, I won't tell you about that – just that the one night was all it took.

I had an easy pregnancy physically – no morning sickness, no swollen feet and ankles, no strange cravings – but in every other way it was horrible. Sarai, though this had all been *her* idea, was *not* pleased when I conceived. She never said that, of course; even *her* denial system wouldn't swallow that mountain! But she found fault, every day, with every single thing I did, or did not do, from dawn until way after dark, and during the night if she happened to wake up.

What really tied her in knots was that I was happy, basically, even though she reduced me to tears three times a day, at minimum! That was because of the baby, of course. That child thrilled me from the moment I knew I was carrying him – and I knew the next morning, though I couldn't prove it until my courses failed to arrive on time.

So I lived inside this warm bubble of joy, cherishing my child, feeling grateful to Abram, and yes, to Sarai, for this completely unexpected gift, and got on with it. Drove Sarai frantic! She knew she couldn't get *in* there, where the baby and I really lived, and she was livid. She even told Abram that I had scorned her ever since I became pregnant, and it was all *his* fault! Poor man

– he reminded her that she was my mistress and that she could do what she liked with me.

So she did. She abused me so much that, finally, I got frightened for the child and ran away. That's when I met the angel. He called me by name and when I told him I was running away, he sent me back to submit to Sarai, telling me the Lord God had heard my cries of distress and promising me that my child and Abram's, a boy to be named Ishmael, would make me the mother of more descendants than anyone could count. He also warned me that my baby would spend his life at war with all his brothers and that everyone would be against him, but I didn't hear that, then.

I went back, of course. You don't say no to the Lord God's angel, not if you know what's good for you! The child was born, Abram named him (and claimed him, in the naming, of course) and all was, relatively anyway, well. Sarai and I rubbed along until my Ishmael was fourteen, a man almost, circumcised by Abram with all the men when God commanded it and named him Abraham and Sarai Sarah.

I thought Sarah might finally forgive Ishmael for existing and me for obeying her and bearing him when she finally bore Abraham their promised son Isaac. Wrong! That's when she really exploded!

It happened at the banquet they gave the day Isaac was weaned. Ishmael was playing with the baby, who really loved him and always laughed when he was around, and Sarah saw them together. She let out a screech like a wounded mother lion and began shouting at Abraham, "Drive out the slave and her son! I won't have him heir with my Isaac!"

Well, poor man, he was really upset. He loved Ishmael (and me, too, for that matter, though he took good care not to show it before Sarah) and he didn't want to cast us out into the desert. He was ready to defy Sarah when the angel told him to do what she wanted, as she was the mother of Isaac who was the son chosen by the Lord God to carry on his name. "But," the angel added, speaking for the Lord God Who had sent him, "I will make a nation from the slave girl's son as well, because he, too, is your child."

And that was it. Abraham packed us food and water and sent us out. We walked south, I guess – deserts aren't good about signposts, or wells, either. Finally, we ran out of water. I found a bush and tucked Ishmael under it to rest, and I went and sat down to wait, far enough away that I wouldn't hear Ishmael crying, if he did, but close enough that I could see the bush and the hem of his robe. I knew we would die without water, and I just couldn't stand to watch that boy, the light of my life, wither before me.

Big as he was, Ishmael did begin to whimper in his fear, and that's when the angel spoke up for the last time. He asked me what was wrong, and when I told him, he said I shouldn't be frightened because the Lord God had been listening to Ishmael whimpering under that bush. He said I should go over, get Ishmael out from under his bush and take care of him. He told me that the Lord God intended to make him into a great nation. Then he showed me the well! I filled the skin and we both drank until we were satisfied. Best water I ever tasted!

How could I have missed it? I didn't. It was not *there,* I promise you, not before the angel pointed to it. At that moment I knew it would all come right, that every promise the Lord God makes He keeps – His way, not ours! I wonder if Sarah ever caught on to that?

[**Genesis 16**: 1-16; **21:** 9-21; **25:** 12-16; **Psalm 83:** 6; **Baruch 3:** 23; **Galatians 4:** 21-31; see **HAGAR** (see also **Abraham's CONCUBINES** and **SARAH, wife of Abraham**); see *SARAH and the End of Patience*]

# HANNAH
# and the Excellent Bargain

It was that time of year again, and Hannah sighed. They were going to Shiloh to offer sacrifice to the Lord God, as they did every year, and she knew Peninnah would start taunting her for her barrenness again, as she did every year. It just wasn't fair, she thought. It wasn't as if her failure to have children was her fault, any more than Peninnah's bearing so many healthy children was to her credit. Everyone knew the Lord God was the One Who opened a woman's womb to receive her husband's seed, or not. He alone gave life, just as He alone took it away. Her barrenness was His business and not anyone else's. Why did Peninnah have to make matters worse?

But even as she asked the question, Hannah knew the answer, heard it almost. "She taunts you because Elkanah loves you best, silly! He's well enough pleased with her, and he delights in her children, but he really *loves* you. Stop fussing, and for pity sake don't show her she's getting to you!" The advice she gave herself each year made complete sense and, each year, did absolutely nothing to ease her pain. But this year, she promised herself, things were going to be different.

They weren't. At the shrine, Elkanah gave Peninnah a portion of the sacrifice he offered for herself, and a portion for each of her children. Then he gave Hannah a single portion, but it was as large as all the portions Peninnah had received put together, because he loved her more and felt sorry for her in her barrenness, and both women knew it.

The portioning seemed to incite Peninnah to renew her taunts. Delivered under her breath so only her rival could hear them, Peninnah's cruel words, as usual, reduced Hannah to tears, as much of rage as of frustration, and robbed her of all appetite for the festal meal, which followed back at the hall. Elkanah noticed her tears and said, as he did every year, "What's making you cry, dear one? What's the matter that you can't eat? What's made you so sad? You have me – isn't that better than having ten sons?"

To that, of course, there was no answer to be made except to smile, and then flee. This year, however, Hannah did not take to her bed. Instead, once the ghastly meal was finally done, she returned to the shrine to confront the Lord God at last. "I can at least *tell* Him how miserable I am," she thought, hurrying along, "and – "

An idea tapped at her consciousness, startling her. Still considering it,

Hannah entered the shrine, passing the ancient priest, Eli, without even seeing him. Maybe, just maybe, – she did not dare to finish the thought. Standing as straight as she could, she faced the altar, the tears running down her cheeks.

"Lord God," she began, her lips moving in the intensity of her silent prayer, and the whole story of her misery tumbled out. When she came to the end of it, she caught her breath and hiccupped, then plunged ahead with the idea that had been teasing at her mind. "Lord God," she said tentatively, "if You will give me a man-child, I will give him to You for the whole of his life, and no razor shall ever touch his head!"

She waited, holding her breath. The silence stretched, broken only by the remnants of her sobs and hiccups. Then a voice, cracked with age and sharp with contempt said, "Woman, just how long are you going to stay here, drunk as you are! Have done with your wine!"

Hannah gasped, her tears shocked to a standstill. "I'm not drunk, my lord! I haven't tasted either wine or spirits!" she protested, her face white. "I'm in serious trouble! All I was doing was pouring my deepest pain out to the Lord God, praying. Don't judge me to be some depraved woman because I'm steeped in misery and anger and praying it out to God!"

Eli felt his face flush. Hannah's sincerity and evident anguish shamed him. He raised both hands in apology and said, very gently indeed, "Go in peace, then, and may the God of Israel grant you what you have asked of Him." He bowed to her most respectfully. She returned his farewell, her heart eased, and walked back to the hall with unaccustomed hope and ate the first cheerful meal she had ever had in Shiloh.

Home in Ramah, Hannah conceived almost at once, to her intense joy. Without complications, she gave birth to a son in due course, and named him Samuel, having asked the Lord God for him. Hannah was ecstatic; Elkanah was delighted, both for her and with the child; Peninnah despaired. "Now she has everything – the man and his child!" she thought, though she was careful to show only a cheerful face to the new mother and baby.

It was when pilgrimage time came again that Hannah delivered her shock. "I won't go this year," she told Elkanah and Peninnah, "not until I've weaned this child. And then I will present him to the Lord God, and he shall stay there forever!"

Elkanah blinked in wonder, but asked no questions. "Whatever you think best, beloved," he said, "By all means, wait until the weaning is done. As for what you have said, may the Lord God make it happen!"

Peninnah was less restrained. "But why?" she demanded, indignant.

"You've waited so long for that child. Why are you going to give him to the priest? That makes no sense!"

Hannah simply smiled. "To the Lord God," she said, "*not* to the priest." and that was all the answer Peninnah got, until, some three years later, the family set out for Shiloh, Hannah and Samuel, now weaned, with them.

Hannah had brought to the shrine, along with Samuel, a three-year-old bull to sacrifice, with an ephah of flour and a skin of wine. When the bull was slaughtered, Hannah approached Eli. She stood quietly in front of him until he looked up, then said, "My lord?" At his nod she continued, "I'm the woman who stood here next to you – praying to the Lord God."

At her words, Eli drew his head back sharply. He recognized Hannah and flushed at the memory of his own mistaken harshness, but before he could speak, she went on, the radiance of her joy warming her tone almost to song, "Yes! Well, this child is what I was praying for, and the Lord God has given him to me! So now I'm giving him back to the Lord God – for his whole life. He is dedicated entirely to the Lord God." Hannah beamed at Eli, who returned her smile, then, turned to the altar and began to sing her song of triumph and grateful praise, *"My heart exults in the Lord God! My horn is exalted in my God! I have swallowed up my enemies – I rejoice in my victory! There is no Holy One like the Lord! There is no Rock like our God!"* [1 Samuel 2:1; NAB]

Peninnah's eyes widened. So *that* was why Hannah was giving her son away! But she said nothing until, back in Ramah, she and Hannah were working at the loom. "That has to be the worst bargain I've ever heard of!" she declared. "Hannah, that made no sense? Why ask for the boy if you had to give him back again to get him?"

Hannah looked at Peninnah for a long moment, then said, "No. That was an excellent bargain! You never lose when you give back to the Lord God something He has given you, and give Him your heart with the gift! And that's what I did. Just wait, Peninnah. You'll see!"

Hannah was right. For every year thereafter, when they went to offer sacrifice, and Hannah brought her Samuel the new tunic she had made, she and Elkanah went to Eli, who blessed them and begged the Lord God to send them a child in place of the one they had given Him. And that prayer was answered. Looking at her three sons and two daughters, Hannah smiled. Truly, it had been an excellent bargain!

**[1 Samuel 1:** 2-28; **2:** 1-21; see **HANNAH** (see also **PENINNAH** and Hannah's DAUGHTERS)]

# HERODIAS
## and the Inconvenient Prophet

Herodias shook her head, her mouth a thin, determined line. There was no help for it she concluded. Prophet or no – and she really wondered about that – John would *have* to go. Soon.

But how was it to be done? "Herod, silly man, is mad about him! Loves to hear him talk, he says. Sends shivers down his spine, he says. What foolishness! Not that Herod will *do* anything about what John is saying, fortunately for me! Fortunately for us all, in fact; we make a good team, Herod and I. No telling what we might manage for Israel when the Romans tire of us – but first we have to survive. *I* have to survive."

And that brought Herodias back to the main problem – how to get rid of John the Baptizer without ruffling Herod's feathers. She had already tried her special version of persuasion, but in this case, exceptionally, without success. Nagging was not her style, and bribery, though her private purse was deep, was out of the question between lovers, particularly when one wished the liaison to continue.

"The problem is," she said to herself, "I'm getting – old." Herodias forced herself to speak the ugly word as she examined her hands, the first place age showed. The skin was soft enough, but it was beginning to loosen and take on the look of crepe, tiny flat plates sliding against each other, making sharp wrinkles where they met.

She made a sudden fist and the skin was smooth again, but she had seen the truth. Her youth was going – "no, gone," she thought. "Let's be blunt about it. So I can't simply overwhelm Herod, make him drunk with my allure and prise that smelly prophet out of his mind and the safety of his dungeon! If I could, disposing of him would be easy!"

Herodias straightened the folds of her skirt so that they sculpted her long, still shapely legs and smiled with satisfaction. Not bad at all. Then her problem with John reasserted itself and she frowned. "I really should have thought more clearly before I engineered John's arrest and forced Herod to put him in that dungeon," she reflected, annoyed with herself. "Getting him out of the public eye only fixed that dreadful man more firmly in Herod's conscience, such as it is – like a burr under a saddle. So the more I fuss about John *now*, the more John's words prick Herod, but if I say nothing, those words can just work on the foolish man undisturbed. *What* am I going to do?" she finished aloud.

"I don't know, I assure you!" her daughter Salome answered, strolling into her mother's room. "About what, Mother?"

"Don't call me that!" Herodias returned automatically. "How many times have I told you, you must always call me Herodias! You're twenty, for goodness sake! If people are constantly reminded that you are my daughter."

"They'll know you can't be thirty the way you always tell them you are. Really, Moth – Herodias! It's so silly! People can count. They can see. You can't fool them! Why do you try?"

"You'll learn," said her mother. "You can't help – aging, but the day you stop *trying* to fight it, the day you let yourself go – skip your exercises, eat what you want, forget your bath oils, let your hair go to rack and ruin, ignore your nails – that's the day you sign your own death warrant as an attractive woman and usher your successor into your house, *and* into your husband's bed. That, dear *daughter,* is the way life is, and I for one, am not going that way gently, nor at all, if I don't absolutely have to." She paused. "And I don't!"

"*Lover's* bed," said Salome, leaning against the back of her mother's couch and examining her rings, turning her hands so that the jewels could catch the light. "Herod is not your husband. Philip, my father, is. *Lover's* bed."

Herodias, her own hands forming reflexive fists, drew in a deep breath. "That," she said, "is why John has to go. He's poisoning everyone. That's *his* charge and I won't have it, particularly not from your mouth!"

"*Uncle* Herod won't let you have John strangled, you know," Salome reminded her. She moved a prudent yard away from her mother and added, "I think *Uncle* might even be coming round to John's way of thinking – water dripping on a rock, you know."

"Yes," rapped Herodias, "and that will mean disaster for us both!" Seeing the girl's eyes widen, she went on smoothly, her voice dripping honeyed venom, "I know you plan a rich marriage here at court, once you've finished your playtime, that is, but if Herod dismisses me it's back to the country *we* go. And that will be the end of everything you hope for. So we have to work together on this, *dear* girl. Don't you think?"

Salome, considerably paler, returned her mother's look steadily. "Yes, Herodias" she said simply. "What are we going to do?"

"Herod's birthday dinner is coming up next week," said Herodias briskly, the plan having risen, as usual, complete in her mind, as she skirmished with Salome. "You'll dance for him once the wines have circulated sufficiently.

He'll be enchanted – he always is – and will offer you a reward. If it's open-ended, we're in. Ask him for John's head. If not, you'll have to work him around to it. Can you do that?"

Salome was back to her lounging cat pose, largely because it annoyed Herodias. "Of course I *can,*" she said, bored. "But what do I get out of it if he gives us John's head? I can see *your* advantage – vengeance – and our gain, safety here at court, but what is my *reward*?"

"My diamonds," said Herodias flatly, and Salome gasped.

"But Moth – Herodias!" she protested. "You have a King's ransom in diamonds!"

"*That* is how important this is," her mother replied. "If that's what it takes to get you to save us both, then that's what it takes." Privately she thought, "And I *loathe* those diamonds, for all their worth; I feel the traces Herod's wife left on them every time I wear them, and I shiver. Take them, darling daughter! Do me a favor!" Aloud she said, "Well?"

"I'll do it," said Salome and straightened decisively. "Veils. I'll use veils..." she murmured, her voice trailing away.

The plan worked perfectly. Salome danced entrancingly and Herod swore in front of all his guests that he would give her anything she named for a reward. "Even half my kingdom!" he declared. Salome, feigning innocence, ran from the room to consult Herodias. On her return, her eyes meeting the King's with a laughing challenge, she asked for the head of John the Baptizer, "on a plate, please!" And so it was done.

Thinking over the matter later, Herodias was almost entirely satisfied. John was dead, his head had been tossed out with the garbage, and she was safe with Herod for as long as she liked, which would be permanently, as far as she was concerned. She did feel a slight uneasiness as, miming a reluctance she did not feel, she gave a complacent Salome the promised diamonds, but dismissed it. "What could she possibly do to harm me?" she thought, and got no answer.

[**Matthew 14:** 3-12; **Mark 6:** 17-28; **Luke 3:** 19-20; see **HERODIAS** (see also **SALOME, daughter of Herodias**); see *SALOME and the Silken Snare*]

# JAEL
# and the Desperate General

It was hot. Jael rubbed at her eyes, stinging from sweat, and reached for the skin of *leben*. She sniffed at it experimentally, tasted it, then nodded and put it back on the shelf. The soured milk was still palatable, its tang refreshing. It would taste good to Heber, her husband, when he returned with the flock. Restlessly, she rose and went to the opening of the tent. Where *was* he?

"Silly!" she admonished herself aloud. "You know he won't be back until just before sunset. Why are you fretting so?"

She knew the answer to that question, though. She was worried, and with good reason. "There's a war going on out there, after all," she reminded herself sharply, "and Heber's likely to land us in the middle of it, for all his alliance with King Jabin of Hazor and his Canaanites. I suppose it was smart of him to ally us with Jabin when we first came here – Israel is a long way away. But now that that Prophet Deborah has finally got a fire lit under prudent old Barak, I wonder. If the Lord God is marching with Barak – and with Deborah involved, I'm as sure of that as I am of my own name – the Canaanites are doomed, even if Sisera *is* the best general Canaan has ever seen. And we'll be doomed with them – unless, of course, the Canaanites overrun us first! *Where* are you, Heber? We've got to get *out* of here!"

Dropping the folded edge of tent flap, Jael checked the opening. Good. Wide enough to tell Heber she was there, but not so wide as to invite anyone else to enter. She hoped. She shook her head, then looked around. There was nothing to do. No way to make the time pass more quickly, or seem to.

From the pile of pegs worn blunt from being hammered into stony ground, she took one, drew her sharp, short-bladed knife from its sheathe and began to work at the tip. The knife took smooth shavings from the peg, shaping it easily. That was the handy thing about being married to a member of a metal-working tribe, Jael thought. Whatever else was going on, Heber saw to it that all their knives were strongly made, of the best metals available, and that they were always sharp, even this little one. And she really needed to get these pegs reshaped if she wanted to be quick about setting up the tent the next time they moved. Besides, it was something to do.

"And we'll be moving soon, anyway," she reflected as her hands went about their work with the ease of long practice. "The pasture land is about cropped out. But I wish we could move away from this coming war altogether.

I wish we were allied with Israel and not with the Canaanites. After all, we are Israelites! Heber is a Kenite, a descendant of Moses' father-in-law!"

Jael sighed. There was nothing she could do about it. Not any of it. "Except pray, of course," she reminded herself, her knife stilling as she closed her eyes. "Lord God, keep us safe, please – and let Israel prevail." She paused, thinking. No, there was nothing else to ask for. "Please, Lord God," she repeated, and shifted on the bench.

Testing the tip of the peg, Jael considered it. What she wanted was a smooth-sided pyramid with a needle-sharp tip. The angle of the first side was good, so far. She would shape the third side and then come back and do the second and fourth. Nodding she picked up her knife again.

Two hours later, when she had finished that peg and eleven others to her satisfaction, she looked up. The sun had reached the red basin, her private mark for an hour before sunset. Jael stretched and rose, then froze in place. Were those running feet she heard? Heber? Quick as breath she was at the tent flap and then outside. A weaponless, helmetless armored man was running full tilt directly at her, wide eyed and gasping for breath. Sweat made mud of the dust on his face and body. He skidded to an awkward stop and Jael, catching his hand to prevent him from falling, recognized him. General Sisera – in flight! The Canaanites must be losing to the Israelites! The Lord God was answering her prayer. All Israel's prayer!

Giving no hint of the jubilation rising within her like a fountain, Jael said, "Come my lord! Into my tent! You'll be safe here! You don't need to be afraid!" Stepping aside, she drew back the tent flap and Sisera plunged in, lost his balance and landed on his hands and knees. Jael bent and entered after him, loosening the flap to let it fall to the ground. Her mind was racing. General Sisera was in her power – and had no idea he was in danger! She had to keep it that way. Glancing around, she snatched up a rug and gestured Sisera to go to the back of the tent behind some boxes. He flung himself there instantly, flat on the ground sheet and Jael draped the rug over the boxes and him.

"Please," he croaked, coughed and tried again. "Please, could I have some water? I'm dying of thirst!"

She nodded. "I'll do better than that," she said, her tone kind, and handed him the skin of *leben*. He drank eagerly, and his breathing slowed as he began to relax.

As she covered him again, he begged her, "Could you just – stand outside by the tent flap there? Then – if they come asking if anyone's here, you can deny it." She simply looked at him. Abashed, he dropped his head. Of course she would know enough to do that! As the rug fell again to the floor, enclosing him in a womb of dark, he sighed and swiftly fell asleep.

Jael stood looking at the rug-covered heap which was Sisera for a moment, then moved to the tent entry. Her mind was churning. What could she use to kill him with? For there was no doubt in her mind that that was what she had to do, why the Lord God had put her in this particular place at this time. Sisera, recovered from his flight and on the loose in Canaan, was more dangerous even than Sisera at the head of his army because he would be desperate, she knew, and desperate men, especially commanders, drew on powers even they did not know they had.

"He'll have another army together in a flash, and this time, whatever Barak did that worked, won't. He's got to die and I have to do it. There's no other way," she thought grimly and looked rapidly around the familiar tent for a weapon. What would kill him most quickly?

She rejected the short-bladed knife she had used on the tent-pegs; while one swift cut across the jugular would bring a quick death, there was always a chance she would not sever the vein. "And then I'll be the one to die!" she said. She thought about the skinning knives and the knife Heber used to slaughter the animals they used for food, but remembered that Heber had taken all of them, and the sharpening stones, with him. "I'll bring you home a kid to fix for supper," he had said, "and I can get the knives done while the flock feeds. You won't be needing them today in any case, will you?' he had said as he left and she had agreed that she wouldn't.

Jael made a face. One never *knew*, she thought resentfully. Then she shook herself. All right. No knives. What, then? "Think, woman!" she urged herself, her eyes roving, touching every item in the tent. Suddenly she stopped, her eyes fixed on the tent pegs she had reshaped. "Lord God!" she breathed. "A weapon! You have put Your enemy in my hands and given me Your weapon! Destroy him, O God! Save Your people Israel!"

Before she moved, Jael listened. Yes, those were snores she was hearing. Swiftly she picked up one of the newly sharpened tent-pegs and the heavy mallet used for driving them. Without a sound, she moved around the pile of boxes to where Israel's enemy, and her own, lay hidden. Turning back the edge of the rug, exposing Sisera's head, she placed the sharpened tip of the peg at the hollow of his temple and with a silent, "Lord God be with me!" struck three blows and drove the peg right through Sisera's head and into the ground. The general did not have time to draw breath to scream.

Some time later Barak came thundering up the hill toward the tent. Jael, pale, light-headed from her body's complete purge of reaction, and still trembling slightly, rose from where she had been sitting outside the tent waiting for Heber. She signaled to the Israelite general. When he got close enough to hear her, she said simply, "The man you're looking for? Come with me. I'll bring you to him." She lifted the tent flap, stooped and entered. A curious Barak followed her.

[Judges 4: 12-22; 5: 6, 24-31; see **JAEL** (see also **DEBORAH, judge and prophet, Sisera's MOTHER** and Sisera's Mother's **PRINCESSES**); see *DEBORAH and the Cautious Commander*]

# JEHOSHEBA
## and the Vanishing King

"Dead? I don't believe it!" exclaimed Jehosheba to her husband, as she sat up in bed and turned up the wick of the oil lamp. "Not Ahaziah! Not my very last brother! He's only twenty-three! He hasn't had time – When? How did it happen? How do you know, Jehoiada?"

"A coded message came in an hour ago," said the High Priest, taking his wife's last question first. He tossed his outer garments at the chest and, as usual, missed. "He was campaigning with old Ahab's son, Jehoram of Israel, against Hazael of Aram. They were besieging Hazael in Ramoth-gilead when Jehoram was wounded, so they retreated to Jezreel. They were going to stay there until Jehoram's wounds healed but Jehu, son of Nimshi, came and killed them both."

"But why? Isn't Jehu one of Jehoram of Israel's men?"

"Yes. But apparently Elisha was told by the Lord God to have Jehu anointed King of Israel and to command him to destroy the whole house of Ahab," said Jehoiada, sitting on the side of the bed with a thump. "Once the guild prophet anointed him and gave him the Lord God's instructions, Jehu and his men went after Jehoram. Jehu tricked Jehoram into leaving Jezreel and meeting him on the road. That's where he killed him – tossed his body into Naboth's field." Uncontrollably, he yawned. "Sorry, Jehosheba. It's been a long day and a longer night. Would you – ?"

As Jehosheba nodded, he turned and she began to knead his neck and shoulders. "And Ahaziah?" she pursued. "Why did Jehu kill my brother? Just because he was fighting on Jehoram's side?"

"I don't think so. More likely for being in the wrong place at the wrong time. The message said Ahaziah ran away, heading for Beth-haggan, as soon as he saw what was happening to Jehoram. I think the only reason Jehu ordered him killed was to keep word of what he was doing from getting out before he got the kingdom under control. Remember, Jezebel is still alive – or she was when the message was sent – and obviously, she's got to be Jehu's next target.. He wouldn't want her to have advance notice that her days were numbered."

"So Ahaziah's really dead," said Jehosheba dully. "Mother will – I don't know what! Does she know?"

"Why on earth do you call that woman *mother?*" her husband asked, turning to embrace her. "She's a horror and no kin to you!"

"Because she makes us, of course, all of us children of Jehoram of Judah," said his wife with a shudder. "She sees us as her property, and since Father died, she's really been hanging onto us. Jehoiada, dearest, you're avoiding the question. Does she know?"

"No, I'm not! Why should I?"

"Jehoiada!"

He gave in. "Not yet. The messenger will arrive at the palace at dawn."

"How did you arrange *that* – no, don't tell me. *Why* did you do that?"

"We needed the time. We absolutely do NOT want a regency! Athaliah would be a sure bet to become Regent for your nephew and that would be a horror. So we had to have the succession arranged before the news got out."

"I agree, Mother as regent for Joash would be a disaster! He's only a year old; she'd have, what, a dozen years' free hand? Brrr! But why the rush to name the heir? There are plenty of candidates among our older brothers' children."

"Enough for a bloodbath that would destroy the Kingdom," her husband answered. Jehosheba drew in a deep breath and let it out softly, nodding. "You're right. If they start picking each other off, Moth – Athaliah can just take the throne when they're done." Suddenly her face went white. "Jehoiada!" she whispered, gripping his arm. "You don't suppose – no. Even Athaliah, raised by dear Jezebel, wouldn't do something like that!"

"Like what?" her husband asked. "Jehosheba! Where are you going?"

But Jehosheba, half-way into her overdress, her feet finding her sandals, opened the door and called, "Keziah! We have to get my nephew! We have to get Joash! How much time does Amos think we have?"

"From the look of the sky, we have an hour – maybe a bit more," a male voice answered, as Keziah, fully dressed, stepped silently into the bedroom carrying a small clay pot.

Jehoiada blinked at hearing his secret messenger speak from Keziah's alcove. He hadn't known about *that* arrangement but, on second thought, he entirely approved. Best to have everything in the family! He started to say so but Jehosheba was still talking to the alcove. "Are you sure, Amos?"

"Yes, ma'am! We got her spies," a fully-dressed Amos said, following Keziah into the room.

"Both sets?" asked the High Priest.

Amos opened his mouth and closed it again, then shook his head. "We only found one set, sir, and they're – gone," he finished, glancing at the women.

"Athaliah always, always has back-ups," said Jehosheba, looking at her husband, "doesn't she?"

Jehoiada nodded. "Then," said his wife decisively, "she knows. We have to act now, before the killing starts. The room?" she asked.

"We just finished getting it ready," her maid replied.

"Thinking again?" Jehosheba smiled tight approval. "Good! Who's on guard at the nurseries?"

"Obed," answered Keziah.

"I can take care of him," offered Amos.

"Good. I can always explain my presence in the nurseries," said Jehosheba. "Can you bring his nurse, Zibiah's Miriam?" she asked Keziah, who nodded.

"Take this with you," she said, handing Jehosheba the small pot. "If he fusses, just rub a little on his gums – he'll sleep till full morning."

"But – " said Jehoiada, and froze. In the still night they heard Athaliah's enraged scream, and then a silence that stretched until it was snapped by the sound of running, armed men.

"No time!" snapped his wife. "Amos – Obed! Then circle back for mop-up at the room." Amos nodded.

"Keziah," she commanded, "Miriam! Use my cloak! And take this signet Zibiah left me. You may need it to convince Miriam, or a guard if you meet one, that you have every right to be in the nurseries and command Zibiah's servant. Straight back to the room?"

Keziah nodded.

All three turned to Jehoiada. "Pray!" they said in unison, and seemed to vanish.

Left alone, the High Priest moved to the window, calculating. If all went well, they could rescue Joash and Miriam and be back in twenty minutes. If not – he shuddered and began to pray the Psalms as, somewhere within, he began the steady count that would measure off what might be the rest of all their lives – and that of the rightful King of Judah.

At four hundred twenty, in the middle of Psalm 27, Jehoiada heard the choked cries of children mixed with the screams of their nurses. His blood froze, but he kept praying *"Hide not Your face from me; do not in anger repel Your servant. You are my helper; cast me not off; forsake me not, O God my Savior…"*

[Psalms 27: 9; NAB]. At six hundred, he heard a sound behind him and turned, horrified.

"You pray well," said Jehosheba, stripping off the dark cloak and her overdress in one motion as she kicked her sandals off and dove into bed. "Quickly!" she ordered. "In! Just in case!"

Her husband was stripped to his tunic and in bed with her in his arms before she had finished speaking, gripping her so tightly she squeaked. "How did you get there and back so fast?" he whispered. "I was counting."

"Secret passage – our floor to the nursery; Father showed me years ago. No one else knows."

"The baby?" he breathed.

"Safe with Zibiah's Miriam, in the secret room; Father had it built, even before the hidden passage. He showed it to me just before he died, told me I was the only one who knew it was there – and you don't want to know where it is or how to get into it," she said as quietly.

"The signet?"

She opened her hand, palm up. "Right here," she said. "Available but not obvious. Pray we won't need it."

A thundering knock shook the front door. They heard the steward answering the door, heard the ominous sound of a sword being drawn and listened as shod feet climbed the stairs. The knock at their own door was much more respectful, Jehosheba thought, snuggling down further among the covers. Jehoiada, who had risen at the first knock, opened the door himself. He was wearing a loincloth only, had mussed his hair and presented the picture of a man of power roused suddenly from sleep and not about to take the interruption lightly.

The knocker was a young member of Athaliah's household Guard, and seeing him, Jehosheba relaxed. This would be all right. The young man was one of Jehoiada's many honorary "nephews," to whom, quite informally, he had been teacher and mentor in the ways of growing up in the royal court and remaining faithful to the Lord God.

"Well, Shaul?" demanded the High Priest, his tone icy.

"I'm hear, my lord," recited Shaul formally, "to search your premises for – any of the royal heirs!" He gulped and dropped his eyes, though his drawn sword was still at the ready.

"Why?" Jehoiada asked, an unfamiliar edge of sarcasm coloring the question. "Are they, perhaps, lost? Who needs them at this hour of night, anyway – and why?"

Shaul took a deep breath, his face white, then said, "The Queen has commanded us to find them – right now – and to, to," and he took another deep breath, "to *kill* them, my lord," he added. "With the sword."

"And have you found any?" Jehoiada asked quietly.

"Yes, my lord," said Shaul, and tears choked him. "Two. Oh, sir, they were – so young! And I had to *kill* them!" Showing the High Priest the blood still staining the sword blade, the young soldier broke out in a cold sweat, turning rather green.

"And now," Jehosheba intervened swiftly, "you have to search our house for more. Well, here at least, you won't have to kill anyone. And if you take your time and do a really *thorough* job, you may not have to kill anyone else. Keziah," she called, and a moment later the maid appeared, swathed in a voluminous night robe, her hair in pins, yawning.

"Yes, my lady?" she asked.

"Would you go with Shaul while he searches the house for some missing royal heirs?'

"Here?" asked Keziah, miming astonishment and insult in perfect balance.

"Here," affirmed Jehoiada. "And take the steward with you," he added, nodding at the man who, in his curiosity, had yet not left the room.

"As you wish my lord, my lady," the servants chorused, and swept Shaul out of the room.

Twenty minutes later they returned, Shaul with his sword sheathed. The young man was white. From the dampness of his hair and tunic, he had evidently cleared his stomach at some point in the course of his search and been restored by Keziah.

"Well, then," said Jehoiada, who had dressed for the day, "you're finished, I take it?"

"Yes, sir," answered Shaul quietly. "For good, I think."

"For good?" repeated the High Priest.

"I really can't do this kind of thing," Shaul declared, "kill innocent people just because they have the wrong blood in their veins. I'd rather work digging ditches!"

"It would be a shame, though," said Jehosheba thoughtfully, "to have all your training go to waste because – someone chooses to – abuse it."

As smoothly as if they had rehearsed it, Jehoiada picked up her thought. "What about the Temple Guard?" he asked conversationally. "We have them guard the house of the Lord God, and He really *hates* politics and all that goes with it. Would that, perhaps, be a solution?"

"But could I — could you, could you really do that?" asked Shaul, hope raising his voice as his head came up. "Soldiering is fine for me! It's what I've always wanted to do. It was just, just that — "

"Transferring you in to the Temple Guard is something I *can* do!" declared the High Priest, interrupting Shaul in what seemed to be headed for, technically, a treasonous statement. "I'll do it in the morning. Well, actually, in an hour, when the scribes will be ready for work. Will that help, my boy?"

"More than you can guess," Shaul replied fervently. "More than you'll ever know!" And he took his leave with a light step.

After the steward had shut the door behind him, Jehoiada and Jehosheba were silent for a moment, then turned to each other for a fierce embrace.

Somewhat later, tucked back in bed, Jehosheba asked, "Now that we've got him safe, what do we do?"

Her husband sat on the bed and hugged her again. "Bring him up in the ways of the Lord God," he answered. "Raise him as a true son of Israel and her King, so that when his time comes, he will be ready."

"Can we do that?" she asked doubtfully. "How?"

"Trust the Lord God Who has given him to us. And then, love him," said Jehoiada. "First, last and always, love him. And live what we want him to learn — to love God above all, and to serve those we care for, even as we teach them."

Jehosheba nodded. "Yes," she said, "yes. We can do that." And she turned over and fell asleep.

[2 **Kings 11:** 2-3; 2 **Chronicles 22:** 11; see **JEHOSHEBA** (see also **ATHALIAH** and **Joash's NURSE**); see *ATHALIAH and the Almost-Perfect Plan*]

# Jephthah's DAUGHTER
# and the Cost of Victory

You know, I never really thought it would end this way – on a beautiful spring day, with the air like wine, the trees in flower, everything pulsing with new life! I never *really* thought I would die like this, before I had begun to live.

So odd, the way it all happened. I keep remembering –

I was so afraid Father – you know, Jephthah – would die in the war, when he'd just been restored to Israel. Not only restored, but named commander of the army and promised authority over all the people if he won! Father *really* hated being exiled, you know, and it was his own brothers who did it. Father was Gilead's son, but he was a bastard child, and when Grandfather died the legitimate sons drove Father into the wilderness – as if it was his fault!

So Father and Mother went to live in Tob. A bunch of men gathered around him and they became raiders. I remember some of that, though all I knew then was that Father had to go away a lot. When he came back, we would have plenty to eat and he would be very happy; so would Mother, but she would be sad when he had to leave again. Then Mother died – two years ago this spring. I do miss her.

Where was I?

Oh, yes. Father came back to Gilead – because they begged him to! The King of the Ammonites had gone to war against them and all Father's brothers were useless as fighting men and leaders. So the elders came to our house in Tob and begged Father to come back and be their leader. It was splendid!

They said, "Come back to us! Be our leader! We have to beat the Ammonites!" Just like that, giving orders.

Father said, just as cool as spring water, "Aren't you the ones who hated me so much that you drove me out of the country? Why should I help you out, now that you're in a mess?"

Well, they squirmed and looked at the floor, but finally replied, "If you lead us in the fight against the Ammonites, we'll make you head of all Gilead." They didn't say what would happen if Father lost, of course, but Father was smart enough to close that loophole – and tell the truth in the bargain.

"*If* the Lord God delivers the Ammonites up to me, you mean!" he said. You see, that put the outcome of the war in the Lord God's hands, where it belonged, *and* it put their promise that he could be ruler in the same place! So they couldn't break their word or change their minds if he won, and if he lost, they couldn't punish him. I told you — my Father is smart!

They agreed and swore to it, of course, and off we went. The first thing Father did was to put his in order so that if anything happened to him, he would be ready to face the Lord God. Also, he wanted to make certain that no one could come down on me for debts, or property, or anything else.

Then he wrote a letter to the King of the Ammonites. I wondered why, but Father said that when you fought the Lord God's wars, you had to be sure your enemy understood why the Lord God was fighting against them, so that, if they had any sense, they could back out fast and save their armies. That would save *our* armies, too, of course. That's why men were so willing to follow Father — he didn't waste their lives.

But the letter didn't work. So Father gathered the army and marched. He was filled with the Spirit of the Lord God, and vowed to Him, "If you deliver the Ammonites into my power, I shall offer up as a holocaust to You whoever is first to come to my door when I get back home."

The reason he did it that way is because, as he always said to me, "When you're offering something to someone, be sure you're giving him what *he* wants — especially if you're asking him for a favor. And when it's the Lord God, make your offer *His* choice, not your own, because only He knows the real worth of what you're asking."

I told you, smart. It never entered his mind that I would be first out the door to greet him, dancing and playing the tambourines — and I never would have been, except that I was so excited and relieved that Father had won the Lord God's war that I just ran to the front of the line of dancers, grabbed Anna's tambourine and took the lead. Normally, I would have been last — highest in rank, you know.

He told me what he'd done — tears running down his face. He was so upset. And I — well, it was odd. I didn't feel anything, not at that moment. Only my head was working. It was perfectly plain that this was the Lord God's doing, that the victory over the Ammonites *and* the rule in Gilead, such enormous favors to our whole people, as well as to Father, were worth any price we had to pay. Father had brought back his whole army practically intact and had subjected the whole Ammonite nation to Israel — more than he had ever dreamed of, more than anyone could ever have done.

I saw, at that moment, that my life was the perfect gift to the Lord God for this great mercy. It would remind Father that the Lord God was God and had done the winning, so that when he was ruling in Gilead he would never make the mistake of thinking *he* was the power. As for me, at that moment, nothing else mattered – Father would be safe; Israel would be safe; I would be with the Lord God.

So I simply said, "You made a vow to the Lord God. Of course you have to keep it! He won the battle! It's all right." Then I asked him if I could spend two months in the mountains with my friends before the sacrifice. I needed the time to put my own heart and spirit in order, to prepare to face the Lord God before I had even lived my life – though of course I didn't say it *that* way. Father felt bad enough as it was. He agreed, of course. And, you know? I never shed a tear – then!

Believe me, I've shed plenty since! I've thrown rocks and screamed, smashed and torn up everything I could lay my hands on, made myself sick I was so furious and terrified. I've bellowed at the Lord God – and not just once! I've screamed at Him, "WHY ME? You knew this would happen – why didn't You warn me? Why couldn't I have tripped and Anna been first out the door?" and everything else I could think of.

I screamed about Father, too – called him every name I could think of for being so stupid as to give the Lord God the chance to take me! What would it have cost for him to add, "except my daughter, Lord!" to his vow? How could he care more for a victory than for me, his only child?

But even with all the screaming, I never really hated the Lord God – not really, nor Father either. You see, I really did understand when I gave that first answer. I think it must have come from the Lord God's Spirit working in me, giving me calm and light when Father needed them.

And now I really *see* it. It *has* to be this way.

That's why the Lord God had me ask for these two months in the mountains and told Father to say yes, I think. He knew I'd need that much time to fight my war and come into His peace.

And – I have. I really have.

Now my time is over – all but a day of it. Tomorrow we return and I will become the offering that seals my father and all Israel to the Lord God, and Him to them.

I hope it doesn't hurt too much.

[Judges 11: 34-40; see **Jephthah's DAUGHTER** (see also **Jephthah's Daughter's COMPANIONS** and **Jephthah's MOTHER**)]

# JEZEBEL
## and the Stubborn Prophet

Her spy had come and gone, bearing word of the death of her son. King Jehoram of Israel had died at the hands of Jehu, one of his captains, and Queen Mother Jezebel was again alone. "Elijah again!" she said to herself, anger rising. "Stubborn man! He's dead! Will his curse never be done?" Her stomach clenched as she recalled the codicil of that curse, and she shuddered.

Then, briskly, she shook herself. "That's not the way. That's not the way a Queen lives. That's not the way to win, at last – win everything! Now it's all in my hands. All that I've waited and schemed for these many years. And *I will have it. All!*"

She would have to inactivate Jehu, she knew, but that would be no problem. She was in possession of Jezreel and had been since King Ahab had brought her to Israel as a bride. She was still beautiful and she had been enchanting men since childhood. That ability was, if anything, more potent now than when she was at the peak of her physical beauty, both because she had learned, down to the last turn of a white shoulder, how to use it, and more important, because she had real power - the most effective aphrodisiac in the world for a man seeking to be a king. She was a genuine Queen, royal by birth and marriage, and Jehu was a usurper. She had both power and legitimacy, and Jehu would need her if he was to rule Israel successfully. She would ensure that he knew that for a fact, and liked it, but she would never, ever, give her power over to him.

"Thank you, Ahab, my sweet love, and thank you Elijah, my stubborn enemy," she murmured with a twist of smile. "Without the two of you, I might never have made the mistakes that taught me that lesson and I would be helpless now!"

Watching her girls prepare the bath she had commanded, she acknowledged to herself, now that it was too late to make a difference, that it had been a mistake to give herself wholly over to Ahab when she married him – that is, if she'd meant to be a real Queen. And wasn't that why she had married the crown prince of Israel in the first place? Handsome Ahab had been a gifted warrior, a charismatic leader of men and the best lover she had ever known. He had been besotted with her - but, as she had discovered to her horror, he was, emphatically, *not* a real King. And she could have been.

Unfortunately, she had been equally besotted with him, "and there went *my* kingdom," she thought ruefully, "with all my fine plans." She shook her head. "Blind. We were both blind. In Ahab's case, that was all to the good, *my* good – but in mine, it was disaster. And inexcusable!" For she had known from before the beginning that a kingdom could have only one ruler and one voice to forge a people to a single will if it were going to survive and its ruler were to thrive. She meant to *be* that ruler, that voice and that will.

To that end, she had planned to – *expand* the Israelites' consciousness and free them from the strictures of their barbaric god by introducing them to the civilizing effects of the worship of Baal and Astarte. Let them once taste the pleasures of *these* gods and they would abandon their own strange, fierce god, hardly noticing they had done so.

And that would eliminate the opposing will, the alternate world-view, which was the main obstacle she faced in creating the single-focus kingdom she intended to rule. A peaceful transition was essential, she knew. Challenge a man's god and you lose him and get yourself a bloody, essentially un-win-nable war, but let him see the benefits of adding another god or two, and he's yours without knowing he's changed. Ideal.

Ahab had agreed with her, wholeheartedly, to her surprised delight. He had joined her in worship, had built Baal a temple and raised an altar to him there, and had enjoyed the change. Jezebel had found, unexpectedly, that she liked having someone to serve as her other half and, pleased with this discovery, had quickly revised her original plan. Israel would have a single focus, but the single ruler would operate in two matched bodies, hers and Ahab's. And everyone would be happy.

"I wish!" she murmured now, allowing her girls to set out fresh clothes for her.

Things had begun well enough, though. Quietly she had had the filthy band of prophets of the Israelites' god, whom most people avoided as crazy anyway, slaughtered.

At that point, of course, she hadn't known about the perfidy of Obadiah, Ahab's chancellor. That – despicable traitor, had somehow gathered a full hundred of the Israelite god's prophets, stashed them in a cave somewhere and kept them alive without anyone at all knowing about them. They began to interfere only a good while later, proving to her satisfaction how wise she had been to do away with the others, but it was small comfort.

In any case, with the prophets and the voice of their god off the scene and out of her way, Jezebel had begun to introduce the Israelites to the cults of Baal and Astarte. She had four hundred fifty priests as the gods' spokesmen, all dependent on *her* for food, clothing and shelter. That *should* have effected the substitution without a bump.

It didn't.

Elijah the Tishbite had arrived on the scene, from where neither she nor Ahab had known, and had declared war on them in the name of his god. There would be a drought in Israel, he had declared; until he spoke to open the heavens again, there would be no rain, nor even dew.

Then he had vanished, not to reappear until three years later. That was when Jezebel had seen the truth about Ahab.

Standing in her sitting room, dripping a mix of rainwater, blood and ash on her carpet, he was all but stammering as he poured out to her what had happened.

"Jezebel," he gabbled, "that fire – I've never seen anything like it! In the first place, Elijah challenged your – our priests to prove Baal is real. He said he'd build an altar to the Lord God and they should build one to Baal. Then he and they would each prepare a beast for a holocaust, but instead of lighting a fire, they should ask Baal to send a fire to consume their offering and he would ask the Lord God for a fire to consume his."

"And?" she asked.

"And," he went on, "nothing happened."

"Nothing *happened*!" she repeated, incredulous. "Look at you! Don't tell me nothing happened!"

"I mean," said Ahab, calming somewhat, "when the priests of Baal prayed. They really worked at it too, Jezebel – cutting themselves, and screaming and jumping around, you know the way they do? And they kept it up, hour after hour, with old Elijah mocking them all the while. Finally, at about sunset, they quit and Elijah took his turn. I tell you Jezebel, I've never seen anything like it. He gathered all the people around him, set up the animal on the altar of the Lord God that he had rebuilt, and then he had them pour four whole jars of water over the whole thing, beast, wood, altar and all. And not just once! Three times, so that the ditch around the altar had it sloshing over the sides."

"Right," said Jezebel sardonically. "And then, I suppose, he waved his hand and got a dry twig or so to light?"

"Dry twig!" exclaimed her husband. "There wasn't a dry twig within a hundred yards of that altar, Jezebel, I promise you! No, he just spoke to the Lord God, told Him that he'd done just what the Lord God had told him to, and now it was His turn, so would He please show His people that He really was God?"

"Did he?" asked Jezebel.

"Did He ever!" Ahab exclaimed. "That's what I was telling you when I came in! That fire just *poured* out of heaven, and it burnt up everything – beast, wood, stones, and even the water in the ditch! Everything was smoke and steam – you couldn't see your hand in front of your face. See this black stuff?" He pointed to smears of ash that streaked his festival tunic. "That's from the stones!"

"I wonder how he did it," mused Jezebel, caught up in admiration in spite of herself. If she could just learn Elijah's secret, she would have a really potent weapon at her disposal.

"The way He always does," answered her husband. "He just wills things and they happen."

"Elijah?"

"No. I meant the Lord God," said Ahab.

Jezebel moved on without comment. Now, she sensed, was not the time to deal with that particular sack of worms. "How did the people react?" she asked instead.

"As you would expect," he answered. "They groveled on the ground and screamed, over and over, that He was God."

"And?" asked Jezebel, aware from Ahab's discomfort that there was more to come.

"And," Ahab continued reluctantly, "Elijah told them to grab the priests of Baal and drag them down to him at the brook – we were near Kishon, you know? And they did. Enthusiastically. And that's where he killed them."

"All?" asked Jezebel in shock.

"Every single one," he assured her. "All four hundred and fifty. He slit their throats. Jezebel – it was awful! I've never seen so much blood. Look! It's all over me! I had to ride by the brook on my way home – splashed through the blood pool! I couldn't see in all the rain. Oh, I didn't tell you. Elijah got us a *deluge* to end that drought."

"How did you kill him?" she remembered demanding, and then impatiently answering his blank look and "Kill who, Jezebel?" with a snarled "Elijah, of course!" She had been thinking about adding "You dolt! Who else? *He* is our enemy! His god would be *nothing* without him! Where are your brains!" when she caught the odd expression on his face. She realized, with horror, that he had been about to see her contempt for him, and worse, her real ambitions for herself in Israel. Definitely, it was time for damage control!

Instantly she had converted her rage to solicitude, laced with a healthy charge of sexual appeal. "But what am I saying?" she had asked and moved in, embracing him and cooing over him. "You're soaked to the skin! You'll catch your death unless we get you out of those filthy wet clothes!" She had summoned her girls and, within minutes, Ahab had found himself in a steaming bath, being soaped and massaged by his tender wife, soft towels and dry clothes at hand and the aroma of a delightful meal coming from the next room. His very tentative mention of Elijah she had stopped with a kiss that stood his hair on end, and that diversion had gotten them safely to dinner and then to bed.

Ahab had never raised the subject of Elijah again, to Jezebel's relief. She herself had sent the prophet a blunt threat, giving him twenty-four hours to flee or be killed as he had killed her prophets, and he had vanished again. But her discovery that Ahab, her ideal lover, was essentially a weakling who instinctively sought compromise when challenged by a single-minded enemy (or ally, for that matter, whom he could not deceive or work around), had left her disillusioned; a change which, after her almost-disastrous misstep, she took good care Ahab should never sense.

Ahab had not killed Elijah, she understood, because the prophet and his god were far stronger-willed in their determination to control Israel than he was. He could not side with the prophet and the god because she, as strong-willed as Elijah and his god together, was equally determined to drag Israel to civilization and to her sole control, by way of the worship of Baal and Astarte, and wouldn't let him.

But there was more to it than that, Jezebel knew. Tucking her hair up to keep it dry, she remembered how deliberately she had set out to enthrall Ahab, body and soul, as though she were waging war. She had succeeded. Ahab admired her body, of course; every male between thirteen and ninety-nine who was conscious did. But even more, he envied her freedom from the fears Elijah was using to keep him and Israel enslaved, her daring in going for what she desired, her ruthlessness in dispatching her enemies and her keen political insight. Those, even more than her beauty and joyous lovemaking, he could not do without.

Nor could he do without Elijah with his link to Israel's god. So Ahab had had to concentrate on keeping them both satisfied, without alienating either; a balancing act that demanded of him the icy nerves of a snake charmer working with two irritable cobras. But, even as she admired his courage and appreciated his inventiveness in maintaining this, for him, essential stalemate between her and Elijah, Jezebel had realized that she had to go back to her original plan – to be Israel's king-in-fact, or there would be no kingdom to rule, for Elijah and his god would have it all.

The girls were ready, at last. Swiftly the Queen stripped off her outer tunic and under garments and stepped down into the perfumed bath, easing her way into the hot water. Her care now reminded her of her only real error in dealing with Ahab and Elijah and she grimaced. She had abandoned caution for the first and only time in that struggle and it was a dangerous slip.

What had deceived her, she had concluded after the event, was the obviousness of what needed to be done, with the infantile simplicity of doing it, and what had undone her – them, really – had been her congenital impatience with shilly-shalliers. That insight had directed the rest of her life as Queen, saving power for her when she was alone, but it had had no effect on the consequences of her error.

"Naboth!" she thought, her eyes tightening as her lips thinned in annoyance. Her girl flinched, but Jezebel, long years in the past, did not notice.

After Israel's prophet-promised second defeat of Ben-Hadad of Aram, the advantageous treaty Ahab had arranged with that king had met with the rebuke of another of the prophets of Israel's god, one of the ones Obadiah had saved, Jezebel assumed, frustrated, and the man's curse had frightened and depressed Ahab. So when he passed Naboth's land and saw, again, the vineyard abutting the palace garden that he had long coveted for a vegetable garden, he had impulsively made an offer for it – land or silver for land. Naboth had flatly refused, claiming it was his ancestral land and not for sale.

Well, that had sent Ahab into a blue funk. He took to his bed, refused food and sulked. Jezebel, hearing this from the servants, had immediately gone to him and, in two minutes, had the whole of the story from him. And there it was – a perfect opportunity to *be* the Queen, where he *could not* or *would not* be the King. She had snatched it and acted. "I'll get you the vineyard!" she had promised Ahab (getting his attention at least, though he did not move from the bed), and had set to work.

She had sent letters of instruction, sealed with Ahab's own seal, to the elders of Naboth's town, telling them to proclaim a fast, call Naboth out in front of the town, have false witnesses accuse him of cursing God and the

King, and have the man stoned outside the town.

When she got word that this had been done, she had gone to Ahab, still sulking in his chamber. "Up you get!" she had caroled, smiling down to her fingertips. "That vineyard you've been so gloomy about is yours! The man who refused to sell it to you, Naboth? Well guess what! He's dead. The land is yours now! Go on! Take it!" And Ahab, in disbelieving joy, had done exactly that.

"And that's where it all fell apart," she mused bitterly, allowing her girls to anoint her body, rubbing cream into her drying skin. Elijah had appeared from nowhere again and had castigated Ahab as murderer and usurper. He told Ahab the dogs would lick up his blood as they had Naboth's and that the Lord God would wipe out Ahab's descendants and every male of his family. Then, almost as an afterthought, he had announced that the dogs would eat Jezebel in the fields of Jezreel.

Ahab had collapsed at this, had torn off his clothes, put on sackcloth, and fasted with every evidence of penitence he could think of. And it had worked, but not altogether. The disaster to the kingdom might have been postponed for his son's kingship, but Ahab himself had finally died the death foretold for him, years ago now, at Ramoth-gilead, in another war against Aram.

As for his family, Ahaziah, the first son to take Ahab's throne, had died of an accident – and of Elijah. Ahaziah had been injured, falling off his balcony, and had sent to consult Baalzebub. Elijah, hearing of this, had sent him word that he would die for this betrayal of their god. He had.

She didn't know about Ahab's baby sister; Athaliah, whom she had raised as her daughter, ruled alone in Judah as Queen, untouched so far, but that was no guarantee. And now Ahab's second son, Jehoram, was dead and his murderer was coming for her. They never forgot, Elijah and his god, though Elijah was dead and his god had neither face nor name. And they kept their promises.

Straightening, Jezebel directed her girls in robing her and dressing her hair. Then, reaching for the kohl and her brush, she began to outline her eyes, reflecting on the difference between Elijah's god and her own. Baal and Astarte never promised anything, never responded to sacrifice. They didn't see people as individuals, didn't seem to care. One offered worship to keep them sweet, or unaware – non-hostile, just in case they were noticing – but really because the rites themselves gave people pleasure; nice to do what you lusted for and have it work for you with the gods!

Elijah's god, Israel's god, on the other hand, saw everything and everyone, and cared intensely about it all. Israel was his people and he rewarded their obedience and worship of himself as the only god, punishing, vividly, their disobedience and the worship of other gods, but he was not *confined* to Israel. He seemed to be *real*, not just a mask for Elijah; certainly it seemed to her that he exercised *real* power in the world of here and now, and that everyone was affected by what he did.

And what if this god was honoring Elijah's curse? Had he *really* killed Ahab and his sons? Was he *really* going to have Jehu kill her? What could she do then?

Her practical mind answered at once, "Do what you can do, of course – challenge Jehu! Throw him off balance! Address him as murderer of his master – that'll label him usurper and give you some leverage." Jezebel shook her head. She would do that, of course – no use quitting before the game was over – but what if stubborn Elijah's god was actually *God*? The only God Who was, or could be? What could she do about *that*?

Meet Him as a penitent, the way Ahab had? He would know it for a lie, would laugh in her face – as she would do to someone with her history approaching *her*.

Then what?

Hearing a shout and a growing thunder of sound outside, she stood. "Meet Him as an honorable enemy, I guess," she thought, "and then – we'll see."

Straightening her back, she walked toward the window.

Afterwards, they found only her skull, her feet and her hands in the courtyard. The dogs had seen to the rest.

[**1 Kings 16:** 31; **18:** 4, 13; **19:** 1, 2; **21:** 1-29; **22:** 53-53; **2 Kings 3:** 1-2, 13; **9:** 4-10, 22, 30-37; **10:** 13; see **JEZEBEL, Queen of Israel** (see also **ATHALIAH**); see *ATHALIAH and the Almost-Perfect Plan*]

# JUDITH
## and the Edge of the Blade

You never can tell about people, you know? Not just by looking, anyway. Not until the blade's edge is at their throats – *then* you can see what they're made of. And sometimes it's a real shock!

Take Mistress Judith, for instance. In all my ninety-six years, I've never seen anyone like my lady - well, she was my lady up until she freed me, and I was her slave during the time I'm going to tell you about. To look at her – small, slender, serious, very quiet, sometimes kind of scared looking, with black eyes twice the size of other people's that could swallow you whole – you'd think she wouldn't have a word to say for herself, not to save her life. You'd think she couldn't lift anything heavier than a scarf! That's what I thought when I first came to serve her. Wrong!

I was ten when I first came to her household in Bethulia – a present to her from her husband, Manasseh. She was all of twenty then, a married lady with an honored husband centuries older than she, that's what I thought then, though he was probably only thirty or so, and she looked, maybe thirteen.

Even at ten, I was as tall as she was – and I soon towered over her. Took after my father, I did, and he topped six feet – and I felt *years* older. I felt I had to take care of her, protect her from – I don't know what all. Anything that would strip her of her innocence and make her face what I knew was *real* – that people can be mean, for instance, or that husbands aren't always right and need to be managed if things are going to go well for the family, or that in the market everyone is out to cheat everyone else, and you have to bargain hard to get a fair price, let alone a good one.

That's what I mean – you can't tell just by looking. The first time I went with her to the market, I warned her before we left about the cheating, told her a couple of dodges that raised her eyebrows, promised her I'd steer her right and help out if she got in trouble. She gave me this funny look – trying not to laugh, I figured out much later – and thanked me in a way that made me feel like a ten-foot-tall bronze-clad hero, and made me determined that she would NOT be cheated, come what may.

And so we went. "Let me try myself, first, Aminah," she said. "Then, when I need help, you can call me aside and tell me what to do."

"Fine," I said, and smiled. "I'll pretend I need your help – I'll have a coughing fit or something."

"Good plan!" she said, and away we went.

Well! She went through that market like a crack troop of Assyrians, may God demolish them, and well, there's no other word for it. She *skinned* those merchants, every single one, even old Simon who has the first coin he ever earned and gets twice the value of his goods when he can't get three times! And she did it never losing her look of a lost fawn! They fell over themselves to give her good value for her money and warned her about each other in the bargain! I've never seen the like! And you know? They never caught on! To the day she died last year at a hundred and five, if she went to the market they lined up to give her their goods, competing to give her the best prices! I've never seen the like!

When we got home and I found my tongue, I said, "Mistress? How did you *do* that?"

"Was it all right?" she asked me, serious as anything.

"All right!" I said. "Mistress, it was a miracle! *No* one gets prices like that! You're amazing!"

"So it was all right," she said, and nodded, not cracking a smile. "Good. You've taught me well, Aminah. Thank you."

And that's all she ever said. I was thinking, "My lady, I never taught you a thing!" but I didn't say a word. If they want to believe you've done well, don't contradict them. That's my motto! Keeps your skin whole when you're a slave and, I guess, even when you're not.

Well, that should have taught me about judging folks by what they look like, but of course it didn't! I still felt I had to take care of Mistress Judith, protect her and all, so I did.

We had a good life, the three of us – she and her husband never had children. Why I don't know. She was kind of sad about that, I think, though she never complained. Once I heard her tell him that he was enough for her and that she was delighted not to have to share him with a houseful of children.

I think now she might have been lying, but then I believed her as much as if she'd said that people get full when they eat every course of a banquet. Manasseh did too, which was the point; a man who thinks he's failed to please his wife by getting her with child and filling his house with babies can come to hate her in short order. Every time he looks at her he sees himself failing her. Men can't live with that very long, especially when it's true. I don't know how she knew that, but I'm sure she did.

And our life went on. It wasn't until three years and some after Manasseh's death during the barley harvest that Mistress Judith really showed what she was made of. It was the thirty-fourth day of the siege of our town by Nebuchadnezzar's General Holofernes. Holofernes was really smart – or someone on his staff was. His forces ringed the town, blocking all the mountain passes so that not even a cockroach could slip out of town, and they controlled our only water source, which flowed out of the base of the mountain. Then Holofernes just back sat and waited for us to surrender.

Our leaders refused, of course; we were the gateway to Jerusalem, its outer defense. Having just gotten the city and the Temple rebuilt after our return from exile in Babylon, we weren't anxious to lose it again. So we prayed to the Lord God, rationed drinking water, and waited for His aid. Eventually though, the cisterns were emptied, the reservoirs ran out, and we were dying of thirst. That's when the people mobbed Uzziah, the spokesman for the rulers of the city, demanding that he surrender our town to Holofernes lest we all die.

Uzziah could tell, I think, that if he refused, they'd kill him then and there and then surrender – a disaster. So he stalled for time, asked them to wait for five more days so the Lord God could aid them, and promised that if He didn't, the leaders would surrender the town.

Well! Mistress Judith was furious! Not that she stamped and screamed – not her style. Mistress Judith *did* things! First, she sent me to ask Uzziah and the leaders to visit her. Of course they did. About fell over themselves getting there, too! Surprised? Don't be. She was rich, and riches talk! But the real reason, I think, was that she had a kind power over people they never fully recognized. If she wanted them to do something, they *did* it, never even questioned it, even if they'd been hot against it five minutes before she saw them. You see what I mean? You never can tell!

Anyway, there they were, standing in the tent on the house's roof – that's where Mistress Judith had lived since Manasseh's death, fasting except for Sabbaths and feast days – and the first thing she did was tell them they were suicidal!

Well, not in those words – she just pointed out, looking like a doe about to lose her fawn, that they had just dared to put the Lord God to the test; that it was that very thing that had got us into Babylonian captivity in the first place; that whether the Lord God decided to save us or let us be destroyed, it was *His* plan and we could not fathom it; that we *asked* the Lord God for favors, we did not command Him like a stone idol; that if we fell, all Judea would follow and the Temple would be destroyed, and *we* would be held accountable for it; that we needed to set an example of fidelity, trust and courage for all our kinsmen; and that, finally, this was the Lord God's test, an honor and an admonition He gives those close to Him.

Now there was nothing unusual in all that, but somehow, when she said it out loud, it became so real you could touch it. And it worked. Uzziah and the leaders agreed at once – then passed their burden to her! They asked *her* to pray to the Lord God for rain for the cisterns so they could continue the resistance. Obviously, *their* prayers weren't working, though of course they didn't *say* that!

That's when I got my second hint of the *real* Mistress Judith! She straightened up slightly and, I swear, she *glinted* like the edge of a sword catching sunlight. "Listen to me!" she commanded. "I'm going to do something that will be remembered forever among our descendants!"

Well, I tell you, *that* made them come to attention! Then she told them to be ready to open the town gate that night so that she and I could get through it – which got *my* attention! She said that the Lord God would rescue Israel by her hand within the five day limit *they* had set for Him. Then, to forestall the thousand questions (and ten thousand objections, all of them beginning, "How can you, a *woman...?*") she told them they were not to ask about her plan, she would tell them when it had been accomplished!

Did they ever stare at her then! If their eyes had been arrows she would have been a sieve instantly! And my *fragile* lady faced them down like a grizzled war commander. You see?

Give credit to Uzziah. Smooth as honey, before anyone else could gather breath, he told her to go in peace and prayed that the Lord God might go with her and work His vengeance on our enemies. Then he cleared out and took all the rest with him. I don't think anyone else could have moved that bunch!

Once they were gone, Mistress Judith looked at me. "To work!" she said and stripped off her dress – she was wearing widows' black with sackcloth under it, had been since Manasseh's death. How she loved that man! Anyway, she poured ashes on her head, and just wearing her sackcloth, went flat on the ground to pray to the Lord God. I got out – none of my business what my lady had to say to our God.

When Mistress Judith was finished, she called me and we went down into the house, and my lady – well! I wouldn't have believed it if I hadn't seen it with my own eyes! She had me fill the tub with warm water, whipped off that nasty haircloth and slid in. When she was finished, she dressed the way she used to for feasts when Manasseh was alive – rich ointments, fancy sandals, ankle bracelets, arm bracelets, earrings, hair up, bound in a fancy net and all her other jewelry on. I began to understand why we were leaving the town after dark! Widow or not, my Mistress Judith, even veiled as she would be, looked good enough to eat with a spoon, and I knew fifty men who'd kill each other to try! And that was just in our neighborhood!

I cleaned up too – put on my best dress, sandals, and veil. Well after dark, I picked up a flask of wine and jar of oil and tucked them into the bag she'd had me fill with roasted grain, fig cakes, bread and cheese, and we headed for the gate. I tell you, the men at the gate were *impressed*! I heard one gasp and try to turn it to a cough. Didn't work! They pulled themselves together, though, prayed for her success and, at her order, opened the gate, and out we went.

Now, I still didn't know what Mistress Judith had in mind. If it had been any other woman, I would have assumed she had tired of the dull life of widowhood and had decided to catch herself a new husband. Holofernes, besides being an important general, was handsome – I mean *really* good to look at! Muscles! You wouldn't believe! And hands – like an angel! When I saw him – well, that's neither here nor there.

But I knew my Judith wasn't "any other woman," and if she had wanted Holofernes for a husband, she would have seen to it that *he* came to *her*! So I was worried, even before we came upon the hidden Assyrian outpost and found ourselves in the custody of the guards. They were polite, but insisted on knowing who we were and where we were going, and I started to sweat! I knew we were in real danger of losing our heads right then, and my mind was blank! Then – I almost fell over! I heard my sweet, shy, helpless Mistress telling the guards the most amazing fairy tale I have ever heard! I know my jaw dropped open – I bit my tongue I closed it so fast!

She told them she was a Hebrew and leaving her people because they were about to be delivered up to the Assyrians, and *then* she said she wanted to see General Holofernes to give him a report and show him a climber's route by which he could capture the whole mountain without the loss of a single man!

And they bought it! Even gave her a bonus for it! They peeled off a hundred men for an escort and brought us straight to Holofernes' tent. Someone went to fill him in while everyone else was drooling over my Judith, who really was looking gorgeous – and absolutely unconscious of the impression she was making. Right!

Anyway, Holofernes' guard came out and ushered us in to the tent – gaudy in my opinion; his bed canopy had crimson and gold netting, picked out with emeralds and other jewels, but what can you expect of an Assyrian? When Mistress Judith was announced, Holofernes bounced off that bed as though he'd just seen his best dream become real, but before he could speak, she fell down flat in front of him. Neat move that – established their relative positions, and made it impossible for him simply to grab her and get on with it. If he had, he would have lost honor with his own people, and they both knew it. So did everyone else, of course. That was the point.

So Holofernes settled for the next best thing – promised she would have nothing to fear from him, said Israel wouldn't have had, either, but they had done this to themselves. Then he asked her why she had fled to his army. Believe me, she could have woven tents for the entire army with the line she spun for him! Marvelously believable she was, too – hand of the Lord God there. I kept looking at her from under my eyelids, to make sure this was still my lady, not some bard in disguise!

She told him the Hebrews, who only lost wars when they turned from their God, had actually deserted Him! They were planning, in their starvation, to eat food He had told them not to eat. And then she said that he, Holofernes, had been chosen by God to destroy them!

Holofernes looked as though he was hearing the best news that had come his way in years, but my lady didn't let him interrupt. She just went on talking. She said that God had told her to go and help him, so she would stay with his army – and that made his eyes light up, you'd better believe! Then she told him that she would go out to pray every night and would report to him when the Lord God told her the Hebrews had committed their crimes. Then Holofernes could demolish the Israelites. She even promised to lead him through Judea to Jerusalem, said she'd set him up in power there over all Israel, and no one would say a word against him, including the very dogs! Oh, she was *good*! And I never thought she had any imagination!

And Holofernes? The experienced warrior? He swallowed that pack of lies whole! Bones and all! Guess he couldn't help it – he was almost losing his eyeballs looking at her as he listened. Soon as he could get a word in edgewise, he promised her he'd convert and she'd have a place in Nebuchadnezzar's court if it all came out the way she said

And then he set about seducing her. He thought!

He invited her to supper – and she refused to eat his food, because it might cause her to sin, she said. He gave way, finally, and we got our own tent to live in. Just before dawn, she sent him word that she wanted to go out to pray, as they had agreed, so he ordered his guard not to hinder her. And down we went to the spring – *our* spring, the one that kept our town alive – in the ravine, where we bathed and she prayed. We did that for three days, got everyone used to it, and by that time I was *really* getting nervous! We had only two more days, and the Lord God had, as far as I could tell, done and said nothing! What could we do?

I got my answer on the fourth night. Holofernes invited my Judith to a private banquet for just his servants – no officers. I smelled a rat, so while she was dressing to the teeth, I packed up all our things in case we had to get out in a hurry.

When I was finished, I went to Holofernes' tent and set out at his feet the fleece that Bagoas, Holofernes' eunuch and steward, had given Judith to use for reclining at table. I took my time, and got the chance I was looking for. When no one was there, I made a slit in the side of the tent behind the spot where my lady's fleece was spread, her usual place. Then I went back to arranging the very last of our provisions on her table, and by the time I was finished, my lady appeared. Holofernes, welcoming her, all but panted audibly, though he kept his courtly manners in place.

That banquet lasted for hours – from before sunset until well past midnight. I served my lady, who ate only our food and drank our wine, though she made two glasses last the night. Holofernes was too busy pretending he wasn't staring to eat, but he made up for it with the wine, which he drank as though all the world's wine would turn to dust at dawn! It did too, for him, come to think of it! Well, when the banquet ended, we servants withdrew and Bagoas closed the tent from outside. I hadn't wanted to leave Judith there alone, but she just shook her head and gestured me outside to wait for her to come out and go with her to pray as we had been doing.

So I went out with our empty provisions bag and watched the others head for their beds as quickly as they could move. When they were gone, I slipped around to the side of the tent to the slit I had made in the wall and peeked through. There was Holofernes, sprawled face down on his bed, out cold, dead drunk – hadn't touched her, obviously. As I looked, Judith got slowly to her feet and walked toward the bed. I knew she was praying, but I couldn't think what she had in mind.

Then – you could have knocked me over with a feather! She went to the head of the bed, drew Holofernes' sword from its scabbard, lifted his hair to bare his neck, whispered, "Strengthen me this day, O God of Israel!" and swung that sword as hard as she could, twice! She cut his head right off his body, rolled the body off the bed and wrapped it in the canopy!

Me? I caught my breath, flew to our tent, grabbed our things, raced back to where I was supposed to be waiting, and unlaced the tent door just as my lady got to it. She was carrying Holofernes' dripping head by its hair, and she looked at me with a kind of – question, you know? So I opened the empty provisions bag and we put the head in it. Mistress Judith had managed to keep most of the blood off her, but I wrapped her in her cloak and veil just to be sure, put on my own, picked up the bag and we headed, not for the spring, but for Bethulia.

Well, you know the rest – Holofernes' head on the ramparts, the rout of the Assyrians and the plundering of their camp, my Judith's procession to Jerusalem with Holofernes' treasures that our people had awarded her, and her sacrifice of them all to the Lord God – it's common knowledge. So's the rest – my lady's prosperity, the peace the Lord God brought to Judah through her, and her reputation and honor among our people.

But what you wouldn't know, unless you'd seen it, was how wonderfully strong and brave and clever she was when she had to be! You see, you never can tell who a person is or what she can do until the Lord God asks her and she says yes! You just never can tell!

[Judith, 8: 1 – 16: 25; see **JUDITH, widow of Manasseh** (see also **Judith's MAIDSERVANT, Judith's WOMEN of Israel**)]

# Lot's DAUGHTERS
# and the Wasted Life

The day was hot. Gazing down over the bleak hills, Lot's older daughter sighed in vexation. She was bored. There was nothing to do here in the cave. Two minutes saw it swept out and the skins that served as bedding spread in the sun to air. The water had been drawn long since, and preparations for a meal could not begin until Lot returned with meat and her sister with the herbs she had gone to gather. She could, of course, go on with her spinning, as she had done every day since they had settled in this isolated place, and probably she would, "but not his minute!" she declared rebelliously. "Not this minute."

They were comfortable enough, she admitted, she and her sister and their father, but she missed their mother. On the flight from Sodom, though the angel leading them away had warned them all not to look back at the destruction of the city by the Lord God, their mother had turned to see what was happening to their neighbors. She had instantly turned into a pillar of salt, hadn't even had a chance to cry out. Not that that would have helped, the girl thought. Once you disobeyed the Lord God, you were finished.

No, what troubled her was the future. For the hundredth time she looked at her prospects – their prospects, really, for her sister and she were in the same trap. Aloud, so she could hear the sound of her own voice, she said, "This is a waste of life! Here we are, two healthy women, and no men in sight to be husbands to us. I want babies! I want to raise a family, have a man to love me, someone to belong to as Mother did Father. I have a right to that – that's what the Lord God made women for. It's not fair. It's plain not fair. Oh how I wish our fiancés had come with us when we left Sodom! Then we wouldn't have this problem."

"Well, they didn't, useless cowards, and they paid for it. They were swallowed up in the fire and brimstone the Lord God sent, and there's absolutely nothing you can do about it," answered the practical voice in her head, as it always did. "Here you are and here you'll stay, childless daughters of a widowed father, until he dies and you follow. Be glad he's alive to hunt for you. Get on spinning!"

It was a week later. A determined rain drenched the countryside and trapped the sisters in the cave. Lot had taken the flock across the valley earlier in the week, and presumably was tucked up in a cave with the beasts, sitting out the downpour. They younger girl moved about the cave, picking up discarded tools and clothing and putting everything in its place. Her sister sat in the doorway watching the rain.

"What's the matter?" the younger finally asked. "You've been sitting there all morning looking grim. Aren't you feeling well?"

Her sister sighed. "Oh, I feel all right. I guess it's just the rain. It makes me so gloomy."

"That's silly!" the younger returned. "Here we are, nice and dry, with food on hand and no real work to do. What's there to be gloomy about?"

The elder shrugged, but said nothing.

"I'll bet I know!" the younger girl announced. "You're thinking about babies again. Honestly, I don't see why you keep torturing yourself that way. You know as well as I do that there are no babies in our future. There can't be. We have no husbands, and we're not going to get any out here. Face it. The only man we'll see for the rest of our lives is our father!"

The older girl sat up suddenly and turned to her sister. "Say that again!" she demanded, and scrambled to her feet. Grabbing her sister by the shoulders, she shook the younger girl. "Say that again!"

"Ouch!" the younger replied, trying to shake free of her elder sister's grip. "Say what again?"

"Say what you just said," her sister repeated, fixing the girl with a stare so intense it should have burned holes through her skull. "About the only man."

"All I *said* was that the only man we'll see for the rest of our lives is our father. It's hardly a revelation! You know it as well as I do!"

But her sister didn't seem to hear her. "That's what I thought you said!" she crowed exultantly. "And it gives me an idea!" She released her hold on her sister's shoulders, and the younger girl backed carefully away from her.

"What do you mean?" she asked cautiously.

"You've solved our problems," said her sister. "You've given us the answer to our problem – our only answer!"

"What answer?" asked the younger girl. "In fact, what problem? I don't have any problem that I know of."

"Children," her sister answered tersely. "Having babies. Getting husbands. Raising families. Doing what the Lord God made us to do. Being real women! Seeing to it that our line continues! That's our job, you know. We have no brothers. Had you forgotten?"

"Wait a minute," said her sister. "I said our father is the only man we'll see for the rest of our lives. Our *father*. How does that solve anything?"

"He's a man, isn't he? And he's able to beget children. And here we are. So he can beget children on us! It's perfect!"

The younger girl gasped and raised her hands in a warding motion. "That's evil!" she declared. "That's no a solution sister, that's a trap! Surely – we *couldn't* do that. Why they didn't eve do anything *that* evil in Sodom!"

"Much you know about it," the elder muttered, but she took good care the younger girl should not hear her. Aloud she said, "There's nothing wrong with it. He's a man. We're women. We're made to bear children, and he's the only man around – you said so yourself. Who else can beget them on us? It's unusual, but there's nothing wrong with it!"

"I don't believe I'm hearing this," her younger sister stated flatly. "You have lost your mind. That's all. Look, Lot is our *father*. You do remember what happened to Noah's son, Ham, after the Flood? He was cursed in all his descendants, and that was only for *looking* at his father's nakedness when Noah lay drunk. Can you imagine what the Lord God would do to us for – for sleeping with our father? I can!"

"Nothing will happen," the older girl asserted, her chin jutting out at a dangerous angle. "We will have our babies and raise our families and all will be as it should be."

The younger girl looked at her sister with consternation. Obviously, this was madness, but she could not find a way to make her sister see that. Finally she said, a little desperately, "How are you planning to persuade him, then? Because he'll have to know, you know! And he'll never, not in a thousand years, consent to such - such desecration."

"It's not desecration. It's necessity," the older girl replied loftily. "And there won't be any difficulty persuading him! You mentioned Ham? Well, Noah was drunk, and he never would have known a thing about what Ham did if Ham's older brother hadn't told him later on, when he was sober. Lot likes his wine. We can do the same thing."

"Don't call him Lot. It's disrespectful," said her sister. "Our father does like his wine, but he drinks to forget Mother. He misses her dreadfully, and I think he dreams about her when the wine puts him to sleep."

The older girl pounced. "Perfect!" she said. "That will make it even easier! All we'll do is be sure he has enough wine to get to sleep, and then I'll slide in beside him and he'll think it's Mother! Then, another night, you'll get your turn. If you're right, and he is dreaming about Mother, it'll really be a favor to him – like bringing her back to him for a while. He'll never know it wasn't a dream!"

The younger girl was horrified. It all hung together so well that she was afraid it would work, and she didn't want it to. "I want babies as much as you do," she said finally, "but not that way. I won't do it, and I won't help you. I'll tell Father!" She was shaking with emotion, but whether with fear, fury or frustration that things were the way they were, she could not have said.

Her sister looked at her quietly. "I don't think you will," she said at last, moving to the girl and hugging her. "I don't think you will. Look, dear one, there's time. Some time, anyway. Nothing has to be done immediately. And you don't have to help me. You don't even have to be here if you don't want to. Let's just be still for a while. You think about it. Then you do what you want. I'd love it if we shared this, of course, if we became mothers at the same time – but not if that will make you unhappy. Promise! Look," she added, "the rain has stopped. Go get me some herbs and just let things settle. I know you don't want a wasted life any more than I do. Out there in the quiet, maybe you'll come to see more clearly."

The younger girl nodded, picked up her basket and ducked out of the cave mouth. She did not look back. Watching her, the older girl nodded and began to smile. "Sooner or later," she said to herself, "you'll see I'm right, my sweet sister. And then we'll do it – we'll get Father drunk, we'll each sleep with him, and we'll each have our babies. Our line will go on as it ought to." She nodded decisively. "That's what will happen. Sooner or later."

It was sooner, in the event. The elder girl named her son Moab, and the younger called her son Ammon.

So the line went on, but not as the girls had expected. The Moabites and Ammonites who rose from their sons were not friends of the Lord God, and were enemies to their kin, the children of Abraham and Sarah.

[Genesis 19: 8, 12-26, 30-38; see **Lot's DAUGHTERS** (see also **Lot's WIFE**)]

# MAHLAH
# and the Challenged Inheritance

"Mahlah! Mahlah!" screamed the little girl running down the path and into the tent. "Oh, Mahlah!" She threw her arms around her eldest sister's knees and began to cry.

"What is it Tirzah? What is it, my love?" Mahlah asked with concern. This was most unlike Tirzah, who was usually most grown-up for five years old, and scorned children who wept as "mere babies" and thought them "foolish things!" Bending down, Mahlah unwrapped Tirzah's arms and lifted the sobbing child into a hug. "Come now! Calm down, get your breath and tell me," she urged. "What's the trouble? What's happened?"

Heaving a shuddering sigh, Tirzah stopped crying. "Are they really going to throw us out of our tent and make us beg from door to door? Are we really going to be beggars because we're only girls?"

"Of course not!" exclaimed Mahlah. "Wherever did you get that idea?"

"Um – " began Tirzah and stopped.

"She's been listening at tent-flaps again, I'll bet!" said Hoglah, the third of Zelophehad's daughters, who had come in as Tirzah was speaking. "And that's what you get, Miss Nosy! You overhear three words and make a war out of them!"

"I'm not making anything!" insisted the little girl, stung. "With my own ears, I heard the Lord Moses and the Priest Eleazar listing all the sons of Joseph for the inheritances, and they never even mentioned Father. Cousin Simon said that meant we couldn't inherit anything because we weren't boys and Father's name would disappear. He said we'd have to leave our tent and beg for our bread, and no one would marry us, and we'd *die!*" she finished in a rush, her voice rising to a wail.

"Thanks, Hoglah, you're a real help!" said Mahlah with a sigh to the twelve year old, usually the most sensible of her sisters. Then hugging Tirzah she crooned, "Hush, little one, hush. That's not going to happen. I won't let it."

"It might, though," objected Milcah, at eight the next youngest to Tirzah. She had been sitting out of the way with her spinning.

"Later, Milcah!" commanded Mahlah, and the other two were silent, waiting for her to soothe Tirzah.

"Later for what?" asked Noah. At fifteen, she was as good as Mahlah with the younger girls, and now she took the calming Tirzah from Mahlah's arms and began to rock her.

Mahlah went to the stew pot over the fire and stirred it. "Discussion," she said finally.

"About what I asked her," explained Tirzah helpfully, wiping at the last of her tears with the back of her hand. "What?" she asked indignantly as all four of her sisters stared at her. "I don't believe it, *now*, but cousin Simon said we'd have to go and be beggars because we're girls and can't inherit the way we could if we were boys. He did! And I'm not making it up!"

"After supper," said Mahlah firmly, and that was that.

Once the remains of the meal were cleared, Mahlah gathered the girls in a circle and said, "Now, let's think. First, Tirzah overheard the Lord Moses and the Priest Eleazar discussing the apportionment of the Promised Land, when we get there."

"And they never mentioned Father at all!" interrupted Tirzah. "And cousin Simon says – "

"Hold that part for now, little one," commanded Mahlah gently, and the child subsided. "Has anyone else heard about this apportionment?"

"It's to be by tribes, by clans, and then by families, to the men whose names were listed as the heads of their families in the census," offered Hoglah. "Aunt Judith told me when I went by to help her with the weaving."

"Whose *names* were listed?" asked Noah. "Then I see where cousin Simon started from. Father died in the desert, before they took the census, so *his* name isn't on that list. And since he had no sons, there's no one carrying Father's *name* who could serve as a family leader, and mark our place in his clan, and be put on that list. Still, though, we shouldn't be left out! We exist! We're Father's family, and we belong to his clan, even though we don't have a brother to lead us. Even though we can't carry on Father's *name,* we should get his portion!"

"But suppose they don't think of it that way," objected Hoglah. "Suppose they just say, 'No sons, no clan, no inheritance,' and split what Father would have gotten among the uncles. Cousin Simon could be right!"

Tirzah screwed up her face to wail again, and Noah picked her up and hugged her gently, while glaring at Hoglah. "They won't, Hoglah. There are five of us, after all, and we're not exactly invisible! Everyone knows us, and all our cousins and aunts and uncles keep an eye on us. *They* won't let it happen."

"Maybe," Hoglah admitted. "But I'd feel a lot safer if we could be sure."

"I don't understand," said Milcah querulously. "What's the fuss about land and an inheritance? Our husbands will take care of us when we marry, and Mahlah and the rest of the family are taking care of us now. What are you so worried about?"

"What husbands?" demanded Hoglah. "Just who do you think will want to marry us if we have nothing to bring with us? And we haven't – not without our inheritance from Father."

"Other poor girls get married," countered Milcah, "and they just bring themselves. What about Anna?"

"There's only one of Anna," explained Noah, "and there are five of us." At Milcah's blank look, she explained, "You see, the first man to marry one of us will make himself responsible for finding husbands for the rest of us. That will be expensive, and taken with the fact that whichever of us he marries will bring *nothing* with her, well – "

"Who could afford it?" interrupted Hoglah impatiently. "It's just too much to ask. Use your head! Why do you think Mahlah is still not married at seventeen?"

"Because she doesn't want to be," returned Tirzah promptly. "She has us!"

"Enough!" said Mahlah with a warning glance that took in Hoglah and Noah. "This isn't thinking – and we need to think. I agree that the family won't let us starve no matter what cousin Simon teases you by saying Tirzah. They won't turn us out of our tent to beg. But the business of the inheritance and of husbands is a concern. I, too, would feel better about it if we could make sure we would inherit Father's share."

"We've got to get the Lord Moses to say so – and we've got to get that decision written down," declared Hoglah. "So the Priest Eleazar has to agree, too. Now, how are you going to do that?" she asked Mahlah.

"I?" her eldest sister asked, eyebrows rising. "*I* am not! *We* are! And you're right, Hoglah. We need it in writing, in the book of the laws. And not just for us – for any girl who finds herself in our position. This is important."

"Do we really have to?" Noah asked.

"I'm afraid so," sighed Mahlah. "I wish it were otherwise, but we really have to

"Then how? You know I'm no good at arguing," said Noah, "and – well, do you really think they'll listen?"

"They'll listen, all right!" said Hoglah, pounding her right fist into her left palm. "They'll listen!"

"I suppose you'll make them," scoffed Milcah, still annoyed about the 'husbands' argument.

"Hush!" said Mahlah. "We have enough trouble without you two fussing at each other. We need to present a united front – go in and face them together and have our argument ready."

"At the same time?" wondered Tirzah. "Like singing the Psalms?"

The others laughed, but Mahlah looked seriously at Tirzah. "I don't think we have time to practice something like that," she said. "What I thought was, we could each say one part of the argument, one after the other. With all of us *there,* and serious, and knowing what we're asking, I think they'll have to listen."

"That's a *good* idea, Mahlah," said Hoglah. "With each of us giving one argument, they'll hear each of our points separately, and because we're all there, they'll have the whole string of beads in their hands at once. Let's do it tomorrow!"

"Tomorrow!" exclaimed Noah. "That soon? It scares me, you know," she murmured to Tirzah, still in her arms.

"Oh, Noah! You don't have to be scared!" Tirzah reassured her, kissing her cheek. "The Lord Moses really likes children! He always smiles at me, and his eyebrows – they're so funny! They wiggle on his forehead like perky caterpillars when he's listening really hard and thinking about what he's hearing, and when he agrees, they fly all the way up to the top and just stay there! You just have to come with us, Noah – say you will!"

Noah laughed and hugged the little girl. "All right, Tirzah, I will. And I won't be scared, at least not with you there! Now, Mahlah, tell us what to say, and how to say it."

The next day found the five sisters, dressed in their best robes, at the entrance to the meeting tent. They stood before Moses and Eleazar with the princes and the whole community.

"The daughters of Zelophehad," announced Eleazar, and they stood, if possible, even straighter.

"What do you wish?" asked Moses kindly, with a smile especially for Tirzah.

"Our father died in the desert," began Tirzah smoothly, her treble voice reaching to the edges of the crowd.

"But he didn't join Korah when Korah and his men rebelled against you and the Lord Aaron," said Milcah firmly. "He wasn't trying to take the priesthood or anything."

"It was for the sins he committed himself," continued Noah, "that he never had a son before he died."

"Only the five of us," Tirzah, leaning forward, whispered to Moses confidentially.

He nodded, meeting her eyes, then looked at Hoglah who was saying, "But is it really fair that our father's name should disappear from the clan for that — just because he had no son?" Moses' eyebrows, wiggling furiously, rose suddenly to the top of his forehead. Noah caught her breath and clamped her lips together trying not to laugh as Tirzah nudged her.

Not noticing the byplay, Mahlah finished the case with, "What we're asking for is that we be allowed to inherit our father's share of the land, just as if we were his sons, because we *are* his only children."

Moses nodded, signaled *wait* and disappeared into the Meeting Tent. There was absolute silence. He soon reappeared, illuminated by his own smile. "The Lord God told me that you were right, and that I should give you, as an inheritance, all the property in the clan holdings that would have gone to you father. Then He said it should be a law that, if a man had no sons, his holdings should go to his daughters when he died."

The girls drew breath to praise the Lord God and Moses, but before they could speak a word, a delegation of their clan's family heads swarmed forward to surround Moses and Eleazar, pushing the girls to one side. The problem was the land itself. For if the girls were to inherit as the Lord God had said, then when they married, the family land would go with them to their husbands families, and would then become part of their sons' heritage. That wouldn't matter if they had married within the tribe, but if they had married men from other tribes, one tribe's land would wind up going to another tribe, and that would make problems. What could be done?

Moses, his eyebrows beetling in a formidable frown, again signaled *wait* and withdrew into the Meeting Tent. He emerged quickly, his face stern, eyebrows level and a triumphant gleam in his eyes. The land would go to the girls, and they might marry anyone they wanted to marry but, and he looked regretfully at the five, the husbands would have to be clan members of their father's tribe. That would keep the tribal division of land intact. His eyebrows angled upward in concern as he looked at them, each in turn.

The girls, all smiles, ran to him and Tirzah flung her arms around his knees. "Oh, thank you!" she exclaimed. "Thank you!" Smiling, he picked her up and looked at her sisters.

"That's wonderful!" exclaimed Hoglah. "A perfect solution! And not just for us!"

"We'd probably have married into Father's clan anyway," said Noah, "so that part's all right."

"Yes! Don't worry about that!" Milcah reassured him. "They're the people we know best, and we already like them!"

"May the Lord God be praised for His mercy, and you for your faithfulness," said Mahlah formally, but with a brilliant smile that warmed his heart. "We shall do what He has decreed through you – with joy!"

And so they did.

[**Numbers 26:** 33; **27:** 1-11; **36:** 2-12; **Joshua 17:** 3-6; see **MAHLAH, eldest daughter of Zelophehad**]

# Manoah's WIFE
# and the Wonder-Son

"I tell you, Manoah, I *did* see him, and he *did* promise me a son! And I'm not drunk, nor am I suffering 'women's foolishness'! He stood there, awesome as an angel of the Lord God and real as your dinner, and spoke to me, just as I'm speaking to you. And no, I *didn't* think to ask where he came from, and he *didn't* tell me his name, so it's no use asking. But he was *here*. And I *saw* him!"

Manoah opened his mouth to belittle her "experience," then closed it again, his eyes on his wife. She longed for a child, he knew, and had done so since the day she came to him as a bride. This — promise, then, was the world to her. Not only a child, but a son! Remembering the nights she had cried herself to sleep, not realizing he was still awake, Manoah felt anger rising within him. For someone to deceive her this way was cruelty beyond belief, and he determined he would kill the man when he found him. But first he had to find out who it was.

"Tell me again," he urged her, putting an arm around her and leading her to their bench in the sun. "From the beginning."

"You don't believe me," she muttered. "And you won't."

"Oh, I believe you," he assured her, thinking *I know something happened, just not its source!* "But I need to be *clear*. Tell me again, love."

She drew in a deep breath, and repeated, "A man of God came to me. He looked like an angel of the Lord God — awesome! He said to me that I would bear a child, a son! He said I had to be careful not to drink wine or spirits, nor to eat anything unclean, because the child I would bear was to belong to God from the womb to the grave. He also told me never to cut the boy's hair. Then he said the boy would be the one who would start the deliverance of Israel from the Philistines. Now, isn't that wonderful! A son! *And* he will free us from the Philistines!"

Noting his wife's rising excitement and the almost-feverish gleam in her eyes as she faced him and gripped his upper arms, Manoah realized that he could not directly challenge her nor discredit her experience — not without doing her serious damage. Then he had an idea.

"Let me pray to the Lord God," he suggested, "so that, when the boy is born, we'll know exactly what we have to do for him. After all, He may need us to do some special teaching or preparation for the boy's mission. Shall I?"

His wife leaned suddenly against him, sagging, he realized, in relief. "Oh, Manoah! Blessed man – dearest husband! You *do* believe me, improbable as all this sounds. You are the best husband a woman could have! And at last, I'll be able to give you a son!"

Manoah kept his counsel, murmured endearments in his wife's ear, and then, his arms still around her, raised his voice to pray, "Lord God, I beg, send back the man of God who came from You, so he can show us what You want us to do for our son once he gets here."

*There,* he thought, *that will do it. If God did send this messenger, we've done the right thing – and if He didn't, I'll ask Him who's taking His Name in vain so I – or He – can punish him.*

Several days later, as the woman was sitting in the field, the angel reappeared. Gesturing "Wait right there!" in his direction, the woman ran as fast as she could to find Manoah. "He's here! The man of God!" she panted when she found him. "In the field! Oh, come!" She tugged his arm so hard as they ran back to the field, she nearly overbalanced them both.

Skidding to a stop before the angel, Manoah found his doubts had vanished, but still he asked, "Was it you who spoke to my wife?"

"Yes," the angel answered, a smile in his tone.

"Well! Um – just what are we supposed to do for the boy when he is born?" Manoah asked, flushing because he knew, as well as the angel, that it wasn't a real question.

"Exactly what I told your wife – no wine, no spirits, no unclean foods. And don't ever cut his hair. That's it," the angel answered with – it was a smile. Manoah was sure of it and his face burned brighter.

"Well – um, could we – could you wait while we fix you a meal? A nice kid?" he all but begged.

The angel smiled but shook his head. "Oh, no! I wouldn't be eating your food, even if I did stay with you. You could offer a holocaust to the Lord God, though, if you wanted to."

Taking heart, and determined to have an answer, Manoah asked, "Please! Could you tell us your name? When what you've told us happens, we'd like to be able to give you credit."

"Why do you want to know my name?" the angel responded. "That's in the realm of mystery."

Blushing again, Manoah busied himself preparing the kid and the grain. These he placed both on a rock, lit the fire, offered the gifts to the Lord God, and stood back, taking his wife by the hand. As they watched, the flames rose in a flag from the holocaust straight to heaven, and the angel, furled in the fire, rose with it and disappeared.

Falling flat on the ground, Manoah and his wife trembled. Finally, raising their heads, they saw only the smoking ash of the holocaust. Manoah blew out his breath. "We're going to die," he said flatly to his wife. "We've just seen the Lord God." And he began to shake.

"Nonsense," his wife returned stoutly, rolling over to sit up. "He accepted the holocaust, after all – you just saw that! What would be the sense of telling us all that and then killing us off? We're not going to die, my dearest husband, best in the world! *We* are going to have a baby!" Briskly she tugged him up, hugged him tight and said, "Well?"

"Well indeed, beloved!' he answered, beginning to match her delight. "Well indeed! Come!"

And back they went toward the house, rejoicing.

[Judges 13: 2-25; 14: 1-9; 16: 17; see **Manoah's WIFE** (see also **Samson's WIFE**); see *Samson's WIFE and the Coils of Betrayal*]

# MARTHA
## and the War for Order

"Get that dog out into the yard or I'll serve him for supper!" Martha screeched as, for the third time, the brown mongrel with the melting brown eyes had nudged against her knee, startling her into dropping her knife on the table. He was looking for a piece of the lamb she was preparing, she knew, and there was no harm in him, but still! How could she cook a decent meal with everything at sixes and sevens and a dog underfoot! It was impossible! She had to have some order around here to cook, and no one, absolutely no one, was helping her even that far!

Mary appeared at her shout and scooped up the dog to rush him outside. The pooch covered her face with kisses as his paws left generous gifts of mud and who knew what else on her best dress.

"Mary, have you no sense at all!" Martha demanded.

"What's wrong?" Mary asked, bewildered, still holding onto the delighted dog. "I thought you wanted him out of the kitchen while you were cooking – and you certainly should be, Lion!" she added to the dog, who cocked his head to one side and seemed to consider her words. "I was just going to take him out."

Hands on hips, Martha growled, "And just look at your clothes! I slaved to get that dress clean the last time, and here it is, filthy again. Well, you'll just have to wear it and look like a, a – disorderly child for the Master! And don't argue with me!"

Standing her ground, Mary said quietly, "I wasn't going to. And the mud will brush off when it dries, so your work won't be lost. But Martha – "

"Get to the point!" she snapped, turning back to the lamb. "Some folks have nothing to do but sit around all day and make a mess, but I have to cook!" A patently unfair remark she had realized even at the time and in the throes of a most satisfying temper display.

"Um," said Mary and stopped.

"What!" Martha demanded, slamming the knife down on the table.

Mary was staring steadily at Martha's skirt. Nodding at it she said, "I think – that might be blood on your skirt? From the knife? When you had your fists on your hips?"

Horrified, Martha turned to her left and followed her sister's gaze down the side of her skirt. There *was* blood on it where the apron had twitched aside. "I think," Mary went on carefully, "I might be able to get it out for you."

"Just get that dog OUT OF HERE!" Martha answered, her voice rising. Mary fled with the dog and, Martha saw, with a couple of small pieces of the lamb she had filched from the pile on the table. "I'll kill her," Martha muttered. "I positively will! But not today. There isn't time. Now *where* has that salt gone to? "

From that point on the day had gone rapidly downhill. By the time the dinner preparations were in their final stages, Martha had reduced Mary to tears three times with constant criticism of her, admittedly inexpert, efforts to help, finally driving her from the kitchen altogether with, "You double my work! You put away everything I'm just about to pick up and lose everything I put down! Have you *no* sense of order at all? Out of my way!"

Lazarus had retreated early to his shop. "Just send Judah for me when you're ready," he told had Mary quietly and disappeared.

Jesus soon appeared – for once without His gang of friends, Mary was happy to note. Judah, stationed at the gate, ran to get Lazarus. Mary flew to greet Jesus, got Him water from the well and settled Him on the bench. And she stayed there, soaking up everything He was saying and asking questions by the dozen, oblivious to the muddy dog-tracks on her dress, her disheveled hair and the tear-stains on her cheeks.

Martha caught just a glimpse of them as she whipped around the table – Mary supremely content, if looking like an unmade bed or a heap of laundry in sore need of a washing, and Jesus entirely focused on her, eyes for no one and nothing else. Martha positively *seethed*, muttering just under her breath, "Company, and who had to do all the work? I did! And who gets to sit down like a lady? She does! It's just not fair!" She deftly slid the hearth cakes onto a platter. Then, with the platter of cakes in one hand and the bowl of stew from the warming hearth in the other, she turned and headed swiftly for the door. The dog, who had slipped back into the house when Jesus and Mary came in, shot between her feet. The bowl of stew went one way and bounced, the platter of bread flew the other and shattered, the dog fled out the back door and she landed on the floor with a solid thud.

And nobody even seemed to notice! The murmur of voices continued undisturbed. "That does is!" Martha thought. She stomped up to the bench, planted both feet and shouted, "Master! Don't you even *care* that my sister has left all the work to me? Make her come and help me!" And to her mortification, she burst into tears. In a flash, He was on his feet, His arms around her, comforting her as, for years, she had comforted the little ones who came her way, beginning with Mary and Lazarus when they were children. It was comfort she had been needing forever.

When her tears quieted and she began to pull away, He gave her a hug and said cheerfully, "You worry too much, Martha. All those details – there's only one really *necessary* thing, you know." He looked at her quizzically, to see if she understood. She did. The one thing was what He had just given her – personal love and direct attention, all of Himself for that moment. She nodded, and He went on, drawing Mary into the embrace. "Mary chose the better part," he said with a smile, but seriously, so she – so they both, would remember, "It's not going to be taken away from her."

Martha wasn't quite sure what happened after that – only that the three of them, and Lazarus when he arrived, worked together, restoring the order she so prized. They reassembled the meal, ate and cleaned up. Judah and the dog also had a share.

Martha knew that, somehow, she herself had been changed this day, had grown into that part of herself she had never let anyone see. Because He loved her and let her feel it, He freed her from the imprisoning, lethal order she craved, so that she could *live* – receive the love Lazarus and Mary and everyone else had been trying to give her all these years and then return it.

After that amazing meal, order gradually became less and less her god, less the air she needed for breathing, and more simply a product of her active giving and receiving of love. She learned to relax and let other people do what they did best without feeling challenged or threatened, because she learned that she could be, was in fact, loved for who she was, not for what she did and how she did it. That was how her service was becoming service in reality, not just a disguise for control nor a means to prevent her own annihilation. That "better part" became her choice as well, thanks to Him. He had given her life back to her when it had died within her.

[**Luke 10:** 38-42; **John 11:** 1-44; **12:** 2; see **MARTHA** (see also **MARY, sister of Martha**); see *MARY and the Costly Nard*]

# MARY
## and the Costly Nard

Sitting where she could see Jesus, Martha's sister Mary smiled. This was perfect. Martha was happy because she was serving a meal that would feed Jesus properly as well as please everyone here, and she had welcomed Mary's help with the preparations, a real breakthrough in their relationship. Their brother Lazarus was happy because he was alive – and was with Jesus who had called him from the tomb. And she was happy because – well, because for now, everything was perfect.

Remembering last month, when everything had been absolutely horrible, with no way to make anything at all better, Mary shuddered. She would not want to go through that time again for any price. First, Lazarus, who was never, ever sick, had felt unwell, and rapidly gotten worse, until he was very ill indeed – for no reason the doctor could find. His fever went sky high and stayed there; his skin was burning to the touch, and bathing him with cool water helped only while his skin was actually wet. He could neither eat nor drink – which was just as well, since he had not been able to keep anything in his stomach for several days before the fever had gotten so high.

Martha had been wonderful. She seemed to have been made for just such crises. She organized those who offered help, so that there was always someone with Lazarus, there was always food for the table, the washing got done, the water was brought from the well and they themselves got some rest.

Neither of them, for a wonder, had gotten sick, and no one who helped out did either, but Lazarus had not begun to heal. Instead, he took a turn for the worse and the doctor warned them that he would die unless something happened soon to change the course of this mysterious illness.

That was when she had thought of Jesus. "We could send word to Him," she had suggested to Martha, boldly for her. "I know He would come to heal Lazarus."

Martha had agreed, and they had sent Him a message by a neighbor. But Jesus had not appeared and Lazarus grew weaker as the fever seemed to eat his substance. Finally, just at dawn, Lazarus had died.

Amid the bustle of preparing the body for burial in the tomb outside of town and dealing with everyone, from the doctor to the mourners, neither Martha nor Mary had time to wonder about what had happened to Jesus, but neither forgot him. They knew, without discussing it, or even thinking about it, that it must have been impossible for Him to come, but the fact that He hadn't been with them still hurt them deeply.

They had been four days into sitting *Shiva* when Jesus finally got to Bethany. Word had reached them almost at the moment He set foot across the town line, and Martha, snatching her veil, had all but run out the door. Mary had simply sat where she was. Jesus, for whatever reason, had not come on time, Lazarus was dead and nothing could be done now to change that, she had thought dully, her tears beginning again. Then had come their cousin Judah, bringing Martha's message, "The Master is here and is asking for you!"

She had gotten up quickly, wrapped her mourning veil properly around her and, tears still falling, had walked down the road, Judah's hand in her own, with all the visitors trailing behind her. Seeing Him standing there, face carved in stone, she'd fallen to her knees at His feet and blurted out the first thing that came into her mind. "Lord!" she had said with deep reproach, "If You'd been here, my brother wouldn't be dead!" She'd clapped both hands over her mouth in horror at the bitterness she heard in her voice, and her tears flowed faster.

Jesus had acted at once, she remembered. He'd helped her up, hugged her tight, asked where Lazarus had been buried and had gone with them to the tomb. And then, standing in the road, looking at the tomb, He'd wept with them.

A voice from the crowd, much louder than the speaker realized, remarked, "Looks like the Master really loved Lazarus!" and another answered, "But then why didn't He keep Lazarus from dying? After all, if He can make a man born blind see..."

Mary and Martha had both cringed at the rudeness, but Jesus had not seemed to notice. Drying His eyes, He had straightened, caught the eyes of two sturdy young men and commanded, "Take the stone away."

Martha grasped his sleeve anxiously. "But – Lord, he's been in there four days! There'll be a stench!"

"Didn't I tell you, you'd see God's glory if you believed?" Jesus asked her, the hint of a smile behind His seriousness.   Martha had simply nodded, bemused, and the young men tugged the stone from the mouth of the tomb.

Then Jesus had stood tall, lifted his eyes to heaven and prayed aloud, "Father, thank you for hearing Me. I know You always do, but I'm saying so out loud so these people will believe You've sent me." Drawing a deep breath, He had looked directly into the mouth of the tomb. "Lazarus!" He had demanded. "Come out!"

Mary shivered, looking at her brother, now vibrantly alive and toasting Jesus. "If I live to be a thousand," she thought, "I'll never forget seeing him, still tied in his shroud with the cloth over his head, hobbling out of that tomb! And we just stood there, looking at him with our mouths hanging open until Jesus reminded us to untie him!" She smiled with such joy that those around her smiled in sympathy, though they had no idea where her mind had been wandering, she knew.

And now the meal was almost over. "I wish," Mary thought, "I just wish there were something *I* could do for *Him*, for a change! People are always asking Him for things — not that He minds; in fact, I think He delights in being able to help them. He says it takes faith to ask and that faith is the first step to God; the first answer to the love God is always offering us. But still — wouldn't it be nice if, just once, someone could do something for Him instead of always taking?
Oh, I wish I could think of some — "

Suddenly it came to her. The alabaster jar of pure spikenard that Uncle Aaron had given her years ago! She'd been saving it, as Martha had told her to, for her own wedding, and when that hadn't happened, she'd just gone on saving it. "Why couldn't I use it?" she wondered now, sitting erect, eyes blazing. "I could — anoint his feet with it! They certainly get enough hard use, so that would feel good. He should get something too, not just pour out himself loving everyone else and never have anyone do more than say thank you, if they remember to do that. He should be loved as much as He loves!"

Before she could talk herself out of the idea, Mary excused herself from the table, ran to the house, snatched up the delicate jar and raced back to the banquet.

No one seemed to have missed her, and Mary slipped into a space that had opened at Jesus' couch, and knelt just by His feet. Swiftly she cracked the neck of the jar and poured its contents out onto Jesus feet. Then, with one hand unloosening her hair with a deft twist and using it to mop up the excess and keep it from the cushions, she used the other to work the nard into his feet, the soles first and then the tops. The odor of spikenard filled the whole house and, within a heartbeat, everyone was looking around to find the source of the perfume.

A murmur of wonder and approval arose from the crowd like the hum of contented bees when they discovered what she was doing. Everyone was delighted; evidently, they too felt it was high time for Jesus to be getting something, instead of always giving.

The feeling was not unanimous, however, and it was Judas Iscariot who became the voice of the envious. "Why didn't she sell that spikenard? She could've given the money to the poor!" he asked with amused contempt. "It would have brought three hundred silver coins!"

Mary felt the bottom drop out of her heart. Stricken, she looked at Jesus. He loved the poor – was He angry with her extravagance and too polite to say so? Had her good idea really been a horrible piece of self-display? Was He angry with *her*? She felt the tears, tight in her throat, begin to spill.

"Leave her alone," commanded Jesus, shocking everyone in the room. "Why are you bothering her?" In the sudden silence, He went on, his tone patient yet resonating strength. "What she has done is one of the Good Deeds. She's done what she could – she's done this early for My burial. You'll always have the poor with you, and you can do good for them," he looked pointedly at Judas, who squirmed in shame but still looked affronted, "whenever you want to. I won't always be here. And I tell you," he added, raising his voice so that no one could miss the message, "what she has done will be retold wherever in the whole world the Good News is preached, as a remembrance of her."

Then He looked down at her, still kneeling, her hands still working the ointment into His feet, and smiled. Her heart sang.

[John 11: 1–20, 28–45; 12: 1–8; Matthew 26: 6–13; Mark 14: 3–9; Luke 10: 38–42; see MARY, sister of Martha (see also MARTHA, MARY MAGDALENE, Sinful WOMAN Who Anointed Jesus' Feet); see MARTHA and the War for Order and The WOMAN and the Shattered Jar]

# MARY
## and the Mothering of God

Donkeys had hard, lumpy spines, even when a nice thick blanket was between them and you, Mary thought, shifting again. She was awkward with child, uncomfortable, and the rain wasn't helping matters. She felt as though she must be growing mildew somewhere, perhaps behind her ears. Impatiently, she shook her head. Rain was rain, even eight days' worth – nothing you could do anything about, so no point getting annoyed about it.

"Trouble?" asked Joseph instantly, hand on hers.

"No," she said, summoning a smile, "just the usual – donkey's bones meeting mine, and all this – this *bulge* I'm carrying. I know now what Aunt Elizabeth meant! I am *so* ready for this baby to be born. Not now!" she added hastily, seeing his look of alarm. "We should be settled in Bethlehem well before time if we keep on at this pace. Don't worry Joseph!"

"That's my wife you're talking about!" he returned sharply, but flashed her a smile, "and that will be *my* baby, too, once He's born – mine to name and claim as the Lord God has given us, mine to cherish as I do you, as I would my own flesh and blood, and mine to educate and protect and send forth into the world! So I *will* worry if I want to!"

"No need, this time," she answered, her smile a real one now. She felt she was riding in a bubble of contentment and peace, in spite of the rain, the donkey's lumps, her own fatigue and – everything else. Joseph was so *good* – thoughtful, responsible, funny sometimes, but above all, loving. Even when he had not known who the Father of her coming Child was, he had decided to spare her – life and reputation both – by arranging a quiet divorce, "so you could marry whoever it was whom you loved more than you loved me," he had explained later. He had said nothing to her, had suffered agonies on his own in coming to that decision, and was fully prepared to implement it when the angel had finally gotten to him, in a dream, and explained everything.

"And about time, too!" she had fumed to the Lord God afterward. "*Why* did he have to suffer so?" She had waited and gotten no spoken answer, but found later that she understood. The Lord God had been testing Joseph, much as He had done Abraham with his firstborn Isaac on the rock of sacrifice, and for the same reason, she guessed – not for His sake, but to show *Joseph* (and, not incidentally, herself and her Son-to-come) that he was a man of absolute fidelity who would not fail those he loved and had committed himself to, no matter what.

Looking at Joseph's strong back as he led the donkey around a really large pothole, she smiled and drifted back into her memory of how this had all begun.

The day was warm for spring. The birds sang fountains of praise to God for the glories of the sun and the trees, of new life to come and of the life they were living. Mary smiled, looking through the open door, her hands quiet among the vegetables.

"Mary!" came her mother's voice and the fifteen-year-old jumped, startled. "Those onions won't chop themselves, you know," said Anna, coming into the kitchen, "and I need them so I can start dinner! You can moon about your Joseph some other time – do your work first." She gave her daughter a warm hug and kiss. "I remember what that's like," she said softly. "Enjoy it while you can! But first get my onions done!"

"Yes, Mother," Mary answered, smiling. "Sorry!" And she began to chop the onions expertly. Her mother had gone about her work and Mary, alone, found her thoughts following her mother's suggestion, drifting to Joseph. How she loved him! He was so strong – at twenty-five, a responsible citizen and full-fledged carpenter making a good living, and a virile young man! "How glad I am that Father didn't find me an *old* husband, a widower even, like poor old Jeremiah, who looks so cross all the time. Mother says it's the pain in his joints, and she's probably right – but I surely am glad I don't have to marry *him!*"

The onions chopped, Mary moved on to trimming the lamb, her mind idling among the spring, Joseph, the birds, the sunlight and the bread she still had to make.

Suddenly there was a presence in the room with her.

Mary felt the hair on the back of her neck rise and her eyes opened their widest to take in this, this – she didn't know! A man? A ghost?

The 'apparition' spoke – a wonderful voice, saying shocking things, as if they were ordinary. Normal even! "Greetings, you who have found God's favor. The Lord is with you."

Mary felt her mouth drop open in shock. *God's* favor? She had found favor *with* God? And He was *with* her? *Here? Now?*

Seeing her expression, the angel said hastily, "Don't be frightened, Mary." And his voice was so kind, so concerned, so – calming - she suddenly cease to be any where near calm. "You *have* found favor with God," he assured her. Then he looked at her intently, as if to be sure he had her whole attention.

*"Behold,"* he said to her solemnly, *"you will conceive in your womb and bear a son, and you shall name him Jesus. He will be great and will be called Son of the Most High, and the Lord God will give Him the throne of David, His father, and He will rule over the house of Jacob forever, and of His kingdom there will be no end."* [Luke 1: 31–33; JB]

He then stopped and waited, looking expectantly at her. Mary guessed she was supposed to say something, but his words, though they had penetrated to the very core of her soul, had left only a jumbled impression on the surface of her mind. So she went back to the beginning – she was to bear a child.

"But," she began, then, in a rush, blurted out, "I'm a virgin! How can all this happen?"

The angel relaxed and leaned toward her, plainly wanting to reassure her. *"The Holy Spirit will come upon you,"* he explained earnestly, *"and the power of the Most High will overshadow you, so the Child to be born will be called Holy, the Son of God."* [Luke 1: 35; JB]

He stopped and eyed her quizzically, and seeing that she still seemed bewildered and troubled, added, almost conversationally, "You should know this, too! Your aged kinswoman Elizabeth? The one they call 'barren'?" Mary nodded. "Well, *she* has conceived a son also. She's in her sixth month! To God, nothing's impossible," he reminded her, using the adage familiar to every child of Israel.

Well, that broke the block. Understanding visibly flooded Mary, filling her first with relief and then with exquisite joy. Unconsciously, she stood straighter, looked directly at this angel and said simply, "Here I am. I am God's handmaid. Let it be done to me as you have said!"

Shifting again on the donkey to see if she could find a less uncomfortable way to sit, Mary remembered she had been filled with a flood of joy so intense it had brought tears to her eyes, so that her vision blurred and she did not see the angel's answering smile, though she felt it like summer warmth, nor did she notice his departure.

The joy had carried her straight to Aunt Elizabeth and Uncle Zechariah's house in Ain Karim. She'd joined the group from Nazareth going to Jerusalem for the Passover, and once there, had gone the further five miles west with a group of Zechariah's kinsfolk. She remembered nothing of the week's journeying except that it seemed to last forever.

Her first sight of Aunt Elizabeth had been a shock. Obviously pregnant, the old woman had glowed with health and joy, and as Mary greeted her, she cried out, "You are most blessed among all women, and blessed is the fruit of your womb! How have I deserved to have the mother of my Lord come to me? For the very moment your greeting sounded in my ears, the child in my womb leaped for joy!"

At that, the flood of joy Mary had been carrying since her meeting with the angel had simply fountained into words, some hers, some from Scripture. "My soul proclaims the greatness of the Lord," she had all but sung, "and my spirit rejoices in God my savior, because He has had regard for the lowliness of His handmaid! For behold, from this moment on, all generations will call me blessed – because He Who is Mighty has done great things for me, and Holy is His Name! His mercy extends from generation to generation to those who fear Him! He has done powerful things with His Own arm. He has scattered the proud in their hearts' judgments. He has deposed the powerful from their positions, and He has lifted up the lowly. He has filled the hungry full with good things, and He has sent the rich away empty! He has raised up Israel, His servant, mindful of His mercy, as He promised our fathers, Abraham and his descendants forever!"

And she had laughed aloud and hugged Elizabeth. "Oh, Aunt!" she had exclaimed, and Elizabeth had laughed with her. "Oh, Mary!" she had echoed, and they had beamed at each other through sudden tears like a spring sun shower.

Recalling the rest of her visit, Mary smiled again. "Oh, Aunt! I wish you could know how much good you've done me," she thought, "what strength I draw from remembering you! I never got a chance to thank you then, but I've never stopped since! I'd never have been able to face this trip to Bethlehem for the Census this close to my time if it hadn't been for my time with you."

She sat a little straighter on the donkey, wondering about the time. The rain was still with them, and there were no shadows on the road, but she guessed it had to be nearly sunset – and there it was, Bethlehem, David's city, and they were going through the gates.

The city – a town, really – was jammed with pilgrims and those coming for the census. There was hardly room to move in the roads, and the fortunate people who were staying with relatives in town were relieved that they wouldn't have to try to find lodging. Mary and Joseph were not among their number, and began their search for a place to stay somewhat anxiously. There was none to be had.

Joseph came to that dismal conclusion several hours after nightfall as they stood in the mud outside the meanest of the caravansaries and the only one they hadn't tried, rain seeping through their clothing and blurring their vision. Joseph knocked again, more forcefully. At last, opening his door a crack, the owner bellowed, "No room! I have no room!" And he slammed the door with a dead thunk.

Joseph looked at Mary apologetically, then froze as she caught her breath and winced. "It's all right," she assured him. "It's just that my labor's started. The pains are coming about two hundred forty slow breaths apart, so it's not urgent, yet. But we really *will* have to find a place to set me down – out of the rain if that can be managed, but definitely out of the road."

Joseph's eyes widened and he whipped around, surveying the area for possibilities. Nothing. "Where's an angel when you need one!" he muttered softly. Mary heard him and smiled wryly, but said nothing.

At that moment a young girl stepped in front of them. She had come out of the last caravansary they had tried, they discovered later, but at that moment she seemed like the answer to Joseph's question. "When are you going to have your baby?" she asked Mary directly.

"In less than an hour, if things go on as they've begun," she answered.

"Well, you can't do it here!" the child declared, in a tone so reminiscent of Aunt Elizabeth's that Mary laughed in spite of herself. "You have to come with me," she said to Joseph, who simply nodded. "We'll go into the hills just over there to our family's sheep cave – where they shelter the animals in really bad weather? Oh, yes. I'm Sarah. Come on!"

Not waiting for an answer, she had bounded up a faint track, leading them to what turned out to be a dry cave with a rack for fodder for the beasts and enough room for them, the donkey and the birthing of the Child.

Sarah had vanished as soon as she settled them in the cave with, "Make a medium-sized fire, why don't you?" to Joseph. Joseph blinked and did so.

"Midwife?" he had asked.

"Too late – unless Sarah's gone to get one," Mary answered. "I know what to do – from helping Aunt Elizabeth and watching her midwife. We'll be all right if you can help me."

"I can," Joseph assured her. "I was the only one around when – " and he was off on an impossibly convoluted story of a time when he had assisted one of his cousins with a birth; a story that had somehow involved a week's wash, a stray goat, a huge mud puddle and a melon that kept rolling into places it didn't belong. He had her laughing between pains as she paced and breathed the way Aunt Elizabeth and the midwife had taught her. He braced her at every pain, he rubbed her back when it cramped, and in between, he unloaded and rubbed down the donkey, unpacked their bedding and settled their things, all the while trailing the story through its twists and turns.

When the story was over, the pains were down to thirty counts apart. Mary said, "Joseph?" and he was instantly at her side.

"Now?" he asked.

"Now!" she replied. At that moment, Sarah arrived carrying a basin of water, clean cloths and a covered pot which proved to contain stew. She put basin and stew by the fire, the cloths on a sheet she spread and said to Mary, "I ran for the midwife, but Martha and my sister, her apprentice, were involved in a difficult birth. It was twins, they said, and there were problems, so neither of them could come. But I've helped them lots of times, and Mother said I should. She's the one who sent me to you in the first place." Seeing their blank expressions, she added, "The caravansary where I met you? That's ours. Anyway, Mother told me to have you come for her," she added to Joseph, "if we had trouble, but we won't."

And they didn't. When Mary, clean and freshly dressed, was settled to rest, her newly-bathed and properly swaddled Child nursing contentedly, she said to the girl, "Sarah, you've done a wonderful job. You've certainly earned the midwife's fee!"

"No," Sarah returned seriously. "That was my gift to you – because letting me help was your gift to me! I really *want* to be a midwife, and now I have a reason Martha will listen to. I can really *do* the work."

"You certainly can!" Mary assured her.

"Perhaps – could we help with the fee for your training, do you suppose?" asked Joseph. "Apprentice carpenters have to pay, I know, and if midwives are the same – "

"Well," said Sarah slowly, "I guess that would be all right."

After they had eaten, she gave Mary a final check and left for the house. They were just about to settle for the night, putting the Baby in the fodder rack to sleep, when the shepherds arrived, babbling of angels. She and Joseph looked at each other. "*That's* where they were!" Joseph had murmured, and she answered, "Except for our Sarah!"

When at last the shepherds had taken their leave, singing songs of glory to God, Joseph looked at Mary and the Child in her arms. "Well," he said contentedly, "that's done. The Baby's safely born and you're healthy! Glad it's over?"

She looked up at him and smiled. "Aunt Elizabeth says the birthing is the easy part. Now comes the hard part — the mothering. And she says that never ends!" She looked down at the Baby and whispered, "Welcome to the world, my Son. Be at peace. I'm here — and I always will be. The mothering never *does* end — and that's a promise!"

[**Matthew 1:** 16, 18-25; **2:** 10-11; **12:** 46-50; **13:** 53-58; **Mark 3:** 31-35; **6:** 1-6; **Luke 1:** 26-56; **2:** 1-52; **4:** 16-30; **8:** 19-21; **11:** 27-28; **John 2:** 1-12; **6:** 42; **19:** 25-27; **Acts 1:** 14; **Galatians 4**; 4; see **MARY, mother of Jesus, Son of God** (see also **ANNA** and **ELIZABETH**); see *MARY and the Quiet Time Between, MARY and the Sword of Sorrow* and *ELIZABETH and the Longed-for Child*]

# MARY
# and the Quiet Time Between

Mary stood in her kitchen on a spring afternoon, kneading bread. It was almost three years since Jesus had left home to begin preaching in the Kingdom of God, and she reflected upon the adventure of his birth and the magnificent simplicity of his name.

And what a name! It had been the Lord God's choice, of course, for Gabriel, the angel, had told her to give it to Him. She had liked it – Jesus, the one who saves – but she hadn't really understood it then, not at all. And she had the feeling that she still didn't. The unfolding of that name had only just begun, and when it was fully revealed, the cost would be everything she, and He, could pay. Maybe more.

But at the time, it had been fine. She smiled and picked up a handful of raisins to work them into the dough. Joseph had arranged everything with the help of Jacob, the innkeeper who ran the caravansary on the outskirts of Bethlehem. The innkeeper's wife had taken them all into her own home and made Mary do more resting that she had done "in my whole life!" she had exclaimed to Joseph, who smiled and said something about the Lord God being thorough when He took a hand. The Baby had done no more crying than the normal boy being circumcised, and Joseph had named Him Jesus, as the angel had instructed, and claimed Him for his own.

They had both been relieved once that was done, and Joseph had decided that, really, there was no point in trekking all the way back to Nazareth when they would just have to turn around in three weeks and make the winter journey all over again so they could go to the Temple for her purification after childbirth and the Child's formal presentation and redemption. "From here," he had explained, "it's a day's journey, and we don't have to push ourselves. From Nazareth, it's ten days on the road, and I doubt the donkey's bones have gotten any softer."

"But we really can't stay here!" Mary had objected. "Abigail was wonderful to give us a room for this long – but another five weeks! We really can't ask her to do that!"

"Of course not," Joseph had agreed. "I've spoken to her – to Jacob, really – and there's a family connection living just outside of town. He's just lost his wife and Abigail says he'll be glad of the company. Sarah will stay with us there for a week, just to be sure everything's all right. She claims we'll be doing the whole family a favor if we stay there until your forty days are over. And Jacob has told me about people who need carpentry done. I've been to see three of them, and they've contracted for work that will keep us in food while we're here - maybe even give us extra!"

And so it was done. The time had passed quickly -- the more so when Sarah returned home, and Mary had the full care of her Son as well as the house. Michael proved an easy man to cook for and a pleasant companion, and he was rather sad when he found them packing for the journey to Nazareth.

"We're not leaving yet," Mary assured him. "We're due at the Temple tomorrow, and we'll stay with your cousin Samuel and his wife over night. Then we'll come back here on Wednesday. I just want to have everything ready – I hate scrambling at the last minute! I forget too much!" Smiling at Michael, she had added, "We're all so grateful to you for giving us your home for this month and more. It's been wonderful! But it's time we went home." With that, Michael had smiled, nodding his agreement.

The experience in the Temple had been – mind-boggling, Mary decided. She set the bread aside for another rising, then began to clean the vegetables for dinner.

First had come Simeon. They had just gotten in to the Temple and were looking around to get their bearings when this old man had just appeared in front of them! Meeting Mary's eyes, he had smiled and extended his arms for the Baby, and she had found herself putting the Child into his embrace.

Then, in a voice that had made her shiver, he had prophesied – she didn't know what else to call it – saying, *"Now, Master, You can let Your servant go in peace, just as You promised; because my eyes have seen the salvation which You have prepared for all the nations to see, a light to enlighten the pagans and the glory of your people, Israel!"* [Luke 2:29-32; JB]
Handing the Baby carefully back to Mary, he had gazed into her eyes and said, continuing his prophecy in the same riveting voice, *"You see this child? He is destined for the fall and for the rising of many in Israel, destined to be a sign that is rejected – and a sword will pierce your own soul, too – so that the secret thoughts of many may be laid bare!"* [Luke 2: 34-35; JB] Then he had bowed and left them staring after him.

Someone passing, having seen but not heard the conversation, hurried over to assure them that Simeon was a very holy man who had been waiting eagerly for the coming of the Messiah and the rescue of Israel all his life. The Spirit of God, quite plainly, rested on him, and he had been promised he would see the Messiah before he died. It seemed he often greeted parents bringing babies to be presented. "Harmless," their informant assured them. "And that, over there, is Anna, a holy widow," he said, pointing to a bent woman just shuffling into view. "She's been here in the Temple forever, just praying all the time. She's waiting for the Messiah, too." He smiled at them, especially at the Baby who seemed to be looking around with interest. "Not a speck of harm in her, either," he said, and took his leave.

"She looks older than Moses!" Mary had whispered to Joseph, gesturing to Anna. Then she jumped, blushing, when that lady had rapped out, "Only eighty-four, my love! You'll be lucky if you live so long, let alone walk on your own! No, no – don't apologize. I *am* old, but there's nothing wrong with my mind -and not much wrong with my hearing, either! Let me see the baby."

That was when it had happened. Mary had opened her shawl and Anna had peered in – and had thrown back her head to praise God in a very loud voice! Next she had started going up to people she knew were waiting actively for the deliverance of Jerusalem to tell them about Mary's Child!

After that, she remembered, she had only had half her mind on what they had come for. Thanks to Joseph, the rituals had gone smoothly. He had gotten their two turtledoves and offered the sacrifice that redeemed this Firstborn to come home with them, and she had undergone the rites of purification the Law prescribed for women after childbirth. It wasn't until the next day, as they came in sight of Michael's house, that she said, "Do you suppose the Lord God thought we needed confirmation of Who this Child is? Or was that all just for Anna and Simeon?"

Joseph had thought for a long moment. "Both, maybe. And remember, all this was happening in His Temple! I think Simeon and Anna were representing all Israel, and it may be their job to pass on the word that the Lord God has kept His promise and sent His Son as Messiah."

"That's – scary, " Mary had said in a small voice. "Wonderful, but – scary. We're only two people and we have to bring up this Child to save Israel! Joseph – how can we *do* that?"

"Hush, love," he had said gently. "How many times have you reminded me that we are not alone in this? That the Lord God is watching over us and protecting us? That nothing's going to happen to this Child that He hasn't planned? Have you forgotten? I haven't - and it's all true! I promise you! We'll be fine, and so will He."

That had been her talisman for the next several years of what she had come to call the quiet time, between the tumultuous beginnings and – well, she didn't know quite what was going to follow this life of preaching and teaching Jesus was leading now. He was the Messiah, but He didn't seem to want people to know about it. At least, He wasn't announcing it. He seemed, these days, to be making a point to tell the people he healed *not* to say what He'd done. Also, she'd begun to notice the growing hostility of the leadership – scribes, Pharisees, maybe even the priests, though she didn't *know* that, not for certain. Well, time enough for that when it happened!

Having finished up the vegetables, she tucked up her skirts and went out to weed her tiny garden. She'd always found working in the earth soothing, and today was no exception. Unbidden, her mind returned to that day of His presentation, to the evening, when she'd *thought* everything new and upsetting was over. That all they had to do was go back to Nazareth and let the whole set of experiences sink in, as they learned to live with each other, and Jesus, and to teach Him how to be a good man and faithful child of God.

But she had been wrong, as it turned out. They'd gone in, had their supper, finished their packing and just blown out the lamp when they heard a quiet knock at the door. Joseph picked up a length of firewood and Mary snatched up Jesus, wrapped Him in His blanket and held Him tightly to her heart. Joseph had cleared his throat and asked, "Who's there?"

"Wise men, Magi, from the East," had come the startling reply in heavily accented Hebrew. "We watched His star rise in the East, and we have followed it here. It stands now over your roof. We have come to pay homage to the Infant Who is King of the Jews."

Mary and Joseph had looked wonderingly at each other, and Joseph had unbarred the door. Seeing the strangers, somberly but richly clad, Joseph had put down the stove wood and stepped outside, turned to face the house and gazed up at the sky. Then he had smiled and, turning, ushered them in, nodding to Mary and mouthing, "It's there all right! Huge!"

The Magi had stopped short seeing her, then, in a single movement, had knelt, put coffers at her feet and touched their foreheads to the ground in profound respect. In response, she had loosened the blanket and stooped, and they had risen to their knees and gazed at Him with their hearts shining through their eyes.

They had told some of their adventures, including their encounter with Herod and the scribes; "Frightened to death!" they had described the King. They stayed the night, of course, but well before dawn they had awakened, conferred with one another in their own language, and then told Joseph that they were leaving at once. "We have had a warning, a dream. We must not go back to Herod. We must take another route when we go home. We will leave at once - we think it best."

Wondering and a little frightened, Mary had fixed a quick meal and offered them food for the road, but they refused it, saying they had plenty, and vanished as silently as they had come. Mary and Joseph had gone back to bed and to sleep, but less than half an hour later, Joseph had sat up and shaken her awake.

"We have to leave now," he announced in a whisper. "I'll pack our things on the donkey if you'll take care of the food, the odds and ends and the Baby. We need to be gone as soon as we can." She had nodded, and they found themselves moving silently down the road some twenty minutes later.

"Angel?" Mary had asked, and Joseph had nodded.

"We're going to Egypt. He says we have to stay there until he tells us it's safe. Herod means to search for Jesus and kill him."

"Kill him!" she had exclaimed. "Why? He's not even two months old! What's He ever done to Herod?"

Joseph glanced at her. "Been born!" he answered. "At least, that's my guess. I think he sees Jesus as a threat to him. After all, the Magi did say He was the new King of the Jews. That can't have made Herod exactly comfortable. Being king is *his* job, and he's just been told he's fired, or will be when the Boy comes of age!"

"I guess," she said. "But Egypt! Oh, it's far away and all, but the Lord God will take care of us. I know that. But Egypt! It's odd, don't you think? Israel's salvation in Jacob's day became Israel's prison, and Moses had to free us - and now Egypt has become Israel's salvation again!"

"The Lord God's like that," her husband had said, smiling. "He takes care of His own, no matter what anyone plans – and He seems to like these, connections, I guess. Anyway, that's what He told the angel to tell me, so that's where we're going. As you've said from the beginning, with Him arranging things, we'll be fine!"

And so it had proved, Mary recalled. They had settled in the Jewish quarter; Joseph had found first the house, and then enough work for them to pay for their stay. The Magi's gifts had proved another special help of God - the gold kept them until Joseph started earning, and then again on their return to Nazareth. The frankincense and myrrh Mary had kept. She wasn't quite sure why, but she was positive that He had given them to her for a reason, and would show her what that reason was at some point.

Mary brushed the sweat off her forehead and straightened up, pausing in her weeding. You wouldn't think that April could be so hot, she reflected. It wasn't, always, but some years it seemed to be part of summer instead of part of spring. It had been like that the year they had returned to Nazareth from Egypt, she remembered. Jesus had been walking by then, and into everything! The journey had been a lively one.

Their return had been – different, she remembered. Everyone had been glad to see them, but they hadn't understood why they'd been away so long. Joseph had passed it off as an unexpected opportunity that they simply had not been able to afford to pass up, at the time. "But," he said, at least a hundred times, "its time was over, so we came back home without regrets." And that was all he would say. She had echoed him and turned the subject to children and their ways, asking advice of the most persistent, which deflected their curiosity nicely, "and got me some really good ideas!" she smiled.

Jesus had been a good Child, no real trouble. Though, with His energy and His interests, ranging as they did over everything He could see, touch, smell, handle or put in His mouth, he could be worrying at times.
Joseph had been wonderful, taking the boy into his shop as soon as He could walk steadily and follow simple directions. He had built the boy a small bench of His own and taught Him to use tools. In fact, Joseph had made Him tools that were small enough for Him to handle, and gave Him real things to do with them. She smiled at the memory. She still had, and used, the bread board He had made for her and given her with such pride. Joseph guided Him as He learned, and always took Him just a little further than He was quite ready to go, so He would learn how to reach beyond His present level for the next.

And that, Mary thought, might have been at least part of the reason for their worst experience in that quiet time of bringing Him up.
It had happened the year Jesus turned twelve. It had been even hotter that year, and they had begun to sweat freely before they had gone a day's journey in their trip to Jerusalem for the Passover feast and for His Bar Mitzvah. Everything had gone smoothly. The Temple services had been splendid, uplifting, renewing mind and heart, and they had rejoiced at being there, and being together. It was on their way home that things had, without warning, fallen disastrously apart. She sat back on her heels, remembering how it had been.

Mary felt the sun, really *warm* for April, shining on her back, and she took a

288 • ALL THE WOMEN OF THE BIBLE

deep breath of the sweet spring air. Watching the children play around the travel group as they made their way up the road, heading for Nazareth again, she smiled. They hadn't lost a single child all the time they were in Jerusalem for the Passover, not even for a hundred breaths, and with twenty-one children from three to twelve, that had to be a record. It had been her idea to have each woman keep track of three youngsters, instead of the usual, haphazard, everyone-watches-all-of-them process they usually used.

"I wonder how Jesus likes travel with the men?" she wondered. "Good for Him, I don't doubt! He'll be an apprentice to Joseph this year and He'll have to move fully out of childhood then; this will give Him a taste of it!" But she admitted to herself that she would be very glad indeed to see Him around the supper fire and sleeping in their tent. "Guess I'm the one who has to let go of His childhood," she smiled. "He's probably itching to be turned loose!"

That evening at the fire, she looked around for her husband and Son, but found only Joseph, who asked her cheerfully, "Was Jesus a help to you today, watching the children?"

"Jesus! He wasn't with us today. Didn't He go with you?" she asked, suddenly anxious.

He shook he head and her heart dropped. "Then where is He?" she demanded, feeling panic rise and clamping down on it. "He can't just have disappeared! Look – you check the fires on that side and I'll check the ones over here. I'll meet you back here. He's got to be here!"

When they met back at the fire, hope died. "We have to go back!" Mary declared. "He's gotten lost along the way, or back in the city."

"Yes," Joseph agreed, "but not tonight. We don't know the roads, and two people alone, at night, with all these strangers about - it's too dangerous. Tomorrow we'll probably meet another group of travelers we can attach ourselves to, and we'll be able to check as we go."

That was what they did. Mary remembered nothing about the day at its end except for the wild alterations of hope and fear -surely they would find Him around the next corner; surely He wasn't lying dead in a ditch someplace down an alley - but maybe He was, and then what would they do? How would they live?

On the third day, having searched the part of Jerusalem where they had stayed and found nothing, Mary declared, "Joseph, I think it's time we got His Father in Heaven involved! If anyone knows where Jesus is, He must!" and they went to the Temple.

She had heard His voice before she recognized Him. As they made their way in, past the groups of remaining pilgrims, their attention was caught by a murmur of voices, and one, rising over the rest, which seemed to pulse with light and love. She remembered thinking, "Now, there's a coming teacher! He sounds nice! And then she had realized who was talking. Transfixed, she gripped Joseph's arm to stop him, and they listened together, then stared at each other.

"Jesus?" asked Joseph, a small frown wrinkling his forehead.

"Yes," Mary replied, "but - where - ?" and she searched the area. "There!" she said and headed to her left, cutting through the crowds like a knife through soft cheese. Joseph followed in her path, arriving with her at the scholars' room, to find Jesus in full flight, talking to all the scholars and doctors of the Law, impressing them with His complete knowledge of the Law and, incidentally, passing an impromptu, stringent oral examination by the religious authority in Jerusalem.

Stunned, Mary stood with Joseph and listened until Jesus had finished what he was saying. Then she stepped forward, her eyes ablaze, her mind churning with all the things she wanted to say to Him, absolutely furious. "Son!" she said sharply and He whipped around to face her, His smile doused in white-faced shock as He realized how very angry she was.

Afterwards, Mary would never be able to remember any more of what she had actually said to Him than the last two sentences, which, really, caught up all her grief, her fear and her wrath. "Why did You *do* this to us?" she demanded. "Your father and I have been frantic hunting for You! For *three days!*" She waited, blazing, for an answer.

Jesus opened His mouth, took a breath - and closed it again, looking very much the child who faced domestic disaster for something he'd never imagined, let alone intended. He swallowed and tried again. "But - but why were you hunting? Didn't you know I'd have to be here, in My Father's house, going about His business?"

Joseph intervened then, stilling Mary's rage with a hand on her shoulder. He gazed at Jesus seriously and shook his head in a tiny gesture, eyebrows flagging a warning. Jesus, eyes widening, gave an equally small nod, then dropped His eyes, said He was sorry to have worried them, asked their forgiveness and waited.

Mary's "We were just so worried!" rode Joseph's "Don't let it happen again, Son," as they caught Him in a hug that brought them all to somewhat damp smiles.

Then He had turned to say good-bye to the graybeards. Some of them had been smiling behind their hands, remembering, no doubt the times they'd gone truant and how they'd had to pay for it. But no one had laughed at Him. They even thanked Him for spending time with them, wished Him well, said they hoped to hear more from Him another time - when He was fully grown was understood by everyone, including Jesus.

And after that - good as gold He had been. He was an excellent apprentice to Joseph, a proper help around the house and a quick learner in everything. Joseph had always been delighted with the way He handled wood, and now, with greater responsibility for the work of the shop, he was really pleased with this Son.

And then Joseph had died so suddenly - how that still hurt, and it was a dozen years ago. Mary shook her head, her eyes blurring with tears she had thought long since shed. "Your best gift to me, Father, except for Yourself, and Your Son, of course."

Jesus had taken over the business, run it well, taken responsibility for her and - "waited, I guess," she thought. "Waited for the Father's moment to begin the work for which He had been sent. I knew it had to come, knew He made arrangements to have the business carried on, so I would be provided for, but still, it was a shock when He left."

Mary knew she would never forget those forty days He was in the desert – all alone. If she'd known where He was, it wouldn't have upset her so. But all she knew was what she'd learned from the neighbors. They'd told her that His cousin John had baptized Him in the Jordan, that a dove had appeared over Him and the Voice of the Lord God, she was sure, had said that He was His Son, and that He was deeply pleasing to Him. Then He'd gone off into the desert.

And then - nothing! When He finally surfaced again, someone ran to let her know where He had been and what He was doing. He had begun to gather some disciples they said, among them the fishermen Simon and Andrew, and their partners, Salome and Zebedee's sons James and John, with Philip and Nathanael.

Then she had begun to relax. These were not wild men; they were the sons of women she knew, practically family; Simon's wife had been a friend of hers and her mother had been one of Anna's friends; Salome was kin, close as a sister in their younger days. So that was all right, she remembered thinking. He would be back. Nothing would really change, nothing - dangerous would happen.

She laughed. "If I had known," she said. "That was the beginning of the end of my quiet time between. Just as well I didn't, though. Just as well, too, that I didn't know what would happen at that wedding in Cana, and what that would start, before I spoke to Him! I'd never have said a word - and then where would we all be? It wouldn't have changed anything, and the poor groom and his new bride would have been humiliated for the rest of their lives. And that's no way to start a marriage!"

Going back to her weeding, she remembered just how it had been.

It was a lovely day, Mary reflected, just the kind of day brides prayed for. She was glad to be in Cana again, glad to be celebrating the wedding of her kinswoman's niece. And the bride was radiant, so full of joy it flowed out of her like streams of living water. Wonderful! There was plenty of food, a reasonable supply of wine, and everyone was having a good time.

And then she looked up. Was that – it was! Jesus had come! She had sent word to Him, but more as a matter of keeping Him up with family news than because she expected Him to appear. This was really a blessing!

She was about to head in His direction when she realized He was not alone. Who were those men with Him? She thought she recognized John, Salome and Zebedee's youngest, so that taller man who looked like him must be James. Were those other two Simon and Andrew? They certainly looked like fishermen - skin like leather, wind-burned and very, very strong. So the others must be Philip and Nathanael? Well, if He wanted her to know them, He would see to the introductions.

Mary had understood that He had to keep His Mission and His private life separate, but it had only now begun to occur to her that with this Mission His private life had ended - which left her where? "Provided for," she answered herself swiftly, "and helping Him this way. Right, Father?" she added to the Lord God. As usual, she got no direct answer, but felt calmer and more peaceful. "So that's a yes," she nodded, and went back to mingling with the guests.

That was why she noticed the problem with the wine. She had just passed the steward of the feast, when she registered the expression of alarm on his face. Glancing toward the table with the wine, she noticed there was only one jar on it, and walking over to it she saw that it was getting very low. Immediately, she looked to where Jesus was. She seemed always to know His position, however dense the crowd, as long as He was in the same place she was.

She saw Peter and Andrew, who had evidently been enjoying the wine, enthusiastically gesturing to James, John, Philip and Nathanael and pointing to the wine table. "They're going to drink the party dry!" she exclaimed, cleaving a path to Jesus through the crowd of celebrating guests. They parted like the Red Sea under Moses' command without even knowing they had moved.

Arriving in front of Him, she planted herself firmly and gave Him a look He had last seen in the Temple at the age of twelve. "Son! They have no wine!" she announced softly.

"What business is that of Mine, Woman?" He asked her seriously, the unaccustomed formality of address affirming her earlier fear that the quiet time of His private life, of which she, and Joseph while he lived, had been the center, was over. "My hour has not yet come."

She caught her breath as though He had doused her with iced water, then stiffened, standing like a queen. Pointedly, she glanced in the direction of His new companions, then met His eyes again. He blinked, startled, eyebrows rising. She pursed her lips, but said nothing, simply nodded and turned away.

She looked for the waiters and beckoned them over. At once they flocked around her, responding to her quiet authority as though they were on strings she held in her hands. "Whatever He tells you to do," she said softly, nodding in Jesus' direction, "do it."

Wide-eyed, they had nodded, and when Jesus came over to them a few moments later and told them to fill up the six stone jugs that usually held water for ritual washing with water, they did so at once. Then, when He told them to draw some out of the jugs and take it to the steward, they did that too, without even blinking.

It was when the steward had tasted the water, which was now rich wine, and complained to the groom that he had been saving the good stuff and serving the poor, that they had understood what Jesus had done.

And that had done it. Word began to spread, people began to flock to Him, He had begun to preach the Kingdom of God as now at hand – and she had kissed her precious, quiet time with Him good-bye, and begun to learn how to live in this new world, when "between" was over.

Rising, Mary gathered her weeds and brought them to her compost pile. Time to go in, clean up, set the table and have her supper. Then she would have to pack. They were leaving in the morning for Jerusalem for the Passover. She hoped everything would be all right.

[**Matthew 1:** 16, 18-25; **2:** 10-11; **12:** 46-50; **13:** 53-58; **Mark 3:** 31-35; **6:** 1-6; **Luke 1:** 26-56; **2:** 1-52; **4:** 16-30; **8:** 19-21; **11:** 27-28; **John 2:** 1-12; **6:** 42; **19:** 25-27; **Acts 1:** 14; **Galatians 4**; 4; see **MARY, mother of Jesus, Son of God** (see also **ANNA** and **ELIZABETH**); see *MARY and the Mothering of God, MARY and the Sword of Sorrow* and *ELIZABETH and the Longed-for Child*]

# MARY
# and the Sword of Sorrow

"This is going to be a long night," thought Jesus' mother, the Widow Mary, settling herself more comfortably in bed in the room provided for her by Joseph of Arimathea. She was sitting up, leaning against her cushions and looking up at the stars through the open window. The brilliant full moon signaling the start of Passover had just begun to move into the frame the window formed, and it seemed to her that she had been sitting there for hours and hours. "No," she corrected herself. "Only since Shabbos dinner ended and the girls helped me get to bed, and that can't be more than an hour, maybe two."

She and the other disciples on Calvary had gone back with Joseph to his house at his insistence, once the Body of Jesus had been placed in Joseph's new tomb on Friday. "Stay with me through the Sabbath?" he had begged them. "I – really need you. I don't think I could bear it alone."

"Neither could we," she thought now. "Yesterday and today have been the worst days of my life. I couldn't have stood either one alone, and I don't think anyone else could have, either." Odd, though, how the core of His closest friends, scattered during the horrors of yesterday, had gathered here, uninvited, by ones and twos as the Sabbath day had worn its way to sunset.

Or maybe not odd at all. They had all loved Him, had become His, really, closer than family. With Him gone, they had to cling together, or be entirely lost. They were all here now, she thought, except for Judas Iscariot who had first betrayed Him by selling Him to the priests, and then had refused even to look for His forgiveness. He'd hanged himself, they'd told her.

"So Judas is buried in the potter's field and my Jesus is buried in Joseph's tomb – and neither rage nor tears will bring either of them back to life, or give either of them another chance." She heaved a sigh, blending pain and impatience. Then, lightly pounding her right fist into her left palm, she said under her breath, "Enough Mary! Enough! You were warned about this when Jesus was forty days old! Simeon, standing right there in the Temple precincts, putting Him back in your arms, *told* you a sword would pierce your spirit – and it has, many times over. But he never said you had to keep turning it in the wound! Now just stop it! Think of something else!"

Mary sighed and sat very still. Focusing all her attention on the stars, she slowly felt herself begin to calm. She slipped through her mind, like beads on a string, contemplating all the times that Simeon's sword, as she thought of it, had made its mark in her spirit.

She saw again that day in the Temple when she and Joseph had brought the infant to present Him to God as firstborn and redeem Him according to the Law. She could still feel the eyes of the ancient Simeon boring right into her soul as he said to her, *"He is destined for the fall and for the rising of many in Israel, destined to be a sign that is rejected – and a sword will pierce your own soul too – so that the secret thoughts of many may be laid bare."* [Luke 2: 34-35; JB]

She had clutched her baby to her then, she remembered, vowing to protect Him from everything, all the while knowing she could not – any more than she had been able to save Him from the necessary pain of His circumcision, though she had seemed to feel the swift cut in her own flesh, and seeing His blood, had seemed to bleed with Him. She had known then that each failure would pierce her through and through as that one had.

The next thrust of Simeon's sword had come that same night – the hideous terror that had accompanied their pell-mell escape into Egypt by darkness, fleeing Herod's soldiers to save the child's life. Their few possessions bundled onto the donkey behind her, the Jesus asleep in her arms, they had fled; Joseph, dear Joseph, urged the donkey to keep up the quick pace he had set.

Their flight had been accompanied, for her at least, by visions of blood and body parts and huge soldiers smashing Him on the rocks. Those visions had persisted even after they were safe in Egypt in a kinsman's house, well out of range of Herod's fury, and with the Magi's gold to see them through until Joseph could get work. "What if?" she'd kept fretting, hearing the screams and feeling the pain, awake and asleep, for weeks.

"It was the helplessness, the hopelessness, the fear that, no matter what we did, we'd fail and He'd die, that gave the sword its edge that time," she saw now. "That was the first time I'd had to face a world where God might – lose! And that's how it seemed, even though I knew better." She shivered.

But, bad as that had been, it was nothing to the time they had lost Him in the Temple. "That's when I learned the next lesson of the sword," she mused, "that I couldn't control *His* choices, even to keep Him safe. I finally saw that I had to let Him go, and that I wouldn't necessarily know where He was, or what was happening to Him. But it took a good while – and oh, how that seeing hurt!"

Stretching, she changed position, trying to find a more comfortable way to settle herself. "And I thought that was the end of Simeon's sword," she remembered. "I should have known better. I should have known!"

There had been no hint, though, that she had been wrong. Their life in Nazareth, after that, had been peaceful, a quiet time when they had grown closer to each other; when they had enjoyed the work they did for each other and for their neighbors.

Then Joseph had died. Somehow, she had never thought of this serious, gentle man, with his enduring strength, absolute steadiness and delightful sense of fun, this husband of hers, this – other half of herself, really, as not *being* there. As dying and leaving her essentially alone in the ways that most mattered. "And I didn't think," she remembered, "not even once, of Simeon's sword. I wish I had – it all might have been easier."

Still, though, they had gone on, she and Jesus, and not much had really changed. She'd begun to relax, then, to think that the work of the sword must be over. After all, she had nothing left to lose! Thinking of that time now, Mary smiled and shook her head. She should have known. Simeon's sword had only just begun its work.

It was the wedding at Cana, innocent, wonderful feast that it was, that had given the sword a place to begin in its next dismantling of her life and her preconceptions. It wasn't so much that word of what He'd done had spread so quickly. Or even that people had started to flock to Him as He began to preach the Kingdom of God as now at hand. That had been fine. She had seen Him, had heard Him preach from time to time, and had been impressed. He was good! His Father would be pleased. That she could have lived with. Cheerfully!

It was what had, so unexpectedly, come with that change that had cut her to the heart. She had gone to visit with Him when He was teaching nearby, taking along some of the family. He'd been inside a house when she got there, and one of the relatives, "who has less patience than a two-year old, bless his heart," she remembered, "sent in that dreadful message, saying I was there and *He* should come out to see *us*!"

She shook her head. The message had interrupted the lesson He was teaching to the people who had gathered around Him to learn about God, and He had *not*, she imagined, been pleased. He'd covered it well, of course, even used it to make another point – for them all!

"Who is my mother? Who are my brothers and sisters?" He had asked from inside the house, but pitching His voice so that everyone in the crowd outside, herself and the family included, could hear Him. "The one who does the will of My Father is mother and brother and sister to Me."

She had gasped in shock. It had felt like a total rejection of her being, of all they had shared and of His whole life with her. A rejection of all the love she, and Joseph, while he was alive, had poured out on Him. It seemed to deny value to everything she had ever done for Him, given Him, taught Him, suffered for Him – everything. Her sense of loss was overwhelming. Jesus had come out after that, of course, and spoken lovingly to her, but they both knew what He had meant, and what He had done. He had, once and for all time, closed the door of the life they had shared in their home, just the three – and now just the two – of them, and sealed it with a stone as formidable as the one they had used today to seal his tomb. And she had been inside. She felt the darkness and the weight of that stone still. She had known, at that moment, that that part of her had died, and that it could never come back to life.

A good deal later, after the numbness had worn off and the pain had become an accustomed and tolerated part of her, residing in the background but never absent, she had begun to understand what Simeon's sword, wielded by Jesus, had been up to that day. He had not been casting her off, nor refusing her love. What He had been saying to His followers, and to her on another level, was that it was following the Father that mattered, and that He meant to include in His family anyone who would do so.

Really, she reflected now, He had *opened* the door to His family, not closed it. He had rolled back that stone she'd been thinking of as permanently sealing her inside what had been their life, leaving her in the dark. He had made everyone welcome who wanted to come in, be one with Him by loving and obeying His Father. It had been a good thing to do – essential, really – and she was the richer for it.

But at the time, all she could feel was Simeon's blade at work, cutting the ties of love and blood that had sustained her. That, unless she *wanted* to be sealed in her past with Him, with only memory to light the dark, had left her with really only one way of going on. She'd taken that way. She'd wanted to be a part of His *present* life of mission, with all her heart, so she had looked around to find the people who had gravitated toward Him. Then, first tentatively, then eagerly, she had seconded the welcome to His family that He had extended them. And gradually and carefully, she had begun to learn how to make them a home, too.

On the surface, she had become just one of the band of women who ministered to Him, but they all, including herself, knew better. So did the men who became His disciples. She was the heart of the group. They welcomed her lovingly, seemed anxious to spend time with her, and leaned on her strength and peace. She had responded to them and had grown glad at the richness of this new and most unexpected life. But the pain - Simeon's sword, she knew now - had never entirely faded.

And then had come yesterday, with that sword dealing pain so close to death that still being alive afterwards seemed hardly a mercy.
She shuddered now, remembering, not just what she had seen and felt and smelled, but what she had not. For they had told her everything – had seemed to need to, as if telling her were all that could make it bearable, that being alone with all that pain would have been too much.

And so she knew about the night they had all spent in the Garden of Olives. It was John who had begun, with Peter and James filling in what they remembered. In their telling, it was as though she had been there with them. Through their eyes, she had seen Him, facing the stark reality of His coming death, coming in a matter of hours, His terror matched only by His courage and His absolute trust in His Father. She saw His sweat pouring down like blood, praying – three times, they said – that the cup, now almost at His lips, might somehow not have to be drunk. She heard Him as they had, voice breaking with unshed tears, telling His Father that if the cup had to be drunk, He would drink it, and He meant it. It was His Father that mattered, and His Father's will alone, that He would do.

They had slept, they confessed to her – couldn't seem to stay awake. His pain had been so intense, they hadn't been able to bear it, and they couldn't help Him. "So we even failed Him there," Peter had declared, still ravaged with grief over his own betrayal of the one he had believed he loved more than his life. His failure had come later, after Judas had led the armed group – both Temple Guards and a small detachment of Roman soldiers – into the Garden and greeted Jesus with a kiss. That was the sign, he had told them, that would mark the man he was betraying, the one the Priests had sent them to capture.

Peter had stayed at first, had even, in trying to cleave the man in two, chopped off the ear of the High Priest's servant, Malchus, with the sword he had brought. "And He healed him! Jesus picked up that ear and put it right back where it belonged – and there it stayed!" said Levi, who'd known the man, as he did most of the Temple servants, from his own days at his post as a tax-collector for the Romans.

But they had all fled from the Garden, they told her, once He had told His captors to let them go if He was the one they'd come for. No one wanted to be there if the soldiers changed their minds. Poor Mark had even left his outer garment in their hands — fleeing naked into the night!

Once the Guard had hauled Jesus off to the High Priest's house, and it was plain that they weren't going to be pursued and taken with Him, they'd begun to make their way back to Him. John had been able to get into the palace itself and, spotting Peter following along, had gotten him into the courtyard.

They had brought Jesus to Annas, first. "That's when the Guard hit Him," John had told her, looking sick. "And all He'd done was tell Annas to ask the people who'd heard Him if Annas wanted to know what He'd said."

And then he had told her about the "trial" Caiaphas and his father-in-law Annas had conducted before the Sanhedrin. It had been a farce, with no witnesses to the charges they were trying to bring, but paid ones — and *they* had not been able to agree. It was only when they'd put Him on oath to say whether or not He were the Messiah, and He told them they'd see Him coming from the heavens, sitting at God's right hand, that they'd been able to move.

"Blasphemy, of course," said John. "That was the charge, and they made it with bells on! And then — then they attacked him and the guards joined in. They beat Him, they spit on Him, they blindfolded Him and punched Him, telling Him to 'prophesy' who had hit Him."

"But," Peter had interrupted, "it was while all that was going on that I failed Him. They asked me three times while I was out in that courtyard if I was one of His men — and I said I wasn't Said I didn't even know Him. I swore it! And then — I heard the cock crow. It was the second crowing, you know, the one just before dawn, and that's when I realized. He *knew* I'd deny Him, even told me when and how many times! And then — they had his hands tied, and they were marching Him out to take Him to Pilate, and — they brought him right past me. I looked at Him, and He looked back at me, right into my eyes. He — He wasn't angry, the way I would have been, or disgusted with me. I certainly was! He just looked so *sad*. It broke my heart."

The tears had come again. Mary thought that maybe there wouldn't be enough of them, ever, to wipe out that memory for Peter. She hoped there would be, some day. *She* certainly didn't blame the burly fisherman, didn't hold his failure against him, and she knew Jesus wouldn't. Wouldn't have, she remembered, wincing.

"Anyway," John had gone on, "at dawn, they marched Him out to take

Him to Pilate, so they could have Him killed."

The priests had made Pilate come out to *them*, John told her, so they'd be "clean" and would be able to celebrate the Passover. When Pilate had come out, they'd accused Jesus of stirring up rebellion, of telling people not to pay taxes to Caesar, and of claiming to be the Anointed One, a king, they said. When Pilate, who knew a jealous charge when he heard one, told them they had no case, they'd started to scream. This man had started spreading His poison in Galilee and now it was all over Judea!

"Well," said John, "Pilate just grabbed at Galilee because that's Herod's jurisdiction. He could send Jesus to Herod and let *him* deal with these people and their charges! So he did."

"Herod!" she had exclaimed. "That filthy man!"

"I know," John said, "but at the time I was almost relieved. I didn't think Herod could give out a death sentence, which is what the elders and priests were determined to have, so I thought Jesus just *might* have a chance. Pilate had already refused the case, so if Herod dismissed the charges, they'd have lost."

"Too bad it didn't work out that way," Andrew had said.

"Don't tell me Herod actually *can* hand out death sentences!" Mary exclaimed.

"Well, he killed John the Baptizer," one of the women said. "Why couldn't he?"

"John was a special case," said Thomas. "He'd been taken into custody, but he was never tried. It was personal — and that's how he was killed, so Herod could keep his word to a — well!" Glancing at Mary, he blushed.

"In any case," John picked up the story, "Herod couldn't get a word out of Jesus, couldn't get Him to do any tricks — miracles, you know — and I think that's what he was looking for. The priests were screeching away, trying to convince him that Jesus was a criminal who needed to die, but Herod just tuned them out. I guess Herod was getting bored. He likes some excitement, you know. So he and his guards started making fun of Jesus, dressed him up in lavish clothes — and then sent Him back to Pilate to deal with."

Pilate had not been pleased. The priests had gotten their second wind, and had recruited a mob they could use to scream and rant and threaten riot. They'd come back with their prisoner baying for blood, and the mob joined in.

Pilate had questioned Jesus at length and had evidently come away convinced that He was innocent, and that His accusers were trying to use

Rome to eliminate this uncomfortable rival for their power. So he'd been determined to free Jesus somehow, "or so it seemed," said John. But he'd reckoned without the persistence and wiles of the priests, who'd used their mob to good effect.

Pilate had begun by saying there was no case against Jesus. Then he'd offered to release Him as the Passover prisoner – gave them a choice of Jesus or Barabbas, a murderer. He'd been trying to appeal to the crowd, for he knew most of the people in Jerusalem who'd heard of Jesus loved Him. "I think," said John, "he hoped they'd turn against the priests and demand Jesus be the one released."

It hadn't worked. The priest-led portion of the mob had screamed for Barabbas, and kept on screaming, until Pilate began to get nervous. It looked as though a riot would break out any minute, and that would mean trouble, not only for Jerusalem, but also for him, with Rome. So he temporized. He found no case, he said, so he'd simply scourge Him and set him free.

"What was he going to scourge Him for, if He was innocent!" Mary had demanded, as if John had been Pilate. "That's the most utter nonsense I've ever heard!"

John had shaken his head. "I know," he said. "It's criminal! I *think* he thought he could appease the priests by punishing Jesus severely, *even though* he'd said there was no case – out loud and in public – and the priests knew perfectly well that there wasn't."

"Like a bribe?" asked Philip. "So they'd go away happy – or just go away?"

"I think so," said John, "because of what he did afterwards."

For the scourging, the soldiers had taken Jesus in to the Praetorium, to the punishment area, and had gathered the whole cohort. They'd stripped Him, scourged Him until there wasn't an unbroken bit of skin on Him, and blood covered him from head to foot. Then they had begun to make fun of Him. They'd dressed Him in a purple robe, set Him down, pushed onto His head a crown woven of thorns, stuck a reed in his hand, and then made their obeisance, greeting Him as "King of the Jews" with raucous laughter. They'd spat on Him, beaten Him over the head with the reed, slapped Him in the face – done everything they could think of to degrade Him.

It was after that, that Pilate had brought Him before the crowd. He wanted them to look at Jesus. He'd thought the ones who believed the priests and were afraid would *see* that He was no threat, if He had ever been one; would *see* that the charges had to be false. He'd thought the rest of the people, the majority he supposed, would be shocked and furious at what He had suffered and would rise up and demand that He be released. None of that happened.

"It was the priests and elders," John explained. "They'd worked up their people in the crowd to such a pitch, they'd scream for no reason. And the minute Jesus appeared, the priests started the chant, "Crucify Him, Crucify Him!" and wouldn't let up. Pilate screamed over the noise that the priests should crucify Jesus themselves, because *he* wasn't going to, but they turned it around. They told him that if he freed a man who claimed to be a king, he wasn't serving Caesar. And *then* they said that Jesus certainly wasn't *their* king, that their only king was Caesar! Can you imagine? Religious leaders in Israel *saying* Caesar was *their* king? Their *only* king? I looked over my shoulder to see if the Temple was still standing! Anyway, that did it. Pilate caved and ordered Jesus to be taken out and crucified. He didn't *like* it, but he *did* it."

"And that was when you came to get me?" Mary had asked.

"Exactly," said John. "I'd waited until then, hoping He'd be freed and I could bring Him back with me. But that didn't happen."

"I'm glad you came," she'd said.

"I knew you'd want to be there, to do whatever you could, and if you couldn't *do* anything, at least you'd want to *stay* with Him as long as they'd let you," John had answered simply.

"I thank you for that," she'd said, "and for staying with me all the way. I don't know how I'd have managed without you, in all that crush."

It had been dreadful. Thinking about it now, she got up, restless, and walked to the window for a breath of air. The moon had moved. It was almost centered in the window, and it seemed to have grown smaller, gotten further away. The day seemed to be trying to do the same thing, but it was not succeeding. Mary sat on the bench beside the window and leaned back against the wall, still gazing at the sky. She knew she was going to have to relive the day.

Just after the third hour, the thundering at the door began. Mary, working at her loom, had gone quickly to the window to look. It was John. She ran to let him in, her heart thudding. Something terrible must have happened, for the usually voluble young man was absolutely silent and white as her sheets. "What is it?" she asked, concerned. "John! Tell me what's wrong! Is it — is it Jesus?"

"They've arrested Him," John said woodenly.

"Who has?' she demanded. "John! Who has arrested Jesus? Where is He?"

Answering her last question first, John said, "On His way to Golgotha, to be crucified. It was the High Priests, first. They sent the Temple Guard, with some Roman soldiers, to the Garden to get Him. They put Him on trial, condemned Him for blasphemy, then took Him to the Romans so they'd execute Him. And they managed to get Pilate to pass sentence. Right now, He should be making His way through the city, carrying His cross."

The bald recital of the horrors was somehow steadying, she found. It left her with only the practicalities to deal with. "What route will they take?" she asked.

"The usual one," he said.

"Take me there!" she demanded.

They moved quickly, using byways and shortcuts that got them around the jams of pilgrims enjoying the capital during the festival, and were able to settle themselves in a secure corner before the first of the soldiers appeared, clearing the way for the following procession.

Catching sight of Jesus, at last, Mary drew a deep breath. This was worse than anything she'd been imagining. Blood was crusted on Him everywhere. Even His outer garments were rusty brown with it, and red blood still oozed around the thorns pressed into His head. Evidently He'd fallen, for mud mixed with the blood all down the front of His clothes, and He limped, though that was hard to tell as He also staggered with weakness under the weight of the cross He was carrying.

She raised one hand to Him as He came abreast of the spot where she and John stood, almost reaching out to stop Him. Catching the gesture, He turned and saw her. An odd expression came over His battered, bloody face, as if He wanted to smile at her and, at the same time, weep in her arms like a hurt child. She looked all her love at Him, but did not move toward Him, knowing that that would shatter His control. He gave her a tiny nod of relief and thanks. He knew she was there, that she always would be. That was all that really mattered – to both of them, she knew.

Mary stepped back against the wall and felt John's arm around her, gripping her firmly, supporting her while he awaited her decision about what they would do next.

"Can we get to the top of the hill before they do?" she asked.

"If we go the long way round," he said. "Sounds foolish, I know, but it'll work. If you want to, we can."

"I do," she said decisively. "More than anything in the world." She stopped. Then she added, "And, like you, least of all."

He gave what was almost the start of a laugh, and said, "Right. Up we go, then."

The moon had been moving steadily, she noticed, standing and straightening her back. Now it was almost to the edge of the window frame. When it had gone, she knew, the sky would gray and the new day would announce itself. "That bench is *hard*," she thought with a grimace. Seizing on the distraction, she looked around the room, then took a pillow from the bed and spent some time getting it on the bench to her satisfaction. Settling back down with a sigh, she went on with her agonizing retracing of the day.

The crucifixion itself had been indescribably horrible. Mary knew she had never seen anything like it, nor come near imagining it, though she'd known that the Romans crucified their criminals from the time she knew her own name.

It had been bad enough watching the two who were crucified with Him — their screams as the nails plunged through hands and feet and the cross–beams settled onto the uprights were beyond bearing. But watching Jesus, her baby, her dearest child, endure the same thing – that was in another world of pain she hadn't know existed until it swallowed her.

She hadn't thought about Simeon's sword, then. She hadn't had breath or attention to spare for herself. She had just suffered with Him, watching Him, unable to reduce the pain by so much as a fingernail's thickness. It had seemed this pain would never end and that nothing could be worse!

"Wrong again!" she thought. "On two counts. That pain *did* end – when He died. And what followed *was* worse."

Worse even than hearing Him give her away to John as his mother, with Salome, his own mother, standing right there, and give John to her as her son, when the only Son she wanted was Himself, hanging on that cross. That pain had been bad enough. It had been a pinprick compared to the rest, and she knew so, even at the time, but somehow it had seemed worse than all the rest. For it was her very self that He was putting from Him, the self she had given Him totally, with her consent to His birth – and now she had nothing left. Nothing at all. A tear had slid down her cheek and, for that moment, all the desolation of the abandoned world was hers alone.

Her mind had understood it, even then, of course. It was simple. He loved her and wanted her taken care of, and John was His dearest friend. So John was the only one He'd really trust to take care of her. The understanding had helped, though it had little effect on what she was feeling – bitterness, the pain of being put aside, rejection - but she'd been able to see that as a ploy of the evil one and thrust it aside to concentrate on *being with* her beloved Son in His agony and dying.

She'd leaned on John, and the young man had seemed glad of it, she'd noticed with a corner of her attention, surprised. With John, she'd watched Him die, breath by breath, the pain growing worse for Him, not better. She'd died with Him as He came to feel that even God His Father had abandoned Him, and her heart had supported Him, as He'd continued to trust the Love He *knew* was there, hidden in the death He was dying.

Finally, it had ended. It was in the silence that followed His last shuddering breath that she'd begun to breathe easily again.

That ease had ended and this new state had announced itself when they'd taken Him down from the cross, good Joseph of Arimathea and Nicodemus, and laid Him in her arms until they could get the linens spread with spices and move His body to its graveclothes. Then she had felt opening within her the same void she had watched Him enter, and perhaps had helped Him struggle through. Abandonment. Absence. Loss of meaning. All of these and more. And less. How could she survive this – death? Why hadn't she – couldn't she have, died with Him?

"I am utterly alone. I am useless," she said aloud now, tasting the words, weighing them for truth.

She found them false.

She wasn't alone, had never been. God lived in her, as He had always done, and loved her. And Jesus, Who, almost with His last breath, had stripped Himself of His only remaining comfort, herself – the very last of His private life on earth – to give her to John, had also given her, she supposed, to the whole band of His followers, to mother them all. They needed her. He needed her to do this for Him. And that was why she hadn't died, couldn't have. Though how she was going to learn how to feel again, she did not know, nor did she think, really, that she could go on without Him. She shook herself.

"Simeon's sword again!" she said. "But what's the point of this wound if there's no *me* left after it's done its work?"

And then, finally, she understood. All of it. Her *me* was still there, stronger than ever. Each sword thrust that had seemed to separate her from Him had actually drawn them closer, made them one on a deeper level. "And this one will, too," she said, "if I will have it so. And I will."

Still gazing out the window, she saw the first hint of gray lighten the horizon and heard movements below her. The girls must be getting ready to go out to the tomb to give His body a proper burial. Last night, she had given them the Magi's frankincense and myrrh, saved all these years, to use with what they had, for she knew their task was beyond her.

"He's in the tomb," she said now. "That part is over. Now we have to learn, together, to live His way without Him. We can't go back. We have to find a way to go forward. And we will. We will." As for the sword, she supposed its work in her would end only with her own life. And that was all right. Who could argue with the Father's plan?

Watching the backs of the women receding as they walked the road to the tomb, she felt a sudden stir of hope rise in the center of her being, like the uncurling green of the first leaf to break dead bark in spring, signing, again, the triumph of life over winter's death.

"I wonder," she whispered, hardly daring to breathe the thought. "I wonder! He did say, *'Destroy this temple, and I will raise it up in three days.'* [John 2:19; NAB] This is the third day! I wonder…?!"

[**Matthew 1:** 16, 18-25; **2:** 10-11; **12:** 46-50; **13:** 53-58; **Mark 3:** 31-35; **6:** 1-6; **Luke 1:** 26-56; **2:** 1-52; **4:** 16-30; **8:** 19-21; **11:** 27-28; **John 2:** 1-12; **6:** 42; **19:** 25-27; **Acts 1:** 14; **Galatians 4:** 4; see **MARY, mother of Jesus, Son of God**; see *MARY and the Mothering of God* and *MARY and the Quiet Time Between*]

# MARY MAGDALENE
## and the Questing Heart

For the third time that early morning, Mary Magdalene made her way down the road that led from Joseph of Arimathea's house to his new tomb. Two days ago, they had laid there the body of Jesus, their Master, Teacher and very center of their collective and individual lives. Of her life, anyway - that she was sure of. Looking ahead, she could just see the puff of dust Simon Peter and John, Zebedee's son, had left in their headlong rush to the tomb to verify with their own eyes the news she had run so fast, and so distractedly, to bring them.

She herself was walking slowly, still holding herself together so she could do this one last thing for Him, bury His body properly. But now there was this complication, and she did not know how long her enforced calm would last.

Complication! Well, that was a kind word for it! They'd gone to the tomb together, she and some of the women, carrying fresh linens and spices. She'd wrapped the Magi's gift, the jars of frankincense and myrrh His Mother had given her to use, in linen, then leather, and tucked them carefully into her sash. And then – the tomb was wide open! Its rock door rolled to one side and no body inside, just the graveclothes! Empty! No one around! That's what they had seen, the three of them, when they'd gotten to the tomb at the break of day. That was the *complication!* That's what she'd told the disciples, tears streaming unheeded down her dusty face and gasping for breath, not five minutes ago.

It simply could *not* be true. It was not, *could* not be possible, or – and she felt her control lurch dangerously. "I can't fall apart now!" she insisted to herself. "I *have* to find His body! I have to use this frankincense and this myrrh on Him and bury Him properly! His body *has* to be there! Has to be *somewhere!* Because if it isn't – if He isn't – !" and she felt horror wash over her, the ground open before her feet and herself begin to fall and fall and fall – .

She stopped in the road and held perfectly still. "Mary of Magdala," she addressed herself firmly, "Stop this! You are looking through the eyes of those seven devils He drove out of you, and if you keep on, they will blind and bind you as they did before. You've been healed! They're gone! But if you let them, they can come back, as He warned you. Hush, now! Remember

Him living. Remember how He healed you and how that felt, and how wonderful life has been since."

"Up until Friday," her listening self interrupted bitterly, and the ground began to open again. "Stop," she said steadily. "Just remember the healing, and let your feet keep on walking. Trust Him. He will not abandon you. He *will* be found. When has He ever failed anyone?"

"Never," her rebellious, terrified self admitted, and obediently she began to remember.

It had been two years ago. She had been suffering for ages, it seemed – not really ill, but in a misery for which there had been no visible cause, having no reason to want to go on living, and no real justification for not embracing the good life she had come to.

Her widowed father, who had found her a good husband, had died contented after a long life. She had mourned him, but with little sense of loss, for they had never been close. She had been his only heir and found, surprised, that she was now wealthy.

Then her husband, a wealthy widower nearer her father's age than her own, had also died. He had been kind to her and they were good companions, but he had never engaged her heart, so she felt her loss as a gentle regret rather than a heart-tearing grief. They had had no children, and the rest of his family had died before him, so she was, again, the only heir. That left her very rich indeed, and independent, in full control of her fortune and her destiny.

Women who knew her had told her frankly they envied her – and then returned to lives that seemed, to her, to be full to overflowing with people and responsibilities and meaningful things that only they could do. But there had been nothing in the world that she had absolutely *had* to do, and there had not been a single soul who really depended on her just to *be*. She had seemed to herself to be living in a thick, clammy fog that kept her from touching, or being touched by, anyone, or feeling anything. That "fog" had made the once solid world a place of dim, fearsome shadows, and the ground under her feet a treacherous bog that might open and swallow her at any moment.

That had been the start of it, and things had gotten worse. There were the symptoms of illness that had no cause any doctor could find – the headaches; the miseries of bowel and stomach; the sudden, lancing pains in every muscle that put her to bed, where she could not remain, for even her skin seemed to hurt; the sudden breathlessness when her heart would pound much too fast, she would pour sweat, her vision would dim and the room would spin. There were the dreams when she slept which were bad, and the dreams, or some odd state, when she was awake yet not awake, which were worse, for in them she heard voices and saw things that she knew weren't there.

And there had been, under it all, waking and sleeping, a leaden sense of hopelessness, helplessness, utter aloneness — and always, lurking unseen, just around the next corner, an absolute, nameless terror into which she would fall and fall and fall....

How long she had gone on this way, gradually worsening, she did not know. During that period, things had seemed to her disordered spirit *always* to have been this way, yet she knew there had been a time when she had been quite well, happy even, though that seemed, sometimes, to have been another person entirely. A person she could not find and could never be again. So, in desperation, she had kept on with her daily routine, seeing no sense in it, but feeling that, somehow, it kept her safe, from both the terrors and from dissolution.

That was when she had come across the Master. She had been passing by as He was preaching, hearing His voice as a background for her thoughts, and suddenly she had come to a dead halt, turned toward Him and listened with all her being. His words had cut through the thick fog she had been living in, and she saw the sun, the sky, the people, smelled the grass everyone was trampling, as *real* again. She felt alive — then, suddenly, in excruciating pain that threatened to tear her body apart. Waves of terror and hopelessness swept over her and she felt the sunlight fading, the sights and odors, sounds and feelings dimming out, though she was not faint.

She had felt, then, as though she would die and had known, with certainty, that there was not one single thing she could do about it. Yet, with dim surprise, she had found herself pressing steadily forward, toward the center of the crowd to where He was. She had not really thought He could do anything for her, did not think anyone could, but her feet had stubbornly carried her forward anyway. Eventually, she reached Him, stood before Him, her gaze devouring Him, pain and nameless, helpless longing flooding out of her like a fountain. She had said nothing. There was nothing to say.

Suddenly He had looked directly at her, then into her eyes, then straight into the depths of her being, and the world around them vanished. She had held her breath, her life in her eyes, her need crying out through her silence, and waited.

Still holding her gaze in His, He had spoken seven times, not to her but to each of the forces that held her captive. The dark powers that had refused to let her live for so long. He spoke with such authority that each of the seven was torn out by the roots, dismissed forever, and she was whole! Herself again!

The tears that had come as she stood there, gaze drowning in His, washed her clean and completed the restoration His words had commanded and effected in her. She could not remember saying, "Thank you!" even, but that hadn't mattered. He *knew*. And when He smiled at her, everything, *everything* was entirely all right.

Leaning on that smile, Mary smiled herself. "How wonderful He is!" she thought and opened her eyes – to see His ravaged tomb, gaping open to the sun, empty forever. The horrors of Friday and the miseries of yesterday, compounded by this senseless despoiling of His grave and the theft of His body, crashed down on her, and she began to weep as she felt her heart break again.

She continued walking to the open tomb, then stooped and entered. Through her tears, she gazed, hoping against hope, at the place where His body had been. Nothing, just as before. Only empty graveclothes. Then the "something different" she had seen and not seen demanded attention. She raised her eyes and saw two blurred figures, dressed in white, sitting, one at the place where the head of His Body had been, the other where His feet had rested.

She opened her mouth to speak, but they forestalled her. "Woman?" they asked. "Why are you crying?"

"Because they have taken away the body of my Lord, and I don't know where they've put Him," she responded, voice thick with grief. Shoulders sagging, she turned around to leave the tomb and saw the gardener standing in the open entry. At last! Someone who might know something! Someone who could help her. She took a step toward him.

He spoke first. "Woman?" he asked gently. "Why are you crying?"

"Oh, sir!" she exclaimed, energized, "if you have carried Him off, tell me where you've put Him, and I will take Him away!" Her hands gripped each other tightly, pressing against the jars of frankincense and myrrh. She held her breath and fastened her gaze on him, willing him to tell her what she needed to know.

The gardener smiled quietly, eyes somewhat moist. "Mary!" He said, extending His hands to her.

She caught her breath at the sound of her own name in His mouth, and suddenly everything changed. Not the gardener! Jesus! Alive! Calling her name! Caught between tears and laughter, she flung herself at Him, crying, *"Rabbouni!"*[John 20:16; NAB] She gripped Him in a fierce hug that made His ribs creak and winded Him.

He wept and laughed with her, then, easing her grip, said, "You don't need to hang on to Me so tightly! I haven't ascended to My Father in Heaven yet!"

She shook her head, laughed and released Him, but kept tight hold of His hands. There was so much she wanted to say, so much she wanted learn – but all she could do was devour Him with her eyes and laugh through her tears.

He smiled back, gave her hands a squeeze and said, in the tone He always used when He wanted a special favor, "Go to My brothers? Tell them for Me, *I am going to My Father and your Father, to My God and your God."*[John 20: 17; NAB] He did not add, "Will you do that for Me?" He did not have to.

Giving Him a smile that put the rising sun to shame, Mary of Magdala, restored to her own life by something she could do *for Him,* returned the pressure of His hands clasping hers, ducked her head to get out of the tomb, kilted up her skirts and ran for Joseph's house, her feet pounding out the rhythm of her joy-filled heart, "Alive again! Alive again! He *is* alive again!"

[Matthew 27: 55–56, 61; 28: 1–10; Mark 15: 40–41, 47; 16: 1–11; Luke 8: 2–3; 23: 49, 55–56; 24: 1–11; John 19: 25; 20: 1–18; see MARY MAGDALENE (see also MARY, wife of Clopas, SALOME, wife of Zebedee, JOANNA, SUSANNA, MARY, sister of Martha, Sinful WOMAN Who Anointed Jesus' Feet, MINISTERING WOMEN of Jesus and the Apostles)]

# MICHAL
## and the Dancing King

David? He might have been King in Israel and favorite of the Lord God and of every man, woman and child in the nation, but to me, on that day he danced before the Ark of God, he was nothing. Nothing at all.

Oh, I *had* loved him – I was besotted with him when I was a girl, to tell the truth! My father was very pleased with that, though I didn't know it. You see, he hoped to use me to trap David and destroy him. He saw David as a threat, even then, though all I saw was this gorgeous shepherd who played the harp like an angel! My! How I wanted him for my own! Until that day of the dance, I never once thought of what it would be like to be *married* to a man for whom God really *was* All in all.

And so it was arranged. David really didn't believe my father wanted him for a son-in-law. He *knew* there was no political advantage in it and he knew I was way out of his class by birth and by wealth, but when my father convinced him that all he wanted was the foreskins of a hundred Philistines for a marriage settlement, the poor innocent went for it. Brought back *two* hundred, in fact, and claimed me!

I was thrilled! My father was furious! He had come to hate David and that hatred increased as David won more and more battles against the Philistines. In fact, when David was playing the harp for him one night, my father tried to run him through with a spear. He missed and David fled, but my father sent his spies to watch David's house for his return so they could kill him. That night, though, he was with me in my room. I warned him about my father's spies and let him out my window so he could avoid the palace guards, and he vanished.

I knew he would need time to make good his escape, and I figured out just the way to give it to him! I grabbed the household idol, tucked it into my bed, made a wig of goat-hair for its head and covered it with David's cloak. Then, in the morning when my father sent the spies up to my room to capture David, I stood in the doorway so they could see around me but not get close enough to examine the bed. "He's sick. He can't go down to my father!" I told them and shut the door. My father sent them right back up with instructions to pick up the bed with David still in it and bring him back with them, so he could kill my David himself!

Well, that finished that! My father was furious when the agents told them about my ruse, and he turned on me. I was terrified! When he demanded, his eyes glittering and that spear in his hand, why I had betrayed him by helping his enemy escape, I lied. I told him David had threatened to kill me if I didn't help him. It was a lie I didn't really need to tell. If I had just been brave and kept my head, I could have done what Jonathan did – told my father that David was no traitor, persuaded him to send for David, something.

But I wasn't brave, and I think it was that betrayal, really, that ended my marriage to David. Because that lie changed everything – inside me. It poisoned me. I couldn't bear to see what I had really done, so I told myself – and began to believe – that my failure was really David's fault. If he had stayed and faced my father instead of abandoning me to his wrath and my fate, I wouldn't have had to lie, I told myself, over and over, so I couldn't hear my conscience saying, "Coward! Foolish girl! You've lost your heart's desire!"

Then my father married me off to Paltiel, the son of Laish – he was a dear man! He was as besotted about me as I had been about David, and he treated me as though I were High Queen, lavishing on me everything I could even imagine wanting, well before I'd even thought of it. Well, that's when the lie's poison finished its work. "This is the way a woman of my rank *should* be treated," I told myself, "and look at that peasant David! A filthy shepherd who abandons me to my father when I need him most! Just imagine what a *marriage* with him would really be like. I certainly wouldn't have all this!"

Which was true enough; Paltiel spoiled me, treated me like a cross between a beloved child and a goddess, though never like a woman and his partner. He never held me responsible for my deeds, never checked my failings, even when they cost him shame and money. He couldn't bear to hurt me, he told me, when my conscience made me apologize to him, occasionally, and ask why he was so patient with me and never scolded me for my foolishness.

But his refusal ever to find fault with me, even when I richly deserved it, did not teach me that I needed to grow up and take responsibility in this relationship if I wanted to be a wife worthy of the name. It only told me that I had done a good thing by betraying David, lying about him and embracing this new husband who was treating me *properly* by letting me do anything I pleased, even shame him, so much did he fear to displease me and lose my love. It was a bad situation, and I never guessed how much harm Paltiel's kindness was doing us both.

Then, when Abner arrived demanding my return to David, I was haughty in my displeasure, angry at David (and terrified to face him, though I couldn't afford to see that, then). Poor Paltiel followed us in tears until Abner sent him home; we'd gotten to Bahurim, I think.

And then David never sent for me at all! I was furious! How dare he! That peasant! And so on – you know how that goes. Anyway, I sat with the rest of his women and simmered, and David finished his conquest of Israel.

It was only when we were all in Jerusalem and David had decided to bring the Ark of God into the City for blessing and protection, that I finally confronted him – and sealed my fate. I was looking out the window with the other wives, watching the Ark being carried down the street – and there was David wearing only a linen loincloth, leaping and dancing before the Ark in an ecstasy of love and joy, welcoming God into His city.

Well! Just the sight of him – virile, alive, beautiful and so in love with God he shone – made me ache with a desire for him that scared me to death. It turned my carefully constructed world of lies upside down and inside out, and I couldn't stand it! I snatched at contempt and rage and hugged them to me, telling myself I was right to be angry because he was demeaning himself before everyone, not acting like a proper king, shaming *me*!

I stormed down the stairs and waited. When finally he came to bless the household, I went out to meet him and said to him coldly, "Well! You certainly did a good job of shaming yourself today, exposing yourself to the gaze of the slave girls as any peasant might do!" And I glared at him, waiting for an answer.

He looked at me, startled, then seemed to look through me, right to the depths of my soul where that first lie sat. His face grew sad, then stern as carved rock. I'll never forget his words. "It was the Lord God I was dancing for, not them," he said softly, "and, as the Lord God lives – the One Who chose me to be leader of His people, Israel, instead of your father and his whole family – I shall 'shame' myself even more and dance before Him again." Then his eyes flashed, and my anger died in their fire. "You may hold me in contempt," he said, grimacing as though he tasted gall, "but the slave girls before whom I 'shamed' myself by this dance will honor me." And he turned and started to walk away.

That was all. It was enough. I saw my lie for the betrayal it was and named it so, knowing I could never be forgiven for it, could never possibly be loved by this man who, of all men, my heart desired and my soul cleaved to. And I saw that without his love I might go on walking the earth, but I would be dead forever as *me*. I opened my mouth to say — I don't know what; it felt like a howl of misery — but it was too late. I could not call him back.

So, here I am, living in his harem, untouched, unloved, childless — longing for what I threw away in contempt and knowing, certain as stone, that he will never touch me again - my dancing, lovely King.

[**1 Samuel 14:** 49; **18:** 20-29; **19:** 10-17; **25:** 44; **2 Samuel 3:** 13-16; **6:** 16-23; **1 Chronicles 15:** 29; see **MICHAL** (see also **David's SERVING GIRLS**)]

# MIRIAM
## and the Younger Brothers

Miriam, prophet and an acknowledged leader of Israel's women, was out of sorts. It was hot – had been hot forever, it seemed – and there was sand everywhere it was possible for sand to be. "And some impossible places, too," she growled to herself. "Oh, how *tired* I am of wading through sand – sleeping on sand, cleaning with sand, *eating* sand!"

It had been two years since the glory days when they had walked through the Lord God's walls of water that her brother Moses had raised through which to bring them dry-shod to freedom, two years since they had watched those walls crash down upon the pursuing Egyptians and begun their march to the Land the Lord God had promised them, following the Pillar, Cloud by day and Fire by night – two years!

"And we're still not there!" Miriam fumed to Aaron, her younger brother by two years. "Just how long is this journey supposed to take!"

She wasn't expecting an answer, not really, and Aaron knew that but still he answered, "As long as it takes, I guess. The Lord God never said – "

"The Lord God never said a lot of things!" his sister interrupted sharply. "Like where this blessed land IS, for instance. And when we're supposed to get there! And what route we're taking!"

"Moses," Aaron began, but Miriam, in full flight, was not deflected from her complaint.

"Moses!" she snapped. "Don't give me Moses! I changed that boy's dirty napkins when he was an infant! Who do you think cleaned up after him when he spit up? Amused him when Mother was exhausted? Bathed him? Dressed him? *I* did – until he was three and went to the Pharaoh's daughter to be raised in her foreign ways. And *I* was the one who watched him when Mother put him in the river in that woven basket in the first place. *I* had the sense to speak to the Princess when her maids found him, and offer to get a "Hebrew woman" to nurse him. *I* was the one who brought Mother back to the Princess, so that we got to raise Moses ourselves and safely. *I* did all that! And what thanks do I get?"

Aaron was puzzled. "What thanks do you want?" he asked her. "Moses knows all that and he's immensely grateful to you for all of it. He's told you so, and more than once. What do you want him to do? Just what do you want?"

It was plain that he really wanted to know, and Miriam blinked. How could he be so dense? Between her gritted teeth she said, very slowly and with emphasis, "Respect. I want *respect* for all I've done. All I'm doing! After all, I lead the women — by their choice! They follow my lead. They consult me and have me intercede with Moses when that's what's needed. I keep them peaceful. And he doesn't even notice! He never says a word — not even 'Thank you Miriam. I appreciate your support.' Nothing!"

"Well," said Aaron, "I think — "

"And don't you stick up for him either!" his sister blazed. "He's just as rude to you! He acts as if you exist for his convenience — when *he* was the one who forced the Lord God to appoint you as his speaker! Has he ever even thanked you for that? Recently, I mean?"

"Recently? No. Why should he do that?" asked Aaron. "He thanked me at the time."

"Because it wasn't a one-time thing, of course! You've been working with him ever since!"

"And you think he should thank me every time I make an announcement for him? Miriam, that's — that's not very sensible, you know. I'm his brother, after all. I *know* he knows what I'm doing for him, and he *knows* I know. What's the point of making a big song and dance over it?"

Seeing that this objection was going nowhere, Miriam changed tack. "Well, I think he doesn't really respect us — either of us! After all, we're both prophets, too! Why doesn't he tell us what the Lord God says to him when they're alone in the Tent? Why doesn't he tell us where we're going, for instance, or how long we still have to travel — things like that. We're the leadership in this community, under him, of course. How can we lead if we have no answers for the people? Why, I bet the people would never have complained about the *manna* if Moses had told us he could call quail for them! And we wouldn't have lost all those people to the plague!"

Aaron shook his head. When Miriam was in one of these moods, reasoning with her was futile. But he had to try. "Moses tells us what he knows, if the Lord God allows it," he reminded her. "I don't think he *did* know about the quail. He just brought the Lord God the people's complaint about not having meat to eat. At that point, he was asking to die — said he couldn't carry the whole people on his back — and the Lord God was more concerned with getting him some help than with telling him His plans for the people. That's why we have the elders who are also prophets — to help Moses lead us in following the Lord God."

He had said the wrong thing, Aaron saw at once. Miriam's eyes grew wide and her breath came quickly. "That's *just* what I'm talking about!" she stormed. "Moses, Moses, Moses! Everything is Moses! Even the Lord God wipes the tears from his eyes and sees to it that he doesn't suffer! What about *us*?"

Aaron opened his mouth to answer her, but she rushed on, "And besides! The Lord God gave us a Law – through *Moses* – and *Moses* is the only one who doesn't have to keep it!"

"Miriam!" Aaron objected. "Moses, of all people, keeps the Law – as nearly perfectly as a man can keep it, too!"

"What about his wife?" demanded Miriam, still seething. "His *Cushite* wife! We're not supposed to marry foreigners, but *Moses,* precious *Moses* can! Is *Moses* the only one the Lord God speaks to? Hasn't He spoken to *us*, too?"

The challenge still rang on the air when Aaron stiffened and stared at Miriam, who stared back at him. The Lord God was summoning them and Moses to the Meeting Tent. Now! White with shock, Miriam ran for the Tent, Aaron close behind her, trembling. Moses, following his brother and sister, was puzzled at their agitation. What was the problem?

As they reached the Tent, the Lord God manifested Himself in the Pillar of Cloud and called Aaron and Miriam, who stepped forward, terror plain in their faces.

"Now listen to My words," He said. "I speak to the prophets among your people in dreams and visions, but to Moses I speak the way one man speaks to another, face to face, and I speak in plain language, not in riddles. I trust him with the whole of My house, and he *sees* the presence of the Lord God. How dared you speak against him, My servant, Moses, then?"

With that, the Pillar of Cloud and the presence of the Lord God abruptly departed. Aaron turned to look at Miriam and almost screamed. There she stood, a leper, her skin white as snow. He turned to his brother. "Moses! My lord!" he whispered. "Do not punish us for this stupid sin we are guilty of. Don't let her stay like this – like a baby born dead with half its flesh rotted away!"

Moses, staring horrified at Miriam, said at once, "Lord God! Please! Heal her, I pray!"

The response was immediate. "If she had only been spit on by her father, she'd be in shame for seven days, wouldn't she? Well, then, let her spend seven days outside the camp. After that, she may return."

On the morning of the eighth day, Miriam, her leprosy gone and her spirit much changed, slipped back into camp and went in search of her brothers. They found her, and before she could open her mouth to speak the apologies and promises the past seven days had shown her she owed, Aaron had hugged her tightly and Moses had embraced both of them.

"Are you all right, sister?" they chorused. "Miriam, are you truly all right?"

She laughed a little shakily, tears in her voice. "Oh, yes! Yes, indeed! My leprosy is gone, thanks to your forgiveness and prayer, Mos – my lord. And my heart is healed as well. I'm glad to be who I really am – your sister and your helper, both of you! And I promise that is what I will always be. If, that is, you wish it so?"

"Of course we do!" Aaron assured her. "Don't we, Mos – my lord?"

"We do," Moses agreed. "And so does the Lord God. That's why He gave us to you as little brothers, after all!"

[**Exodus 2:** 4-10; **15:** 20-21; **Numbers 12:** 1-16; **20:** 1; **26:** 59; **Deuteronomy 24:** 9; **1 Chronicles 5:** 29; **Micah 6:** 4; see **MIRIAM, sister of Aaron and Moses** (see also **JOCHEBED, Pharaoh's DAUGHTER**)]

# The PATRIOT WOMAN of Thebez and the Grasping General

Looking down from the Tower at the boiling of dust approaching the gate, the woman pursed her lips. This was not good.

"We've trapped ourselves," she remarked to the man standing next to her, an important figure in the town, she knew. "All Abimelech has to do is get close enough to set the Tower on fire and we'll serve as the roast for his victory dinner!"

"He won't do that," her companion assured her. "We can defend ourselves for longer than he can keep up a siege. Remember, we have the advantage of height!"

"Which means?" she asked

"Which means we can shoot arrows at him and kill off his men before he can do us any real damage. And we can throw things down on his forces and kill them off before they can kill us. No, you have nothing to worry about up here!" the man declared and made his way to a knot of important people near the center of the Tower.

The woman looked again. She saw the man's point, but she also saw, looking to where the archers were standing to fire, that the supply of arrows, while large, was not going to be enough to kill off every man in Abimelech's army. She also noticed that the arrows which went astray, as well as those which killed men, were being gathered up by the enemy for use by their own archers. She shook her head and made her way over to the knot of people the man had joined.

On her approach all conversation stopped and they greeted her politely. "We're in a trap," she informed them baldly and repeated her conclusions about the arrows.

"Don't worry," they told her. "We can outlast them. They'll be gone before we run out. Their supply lines are too long."

"They control the stream and the well," she reminded them. "What about water?"

"We have an ample supply stockpiled to keep us, if not in comfort, at least alive and fighting for longer than they'll stay."

"But when that's gone," she began, and they hushed her.

"Don't fret. It will be all right. Why don't you go and help the other women with folding bandages, just in case?" they said and dismissed her.

She went away, fuming. Such stupidity! Such complacence! Abimelech was not going to "go away" – not with this town unconquered. He was drunk with blood! Had he not just routed Gaal of Shechem and burnt the crypt of the Temple E-berith with about a thousand people of Migdal-shechem inside it? There was no way Abimelech would ever let poor little Thebez beat him!

Once more, she went to the important men. "At least," she said, when they finally deigned to look at her, "plan an escape route for us. I promise you, once Abimelech gets close enough to send a fire-arrow into the Tower's base, we're done for unless we have another way out besides the stairs. Or can you teach us to fly?"

That annoyed the men, and they shooed her away like a distraught chicken. The woman was furious. They were wrong, and by rights ought to be allowed to pay for their blindness with its consequences. "But I don't want to die with them!" she reminded herself, "and I, at least, can *not* fly!"

So she began to look around for a weapon, anything that might change the course of events. "Abimelech," she said to herself. "Concentrate on Abimelech. If he dies, so will the attack." Looking toward the center of the Tower where the lookout shelter stood, she suddenly stopped. "Is that – it is! The top half of a broken grindstone! But what's it doing here?" She went over to the stone and bent to shift it. "Possible," she murmured to herself. "Possible!"

Suddenly the noise of the crowds on the Tower as well as that of the attackers changed. Looking out, she saw Abimelech cleaving a path straight toward the vulnerable Tower door. Quicker than lightening, she snatched up the grindstone, caught her balance, hurtled with it toward the Tower's outer wall and, with all her strength, pitched it over.

The grindstone landed squarely on Abimelech's head with a hollow crash, breaking his skull as it drove his own helmet's fragments into the brain. In the shock of silence that followed, Abimelech's voice could be heard, begging his armor bearer to run him through with his sword, "or they'll all say a *woman* killed me!"

As the armor-bearer obeyed, the woman slipped back into the crowd which had begun to rejoice at the defeat of this enemy. She wanted no praise, no public notice. It was enough that her people had been saved and their enemy destroyed. *She* would know how it came about, and that was enough!

[Judges 9: 50-57 (see also **2 Samuel 11:** 18-24); see **PATRIOT WOMAN of Thebez**]

# Potiphar's WIFE
# and the Respectful Slave

Potiphar's wife was lovely — a breath or two past lush, in truth, but unaware of it. She loved to pamper herself, and her husband, who delighted in her and, truth to tell, could scarcely believe his luck in having secured her for himself, spoiled her, as she intended he should. Everything in her world was as she desired it, and if she saw anything she wanted, she had only to stretch out her hand and it was hers. All in all, an entirely satisfactory state of affairs — or so it had been until this Hebrew slave, Joseph, had come into the household and taken over its management.

Thinking of Joseph, Potiphar's wife smiled, rather like a cat thinking of a plump mouse. Now *there* was a man worth taking a little trouble over! Tall, ruddy, handsome, strong — she shivered a *frisson* of delight. She wanted him, no doubt about it. Well, that would be easily remedied.

The first encounter was not, however, exactly what she had expected. She had bathed and had her hair dressed with jewels, had worn the almost-transparent linen robe that revealed more than it concealed, serving, indeed, as a frame for her loveliness rather than its veil, and then she had approached Joseph, now the household steward by her husband's command.

"Mmm!" she'd whispered, hand on his shoulder, mouth near his ear (which blushed scarlet). "You're delicious. I could eat you up! Come. You shall know the delights of the gods. Come to my bed and love me!" She'd wafted a sigh into his ear that made the hair on the back of his neck stand up, she saw with satisfaction. She'd started to tug on his shoulder — and suddenly found herself facing him, no longer in control of the situation.

Very gently he had slipped out from under her grasping fingers and looked seriously into her eyes. In a tone cool as rocks before dawn, and about as yielding, he had said quietly, "My master worries about nothing in the household as long as I am here. He has given everything in the household — except yourself, of course, for you are his wife — into my care, and I wield his own authority over it all. How then, can I betray him by stealing you, his greatest treasure, from him? I would be condemned by God for such a sin!" And before she could catch her breath to answer, he had vanished to go about his work and she had seen nothing further of him for several days.

She was furious, of course, but that had only whetted her appetite for this magnetically attractive slave. "Denial is a sharper sauce for desire than satisfaction," her nurse had reminded her, but she ignored the old woman and began to plot her campaign in earnest.

Repeated invitations, direct or subtle, had had no effect. Joseph might as well have been made of glass, for they slid off his person without leaving a trace beyond somewhat heightened color and more rapid breathing – which could equally well have been accounted for by the heat. Mostly, she had not seen him, for he took good care not to cross her path if he could foresee doing so, and his foresight in this regard was becoming both legendary and a true nuisance.

It was time to take action! Potiphar's wife set up the plan that was to gain her success, she hoped, to take place on a day when all the household servants would be working outside the family quarters, within earshot of course, but not able to see anything that might happen. She dressed in her most alluring gown and, glowing with anticipation more than cosmetics, she stood in the doorway of her bedroom and waylaid Joseph as he came past. Clamping one hand on his shoulder, she said, a faint, enticing growl underlying the words, "Come now, my shy one. Make me the happiest woman on earth and yourself the happiest man who ever lived! Lay with me now!" She breathed the words in his ear and tugged at the fabric of his cloak.

Quick as a fox, Joseph whipped around, leaving the cloak in her hands and fled for the safety of the public corridors of the building. But Potiphar's wife had planned well, even for this shaming eventuality. She took a deep breath, threw back her head and screamed for all she was worth. "Help! Rape! Help me!"

Her servants tumbled out from everywhere, flooding the bedroom where she was standing, shaking, tears (of frustration, but they weren't to know that) streaming down her face, as she sobbed, "Look what that Hebrew slave my husband has brought in here has done to make fun of us! He broke in here and tried to rape me, but when I screamed for help he ran away, leaving his cloak beside me."

Soothed and put to bed by her nurse, she took good care to keep hold of the cloak, and when her husband came home, told him the whole story with all the considerable drama and pathos at her command, ending "Get rid of him, beloved! I never want to see him again!"

He believed her, of course, and firmly squashed his tendrils of suspicion in his great need that she be pure and wholly his, as he was wholly hers. Joseph was put in the royal prisons, and she never did see him again, at least not in their household.

She did not have to wonder, however, why that did not make her happy.

[**Genesis 39:** 7-21; **41:** 44-45; see **Potiphar's WIFE** (see also **ASENATH**)]

# PUAH, SHIPHRAH
# and the Thwarting of the Pharaoh

"But what are we going to do, Puah?" asked her assistant Shiphrah, wringing her hands. "What are we going to do?"

"About what?" responded the elder midwife.

"About what the Pharaoh told us to do! About killing the baby boys born to the mothers of our people!"

"What do you *think* we're going to do about it?" asked Puah, frowning in concern. "Really, Shiphrah, what kind of a question is that?"

"What do you mean?" protested the younger woman. "We'll be killed if we don't do what the Pharaoh says. But how can we kill all those babies? I certainly can't! Can you? And if you can't and I can't – what are we going to *do*? Because he'll find out we haven't! And I don't want to be killed!"

"Neither do I," said Puah, calmly continuing with the meticulous cleaning of her midwife's kit. "Now, Shiphrah, think! We both know that killing the babies is out of the question. It would be even if we weren't Hebrews, because we're midwives. Remember? Midwives help mothers give birth, help the babies to live and the mothers, too. Midwives do not kill mothers. Midwives do not kill babies, not in their mothers' wombs nor outside them. Right?"

"Right!" agreed Shiphrah. "But – "

"So tell me," interrupted her partner. "How do we stay faithful to our trust in this situation?"

"The only thing I can think of," admitted Shiphrah, "is that we just not to go to the Hebrew women when they are giving birth – but that's wrong too. Puah, there's no way out! What are we going to do?"

"You just gave the answer," said Puah, a smile spreading from her mouth to her eyes. "Blessed girl, you just gave us the answer!"

"What did I say?"

"You said that 'we just not go to the Hebrew women when they are giving birth'!" crowed Puah. "Well, we will go, of course – we have to. And we'll help with the birth. After all, we're midwives. But tell me, who will *know* we've gone? Or gotten there on time?"

"The husband," offered Shiphrah.

"Bah!" retorted Puah. "You know that most of them don't know if they're standing on their heads or their feet at that point! They're frantic about their

326 • ALL THE WOMEN OF THE BIBLE

wives, or terrified by the screaming. They vanish after they send for us."

"The maids, then."

"And you think another woman would tell tales, if we *said* we got there too late, that the baby had already been born?"

"Sometimes the husbands stay, though," Shiphrah objected. "What then? They won't lie for us. They're men!"

"And whose *son* is it that we've just let live? Of course they'll lie for us! And they'll make their households swear we never set foot in the tent until well after the first cries of the baby!"

Shiphrah thought it over. "Well, it might work," she said doubtfully.

"It will," Puah assured her. "Remember, the Lord God has a stake in this, too. We are His people, after all! And if push comes to shove, I think we're safer obeying Him than ten Pharaohs standing in a line! Watch and see!"

Puah was right, as far as the Pharaoh's order to the midwives was concerned. When he asked them why Hebrew boys were still being born and being allowed to live, the women claimed that Hebrew women were hardier than Egyptians, and that they gave birth before the midwives could get there.

The Pharaoh accepted the story – and changed his tactics. He ordered all his subjects to murder newborn Hebrew boys by throwing them into the Nile, counting on the discontent between the Egyptians and Hebrews to ensure his success. And that was the condition when Puah and Shiphrah were called to minister to Jochebed, wife of Amram, and mother of a girl, Miriam, now eight, and a boy, Aaron, six. They had delivered both children, and Aaron was one of the first group they "hadn't gotten to on time," so Jochebed was confident that, whatever happened, she could count on the aid of these two good women.

In the event, the child was a boy, and Jochebed planned to hide him at home for as long as she could. "And then?" asked Shiphrah, though Puah glared at her.

"And then," said Jochebed steadily, "I shall have to put him in the River Nile, like an obedient subject of the Pharaoh." She did not look unhappy, merely thoughtful. "The Pharaoh's law says the boy has to be put into the River Nile," Jochebed said, "but –
it doesn't say *how,* does it?" She held her breath, then relaxed as Puah's smile broadened.

"No," she said, "it doesn't say a word about how!"

For a moment they were both still. Then "reeds and bitumen and pitch" murmured Jochebed to herself, giving Puah a sidelong glance.

Puah smiled still more broadly and said to Shiphrah, "Doesn't Jochebed make a wonderful mother? So *prudent* and *clever*, even *inventive*! No wonder her daughter and *son* have grown up so well! I think we can count on this new child's doing the same, with *that* kind of care, don't you?"

Shiphrah had no idea where all that had come from, but she knew a "Yes, ma'am!" cue when she heard one and agreed heartily.

Come, then," Puah said briskly to Shiphrah. "We still have to check on Bithiah. She'll probably be overdue in the end, but we must check. The Lord God's peace be yours, Jochebed, and on *all* your family!"

[**Exodus 1:** 15–21; see **PUAH** (see also **JOCHEBED**)]

# RACHEL, LEAH
# and the Duping of the Bridegroom

"How can you be so dense?" demanded Laban's daughter, Rachel, of her sister Leah. She spoke in an undertone, but her intensity burned holes in the floor, it seemed to the older girl. "Jacob doesn't love you! He loves me! He has loved me since he laid eyes on me at the well the day he arrived. He rolled the stone away from the well, watered all our sheep, and then he took me in his arms, and kissed me!" Rachel flushed at the memory and a dreamy smile replaced her fierce frown.

Leah's mouth twisted slightly as she looked at her younger sister, but she spoke gently, "I know that, silly! He's also spent the last seven years working for our father, so that he can take you to wife. I also know," she went on before Rachel could interrupt, "that you love him just as much as he loves you. When the two of you are in the same room the rest of us might just as well not exist. He will have you for his wife, no matter what anyone may say. Or do," she added and braced herself for a storm.

None came. Rachel just gazed speculatively at Leah. "And father knows all this?" she asked quietly.

"Of course he does!" snorted Leah. "When did you ever know him to miss a bargaining point? Jacob will do absolutely anything for you."

"I don't understand," her sister returned. "What bargain? He's already served seven years for me!" Then, straightening suddenly, she fixed Leah with what her older sister privately referred to as her gutting knife look, the one that would get to an answer that satisfied her if she had to shift entrails to do it. "What other bargain was there?" she asked dangerously.

"None!" Leah assured her hastily. "At least, none that I know about." She turned to Zilpah, her favorite among her father Laban's slaves.

At once, the girl said to Rachel, "There were none, mistress. I promise! Ask Bilhah!"

Without waiting for a further cue, Bilhah, who was Rachel's favorite among the slaves, said calmly, "Rachel, you know there was none. You were there the whole time. This is something – else." She looked at Leah meaningfully, her eyebrows raised, and the older sister blushed. "You must tell her, Leah," the slave said, so softly that the words might have come from Leah's conscience.

Leah dropped her eyes, drew a deep breath and then met Rachel's eyes.

"This was our father's idea," she said, "not mine. He knows, and you know it too, Rachel, that you are the beauty of the family and I – am not. And I never will be. So my hopes of a husband are – they aren't."

"But," Rachel interrupted her, "but Leah, you're really nice – much nicer than I am! You're always patient and you always do things properly, and you never forget, and you're so kind, so thoughtful, so – loving!"

"When you're not pretty," her sister answered, the twist in her mouth more evident, "you have to be kind and patient and proper, and all the rest. You have nothing else to please a husband with. But he has to look at you first. And if what he sees sends him running into the wilderness, he'll never know what's inside, will he. So I won't be marrying," she finished, a knife edge entering her own tone, "unless this works."

"Jacob is mine!" Rachel insisted, pouting, which simply made her look bewitching. Leah sighed.

"Jacob is yours," she agreed with a nod, "and he always will be, as you will always be his. But I can become his wife, too, and you won't lose a thing by it. In fact, if you cooperate, he'll never know a thing about it until after it's over."

"But how – " Rachel looked at Leah, puzzled, going over the older girl's words. Then, light dawning, she said, "Oh! Right. I forgot about the wedding veil. But Leah," she challenged, "what about when morning comes? Because it will, you know, and you can't wear that wedding veil forever. And then what! He'll hate you, and he'll hate me too, for tricking him! No, I won't do it. I'll tell Jacob!" and she headed for the door. Leah grabbed her left forearm as she swung past and pulled the girl toward her as Zilpah snatched Rachel's floating veil and used it to bind her mouth.

"No, dear sister, you will not," grated Leah. "This is my only chance for a husband and I mean to have him – even though I will have only one night of unforced loving from him. I know perfectly well what will happen when morning comes." She winced, but went on steadily. "He'll be horrified when he sees me, not you, and furious that our father has tricked him. But I will still be his *actual* wife, whoever he *thought* I was. So he'll roar at Laban, but he will also have to bargain with him to get you as his second wife. And that is what our father is counting on. I'm not sure what else he wants from Jacob, but whatever it is, he'll get it, because Jacob really *will* do anything to have you. So Laban will be happy, and I'll be happy, and you two will be where you both want to be, married, with the approval of the family."

Rachel suddenly stopped struggling and Zilpah carefully released the scarf. But there was no shout left in Rachel, who was looking at the unthinkable and finding it only too possible. "Suppose," she said in a very small voice, "suppose he *doesn't* want me for a wife, once he's taken you? Suppose he *doesn't* really love me? Suppose he thinks I'm only a child! Oh, Leah, how could you!"

"And if he doesn't want you, what's the loss?" asked Leah briskly, though at the thought, her heart took wing and began to sing. "You'll be well rid of a man who has no spine, who won't risk our father's anger to demand what is his by rights – better to have that happen before the wedding than after! And you'll have no trouble finding another; a better man than Jacob, who *will* fight for you if he has to."

Tears slipped down Rachel's cheeks slowly. "But I love Jacob," she said.

Bilhah moved to Rachel and put her arms around the girl, who turned into the hug to weep, desolate. "Hush, now," she crooned. "Silly mite! To get so upset over something that will never happen, no more than a camel will turn green and produce coconuts for us! Jacob loves you, and no matter what happens, he will have you. I promise!" Over Rachel's head, Bilhah fixed Leah with a look of silent, implacable demand. "Won't he, Leah," she finished, and Leah found herself nodding, though inwardly she was about to scream with rage and disappointment as her half-formed plans to keep Jacob from confronting her father melted and vanished.

"Yes," she said calmly, "Jacob will have you, and you will have him, and you will both be happy." She struggled to control the bitter twist of her mouth for a moment, then, her face its usual placid mask, said gently, "And I shall be a wife, no longer an unmarriageable daughter, so our father will be pleased. But," she added, "we have to do it this way. Can you see that?" She held her breath.

Slowly Rachel looked up from Bilhah's shoulder. "Yes," she said, looking at her sister. Leah shivered. The look was one she had only seen once – an absence of living expression that betokened the departure of the body's life – and for an instant, Leah quailed. She was about to tell Rachel that they would not work their father's plot, that Jacob was hers alone and she could marry him tonight, be the consequences for Leah what they might, when Rachel spoke.

In contrast with her look of death-come-calling, her voice was steady and entirely practical. "You must wear the gown Jacob gave me, the one with the wilderness of flowers embroidered on it," she said, "and wear the veil that goes with it. Oh, yes, and my necklace!" She removed the silver garland with the enameled blue, red and yellow flowers from her neck and handed it to Leah. "Put it on," she commanded. "He knows I have never taken it off since he gave it to me, and that will guarantee to him that you are me. As for me, let me wear your yellow festal gown and veil. We are enough of a size that no one will recognize me, and I'll keep well clear of you both."

This was going to be the longest night of her life, Rachel decided as she helped with the serving, wearing Leah's unfamiliar robes. Even veiled, Leah radiated joy and satisfaction, and Jacob had eyes for no one else. He touched the necklace of flowers lightly and whispered something to his bride. Rachel ground her teeth, sorely tempted to upend the pitcher of wine over her sister.

"Remember, that's *your* dress and veil you're thinking about ruining!" Bilhah whispered to her in passing, and Rachel jumped. But Bilhah had always been able to read her mind, and this was not the first time that the slave had interposed a realistic, often ironic, comment between Rachel and her passions before she destroyed something really valuable. Catching Bilhah's eye, Rachel nodded, then concentrated on being Leah for the assembled family and guests.

All too soon, the bride and groom rose from the feast and retired to their bridal chamber in which they would spend the first seven nights of their marriage. Rachel gripped her self-control in both hands, endured the rest of the feast and helped with the clearing up, trying not to think of what was going on elsewhere. When, at last, she retired and Bilhah helped her undress, she was exhausted but nowhere near sleeping. "Suppose," she began, but Bilhah interrupted her.

"No point in it," she said. "You'll want to get a good night's sleep tonight, so you'll look your best tomorrow." At Rachel's open-mouthed stare, the slave grinned impishly. "You know perfectly well that, come the dawn, Jacob will be roaring at my master Laban's door, if he doesn't take it down altogether, and he will be demanding you for his wife, NOW! This time tomorrow night, you'll be sleeping with Jacob, or I miss my guess! You don't want to fret and cry all night – and for no reason at all, either – and then look as if you've been parboiled for your own wedding, do you?"

As Rachel began to giggle, Bilhah smiled. "That's my brave girl!" she said. "You've done well, so far. Now let's finish the job!" She popped Rachel into bed, pulled up the covers and kissed her. "Sleep well, dear heart," she whispered, and that was the last thing Rachel heard until sunrise.

She woke to see Bilhah in the doorway carrying a plate of fruit and bread. "Quick!" the slave hissed. "Up and dress! You have to take this to Leah!"

Rachel blinked. "What – why me?" she asked querulously.

Bilhah sniffed impatiently. "Haven't you been listening to all I've told you about your kin's etiquette for weddings and the wedding week? Only family may wait on the bride and groom, remember? And that's you! You certainly wouldn't want to disgrace yourself before the entire family would you?"

Rachel shook her head slightly to clear her thoughts. Morning had never been her best time. Automatically, she reached for her robe, and found the one she had taken off the night before. "But this is Leah's," she objected, and Bilhah all but stamped her foot in impatience.

"Of course it is!" she snapped. "Remember? You are Leah – at least as far as the rest of the family is concerned! And you have to get to the bridal chamber before Jacob rouses everyone in the house shouting at Laban, or everyone will lose face, and you will lose your bridegroom! Now hurry!"

Rachel's fingers flew as she donned Leah's gown and arranged her sister's veil to conceal her face properly. As she rushed past Bilhah, still in the doorway, the slave stepped aside and deftly slipped the loaded plate into her hands. "Hurry, now!" she whispered and Rachel nodded, moving as rapidly as she had ever done in her life.

At the door of the bridal chamber, she found Zilpah. "Am I glad to see you!" said the slave. "Jacob has torn out of here breathing fire! Hurry! Get in before he wakes everyone – no need for the world to know how he was tricked, or how desperate Leah was for a husband!"

Slipping in the half-opened door, Rachel accustomed her eyes to the dimness. "Leah?" she said softly. She peered around the screen to find her sister sitting up in bed, illumined by the single ray of sunlight that had worked its way through the tiny gap in the curtains. She had a robe about her bare shoulders, her hair was glorious in disarray and a beatific smile transformed her face. Rachel caught her breath. "Leah! You – you're gorgeous! I've never seen anyone look so beautiful, or so happy!"

"Loving will do that for you," Leah replied, "even when you know it's not really meant for you. Somehow, you hope it is – and then you forget everything – " her voice trailed off. Slowly the smile faded. "And then comes the dawn," she said, her voice flat.

"Was he very angry with you?" asked Rachel.

"No," she replied. "Not with me. Not at all. He got up and twitched the curtain there, you see? He whispered, 'At last we meet face to face as husband and wife, my beloved!' And then he turned around. I felt the sun on my skin, and I closed my eyes. I didn't want to see his face."

"What happened?" breathed Rachel, sitting on the bed beside her sister.

"For a long minute," she said, "absolutely nothing. I finally opened my eyes. I couldn't stand the waiting. He was looking at me, and his face was – just so sad. There was anger, a lot of it, but that was underneath. He met my eyes and said, 'Oh, Leah! I am so sorry, my dear! I wish I could be truly your husband – but I am Rachel's, and she is mine, and there's nothing I can or want to do about that.' And then," Leah gulped, tears streaming down her face, "he said 'We are married, of course, you and I, and you have given me much joy. This thing is not your fault. I shall not put you aside, Leah. But I will have Rachel!' Then he grabbed some clothes and flung them on as he ran out the door."

Rachel put her arms about her sister and held her as she cried. Then, hearing Jacob's roar, the sound of his fists battering Laban's door and then a sudden silence, Leah stopped weeping. Sitting up, she wiped her eyes. "And now the bargaining begins again," she said wryly. "Poor Jacob! He hasn't got a chance this time. He will have you for his bride, at once. But he'll never trust our father again. And somehow, some day, he will get his own back. I wouldn't want to be Laban when that day comes! Come on. We'd better put the chamber to rights. You'll be using it tonight."

As it happened, Leah was wrong, and Bilhah did miss her guess. Laban had no intention of allowing his trickery to become common knowledge in the family and the village, not so much to keep Leah from shame as to preserve his own reputation as a wealthy father able to provide husbands for both his daughters. So he insisted that Jacob complete the marriage week with Leah. "Then," he said, "I will give you Rachel, too, if you will work another seven years to earn her!" Jacob agreed grimly, determined that this was the last time Laban, or anyone else, would ever trick him. And he was right.

[**Genesis 28:** 2; **29:** 6-14, 16-35; **30:** 1-8, 9-21, 22-25; **31:** 4, 14-16, 19, 26-35, 31, 41, 43, 50; **32:** 1, 12, 23; **33:** 1-7; **35:** 16-21, 23, 24-26; **37:** 10; **43:** 29; **44:** 20, 27; **46:** 5, 15, 18, 19, 22, 25; **48:** 7; **49:** 31; **Ruth 4:** 11; **1 Samuel 10:** 2; **Jeremiah 31:** 15; **Hosea 12:** 12; **Matthew 2:** 18; see **RACHEL** and **LEAH** (see also **BILHAH**, **ZILPAH** and **Rachel's MIDWIFE**); see *DINAH and the Importunate Brothers*

# RAHAB
# and the Scarlet Cord

When the two men of Israel from Shittim came to the house of Rahab the Harlot for lodging, she grew thoughtful. True, Jericho was a growing city and drew all sorts, but these men were different from any she had met and entertained before. They were not particularly interested in her, for one thing, and they were extremely alert and "watchful," she said to herself. "They miss nothing of what goes by the house in the evening – take tonight – and they've been looking all over the city. They're not looking for someone, I'm sure, or they would have asked me, but they are. They seem to be *counting* things, looking at the walls and the city's defenses, and all the while moving with less stir than shadows. They're spies or I miss my guess! But who's paying them? Who would want to spy on Jericho, the Unconquerable?"

"Someone who wants to conquer it, obviously!" she answered herself, "and that leaves only one possibility. Joshua, son of Nun, a servant of One Whom Israel calls the Lord God Himself, is looking to take over the city, and these are his men. Not good!"

Rahab shuddered, remembering all she had heard about the Lord God and His dealings with His people, and with His people's enemies. You *really* didn't want to be on the wrong side of a quarrel with Israel; their Lord God was just too powerful. After all, He had parted the waters of the Sea of Reeds so they could escape dry-shod from the Egyptians who pursued them – and then hadn't He drowned every one of those pursuers when He released those banked up waters? And hadn't He annihilated the Amorite peoples of Og and Sihon from beyond the Jordan on Israel's behalf? If He wanted Jericho for His people, there was nothing anyone could do to stop Him.

"And if I can figure that out, so can the King, or his advisers, anyway. And they will, the second they spot this pair. I'm going to have to hide them tonight and get them out of town at dawn, or I'll be taken up with them and killed too! I hope I haven't left it too late!"

Giving herself no time to think, Rahab went to the room where her "lodgers" were and found them deep in almost-silent conversation. "You have to hide," she announced flatly. "Now! Your lives are in danger, or will be soon. Come with me!"

The two asked no questions. Exchanging a single glance, they moved as one, gathering their things with a swift economy of motion she admired, even as she swept them out of the room and up the ladder to the rooftop. "Under there," she said, gesturing to her drying racks, laden with long flax stalks, and they slid under as though they had been doing this every night of their lives.

She was just about to offer an explanation when a peremptory thundering at the door made her catch her breath. Lightly gripping the ladder's sides, she slid down to the floor (something she hadn't done since she was a child), hurried down the stairs and opened the door. Facing her were three burly Palace Guards, fully armed and not happy.

"Throw your *visitors* out in the street!" commanded the one who was plainly the leader. "They're spies! They've been checking out the entire countryside!"

"I can't!" Rahab cried in dismay, meeting the leader's eyes with absolute candor. "They *were* here, but they've already gone. When they asked me for lodging, I had no idea who they were," she explained earnestly, "and they left here just as the city gates were about to close for the night. I don't know which way they went from there." She kept her eyes fixed on the leaders, her expression one of helpless concern. "You'll have to go after them quickly, if you're going to catch up with them!"

Giving her a short nod, the leader said to his companions, "To the gates, now! They're probably heading for the Jordan fords." And off they marched.

Once the city gates had shut behind the soldiers, Rahab went slowly back into her house, her mind working furiously. This might just be her chance – the only one likely to come her way – to save both herself and her whole family from the death certain to follow upon Israel's invasion of Jericho. It all depended on "her" spies, and on how good a bargain she could strike.

Moving quietly onto the roof, she cleared her throat and said softly, "They've gone. You can come out." She saw no movement, but suddenly the two crouched before her, ready to attack, rush the stairs or settle for conversation. She did not move a muscle, waiting for them to choose their course. After a two-breath pause and a glance at each other, they settled as one man.

Rahab sat facing them. They were all, she noticed, tucked well out of sight from anyone on a neighboring roof and from the street as well. They looked at her, waiting, and she repeated to them the conclusions she had reached about the Lord God, earning a grin from the younger man. She ended, "Now, since I've done you a favor, I want you to do me one! Give me some signal or sign I can use, so that my whole family and I will be safe when your forces take over Jericho."

The elder of the spies nodded. "Of course," he said, "we swear – provided you don't betray us or tell anyone why we were here."

She shook her head impatiently. "Of course not!" she snapped. Then, in a business-like tone, she went on, "They've gone to search the Jordan fords, so you'll have to go into the hills and hide there. Three days will do it, I'd say. Then it'll be safe for you to ford the Jordan and rejoin your forces. Now, as for getting you out – that's simple enough! The window in my room is set into the city wall itself. You can slide down a rope attached to the window bar and be on your way now, while it's still dark, with no one the wiser. Will that do?" They nodded. "Let's go, then. The sooner you go, the safer you'll be!"

In the bedroom, the younger of the spies took charge of the rope, showing her the knot he was tying so that she could undo it again rapidly. The elder cleared his throat and she looked at him. "Here," he said, and handed her a broad strip of brilliant scarlet a yard long. "When our armies enter the city, tie this streamer to the bar of this very window from which we're escaping. That will be our sign to spare you and yours. Gather every member of your family and keep them in this house. I swear to you, everyone inside this house will be spared, and we will take the responsibility if anyone is harmed, but if any of your family leave it, they'll be killed, and their deaths will be their own fault. Of course if you betray us, our oath and responsibility end!"

"Of course!" she agreed. "I agree. Now, go quickly and safely!"

Nerves were fraying in Rahab's overcrowded house by the seventh day of Joshua's siege, and children were scrapping with one another as their elders fretted in their own fashion.

"You're *sure* they'll honor their pledge?" her aunt asked Rahab for what seemed like the four hundredth time in the past eight days. Getting a fresh grip on her temper and her manners, Rahab assured the old lady that the pledge would be honored, the red streamer would be seen, no one would be harmed and all would be well under the rule of Joshua, while under the flow of soothing speech, her own uncertainties rattled a bit, like pebbles in a moving stream. She hoped the siege would soon be over, and thought today might see the end of it, yet feared that very thing.

"What are they doing?" her mother asked, a tremor in her voice that startled Rahab. "Today they just keep on circling the city blowing that awful horn! They're on their seventh circuit, and it's giving me a headache! Why don't they stop?"

Rahab drew breath to answer — something, she didn't know what, was about to happen. She felt it. But before she could say a word, there was a tremendous shout from Joshua's army and the city walls seemed to fall in upon themselves, collapsing in a heap. Everyone in Rahab's house rushed to the windows on the side of the house that had been up against the wall to watch the invaders storming the city and speculate on how, and whether, Joshua would rescue them from the slaughter.

Then there came a thunderous knock at the door. Everyone shrank back as Rahab opened the it — and smiled. There stood "her" spies, dusty and blood-spattered but otherwise unharmed. "Joshua sent us," the younger announced with a broad smile, "so we could keep our oath to you! The scarlet streamer showed up like a beacon!"

The elder nodded. "Now," he instructed, "you're to come with us. We're to bring every single person in the house with us outside the walls to the camp, where you'll be safe."

"The city?" she asked hesitantly.

"It will be burnt to the ground with everything in it — except the treasure which will go to the treasury in the House of the Lord God. But you and yours will be safe, as you saved us."

"That will be enough and more than enough," Rahab agreed, and turned to organize her kin for the rescue. Who knew what tomorrow might bring? She smiled. The Lord God, of course! Who else?

[Joshua 2: 1-21; 6: 16-25; Matthew 1: 5; Hebrews 11: 31; James 2: 25; see RAHAB (see also Rahab's MOTHER and SISTERS)]

# REBEKAH
## and the Camels of Courtship

It seemed to Rebekah entirely amazing that she should find herself riding on a camel in the middle of the desert wearing a half-shekel-weight gold ring in her nose and two five-shekel-weight gold bracelets on her arms, when, two weeks ago, she had assumed her world ended at the well and always would.

Two weeks ago, she was only the younger sister of Laban, charged by her mother with going to the well for water and helping with the household chores. She was looking forward to being married to whichever man her father, Bethuel, selected for her. "Or that Abba was pushed into choosing by Laban!" she added to herself realistically. Her brother was bossy as he could be but, much as she sometimes resented what she thought of as his arrogance in managing the family, he had a gift for choosing the paths and courses of action that would bring them all the most profit with the least grief. For that his father valued him, and she and her mother held their tongues.

"But that was ten days ago!" she reminded herself. "That was before I went to the well and gave a drink of water to that leathery old traveler I felt so sorry for and watered his camels. And he turned out to be the servant of Abraham, my Abba's father's own brother! And he was looking for a bride for Abraham's son Isaac! And that turned out to be *me*! Who'd have thought watering some camels for a stranger, and that's just ordinary hospitality, would bring me such a golden opportunity, thanks to the Lord God! *And* I've taken it! My, how the world has changed!"

She bounced a little in her delight, then settled back into the rocking rhythm the camel's steady pace set up, savoring for the hundredth time on this journey just how it all had happened, and shivering a bit at how nearly it had not.

The day had been hot, of course. It always was. But in this area, Aram of the Rivers they called it, there was water in plenty, and Nahor, their town, named for Grandfather, had a capacious well. No one worked during the heat of the day, except for the women of course, but they only did the gentle labor that could be accomplished indoors. The young women went to the well to draw their water early in the morning, returning to draw more in the early evening, and it was then, as the sun was setting, that Rebekah had met the traveler there, dusty from his desert journey.

"Suppose cousin Hannah or cousin Miriam had gotten to the well first," Rebekah mused. "One of them could be here riding my camel, going to marry my Isaac!" Then she shook her head and said under her breath, "No. That would never have happened. Even if the servant had learned about Hannah and Miriam, it wouldn't have changed a thing. I'd still be riding this camel, wearing this gold, betrothed to Isaac, no matter what." Her eyes narrowed and her mouth firmed. "I don't know how, but I would have managed it and no one would have stopped me. Isaac is mine!"

Then, her fears forgotten, her eyes brightened with curiosity. "Isaac – I wonder what he looks like. I wonder if he'll like me!" She paled a little at the thought, but then relaxed, smiling with the simple confidence of a child who had, for all of her short life, been the cherished center of her family and the delight of all who knew her. "Of course he will! Everyone likes me! Why would he be different?"

Briskly she shook her head. "What nonsense you do waste your time with, Rebekah!" she told herself, amused. "As Abba is forever saying, the Lord God is in charge, and nothing but what He wants is going to happen. Relax!" And, remembering the scene at the well, she began to chuckle quietly, nodding.

It seemed, from the story the traveler told the family later, that her perfectly natural gesture – giving this parched traveler water from her pitcher to drink, and watering his ten camels for him – was precisely the sign he had asked of the Lord God to point out the bride He had chosen for Isaac. Even the words she had said were the right ones, and she hadn't known a thing about it! When she had finished watering the camels, the traveler had pulled out the gold nose-ring and bracelets and put them on her, to her open-mouthed astonishment. Then he had asked her father's name and whether there might be room at her father's house for him, his companions and his camels to spend the night.

"I'm Bethuel's daughter," she had answered promptly, if somewhat breathlessly. "He's Nahor's son? The one who's Abraham's brother. His wife – my Grandmother – is Milcah. We've got plenty of room for you and your people, and for the camels there's plenty of straw and fodder, much as you need." Before she could add, "I'll tell my father you're here so he can come to greet you properly," the traveler had bowed his head to touch the ground and begun to pray aloud.

"Blessed be the Lord God of my master Abraham!" he exclaimed. "He keeps on showing such kindness to him!" Rebekah had backed away, startled, and as the man continued, "It is He Who has brought my footsteps to the home of my master's own brother." She ran for the house to tell her mother what had happened, leaving him there by the well with his companions and his camels, his face to the ground.

"That was rude of me," she thought now. "But, really, what could I do? The other girls had left, so I couldn't ask one of them to take a message, and that would have been wrong, too. Family business needs family to do it. Anyway, it all worked out." She began to grin. "Laban almost split himself in half when he heard my story and saw all the gold I was wearing!" she chuckled quietly. "He wanted to run to the stranger to find out what was *really* going and, at the same time, run to my father to tell him what to do. As if Abba would have needed that! He spoils Laban, letting him be so bossy. Abba always does what's right, and with none of Laban's pushiness."

Laban had run out and brought the stranger and his camels home, acting, thought Rebekah, as if he had invented hospitality and owned everything in the house. "He did shake down the straw for the camels and give them fodder," she admitted, "but the way he ordered mother and me around! You'd think mother had never seen a guest, and that I was a half-wit who knew nothing about feeding people! Ooh! He makes me so angry!"

Rebekah laughed aloud. "And now who's he going to boss around!" she crowed, but silently. She didn't want to shock her escort, or let them think she was less than a lady, for then her great-uncle's servant might change his mind and turn around and take her back to her father and mother, finding her unfit to be Isaac's bride. And *then* what would she do!

"I don't think he can do that, though," she thought. "According to what he told us, he had to swear to Abraham to bring home a woman of Abraham's own kin to be a wife to Isaac. And he's made the commitment to my family for me so, even if he did come to think I'm not as perfect as he seems to think I am, he really couldn't renege. Of course, he *might* come to learn that I'm not the only one of marriageable age still unpromised among the children of Nahor's twelve sons – though I'm certainly not going to tell him! But still, it would be very awkward for him to change his mind now, even if Laban would let him. And Laban never, ever, lets go of something, once he has it in his hands. No, no danger there."

She blinked. "What am I getting so upset about?" she wondered. "Here I *am*! I've said I'll marry Isaac, and the servant said that by the terms of his oath, if the woman agreed, he had to bring her back to Canaan with him. It was only if the woman said no that he would have been free of his oath. And I certainly said yes! Catch me saying anything else! This is my golden opportunity! But that was a near thing, come to think of it," she mused, "and

I never saw the danger until it was almost too late!"

Everything had been just fine that first evening, of course. The servant told his story and even Laban could see the hand of the Lord God at work in it. Her father had been pleased. Her mother had not been visibly unhappy, though she hadn't exactly been thrilled at the thought that her grandchildren would be living halfway to nowhere, in far Canaan

Rebekah shifted to a more comfortable position on the camel's back and went on remembering. "I wish Abba had done the speaking, though, instead of letting Laban take over," she muttered, still angry as her brother's interference. "I suppose he would have had to stuff a camel-blanket in Laban's mouth to shut him up, though, and that would hardly have done!" But at least Laban admitted that this was the Lord God's choice, and no one had the right to contest it. Although she was sure the servant's rich gifts to him and Mother had something to do with that! And he didn't try to be anything more than their father's obedient voice — not then. Rebekah tried to be grateful for that, with minimal success as the memory of the next morning burned up in her.

That was when things had almost come unraveled. She felt a chill run down her spine at the recollection. At breakfast, the servant had asked to take his leave and Rebekah had jumped up and run for the baggage she had spend a good part of the night packing — all the gifts the servant had given her from Isaac, with all the things of her own she was unwilling to leave behind. Then Laban, "that snake!" she hissed, still furious, had used their mother to try to take control of the situation. "He just wanted more gifts, or money from the servant, or a bribe, or something," she fumed, still silently. "Maybe he just wanted to be mean! Or to make trouble for me — just because he could! Or maybe he even wanted to prevent the marriage altogether, so he could keep me under his control! And he could have," she acknowledged. "Abba wouldn't ever fight him, even for my sake."

Fortunately, as she neared the door, carrying her three bags, she had caught the tone in her mother's voice that announced that what she was saying were not her word but someone else's, even before she could distinguish the words. Obediently her mother had been reciting, "Do, please, let the girl stay on with us, just for a few more days — maybe ten? Then she can go with you."

Ten days! Rebekah had stopped short, just out of sight of the people in the room, horrified. That meant indefinitely, she knew; it was a bargaining ploy with which she was familiar, though instead of shekels they were using time. Who was trying to interfere with this marriage, with her life? Suppose the servant of Abraham refused to have her for Isaac's bride because of their greed! She was about to thrust herself into the room, screaming in rage, when she heard the servant's quiet voice, steady, smooth and implacable as the force of the Great River. "Don't hold me back!" he warned them. "It is the Lord God Who has given success to my quest. Now, allow me to depart from you and go back to my master."

Though the words were phrased as a request, they were really a command, and their power was that of the Lord God Himself. Rebekah heard her mother's gasp, almost covering Laban's unmistakable "Tch!" of disapproval curbed by fear. She took a fresh hold on her bags and stepped forward, drawing breath to shout at them all, demand her rights, denounce them all for cheats – do *something* to prevent their spoiling her golden opportunity and ruining her life! Then she heard Abba clear his throat. "Why don't we call the girl and ask *her* what she thinks?" his quiet suggestion as much a command, as one enforced by a sword.

It was as if someone had poured a jar of cold well water on the company. Everyone froze in shock, except Rebekah, and as someone, her nurse probably, broke free and called her name, she was already striding into the room, bags in hand, lips compressed, her whole being shining like a burnished knife blade. She glared at them all, then focused on Laban. If a look could have done the work, Laban would have become a grease spot on the floor!

Taken aback, her brother had looked away and glanced to their mother, who gave him a single unreadable look, modestly dropped her eyes and began to smile, slowly and with utter satisfaction. Shocked, Laban had turned to Abba, who regarded him impassively, with something almost like contempt, and then gave him the customary indication that he should speak for the family – very carefully.

Laban had drawn a deep breath, then blown the air out through his mouth without speaking. Then, almost diffidently, he asked her, "Do you – want to go with this man?"

"I do!" she had announced, her voice golden and sure as a blare of trumpets, declaring war on anyone foolhardy enough to step between her and her marriage. She seemed to blaze with triumphant joy and utter determination, and Laban, meeting her eyes, understood, however unwillingly, what those eyes were telling him. Here was a woman who would never be his, or anyone's, to command. For love, she might do anything, but not for fear, and to anyone who might think to threaten, or use, or control her or hers, she was an enemy to the death. And she would win. She would always win.

Involuntarily, Laban had stepped back a pace, then shrugged and, his hands down, palms open in entreaty, had turned to Abba. Her father had nodded quietly and begun the traditional blessing with a special smile for her. *"Increase to thousands and tens of thousands! May your descendants gain possession of the gates of their enemies!"* [Genesis 24: 60; JB]

Then he directed Deborah, Rebekah's old nurse, to go with his daughter and stay with her in Canaan, an order that made the old woman smile with delight and hurry to get her few possessions. Truth to tell, Rebekah and she had hoped this would happen and they had packed for the nurse as well as the bride. In less time than she had imagined, Rebekah and her nurse were mounting their camels and waving to the rest of the family as the group took its leave.

"And that's how I got to be riding on this camel wearing all this gold!" she smiled. Suddenly, she looked up. They had come to the fields near the well of Lahai Roi, and Rebekah saw someone approaching them on foot. She dismounted from her camel and tugged on the servant's sleeve. "Who is that man walking through the fields to meet us?" she asked, breathless, and the servant smiled.

"That is my master," he answered, and Rebekah covered her face. It couldn't be Abraham, she knew, for this was a young man. It had to be Isaac. She arranged her veil so that she could see his features, and she watched him as the servant told him the whole story. Acted it out, really, she thought. "That's Laban to the life, being pompous, and that's mother, and that is Abba."

She all but laughed out loud as she caught the twinkle in Isaac's eyes at the perfectly proper and entirely irreverent report he was receiving. "He's going to be a wonderful husband," she thought, "and what fun we'll have!"

Isaac turned to her. He held out his hands, and she stepped forward, head held high, smiling with all her being, as if he would be able to see her joy through the veil, and put both of her hands in his. "Come," he said, his voice like complicated music, "Rebekah, my wife! Come with me!"

And she did.

[**Genesis 22:** 23; **24:** 15-67; **25:** 20-28; **26:**7-11, 35; **27:** 5-17, 29, 42-46; **28:** 2, 3, 5; **29:** 12; **35:** 8; **49:** 31; **Romans 9:** 10-13; see **REBEKAH** (see also **DEBORAH, nurse of Rebekah, Rebekah's MOTHER, Rebekah's MAIDS**); see *REBEKAH and the Golden Opportunity*]

# REBEKAH
## and the Golden Opportunity

Alerted by the rumble of voices, Rebekah, wife of Abraham's only son Isaac, mother of twin sons Esau and Jacob, moved to the slit formed by the edge of the curtain closing off the kitchen area and the tent wall proper. She could not really see, but that didn't matter in this case, for she recognized the hearty voice of Esau, unnaturally subdued by the presence of his father and the instructions the old man was giving him.

"Son, it is time," Isaac was saying. "At my age, there's no telling when I will die. So go and hunt, then prepare me a dish from the meat you kill so that I may eat and bless you, my firstborn!"

"Yes, father. Right away father!" said Esau obediently, sitting firmly on a whoop of delight. He headed for the outdoors all but running.

Rebekah stepped back, her eyes alight. This was it! This was the golden opportunity she had been looking for since the boys had grown enough to develop their own characters and she had discovered that, where Isaac, never a warrior himself, admired the first born of the twins, who was physically all his father had never been, she herself preferred Jacob who, to her eyes, was his father's very self when Isaac had been his age — well before she had met and married him.

The thing was – the Blessing of the Firstborn was irreplaceable and only one son could receive it, for with it he would also receive power over the whole clan, including his twin and his twin's offspring, and that forever. Getting Jacob in to Isaac with a dish prepared as he liked it was no feat. Getting Isaac to accept Jacob for Esau was going to take every scrap of cunning she and Jacob possessed between them, for Isaac, though blind in his old age, was far from his dotage and would be suspicious of Jacob's trying this very trick.

"Why do I bother?" she asked herself. "Why do I interfere? Why am I helping Jacob obtain the Firstborn's Blessing which is Esau's by right?" She remembered the glee with which Jacob had come in to her some years earlier, whispering the "great news" that he had just purchased that blessing for a dish of lentils from an impatient Esau, wet and hungry after a long, unsuccessful hunt.

"You can't do that!" she had protested, even as her heart rose up in hope. "Esau can't sell what he hasn't gotten, and once he has it, it's too late!"

"But Mother," he had answered quickly, "I have the *right* to the Blessing now. He sold it to me! So if I can just get in to Father and *get* it, it will be mine in fact as it is in right! It's a golden opportunity in the making, isn't it?"

She had had to agree. The phrase "golden opportunity" had been her own, the phrase she had always used to describe to the boys the process by which she had come to marry Isaac and they themselves had been born. For when her family had tried to keep her from going with Abraham's servant to be Isaac's wife, and they had been forced to ask her if she wanted to go with him there and then, she had said instantly, "Oh, yes, please!" – and she was already carrying the bags she had packed the night before. "Just in case," she always said when she told the story, "my golden opportunity would leave without me in the morning if I were not ready! Be ready," she had always ended the tale, "for you never can tell when your golden opportunity will show up at the door!"

She shook her head, thinking of the wondrous, and sometimes peculiar, unfolding of her own golden opportunity, that had brought her to this morning and this – dilemma. The memory always had the power to calm her, no matter what was going on, and she entered it willingly now.

The wedding night had been wonderful. The next morning Rebekah awoke slowly, aware first of a strand of music dancing somewhere within her, and then of a warm presence beside her in the darkness. As her eyes took in the details of the tent, the rest of her memory replayed last evening for her – the splendid feast which followed the warm bath and donning of fresh garments, all the happy people who were intent on greeting her and making her feel welcomed, and Isaac! He was beside her at every turn, it seemed, focused entirely on letting her know how wonderful he thought she was, but without using words that he preferred not to speak in company. She could see them, though, hear them in the center of her being, and she returned her own in the same way, as well as she could.

The words came later, after they had been led to their tent and left there by the servants, smiling at them with knowing looks. "Beloved," Isaac had begun, and she had replied with singing joy, though what he had said and what she had answered were gone from her mind as they faded from her hearing. And then had come their marriage union – a splendor she had never imagined could happen to anyone, and a fulfillment that left her more fully alive than she had ever been before. Rolling over to look at Isaac that next morning, she had found him already awake, watching her. "Good morning!" they said together, then laughed at the chorus they had made.

"So, we are truly married!" Rebekah said.

"That we are, my dearest one," Isaac answered her with a smile that made him radiant as she. "Can you doubt it?"

"Only that it was so much – so very – so wonderful! And it's for always!"

"Yes!" he laughed, "for always!"

"And when will the children be born?" she asked him.

Isaac blinked at that and looked sharply at her to see if she were serious. "Ah," he began, uncomfortably, reddening "like a boy – and he's forty years old!" she thought, amused, then, aloud, hastened to assure him.

"Oh, I know about pregnancy and all that," she said. "Nine months, more or less. But I don't know about conception. Did we, do you suppose, last night? I don't *feel* any different, but I don't know how I'm supposed to feel – except for morning sickness, but that comes a bit later."

"Can't help you out there," Isaac answered with a smile. "That's one of the things they never tell us! And you're my first and only wife, so – I guess we'll have to learn together."

"And meanwhile, wait and see, I suppose," she said with a small grimace of distaste. "Oh, how I wish things were settled! I want to know now! I'm not very good at patience, I'm afraid."

"Now you sound like my mother!" he told her, laughing. "She was always complaining about her own impatience – and she was right! Anyway, since we have no choice," he went on, "let's get some breakfast, and then we can work on getting to know each other while I help you explore this new world you've come to."


And that's what they had done. Isaac was a wonderful teacher, Rebekah had discovered as the weeks and months passed, eager to show her all he had built in this settlement near the well of Lahai Roi since the death of his father Abraham, eager to tell her all about his branch of their family with its complicated history. In her turn, Rebekah had talked about Bethuel and his eleven brothers, her uncles and their families, her cousins, about her brother Laban who was not yet married, and about their mother whom she missed more than she had realized she would.

And of course, wherever the talk began or wandered, there was the presence of the Lord God, a presence Isaac cherished and Rebekah respected but found that she did not entirely trust. She had had no direct dealings with Him herself, nor had any of her people as far as she knew, though, of course, they all respected Him. And that, she thought, must be the difference. How could you love Someone you didn't really know?

That there were no children did not weigh on Rebekah as, apparently, it had on Sarah. "No children means the Lord God can't test us by taking them away," she frequently reminded herself, remembering Isaac's hideous ordeal at the hands of his father Abraham. "Maybe even kill them! I could never stand that. Better not to have them than to lose them."

Of course she had given no hint of that lingering mistrust of the Lord God to her beloved Isaac. "It would only worry him," she told herself. Usually, she concealed it even from herself. And when, marveling at her unfailing sweetness of temper with him and everyone else, in spite of this burden of barrenness, he asked her if she were worried, all she would say was, "In the Lord God's time, He will send us children, love. No use getting all worked up over it – that will only make us miserable, and from what you've told me, it won't make Him hurry. When the children come, it will be marvelous but, until they do, we have each other. What is there to complain about?"

And then, as their twentieth year of marriage started, it had occurred to Isaac, as he told her afterwards, that it might just be that the Lord God was only waiting until they asked for a child before He sent them one. So he had gone to the Lord God to ask for an end to Rebekah's barrenness and the gift of their child, the next generation of the promised descendants of Abraham. He had been right, it seemed. Rebekah had conceived shortly afterward, and they rejoiced as though the world had been newly recreated for their private delight!

Their joy lasted until the child quickened in her womb and proved to be, not one, but two, and two who were, apparently, at war with each other. Vividly remembering those days, Rebekah shivered slightly, even as she laughed quietly. Her morning sickness had been spectacular.

"This," said Rebekah, collapsing on a bench by the empty hearth and wiping her mouth after her third trip out doors to empty her stomach that morning, "is ridiculous. These children will tear me apart if they don't dismember each other, and they roil so I can't keep a thing down! And I have how many months more of this? There's got to be a better way – " and she dashed for the door again. Isaac followed her this time, bringing with him a dampened cloth and a cup of cool water just touched with lemon.

When he reached her, she said, "Dry heaves. I knew I couldn't have anything left! Oh, a wet cloth! You dear man!" She wiped her eyes and face, then cleaned up her mouth. "And lemon water! Marvelous!" She rinsed her mouth, wiped it with a clean corner of the cloth and then took the smallest of sips from the cup. "Maybe that'll work," she said, then looked at her husband. "Ouch!" she exclaimed suddenly, glancing down. "That hurt!" Then looking again at Isaac, she said, "Love, we've got to do something. I can't stand much more of this. I think," she continued as he was drawing breath to answer, "I'll go to consult the Lord God myself. These are the children He's giving us, after all. He surely can tell me what to do!"

Isaac closed his mouth with a startled expression. Then, a smile spreading over his face he said, "Excellent idea, my dearest love! Do you need me to go with you?"

"No," she returned briskly. "I know exactly what I need to know. I'll do it." And she headed off to the cave near them, where Isaac had always gone to pray.

Once there, settling into the dim stillness, Rebekah felt her desperation fade away, taking with it her constant nausea and seeming to still the struggling children growing in her womb. She relaxed and, finding no words, simply opened herself to the Lord God, *being* the questions she wanted to ask, and waited. Time passed unremarked. Then, into the pooled quiet she had become, His words had fallen, one by one, each a drop of distilled peace, though the message as a whole was disturbing. "There are two nations in your womb," He had said. "Your issue will be two rival peoples. One nation shall have the mastery of the other, and the elder shall serve the younger." And that was all.

Slowly Rebekah gathered herself together and rose to return home. She was at peace and so, for the moment, were the children. An immense wave of well-being washed over her, taking with it every trace of her nausea, and she knew, though she did not know how, that *that* misery, at least, was gone for good.

As for the wars to come once her children were born and grown, well, that trouble would keep for its own time. No need to trouble Isaac with it. "For now, we've got to get them born," she thought, and knew that by "we" she meant, not just herself, Isaac, the midwife and the female servants, but herself and the Lord God. Somehow, she had taken the first step into the wonders of union with Him that Isaac had spent almost twenty years talking to her about and, judging from the well of peace that had established itself at the core of her being, she knew it would not be the last. She wanted more!

That peace did not desert her, even when the children resumed their wars within her. True to her intuition, the nausea did not return and, though she was uncomfortable and longed for her delivery, pain or no pain, she felt grounded, entirely secure. "So that's what Isaac meant," she thought. "Yes, I can see that."

Her delivery was timely and, the midwife assured her, easy. "Easy! Hah! You weren't in here!" Rebekah thought but did not say, as she gazed at the wonder of her twins, laughing in delight. The firstborn, his skin bright red, was also a redhead. In fact, the whole of his strong body was covered with a red-gold pelt. And because of the redness and the hair, they had named him Esau. His brother, dark-haired, olive-skinned, had emerged right behind him, gripping Esau's heel, immediately earning himself the name Jacob, a name which suggested "supplant" as well as "heel."

"I wonder," she remembered musing in the weeks that followed their birth, "whether Jacob really *will* supplant Esau – and how, if he does it! And now, here she was, standing in the middle of the kitchen portion of the tent, holding that supplanting, Jacob's golden opportunity, in her hands.
She found herself holding her breath in indecision. Should she do this thing, or no? Risking – what? Isaac might be angry, but Rebekah knew in her heart of hearts that Jacob would be a better leader for the clan than Esau. She shook her head decisively and walked to the back entrance of the tent, right beside the oven. She had her hand out to the flap when it lifted and Jacob slipped in. "I've brought your herbs," he announced, then looked sharply at her. "Mother? What's wrong?"

"Not a thing," she answered, looking at him oddly. "Your golden opportunity is here, that's all. Your father has just sent Esau out to hunt some game and fix him a dish to eat so that he can give Esau the Firstborn blessing. Go quickly to the flock, pick out two nice kids, slaughter them for me and I'll fix a dish for *you* to bring him, instead!"

Jacob caught his breath. "Mother!" he whispered in joy. Then his face fell. "But Mother," he said, "Esau's covered with hair – hands, arms, legs, chest, everywhere! And I'm about as smooth as a boiled egg! If he rubs my skin, he's going to feel smoothness, and he's likely to curse me for mocking him in his blindness."

"Just get me the kids," his mother replied, "and I'll take the curse. Hurry!

Do what I told you!"

Jacob blinked and obeyed, returning in record time with the kids, and Rebekah, having made the dish and left it to simmer, took the skins of the kids, scraped them clean and fastened them to Jacob's neck, chest, back, arms and legs, covering the backs of his hands and the tops of his feet as well. Then she slipped Esau's best tunic over Jacob's head and checked the result. It wouldn't have fooled a seeing man for an instant, but a blind man? "It will do," she said to Jacob. "Now, take this dish and this loaf of bread, go in to your father and be Esau. Don't try for his voice – you'll not be able to match it – but match his spirit and his words. Trust me, this will work!"

His eyes larger than usual, Jacob nodded, carefully took the warm dish from her and slipped out the back of the tent and around to the front. Rebekah caught her breath and moved to the kitchen slit. She was just in time to hear Jacob, in Esau's very phrasing, announce his presence to Isaac and invite him to eat.

Isaac was suspicious. He asked how "Esau" had slain the beast and prepared the meal so quickly; asked "Esau" to come closer so he could feel "Esau's" skin and make sure he really was "Esau"; and remarked dubiously when he felt the hairy kidskin transforming Jacob to Esau. "That's Jacob's voice, but these are Esau's hands!" Isaac was silent for a long moment, then demanded, "Are you really my firstborn son, Esau?"

"Of course I am!" said Jacob stoutly, and that seemed to settle Isaac's doubts. He accepted the dish and ate. Rebekah and Jacob exhaled simultaneously in relief, but Isaac had one last test to make.

"Come over here and kiss me, my son!" he invited, and as Jacob bent over and embraced him, he took a deep breath. "Ah!" he said, satisfied at last. "That's Esau's scent all right – just like a field blessed by the Lord God!" Then he intoned, *"May the Lord God give you the dew of heaven and the richness of earth! May you have an abundance of grain and wine! Let nations serve you and peoples do homage to you! Be your brothers' ruler, and let your mother's sons bow to your authority. May anyone who curses you be cursed himself; may anyone who blesses you be blessed!"* [Genesis 27: 28-29; JB]

And that was it. Jacob had the Blessing of the Firstborn. He picked up the empty dish, said goodbye to his father and left the tent, still being "Esau" as his mother had instructed him. Quickly, he slipped into the back of the tent, where Rebekah met him, took the dish and helped him strip off "Esau" and become Jacob again. Then he headed for his own work, while Rebekah braced herself for the real Esau's return and what would follow.

It was about a week later that Rebekah sent for Jacob, again on the pretext of bringing her herbs. Esau had been furious with Jacob, had planned to murder him once Isaac died, and

had been rash enough to say so in the hearing of one of the family servants, who promptly came with the story to Rebekah as the only one who could deal with it.

"You've got to leave," she announced to Jacob as he stepped into the kitchen carrying the herbs. "Go and stay with my brother Laban until Esau calms down and I can send for you. If you don't he'll murder you, and then he will die for it – and I see no reason to lose both my sons on the same day!"

Jacob nodded. "But how – " he began.

"I've been complaining to your father about your brother's Canaanite wives, telling him that if you marry a Canaanite I'll have no reason to live. He should be summoning you tomorrow, to send you to Laban to get a wife from my kindred, probably with a blessing for children, so that you and they can possess this land which the Lord God gave Abraham. When he does – "

"I'll act surprised and pleased," Jacob responded, "and I'll be out of here within the hour! I'll pack now." He looked at her and an impish smile curled his lips and lit his eye. "After all," he said, "if I'm not ready, my golden opportunity just might leave without me!"

She answered his smile with her own and a playful swat.

Her tears she held until she saw the last of the dust of his passage settle on the road that would bring him to a future she would not live to see – her golden opportunity come full circle.

[**Genesis 22**: 23; **24**: 15-67; **25**: 20-28; **26**:7-11, 35; **27**: 5-17, 29, 42-46; **28**: 2, 3, 5; **29**: 12; **35**: 8; **49**: 31; **Romans 9**: 10-13; see **REBEKAH** (see also **DEBORAH, nurse of Rebekah, Rebekah's MOTHER, Rebekah's MAIDS**); see *REBEKAH and the Camels of Courtship*]

# RHODA
## and the Knock at the Door

Rhoda was frightened. She twisted her hands in her apron until it was a mass of wrinkles, noticed what she was doing and tried to smooth the fabric. She lost track of the attempt as her fears reasserted themselves, and twisted her hands again, this time in the opposite direction. What would become of them? Would they all die? Worse, would they all be imprisoned as their leader was? And then what would happen?

Peter had been imprisoned for most of this Passover week. Once Herod had beheaded James, John's brother, and discovered that the death pleased the leaders of the Jewish people, he had looked around for another victim and had found the leader of Jesus' Church on earth. The church itself had gathered in various houses, particularly this one, where her mistress, John Mark's mother Mary, had always kept an informal open house for the community. Now they were upstairs praying for Peter, as they had been doing all week, and Rhoda, one of the maidservants of the house, was down taking the porter's place, waiting to answer the knock of anyone who might come to the door and trembling at the thought.

"It's so dark," she thought. "Anybody might come to the house. I hate this job! Even Miriam says it's no job for a woman, and she doesn't much like me! Oh, I *do* wish Timon hadn't gotten sick!" But he had, and the Lady had said she was to answer the door this evening.

"It's important to have someone ready to answer the door," she had said. "You never know who might come to the house needing the community, and what might happen if no one were there. So do a good job for me Rhoda, as you always do!" Well, how could you argue with that – if you were foolish enough to try arguing with the Lady in the first place! For though she always *said* she was "just another Christian, superior to no one!" and really believed that was true, the Lady ran the house better than an officer ran his section of the army, at least as Rhoda saw it, and with three older brothers in the Legions she ought to know.

"What was that?" she whispered in terror. She listened again. Yes, there it was. A rattle? A bit of rubbish blowing against the door? No! It was a soft knock, and – there it was again! Rhoda moaned. She did not want to open that door! And then she remembered the peephole. Swiftly she stepped up on the stool and peered through it. Whoever it was at least was alone, she saw with relief, and he wasn't from the army or the Temple Guard. He was wearing a worn cloak and covering his face with it as he stood in the deepest shadow the doorway afforded. He knocked again, this time a little harder.

Rhoda made up her mind. Stepping down from the stool, she reached for the bar to slide it back and heard the one knocking say quietly but with intensity, "Let me in, please!"

The world for Rhoda suddenly turned to bright sunlight! She turned from the door and ran as fast as she could, taking the stairs two at a time, and slid on the threshold rug into the room where the community had gathered to pray. The rug took her halfway to the windows, and she was only able to stop herself by catching the edge of the heavy table. "He's here! He's here!" she gulped, panting for breath.

"Who's here?" demanded an elder.

"Sir!" she answered.

"Who's here?" he repeated impatiently.

"Sir!" she said again.

"Which 'sir' do you mean, Rhoda?" asked her mistress quietly. "Calm yourself and tell us. Has someone come to the door?"

Rhoda composed herself and stood straight as Mary had trained her to do. "Ma'am," she said, "Sir – I mean Cephas, is at the door."

The community erupted.

"Impossible!" snorted the elder who had first questioned her. "Peter is well and truly locked up in Herod's prison – chained between two soldiers."

"Double chained," offered another. "My uncle knows the guards."

"He is too here!" said Rhoda.

"Silly girl!" said a woman. "Giving us a fright like that! How can he be here?"

"I don't know, but he is!" insisted the maidservant.

"You've lost your mind," said a third community member, "or are lying for attention!"

"I'm not!" insisted Rhoda, tears starting. "I'm not! He's really here!"

"I'll bet it's his angel," another suggested, but Rhoda shook her head, growing more upset with each objection.

"Enough!" commanded Mary, and a sudden silence fell as the community gaped at her, startled. "Rhoda does not lie, and she doesn't have enough imagination to make up stories. If she says Peter is here, he is. Where is he, child?"

Rhoda's hands flew to her mouth. "Oh!" She gave her mistress a horrified look. "Still at the door, ma'am!"

"Inside?"

"Oh, no, ma'am! Of course not!"

Mary looked at her, started to speak, then simply nodded. "Well done, Rhoda," she said. "Now, go down, unbar the door, and let Peter in. Then bring him up here. Please."

Rhoda found herself unbarring the front door before she knew she had left the room. As Peter came in and she began her "Good evening, Sir! My mistress says – ," Mary interrupted.

"Peter!" she exclaimed, embracing the burly ex-fisherman, tears streaming down her face. "How did you get here? Are you all right?" She was not alone. The community had swarmed down the stairs behind her, and everyone was babbling, asking him the same things, caught between tears and laughter.

Peter, his own eyes damp, raised his hand and, in the silence, told them about the angel and the eerie walk through the prison and out its gates that he had thought a dream. "Get the word to James and everyone else!" he ended and slipped back out the door into the night.

As everyone, still chattering, went back upstairs to give God thanks, and young Samuel left to bring James with the message, Rhoda looked with an odd expression at the door she had just closed and barred.

"So the Lady was right," she whispered to herself, eyes shining. "Having someone standing ready to open the door is *very* important – it can be a matter of life and death!" She stepped back into the porter's place and stood even straighter, waiting eagerly. Why, anyone might come!

**[Acts 12:** 13-17; see **RHODA]**

# RIZPAH
# and the Bones

The news caught Rizpah, the daughter of Aiah and King Saul's concubine, like a blow to the heart. "My sons?" she asked the messenger. "Armoni and Meribbaal? What does he want with them?" For Rizpah expected nothing good of King David, the stripling rebel who had supplanted her lord when Saul died at the hands of the Philistines.

"He says the Lord God requires us to make peace with the Gibeonites in order to restore Israel to His favor and end this drought."

"My sons?" she repeated. "Just *my* boys?"

"No, ma'am," the messenger answered. "King David sent my brother to the house of King Saul's daughter, Merab, and her husband Adriel, with a summons for their five sons as well."

"But why them? Why my boys? What has either of *our* families to do with making peace or ending the drought? We have done nothing, right or wrong, of any power in this land since my lord Saul was slaughtered. This is David's business! He wanted to be King! Let him pay the price!"

The messenger waited, eyes on the ground, until she had finished. Then he looked at her, expressionless, and said, "Those are his words, my lady."

Rizpah drooped. She knew as well as the messenger did that she had no power to oppose King David, though she dearly wanted to. She was helpless, owing her life itself to the mercy of this new King, to say nothing of the roof over her head and the clothes on her back. David had refrained from taking vengeance on Saul while the King lived, and continued to show the King respect by protecting Saul's family. If now he needed her sons, it was because they were Saul's, she understood, just as he needed Merab's five sons because Merab was Saul's daughter, and her sons were Saul's grandsons. Saul's blood was the connection between her sons and Merab's, the connection that the messenger was being too tactful, or too prudent, to name directly.

Rizpah sighed, capitulating. "Well, then, if they must go, they must. Will you take them or shall I send them with my servants?"

"I am to escort them, my lady," the messenger answered, relief in his tone.

"And you will leave – when?" she asked.

"We are to leave at once," he said apologetically. "The King says the matter is urgent."

Half an hour later they were gone, leaving Rizpah alone to face her worry and wrestle with it until her sons should return.

It was two days later that Rizpah found out how her sons and Merab's had made the peace the King sought, not from a court messenger this time, but from one of the men loyal to her because she was of Saul's family. He came at night, in secret, to tell her that the seven young men had been handed over by King David to the Gibeonites who had taken them and impaled them on the mountain of the Lord God in Gibeon. This was their blood vengeance for Saul's attempt to slay them all, in spite of the treaty Israel had signed with them in Joshua's day in the Lord God's presence. The Gibeonites had cursed Israel for King Saul's deed, and with Saul already dead, the blood vengeance could only be paid by Saul's blood. "They died bravely, my lady," he finished. "King Saul would have been proud of them."

"And their bodies?"

He looked at her, puzzled. "On the mountain, my lady. They are sacrificed in the sight of the Lord God."

Late that night, after weeping furiously over her helplessness in the situation, Rizpah dried her eyes, her mind still as rock in her decision. "They are, after all, *my* blood as well as Saul's," she declared aloud, so she could hear the words. "And it was *my* honor, and theirs as well, not just their lives, that has made this peace for Israel with the Lord God, so that He will end the famine that punishes us. It is not — fitting, not for any of us, that their bodies should be eaten by scavengers, bird or beast."

"And what are you going to do about it?" asked her sons' former nurse and her own closest friend, coming in with a bowl of broth which she set by the fire. "You think King David will listen to you?"

"Deborah!" exclaimed Rizpah. "I had no idea you were still awake!"

"How could I sleep?" Deborah returned quietly. "They were my boys as much as yours, so I've always felt. And I agree with you. They oughtn't be dishonored that way. They ought to have a proper burial and be mourned as heroes. Because they were. Heroes, I mean. They died for Israel and they died to restore their father's honor — what more could anyone ask? But what are you going to do? What *can* we do?"

"I — we?"

"Well, you're not going alone, whatever harebrained scheme you've come up with! I won't have that!"

"Harebrained! You haven't even heard my plan!"

Rizpah was indignant, and Deborah smiled inwardly, glad her attack had brought her mistress back to the practical world. "Then there *is* a plan. Good!" she said, and sat down. "I'm listening. Come! Drink your broth!"

Rizpah picked up the bowl, then sat next to her. "*I,*" she declared, "am going to where they've staked out my sons and Merab's, and I'm going to keep off the scavengers." She drank from the bowl.

"You're not going to bring the bodies back here, then?"

Rizpah choked on a mouthful of broth. "You think I'm stupid enough to get us into a *real* war with Gibeon — and the Lord God as well?" she sputtered. "Deborah, they see the bodies as the blood vengeance their honor demands for Saul's treaty-breaking — and their satisfaction is the condition the Lord God has set for His lifting the drought that has plagued us these three years. If I took the bodies — well, you can just imagine!"

"*I* can, certainly," returned Deborah, "but it relieves me to hear that you can as well. So when do we leave, and who, besides me, are you bringing along?"

"Um," said Rizpah. "Well, *I* mean to leave before dawn. By myself!" She finished the broth. "With a donkey, I thought. And sackcloth to sit on. I can flap it to scare the birds and light a fire at night to drive the wild beasts away."

"And how long were *you* planning to do this?"

"Until the bodies are just bones. Then — well," and she shrugged.

"Let's see," Deborah calculated. "The barley harvest is just starting, and with no rain and exposure to the air, the heat will work on the flesh — a season, maybe? Or more? And you'll be living out there in the open? Alone?"

"Yes, I will," said Rizpah, lifting her head and jutting out her chin. "I'll stay as long as it takes."

"Won't work," declared Deborah, "In the first place, you can't stay awake all day and all night too. You'll die. And don't tell me it would be worth it. It wouldn't. Not to me! So you'll need me to do the other half of the watch — split the days and nights with you, so we can both get some rest. And we'll need Jotham — for protection as well as for doing what we don't have the strength to do. One large tent, one small tent, water, grain, dried fruit, money to buy provisions, three donkeys. Dawn you said?"

"Before dawn!" repeated Rizpah.

"All right," said Deborah. "Before dawn it is. Now lie down and get some rest. I'll call you in two hours."

Deborah was a good as her word, and Rizpah found herself established beside the bodies, their camp nearby, driving off the scavenger birds as the sun was coming up. She and Deborah soon fell into a routine, and with Jotham's faithful and clever help, the three were almost comfortable. The days and nights marched peacefully along as the bodies were slowly reduced to their bones, and then came a sudden rain, followed by King David and his men. Someone had told the King of Rizpah's honoring of the dead and he had been moved. When the returning rains signaled the Lord God's forgiveness, he had the bones of Saul and Jonathan collected and buried with the bones of Saul's seven descendants in Saul's father Kish's tomb, with all honor.

Home again, Deborah sighed, "Well, that's done, and well done, too!"

Rizpah nodded. "Indeed. But I wish – I wish the doing had never been needed."

[**2 Samuel 3:** 7; **21:** 8-11; see **RIZPAH**]

# RUTH
# and the Unexpected Gleaning

Ruth straightened up, hand pressed to the small of her back, and fixed her shoulders. Gleaning behind the reapers was harder work than she had imagined it would be, even though these harvesters were leaving her grain to glean, not stripping the ground bare as they probably ought to do. She went to the water jars, dipped herself a cupful and downed it practically in one swallow. It scarcely cut the dust that seemed to coat her mouth and throat, but even so, it was a blessing she was willing to rate up there right next to air to breathe. Truly, Boaz had been as good as his word.

Bending to her work again, she remembered the twisted path which had brought her to this grain field in Bethlehem, gleaning grain so she and her mother-in-law Naomi would have something to eat.

Naomi and her husband Elimelech had fled from Bethlehem of Judah with their two sons, Chilion and Mahlon, to escape the famine that afflicted the countryside, and had settled in Moab. After a time, Elimelech died and Naomi kept house for her sons until they married. To the delight of her family, Mahlon chose Ruth, while her best friend Orpah was given to the eager Chilion by her family. They lived in harmony for ten years. She and Orpah had found in Naomi a real mother, and spouses who had learned from their father how to be good husbands, and from their mother how to treat women respectfully, yet keep them secure. She and Orpah had agreed they had gotten treasures in their marriages.

Then the unthinkable had happened. Without warning, and within days of each other, Mahlon and Chilion had died, leaving the three women bereft, clinging to each other in their grief and desperation, with no idea how they were to go on living without the young men's presence and support. Ruth shuddered, remembering their desolation. For her, Naomi had been the only island of safety in the world, and she'd found that her mother-in-law leaned on her and Oprah even as she sustained them.

The ending of the famine in Judah was what had finally resolved the tangle left by the deaths of Mahlon and Chilion. Naomi, who had taken to calling herself *Mara*, which meant *bitter one*, after the tragedy made her own name, meaning *fair one,* too hard to bear, packed up the household, and with Ruth and Orpah, set out on the road back to Bethlehem.

They had not gone far down the road when Naomi had stopped and faced them. "Go back to your mothers' homes," she had said, freeing them from the responsibility for her which had come with their marriages to her sons. "May the Lord God be as good to you as you have been to my sons who have died. May you each find a good husband and a home." She had hugged and kissed them each in turn, and tried to step back.

Of course they had protested that they would not leave her, saying they would go with her to her land, but Naomi had insisted, "I can't give you more sons to marry – and even if I conceived sons this night, would you wait until they were grown up enough to marry you? That makes no sense! Go, my dears!"

At that, Orpah had kissed Naomi and gone home, but Ruth could not bear to leave. "Don't make me leave you," she had begged, tears in her eyes. "Please!" Then, as Naomi hesitated, she had declared passionately, *"Wherever you go, I will go! Wherever you dwell, I will dwell, too! Your people will be my people! Your God will be my God! Where you die, I will die and I will be buried there!"* [Ruth 1: 16-17; JB]

Ruth had paused, thinking over what she had said, then nodded, adding firmly, "And may the Lord God do whatever He like to me, if we are parted by anything except death!"

At that, Naomi had given way and they had traveled to Bethlehem, arriving at the start of the barley harvest. Once the stir their arrival caused had settled, Ruth and Naomi had set up housekeeping, and Ruth, seeing the harvesters, asked Naomi if she might join the gleaners to get them some grain. Naomi had agreed and Ruth had come to this field and begun to glean.

That had been almost a week ago. Ruth smiled, remembering how kind the owner of the field, Boaz, had been to her. He had discovered her among the gleaners about mid-morning on the first day, learned that she was Naomi's Moabite daughter-in-law, and instructed her to stay in his fields to glean for the rest of the harvest. He told her that he had ordered his servants to protect her, and that she could drink water his servants had drawn whenever she was thirsty.

At noon, Boaz had called her over to eat with his reapers and had given her a heap of roasted grain so large that when she had eaten her fill, there was enough left over for her to bring home to Naomi. She learned later that he had secretly given his reapers instructions to let her glean among the standing grain and told them to drop a couple of sheaves so that she could pick them up. And so she had found, when she winnowed the grain that first day, that she had a full *ephah* of barley to bring to Naomi.

When she got home, Naomi was delighted, and even more pleased to learn that she was working with the reapers of Boaz. "May the Lord God bless him!" she had exclaimed. "And he's our nearest kinsman. Do as he says. Work in his fields with his people until the harvest ends."

Soon the harvest was ending. Ruth wondered how she and Naomi would live, once the barley she had gleaned was gone, but thrust the anxiety aside. "The Lord God has taken us this far," she thought. "He will not abandon us now."

Still, she was not prepared for Naomi's suggestion that evening. "My daughter," Naomi began, "you know, don't you, that it's my duty to provide a good home for you? And I've told you that Boaz is a close kinsman of ours, haven't I? Well, then! This is what you have to do. Boaz will be on the threshing floor, winnowing his harvest. Go and bathe, anoint yourself and put on your best clothes. Then go to the threshing floor — but don't let Boaz see you. Watch where he settles for the night, and then go to his pallet, uncover his feet and lie down there under his cloak." She told Ruth what to say, adding, "He'll tell you what to do from there!" and closed her mouth with a wonderful smile, like one who had just engineered the world's best surprise, refusing to say another word.

Seeing that she would get no explanations from Naomi, Ruth stopped asking questions and did what her mother-in-law told her to do. Finding Boaz was easy; finding his resting place was a little harder in the shifting shadows, but the really difficult part was getting herself to lift his cloak and slip under it. "What if he hates me? What will he think of me? Suppose he thinks I'm just a Moabite whore?" Sternly she told herself, "Ruth! Stop that this instant! Do as Naomi said. She would never, ever, put you in harm's way. Trust her as you trust her God!" And she did.

It was the middle of the night when Boaz suddenly sat up, aware of something strange. Flipping back his cloak, he saw the figure of a woman lying at his feet. "Who are you?" he asked, bewildered.

"I am Ruth, my lord," she answered, catching her breath. Remembering Naomi's instructions, she recited, *"Spread the skirt of your cloak over your servant, for you have the right of redemption over me."* [Ruth 3: 9; JB] Then she held her breath.

After a pause, Boaz exclaimed, "Wonderful woman! May the Lord God bless you! This act of loyalty is even greater than your first one, for you have not run after younger men, rich or poor. Trust me! I will do what you ask!

Everyone knows what a worthy woman you are! There *is* one of our kin who has a closer claim on you than I, but I'll deal with all that in the morning. For now, stay here and be at peace. If he does not redeem you, I promise I will!"

With that, he gestured to her and she curled up again at his feet. He spread his cloak over her and, though neither slept – Ruth for excitement, Boaz planning his strategy for the morning – they were at peace. When the skies began to gray, Boaz roused her. "Come," he said, "no one must know you have come to the threshing floor. But you can't go back to your mother-in-law with empty hands. Take off your cloak and spread it out."

Wondering, Ruth rose and spread her cloak on the floor. Boaz took his scoop and began to fill it with grain. At six measures he stopped, tied the ends of the cloak together to make a manageable bundle, and sent her back to Naomi who welcomed her eagerly.

"What happened? How did it go?" she questioned.

Ruth told her the story and Naomi settled back with a satisfied smile. "That's all right then! Boaz won't rest until he has the matter settled – and that will be today!"

And so it was. Ruth bore Boaz a son, credited to Naomi and Elimelech, and he was named Obed by the women of the village. Naomi was a delighted grandmother, Boaz was a proud father and tender husband, and Ruth the Moabite smiled with special delight whenever she saw growing barley and thought of this most unexpected gleaning of all.

[**Book of Ruth; Matthew 1: 5**; see **RUTH** (see also **NAOMI** and **ORPAH**)]

# SALOME
## and the Silken Snare

Surveying her nails with a critical eye, Salome added just a touch of powdered gold to her left ring-finger. "That'll do," she decided, putting her brush in its holder and turning to face the mirror. "Very nice indeed! A hint of shine, suggesting everything, stating nothing. Mother might even approve!"

Thinking of her mother, Salome saw her mouth twist to match the rage and bitterness Herodias had always been able to rouse in her. Immediately, she reformed her grimace into a pleasant half-smile, lifted her head proudly and murmured, "Oh, no, Mother! I'll not waste *my* looks in fretting over what cannot be!"

Then, still watching herself in the mirror, she continued the series of imaginary confrontations she had been having with Herodias from the age of six, "I won't give you the satisfaction!" she sneered, deliberately provocative. "You *know* how much I hated your leaving my father to cleave to that *slug*, Herod, an then dragging me along with you to this benighted place. At that age, I couldn't help but show what it was costing me. But I'm grown up now – twenty. Now I won't *let* you see how furious and helpless you make me feel every minute I am with you. I'll get even instead – just as you taught me, Mother dear, and I will use *you* to do it, just as you have used me and everyone else along your path, all you life! And you'll never know it's happening, not until you're destroyed!"

Salome closed her eyes. "Every time I think of that woman," she sighed, "I get a headache from grinding my teeth. And what good does that do me?" She shook her head. "None at all. Herodias wouldn't care how I feel if she knew. She certainly wouldn't *change* anything, not just because her only daughter needed – no, *wanted* her to; I don't *need* anything from Mother. It's too late for that. In fact, if she knew how upset she makes me, she'd be glad – she'd think it was another victory!" The girl blew out her breath in frustration. "I tell myself I'll get even with her, for everything, but how? Mother holds all the cards and calls the games – and Herod pays up! Besotted! Some king! Father would make two of him without breathing hard."

She stopped. This was getting her nowhere – it never did and never would. Time to do something. She headed for her mother's room, driven by a vague idea of challenging Herodias at last driving her, but at the doorway she stopped short. Herodias was sitting at her dressing table, apparently examining her hands and frowning her dissatisfaction. Suddenly she balled them into fists, looked relieved, then relaxed them again and frowned, her lips moving in what was evidently serious, somewhat frightened, conversation with herself.

Salome was fascinated. This was the first time she had ever seen Herodias in less than perfect control of herself and everything around her, and her mother was plainly in real distress. "Old age, probably; it shows in the hands first. But something else is brewing – best I not appear!" She was moving back into the hallway when she heard Herodias say, "*What* am I going to do?"

How amazing! *Mother* not know what to do? Impossible! Salome reversed direction. "I don't know, I assure you," she drawled, strolling into the room in the way her mother found most annoying. "About what, Mother?"

"Call me Herodias!" Herodias flared up as usual, and her daughter hid a smile. Herodias hated to have Salome call her mother; it made her feel old, Salome knew, though her mother never admitted that. She was always saying, "Herodias is my name. You're grown up now! Use it!"

And when the storm warnings were up, Salome did. Today they were whipping in a wind that was close to a gale, Salome sensed, and the eye of the storm seemed to be that prophet, John. Herodias hated him with a passion that blinded her to all else.

That, Salome knew, was because the prophet, though a crude man, was more powerful than anyone she had ever seen or heard. In spite of his redolence in that camel's-hair tunic, John had dared tell Herod to his face that he had no business taking Herodias to wife, that she belonged to Herod's brother Phillip, who was Salome's beloved father.

Left to himself, Herod might not have acted, but Herodias had been furious (and, Salome suspected, terrified, lest Herod be swayed by John). So Herodias had exerted herself, and Herod had yielded and sent John to the dungeons, though he still listened to the man. "To *annoy* Mother?" Salome asked herself now, amazed and delighted at the thought, then put it aside to listen closely to Herodias who had calmed down a bit. It never did to ignore her mother, she had learned over the years, sometimes the hard way.

Herodias was saying now that John had to go; he was poisoning everyone, and if he succeeded in having Herodias cast aside, Salome herself would be thrust from the court, her plans of a rich marriage in tatters. Salome watched spittle form at the corners of her mother's mouth. There was a slight tremor in her hands, a hint of disorder in her hair and a carelessness in the drape of her garments. Mother, Salome observed, who was normally as imperturbable as a marble statue and as perfect in the arrangement of her clothing as its carved drapery – was alarmed.

"What are we going to do?" she asked quietly, and listened in astonished disbelief as Herodias unfolded her plan. It was to have Salome dance for the King for his birthday feast in such a way that Herod would be moved to reward her with anything she wanted. Then they could ask for John's head. If the reward were not open-ended, Herodias finished, "you'll have to work him around to it. Can you do that?"

Salome almost stood up and cheered. At last! Herodias and her cherished plan, her life as a queen, even, were in her daughter's hands. She felt a rush of exultation that left her dizzy. "So *this* is what power feels like!" she thought. She wanted to say no, just to see what Herodias would say, but common sense told her that folly would be far too expensive for her and would do her mother no real harm. Herodias, she knew, would just find another way, and Salome would have lost her only opportunity for vengeance, or at least for getting some of her own back from her mother. So her answer would have to be yes. But that could do her service too, if she played the scene well.

That rush of thoughts had flashed through her mind in the space of a single breath. Salome, her outward expression unchanged, slipped into the lounging cat pose that had annoyed her mother for years and drawled, "Of course I *can*, but what do I get out of it if he give us John's head? I can see your advantage – vengeance – and our gain, safety here at court, but what is my *reward*?"

Salome raised her eyebrows in inquiry, smiling but keeping her eyes fixed intently on her mother's. She felt the sweat trickling down her back at her own boldness. She *thought* she had the upper hand, but with Herodias, you never really *knew*.

"My diamonds," Herodias declared flatly, and Salome was so shocked she stopped breathing for a moment. The diamonds were worth millions, a King's ransom! With them she need never again fear her position or her safety. With them she would, at last, be truly free of Herodias – forever!

As Salome voiced the expected shocked protest and listened to her mother's response, she was beginning to realize just how much she wanted that freedom, and the diamonds that would give it to her. Suddenly she knew that she would do anything, absolutely anything, to make the plan work, to earn her reward, and in the same breath she *saw*, for the first time, what had made Herodias the way she was. She froze with the insight. Was she that much her mother's daughter? Was she in fact, *becoming* her mother? It was not a comfortable thought.

"Well?" her mother snapped, and Salome jumped inwardly, though she gave no sign of it, or of what she had been thinking. Instead, tucking away the insight for later consideration, she said, "I'll do it!" and began to plan her dance.

It had been a sound plan to use Herod's birthday dinner as the occasion for disposing of the inconvenient John, Salome reflected as she did her stretching exercises several weeks later. Dancing was something she did well, and Herod had enjoyed watching her – rather more, in fact, than Herodias realized! The dance she had crafted had been the turning point – not just for John, who had lost his head, nor for Herodias, who had received it, but for her, and for Herod, though the poor man had not yet understood that.

Thinking back on the birthday feast, Salome smiled and moved into her acrobatics. It had been splendid! Herodias had taken charge, and the banquet had been exquisite and plentiful, the guest list distinguished and the entertainment rather well above the ordinary. Salome's own dance at the end was obviously intended as the highlight of the evening, and it definitely had been!

Planning the dance, Salome had decided it must show her as virginal but ready to be awakened, and worth the awakening! The image of the unfolding bud had served as her framework, and her costume, seven layers of diaphanous material artfully draped, moving with her and floating free at the same time, had made the image a reality. The outermost layer had been the transparent Egyptian linen favored by their royalty, white over other materials or folded on itself. Successive layers had also been thin – a cream, a white gold, a whisper of green, a pale blue, a faint pink, and closest to her skin, a silk that ranged from ruby and violet through orange to gold, like living flame.

In the course of the dance, choreographed to a breath, blocked out step-by-step in the dining hall and practiced until her bare feet ached, Salome had become the unfolding bud as, layer by layer, she had shed the shrouding veils. Her movements had shown both the bud's opening to full flower and the child ripening to willing, joyous womanhood – all without crossing the gossamer line between the chastely erotic and the blatantly sensual. It had been a masterpiece, she knew, and had done her work as well as won for her mother the prize of the prophet's life.

"Dropping the Egyptian layer in front of Herod's couch was a touch of genius!" she complimented herself. "That way, when the music stopped short at the end, I could fold down in front of him and rise wearing white again – innocence triumphant! So he, and everyone else, could see through the white to the flame, and I could look like the dawn, utterly unaware! Genius!"

She smiled with total satisfaction. "And running like a small child over to Mother where she was lurking in her alcove behind that curtain, and asking what I should ask Herod for," she went on, pausing to catch her breath and swallow some cool water. "Oh, that was good! Everyone knew whose request that really was – especially when I added 'on a plate!' as if I had just remembered about the blood and my costume!"

"And now," she added, counting on her fingers, "Herodias is satisfied. John is no longer a threat to her. I have the diamonds and some security, at last. Herod feels guilty about John, annoyed with Herodias, not me, for trapping him in a public oath before guests he rather fears, and he is more than a little intrigued with me! Maybe, just maybe, I can *really* get even with Mother for once!" And with the hint of a laugh, she whirled herself across the room in a series of pirouettes.

[**Matthew 14:** 6-11; **Mark 6:** 17-28; see **SALOME, daughter of Herodias** (see also **HERODIAS**); see *HERODIAS and the Inconvenient Prophet*]

# The SAMARITAN WOMAN
# and the Meeting at the Well

The sun at noon blazed in a cloudless sky. The woman sighed, picked up her water jug, balanced it with accustomed ease and headed for Jacob's well. It would be nice, she thought, to do this before sunup when the air still held a faint trace of moisture and moved gently. But that could not be. She grimaced. "You choose your miseries," her mother had always said, and she had been right.

But she was not sorry she had taken up with Matthias – and *very* glad she had not married him – though the liaison had earned her what looked like permanent exclusion by the fear-filled women who had once been her neighbors, and was the cause of her having to draw her water at noon when they were all in their homes feeding their families. Being loved as Matthias loved her was worth every jug she had to fill, she thought, and smiled, then frowned. The relationship itself was turning out to be the same disappointing mixed-bag she had experienced, and rejected, in each of her five marriages, and she didn't really see why.

"Is it asking too much to love and be loved? To be happy in loving?" she wondered. "All I ever wanted was that – to be seen as I am, and to be loved anyway. And not to have that love change or diminish or grow stale. Other people seem to manage – and on the first try! What's wrong with me?" She shook her head impatiently. This was an old problem, one she had worried at for years and still could not solve. "Focus on the next thing," she told herself. "Just take the next step. That's all you have, so do it."

Coming in sight of the well, the woman stopped short. Sitting on the well-curb was a traveler. A Jew by the look of him! What was he doing out in the noonday sun, sitting all alone by the well?

"Would you give me a drink?" he asked her as she approached, cautiously but with interest. She blinked.

"You're asking *me* for a drink of water? You, a Jew? Me, a Samaritan?" she queried, even as she lowered her water jug to fill it, then filled the cup that sat by the well and handed it to him.

He took the cup from her hands, drank thirstily, then returned it to her, smiling. "If you knew who was asking you for a drink, you'd ask him for one, and he'd give you living water!"

Her jaw dropped. Then she began to laugh. "Living water?" she asked.

"How? Where's your bucket? That's a deep well! Jacob, our forefather, gave it to us — he and his children and cattle drank from it. You're saying you're greater than Jacob?"

The man smiled at her, and she felt suddenly safe and warm — as though he had dissipated the gray chill that had come to live at the center of her being so long ago she could not remember being without it. "Drink this water," he answered, gesturing toward the well, "and you'll get thirsty again. Drink the water I give you and you'll not only never be thirsty again, you'll have a spring of living water rising up in the center of your soul, giving you eternal life!"

"Give it to me!" she said at once. "How I'd love never to be thirsty again, never to need to draw water from this well again!"

He looked at her, still smiling, and suddenly she felt that he was seeing through her eyes into her very soul, that he *knew* her as she did not even know herself. Strangely, that neither frightened nor angered her. She took a step forward, hands extended toward him. "Get your husband," he said, nodding, "and come back here with him."

Her hands dropped, and she took two steps back, feeling the new warmth in her soul pour out as the gray cold returned with a vengeance. "I don't have a husband," she said flatly, retreating with her pain behind an immobile face.

His eyebrows shot up. "Right you are!" he said, almost with a laugh. "You've had five, and you're not married to the man you're living with now. So you're telling the truth when you say you haven't got a husband."

She gasped. How did he know *that?* And, knowing it, why was he still speaking to her? Then both his tone and his expression registered. He was challenging her, not condemning her! He wanted to see what she would say! Her head came up and her eyes glinted. "Prophet, are you!" she said. "Well, our fathers told us to worship here on this mountain, but you Jews say we're supposed to go to Jerusalem to worship!" Her unspoken, *What do you say to that!* rang between them with the clash of steel on steel.

He straightened and met her gaze. "We're coming to the time when you'll worship neither here nor in Jerusalem," he told her. "You worship what you don't know; we worship what we know — salvation *does* come from the Jews, after all. But the time is coming — it's here, in fact — when the true worshipper will worship the Father in spirit and in truth. Those are the worshippers the Father is looking for. You see, it's because God is Spirit — people who want to worship Him have to worship Him in spirit and in truth." He sat back, satisfied, and cocked an eyebrow at her, waiting for her reply.

She thought for an moment, but found no answer for this new idea, so she fell back on the only graceful way she could think of to end the discussion without conceding the argument. "Well, I do know that once the Messiah comes, he will tell us everything we need to know," she said and bowed slightly, smiling.

He sat very still, looking intently into her eyes. She stirred and was about to ask him what troubled him when he said quietly, pointing to himself, "I *am* he – the one speaking to you."

Suddenly, all the chill gray left her soul, she knew, forever. She wanted to laugh and to weep, to speak, to throw herself at His feet – to shrug off her body and dance in her soul! But before she could do any of these things, an approaching cloud of dust and the sound of male voices coming toward them announced the immanent return of the man's – the prophet's – no, the *Messiah's* – companions.

The woman glanced around for an escape route, found it, and with a quick wave of her hand, fled, leaving her water jug where it stood by the well. Running, she headed for the workshops. She had to tell them, all of them, the good news!

"Jonah!" she panted at the wheelwright's shop. "Come! You have to see him! He's at the well! He's just been telling me every single one of the things I've done in my life! Do you suppose he might be the Messiah?"

Not giving him a chance to answer, she headed down the row of workshops, delivering the same message, and by the time she had reached the end, every man in the village, followed swiftly by the women and children, had converged at the well. They were pelting the stranger – the *Messiah* – with questions, and listening, rapt, to His answers. The woman, gazing at the result of her work, smiled. Good! They had gone to Him because of her but they would stay because of Him, and that was what mattered. They all needed His *living water*, needed this change she had experienced and this joy that would never leave any of them.

Slipping past the enthralled listeners, she retrieved her water jug. Having His *living water* wouldn't excuse her from drawing well-water, she knew, but after this day's meeting, that chore, like herself, would never be the same.

[John 4: 5-42; see *WOMAN at the Well*]

# Samson's WIFE
# and the Coils of Betrayal

This was harder than she had thought it would be. Samson's Philistine wife of seven days frowned. She was beautiful. She knew that. Everyone, male and female, had told her so since she had turned five, the age at which she had learned what beauty could be used for. Then, she had used it to escape punishment, to get extra sweets from her father, to have her mother extend her play time, and to avoid eating disagreeable vegetables her nurse wanted to insist on. From there, as she grew older, she extended her powers, so that now, at eighteen, she had learned how to get anything she wanted from anyone who had it, and she had a large collection of jewels and silks to prove it.

But Samson was different. She had tried every wile she knew and had invented a few new ones, but he still had not told her the answer to the riddle he had proposed to the thirty guards, given them by the city as a wedding honor (but really to protect everyone from Samson, who terrified them all). He'd said he hadn't even told his parents and asked why he should tell her, but her answers made no difference. He was just teasing her, she knew. He wouldn't tell.

The guards were getting angry with her, a first in her experience, and she was getting really nervous. They had even threatened to burn the house down with her and her family inside unless she got the answer for them! Samson just *had* to give her the answer so she could tell the guards and they would not have to give Samson thirty festal garments apiece, the price of failure. Well, this was her last chance. She would have to make it work.

Going to Samson, who still sat at his ease, she coiled herself around him, caressing him and allowing an artistic tear to drop on his cheek. "Beloved," she purred, "why won't you tell me the answer to that silly riddle? What harm can it do?" She rubbed up against him like a cat. "Then we can stop worrying about it and get to better things. Unless, of course, you really don't love me after all!" And she began to weep in earnest, but kept one eye slitted in his direction to gauge her effect on him. Aha! At last!

"Well," rumbled Samson, as he stroked her pliant body, "I suppose it can do no harm now. *The one who eats* is a lion, and *the sweetness that came out of him* is honey." And he told her about killing the lion with his bare hands on the way to arrange their marriage, and finding the full honeycomb in the carcass on his way back home. He thought it an apt metaphor for their marriage, he said, and she agreed wholeheartedly, much to their mutual delight.

Later, when Samson was asleep, she slipped out to the guard on duty and passed on the riddle's solution. She felt uneasy doing so, for she had never forgotten what her grandmother had told her when she was six, gripping her cheeks and staring deeply into her eyes. "Granddaughter, betrayal is a trap, not an escape! For when you untie the knot that joins you to another, its coils will drag you both to your deaths, and everyone and everything else with you!"

"But it's not really a betrayal," she told herself. "At least, not a big one – and I *have* to, or we'll all die!"

That night at the last of the seven wedding banquets, the guards, smirking, told Samson that the strong one was a lion, the sweetness honey, and demanded that he pay the wager.

Samson was enraged. "If you had not plowed with my heifer, you would not have guessed my riddle!" he shouted and stormed out of the house and down to Ashkelon. There he killed thirty men, stripped off their garments, brought them back, thrust them at the guards, and stormed off to his own home.

Samson's bride felt her stomach drop to her feet. "Grandmother's coils!" she thought in terror. Desperate, she turned to her father, by old habit giving him her best *poor baby* look and mournful tone. "What's to become of me now that my husband has left me?" she asked him. "I really wanted to be married!"

Her father cleared his throat. "Well, what about young – you know! The one who was Samson's best man? You like him, I know!"

"Oh, father!" she caroled, lightheaded with relief. Grandmother was wrong – there were no coils here that she need fear.

Several nights later, Samson arrived carrying a small goat as a bride-gift and asking to be shown in to his wife in her room. Her father refused, explaining that he had thought Samson had rejected the girl, so he had given her to Samson's best man instead. "But she has a younger sister, much more beautiful than she. Why don't I give her to you?"

Samson simply stared at the man, turned on his heel and departed. "This time the Philistines have earned a punishment," he thought, "so they can't blame me for giving them one!"      In the event, the punishment was the complete destruction of all the standing grain, the shocks, the vineyards and the olive trees of the Philistines, which prompted them to set fire to the house where Samson's bride and all her family lived. All the bride had time to whisper before the flames devoured her was, "Grandmother's coils!"

[Judges 14: 1-20; 15: 1-8; see Samson's WIFE (see also DELILAH, Manoah's WIFE and Samson's SISTER-IN-LAW); see DELILAH and the Deadly Lure and Manoah's WIFE and the Wonder-Son]

# SAPPHIRA
# and the Better Bargain

"That's ridiculous!" declared Sapphira, putting her cup on the table with a definite click. She folded her arms and looked at her husband sitting across from her. "You can't be serious, Ananias!"

"But I am!" he assured her. "You know how we live – everything belongs to all of us, so everyone gets what he needs to live on every day. So when anyone sells property or anything else, he gives all the money he gets to the Apostles, and that's how the community keeps going."

"*All* the money?"

"Yes, but they'll take care of us both for the rest of our lives, you know. I think it's a good bargain!"

"That part is," Sapphira agreed slowly. "With no children, we'd have a hard time of it in our old age. And living in a community means less work and lots of company. That's good now and it will be a comfort later on. But – give them *everything*? Suppose things change? Suppose the leadership decides to shift us over to pay-as-you-go? What would we do? How would we live?"

"Even then, they couldn't just put us out, Sapphira!" her husband insisted impatiently. "We're Christians! Family! No, we're safe enough – but I was thinking ..."

"What? You've thought of something! I knew you would! What is it?" his wife demanded eagerly. She had learned over the years that Ananias *always* had a backup plan. She had also gotten used to being the one who made the objections, voiced the need for security, so that he could rescue them without having to admit he was as frightened of risk as she was. It annoyed her sometimes, but it worked, and she was not one to fix what was not broken.

"Well," said Ananias, drawing out the words, "I was thinking, we could sell the land as we planned and bring part of the money to Peter, but we could tell him it was all we got. That way, we'd have something to fall back on if things ever went – sour."

"Of course!" said Sapphira. "That's perfect! That's a much better bargain. And it'll work! After all, what would a failed fisherman know about city land prices? And the others – the ones who aren't Galilean yokels are poor people who wouldn't know a mortgage from a fish wrapper. Ananias, you're a genius!"

Ananias smiled at her complacently. "I'm glad you agree!" he said.

The following week, Ananias appeared at the community house early enough to catch Peter before the chief of the Apostles left to go preaching. He knelt at Peter's feet and handed him the soft leather sack, which clinked with the movement of the coins within it – one-half the money he had received for that choice bit of land he had sold to the man who had been pestering him for it. He was opening his mouth to offer the gift with the formula usual in the community – "I have received this money for the sale of some of my property, and I give it to you for the good of the Community" – when Peter suddenly spoke.

His eyes drilling holes in Ananias, the chief Apostle rumbled, "Ananias! How has Satan managed to get such a grip on your soul, that you would tell lies to the Holy Spirit, giving us only part of the money for your land and keeping the rest for yourself?"

Ananias felt his mouth drop open in shock. He looked for something to say, found nothing and closed his mouth again, his eyes opening even wider. Somehow, the *better bargain* was twisting into something else, and he didn't know what to do about it.

Shaking his head, Peter went on, "Before you sold the land, it was yours entirely, right?"

Ananias nodded.

"And when you sold it," Peter continued, "all the money you got for it was yours entirely too, right?"

Ananias nodded again, still finding no words.

Planting his fists on his hips, Peter glared at the man. "So what on earth," he demanded in the muted roar he had developed over years of outshouting a stormy Sea of Galilee, "ever possessed you to try this trick? You were telling lies to God, not to men!"

Transfixed by the words and shocked to the core of his being by the reality they blazed in his understanding, Ananias drew one single breath through his opened mouth – and fell over dead.

The community, which had gathered as the scene unfolded, gasped in unison, terrified at the Power that had just been unleashed. Peter grimly shook his head, then beckoned to a couple of the young man standing with the group. Swiftly, they moved to the corpse, covered it with a sheet one of the women handed them, picked it up, carried it outside and went to bury it in the local graveyard.

Peter did not go out to preach that morning. Instead, he sat in a stillness no one dared either interrupt or question. It was about three hours later that Sapphira, wondering how Ananias had fared with their *better bargain*, slipped into the community's common room. She jumped, startled, when Peter addressed her.

"Tell me, Sapphira," he said, his tone casual, "was one hundred silver pieces the amount your land sold for?"

Sapphira felt her heart speed up and her mouth dry. Giving the burly fisherman her best smile, she nodded, saying cheerfully, "Yes, it was! One hundred silver pieces exactly!"

Slowly Peter rose, seeming to grow taller and broader as he did so. "Why did you two do this thing?" he asked her, his voice cold and unyielding as an iron bar, his eyes looking, it seemed, into her very soul. "Don't you understand? That was the Spirit of the Lord you were testing with your lie, not men! Listen – do you hear those footsteps? Those are the men who have just buried your husband. Now they will bury you."

Horrified, Sapphira broke from Peter's gaze with an almost audible snap, whirled to face the door – and dropped dead at Peter's feet. When the young men came in, they sheeted her body as they had her husband's, carried her out and buried her as well. She never learned, in this life, the real cost of her *better bargain*.

[**Acts 5:** 1-11; see **SAPPHIRA**]

# SARAH
# and the Bridal-Night Demon

Sarah, Raguel and Edna's daughter, was afraid the feast would never end. Then again, that was what she was hoping for because what would follow – well, it terrified her. Certainly, the marriage pleased her, or would have, anyway, had her recent history been anything but what it was. And plainly Tobias was delighted, even though Raguel had taken pains to rehearse that history for him before he finalized the match Tobias was asking for. So here they were – trapped.

She caught Tobias' eye and he smiled at her encouragingly. That made matters worse, somehow. She *liked* this young man who had appeared, it seemed, from out of nowhere, to put forward the claims of kinship and ask for her hand in marriage. And now he was going to be dead, too. How had he gotten into this doomed marriage?

It ought to have been impossible – yet, here he was. Here they were. Oh, she had been there the whole time he was explaining who he was, and her father was unraveling the kinship lines to establish that he *had* to give her to Tobias, that by the Law she belonged to him, but it still seemed impossible. She had heard the words of commitment her father had spoken over them, had seen the contract drawn up, had joined the feast – and still it all seemed unreal.

What *was* real, hideously real, was that she was married – again, and her bridegroom was going to be slaughtered by the demon Asmodeus – again. "For the eighth time," she reminded herself. Seven of their kin, one by one, had married her, and seven bridegrooms, one by one, had been slain by the demon on the night of the wedding, before any of them could bed her.

People had talked, of course, though they had taken good care that no one in the family heard what they were whispering. The family maids had been less discreet. One, indeed, had been bold enough to mock her to her face. The girl had accused her of killing the grooms herself and of using their deaths as an excuse to punish the maids. That had been too much. She had rushed to her father's room, intent on hanging herself, so intense was her pain.

But then she had thought of what *that* would make people say – and of how her death would break her father's heart, to say nothing of what the reproaches of the townsfolk would do. She had decided to ask the Lord God to take her life, or to look on her with pity. The prayer had calmed her, and she had thought she was recovering – until Tobias had showed up and this new marriage had been made.

Sarah looked up to find the eyes of everyone at the table upon her. Flushing, she said, "I'm sorry, Father! Did you say something to me?"

Raguel smiled tenderly at her, though tears beaded his eyelashes. "No, dear one. I just cleared my throat. I told your mother to prepare the bridal chamber and then take you there, and I think she's ready for you."

"Oh!" she answered, and looked up to see Edna standing in the door-way beckoning to her. Taking a deep breath, Sarah gripped her skirts and her courage in both hands, slid out from behind the table and followed her mother.

Once dressed for bed – and oh, how that too-familiar ritual had twisted into a horror for her – Sarah faced Edna, who was in floods of tears. The mother embraced her daughter, weeping over her. Then, wiping away her tears briskly, she helped Sarah into the bed, saying, "Courage! Have courage, my daughter, and may the Lord of Heaven give you joy to make up for all your sorrow!" Then she left Sarah to herself.

It seemed only a few moments before Tobias arrived. As had been sug-gested by his companion, "Azarias" (*the Archangel Gabriel in disguise and Tobias' kinsman, though neither he, nor Sarah, knew that then*), Tobias was carrying an odd, lumpish something in his right hand. He unwrapped it and, still con-tinuing to follow the advice of "Azarias," he placed it at once in the incense burner, laying it directly on the coals. The stench was horrendous. To Sarah, it smelled like burning fish innards – liver, heart, something like that. She sneezed.

A stunned Asmodeus, present though invisible to the humans, looked at the incense burner with horror and at Tobias with loathing. But there was no help for it; the demon simply could not bear to be in the same room with this, this – abomination, so he fled to Egypt. (There, Raphael the archangel bound him briskly.)

Then, still obeying "Azarias," Tobias reached for Sarah's hand. "Before we lie down, beloved," he said softly to her, "let's pray to the Lord God and ask His protection." And so they did.

At midnight, Raguel could stand the suspense no longer. He had been hop-ing that Tobias would be able to bring his marriage to Sarah to its longed-for completion, but suppose his young kinsman had failed! Well, if that had happened, he would just have to bury the body before anyone in town even knew the boy had been in the house. Quietly he called two of his servants and told them they were going to dig a grave in the garden.

"In the usual place?" the elder asked him.

Raguel nodded. One more grave in that patch would go unnoticed, and the soil, from having been disturbed so often, would be easy to dig out quietly.

It was. Once they'd finished and the tools were put away, Raguel came in, washed, then went to their bedroom. "Edna!" he whispered.

She had not been asleep. "What is it, dearest?" she asked.

"I think it would be a good idea if you would send one of the maids in to take a look in the bridal chamber," he told her. "Just tell her to look, and then to come back and tell us — whatever she's seen."

Edna looked at him, frowning. This was most unlike Raguel. "Bad news won't keep until morning?" she asked with some asperity.

"In this case," he answered slowly, "I'm afraid it won't. I thought — well, if he *did* die, it would be just as well if we got him buried before anybody even knew he'd been here. That way we'd avoid problems. There's been so much talk as it is …"

"I know," she said. "Sarah would never be able to live it down — and we might find it impossible to keep on living here. Let me get Naamah. She's got good sense — won't scream the roof off if Tobias is dead, God forbid."

"Amen!" returned her husband fervently.

Edna returned to the bedroom, having sent Naamah on her errand, and gripped her husband's hand. "She should be back in five minutes," she told Raguel, and together they waited.

Three minutes later, the door opened and Naamah came in, wreathed in smiles. "Sleeping sweetly as infants, the two of them!" she said. "Breathing just as nicely as you please, wrapped around each other. They practically glow! Go to bed, master, mistress! The trouble's over!"

"Thanks be to God!" whispered Raguel, beginning a prayer of thanksgiving to the Lord God for His mercy in bringing Tobias to Sarah and delivering her from the demon. Then, still smiling, he went to tell the servants to fill in the grave they'd dug. "We don't need it!" he all but sang. "Everything's all right!"

"Never thought I'd feel so good about wasted work," murmured the younger to the elder, shoveling with a will as Raguel went back into the house with a bounce in his step.

The following morning, sunlight was streaming into the bedroom well before the couple awoke. When they did, Tobias smiled at Sarah, who laughed out loud in her delight and rolled over to give her new, and very much alive, husband an enthusiastic hug. "The Lord God has heard us!" she exclaimed. "Oh, my husband – I was so frightened! But you are alive! Asmodeus, my bridal-night demon, has lost! And here we are, on the first day of the rest of our lives together. How wonderful! How very good the Lord God is to us!"

"More than you know, beloved," returned her husband. Thinking of "Azarias" and all that had happened, and would surely happen, because of this chance-met companion, and realizing that "chance" had had nothing to do with the encounter.

[**Tobit 3:** 7-17, 25; **6:** 11-18; **7:** 8-20; **8:** 1-8, 20-21; **10:** 7-13; **11:** 3, 15-18; **12:** 3, 12-15; see **SARAH, wife of Tobias** (see also **EDNA, ANNA, wife of Tobit, Raguel's MAIDSERVANTS** and *WIFE of Seven Brothers*); see *ANNA and the Homecoming*]

# SARAH
## and the End of Patience

Patience, Sarah reflected, rubbing the ache in her lower back and shifting her position, had never been her strong suit. All her life to date had been one continuous lesson designed to inculcate this virtue in her. "Or kill me outright!" she added, grunting slightly.

Even this long-promised pregnancy, the fulfillment of her and Abraham's heart's desire, was a test of her patience. She knew she was just enduring what every pregnant woman since Eve had and, like them, was looking forward to the hardest struggle and worst pain in her life as a welcome relief to this uncomfortable, interminable *waiting!* With the child, the Lord God's promise would be fulfilled, and her curse of barrenness ended! It had been her burden since she had come as wife to Abraham – Abram he was then, as she had been Sarai.

Remembering those long-ago days, Sarah shook her head. "What a waste!" she thought. "We could have had this child years ago, when we were young and energetic enough to enjoy him and be proper parents for him. It's not the way I would have done things!" she added, addressing the Lord God with the blunt respect and affection she had always used when she spoke to Him in her spirit.

She settled back against the cushions to watch through the tent-flap as the shadows crept across the yard. It had been a long haul, this marriage and the life that had gone with it, sometimes difficult, sometimes painful. But there had been a lot of joys, sudden surprises and steady contentments both, and it had never, ever, been dull! And Abraham had been wonderful, always.

But there had been no children for her. Sarai had not been worried, at first. Everyone said marriage took some getting used to, and that once she and Abram had settled, the children would come. "Enjoy your freedom!" they had told her. "Once you have children you'll never stop working, or worrying!" She had laughed with them.

Then had come the moves, first from Ur to Haran, and then, following the Lord God's promise to Abram to make a great nation of him, to Shechem in Canaan, the land He showed him, where they settled for a time at the holy place, the Oak of Moreh.

All the upset of the move surely explained her continuing childlessness, they had said comfortingly. She had believed them unquestioningly, and the time passed quickly, for she lived in anticipation. Next month, surely, the child would be given! The Lord God had promised! But somehow, next month never came, and Sarai began to fret that Abram might put her aside for her barrenness. And that would have been like dying, she knew, for she had come to love her husband more and more fully.

Abram, however, had simply loved her the more tenderly, making the deepening of his love for her entirely clear. Not only had he made no complaints, never even mentioned the word "barren," he had refused to allow anyone else to do so either. It was at that point, Sarah remembered, that she had first begun to realize the steel of which her quiet husband was made, and to understand that to cross Abram seriously would be dangerous. This realization had increased her respect profoundly, and had even curbed her temper and her tongue on occasion.

But still no children came. It was as they followed the Lord God, moving from Shechem to Bethel and, stage by stage, to the Negeb, then back to Canaan, that Sarai had begun her own increasingly impatient conversations with the Lord God. She had never received an answer, nor had she conceived, but somehow, just talking to Him had helped her go on. Strange, she had thought, even then.

Once in Canaan they had kept traveling as the Lord God led them, ending back at Bethel where Abram had built his second altar, and the Lord God had repeated His promise. Abram had moved them to the Oak of Mamre at Hebron, built an altar to the Lord God and settled there in peace. But Sarai found no peace, for there were still no children, in spite of the promise.

"It was really hearing the promise again and again that made things so hard," Sarah reflected, shifting her bulk and arching her back with a small grunt. "It might have made things easier for Abram, but for me it was like rubbing salt in an open wound. I felt I was failing to do something every other woman could do – and it wasn't my fault. It made me want to scream – at Abram, at God, at everyone!"

When they had been ten years in Canaan and the Lord God had appeared to Abram again, repeating His Promise of protection and reward, Abram had asked Him what that reward would be. "I have no children," he had said. "You haven't given me any, and with no children to inherit, one of my servants will have to get everything." He had waited in silence for a response.

Telling the story to Sarai, Abram had whispered in awe. "He told me I wouldn't have to have a servant inherit my property, that I would have a child from my own body to inherit! We went outside then, and He said, '*Look up to heaven and count the stars if you can. Such will be your descendants!*' [Genesis 15: 5; JB] and then He promised to give me the land."

"And that's all?" Sarah remembered how angry she had been. "That's it? It will happen? Did He say how? When? That's what I want to hear! It's not as if we have forever, you know!"

"He didn't say. He told me that I would die in peace, and He made a covenant with me to give me the land, but – He did not say when the first child would be born."

"Wait a minute! He said *your* descendants?" Sarah had asked sharply. "*Your* descendants? Not mine? Not ours? He just said *your* descendants?"

"Well, yes," Abram had answered, puzzled. "But you're my wife! They'd have to be yours as well!"

At that point, Sarah remembered, she had lost her grip, both on her patience and on her common sense. She stood to stretch. Oh, to be at ease in her own body again! It had never once occurred to her, during all those years she had spent watching other women and waiting to conceive her own child, that steady discomfort might become her companion when the waiting ended.

Yes, that was when she had decided that, since the Lord God was obviously not going to give her a child, but the land was still to go to Abram's descendants, He must mean for her to use a surrogate to bear the heir. And so she had insisted Abram use her maidservant Hagar in her place, saying that she would claim the child as her own.

"And that was the worst mistake of my life," she said ruefully. "That girl has never let me forget that she gave my husband the Lord God's child he longed for, the child I could not conceive. *Why* didn't I trust Him just a little longer?"

But she had not, and Ishmael, now thirteen and the darling of his father and his mother, was the thorn in her foot even now, as she waited for her own child to be born. She had had to take the insolent Hagar back, even after Abram had said she could do as she liked with her maid, and she had beaten the girl until Hagar, pregnant with Ishmael, had fled. But the girl had returned, saying she had seen an angel who told her to.

Sarai had been ready to beat Hagar again, but Abram had a question. "It was the Lord God Who told you all this?"

Hagar had nodded. "El Roi," she said. *"I have seen the One Who sees me."* [Genesis 16: 13; JB]

Abram stood very still. "Yes," he said, finally, "yes."

With that, he had turned and looked directly at her, and Sarai had known that, like it or not, she would have to put up with Hagar and care for her and her child, who was plainly the child of the promise. So she had, and their truce had lasted fourteen years, so far.

"Longer than I thought it would, or wanted it to," Sarah reflected honestly, as she stretched and extended her legs, trying to prevent them from cramping and her back from locking up.

And then, when she was eighty-nine and Abram ninety-nine, the Lord God had spoken to Abram again. Reporting the conversation to her, Abram all but babbled in excitement. He was to be called *Abraham, father of a host of nations* [Genesis 17: 5; JB], she was to be called *Sarah, princess,* for she would mother kings [JB note f on 15-16] and she herself was to bear Abraham a son whom he was to name Isaac.

That Covenant, Abram – now Abraham – had explained to her, was to be sealed now by the circumcision of every male in the household and of every new male child at the age of eight days. The land of Canaan was to be theirs to own forever, and the multitudes of their descendants were to be the Lord God's people as He was to be their God, also forever. As for Ishmael, he was to be the father of twelve sons who would be rulers, and the Lord God was going to make him into a great nation.

At Sarah's disbelieving, indignant stare, Abraham had stopped short, raising his hands, partly in alarm, partly in apology. Then mumbling a little, he confessed that he had asked a blessing for the boy, not really believing that, at their ages, they could actually have a child. But the Covenant, he assured her rapidly, the Lord God had said that was for his descendants through Isaac. And Isaac would be her son, born of her body.

Sarai, now Sarah, had not exploded about Ishmael's blessing. In truth, nothing of what Abraham had been exclaiming about seemed really *real* to her, any more than had her own new name, or the mass circumcision of the males in the household, Abraham's response to the Lord God's word. She found herself suspended, not daring to disbelieve the Lord God and not daring, not really able, to hope anything at all. As for the Promise, that had been sealed in mystery, and she had no key to unlock it.

Several days later, they had had visitors. It was noon, and Abraham was sitting at the entrance to the tent when he saw the three men. He leaped up to offer them hospitality, had the servants wash their feet and told her to make bread while he had a tender calf killed and prepared. He served the visitors himself, as was proper, and when they had finished the meal, one of the visitors had asked, "Where is your wife, Sarah?"

"In the tent," he had replied.

"I'll be back next year," his guest had told him cheerfully. "She'll be caring for her new baby boy by then!" Sarah, following the conversation from where she sat near the tent flap, had given a short, bitter laugh well under her breath.

"Right!" she'd thought. Memories of all the years and all the dead hopes weighed on her spirit like so many stones. Who knew what the Lord God meant by His Promise? Not she. But this was unreal. It had to be.

Then the guest had asked why Sarah had laughed at the idea that she was going to bear a child in her old age. After all, he added, God could do anything!

Sarah had gasped. He was reading her mind! Frightened, she had blurted out that she hadn't laughed, forgetting that she was eavesdropping and should not have heard the question, much less have been bold enough to answer it!

"You did so laugh," he has said to her with a calm assurance that had sealed his authority in her eyes. He *knew*, everything, and if he said she would have a child by next year, she would. Finally the revelation Abraham had received began to become real to her. Isaac! Isaac would be her son! Isaac was to be the child of the Promise, and all else would follow.

Sarah grimaced, her thoughts returning to the present. When would this child be born? She shook her head. "Patience! Patience! I'm sick of it!" she murmured with a rueful smile. "I never change!" Then her eyes widened and she caught her breath at the sudden, intense pain. She knew what it was. The child, finally, was coming.

When sequential thought returned, Sara found herself holding her newborn, who was eagerly nursing. Isaac, at last — her promised son! And the name the angel had given him meant laughter or God has smiled. "God has given me cause to laugh," she said, laughing herself in her joy, "and everyone who hears about it will laugh with me. No one would ever have told Abraham that his Sarah would nurse children. Yet, here I am! I've given birth to his son in his old age!"

[Called **SARAI** in **Genesis 11**: 29, 30, 31; **12**: 5, 11–20; **13**: 1; **16**: 1–9; called **SARAH** in **Genesis 17:** 15–22; **18:** 1–15; **20:** 1–18; **21:** 1–12; **23**:1–2, 5–20; **24**: 36, 67; **25:** 10, 12; **49:** 31; **Isaiah 51:** 2; **Romans 4:** 19; **9:** 9; **Galatians 4:** 21–31; **Hebrews 11:** 11; **1 Peter 3:** 6; see **SARAH, wife of Abraham** (see also **Abraham's CONCUBINES** and **HAGAR**); see *HAGAR and the Impatient Wife*]

# The SHUNAMMITE MOTHER
# and the Promise Kept

Life was blessed indeed, the woman thought as she waved to her five-year-old son who was, this year, going out to the reaping with his father for the first time. She had never thought to have such a wonderful son – nor any child at all, when none had arrived during the first years of her marriage to her gentle husband, who was twenty years her senior.

But then Elisha had come by and she had gotten the idea of building him a room on their house roof, so the Man of God would have a place to stay when he was in their neighborhood. Her husband had agreed eagerly, for, having failed, as he saw it, to give her children, he was anxious to do anything at all that might please her and give her some comfort.

Elisha had been delighted to have the snug retreat with its comfortable bed, table, chair and lamp, and some time later had offered to do for her whatever she wanted, using his influence with the King and the army commander. Of course, she had refused his offer, but he had consulted his servant Gehazi, and then promised her this child.

She had been afraid then, she remembered, had even demanded of him that he not tell her lies – she could not have borne to hope for a child again, and again have that hope snatched from her. And now, here was that very child, sturdy and cheerful, bouncing along beside his elated father to help with a man's work! She felt her cup overflow with joy.

About mid-morning, a commotion in the yard brought her to the back door, where she saw what she could scarcely believe – and had always, somewhere in the depths of her soul, feared. Her son, limp and pale, was being carried to her by two of the reapers.

"Ma'am," said one of them, "the boy came to his father this little while ago, crying. He said, 'Oh, Father! My head! My head hurts!' and he began to sway. The master caught him and picked him up, but the boy didn't seem to notice. He just kept whimpering. So the master told us to carry him straight to you." He blew out his breath and looked at her.

The mother nodded. She beckoned the reapers to bring the child indoors and put him on the kitchen table. One of them handed her a pitcher of well water. The other looked around, then brought her a bag of clean rags for bathing and a pile of towels. She nodded her thanks and they melted from the room. Urgently, she snatched the rags and, very gently, used the cool water to bathe her son. He did not stir, seemed not to notice, though his body relaxed a little and the heat she felt in his flesh began to cool.

Grasping this faintest breath of hope, she snatched her softest blanket from the chest and wrapped the boy in it, then sat in her chair by the open door with him cradled in her lap. She rocked him a little and crooned his favorite lullabies, shifting position very gently when she had to, and made her mind a blank. If she did not give way to the gibbering fears that clawed at her sanity, he would live, she thought without using the words.

Just at noon, the boy stiffened in her arms, arched his back, and then seemed to fall in upon himself, his breath ceasing between one heartbeat and the next. She did not scream. She did not weep or storm at God. She had no breath to make a sound and, in any case, no time.

Gently, gently, she rose and carried her dead son up the stairs to the roof, placed him in the Man of God's bed and closed the door. Then she called her husband. "I need a servant and a donkey," she announced. "I have to get to the Man of God *now* – I'll be back!"

Signaling the groom, who hurried to do his mistress' bidding, he asked, "But – why do you have to go today? It's not New Moon! It's not Sabbath!"

"I just do!" she snapped, then hugged him fiercely, mounted the donkey the groom had brought to her and commanded, "Go! Don't stop until I tell you to."

Infected by her urgency, the donkey cooperated and they moved out at a brisk pace that soon brought them to Mount Carmel where, ignoring Gehazi's questions about herself, her husband and her son, she flung herself at Elisha's feet and clung to him with all her strength. Gehazi was indignant and tried to pry her loose, but Elisha said, "Don't. Let her be. She is in dire trouble, and the Lord God has not let me see what it is."

Catching her breath, the mother screamed, "Was it *I* who asked *you* for a son? Didn't I *tell* you not to tell me lies?"

The silence that followed was painful. Elisha paled, then said to Gehazi, "Quick! Knot your garments up, take my staff and get to her house as fast as you can – and don't stop to talk to anyone on the way! When you get there, go to the child and lay my staff on his body."

But the mother was having none of that dismissal. "I swear on God's life and your own, I will not let you go!" she shouted, and clung to him all the more tightly.

"Right," said Elisha. "Come. We'll go, too."

They met Gehazi, returning from the mother's house and looking very unhappy. "I did what you said," he reported to Elisha, "but nothing happened." The mother stiffened and her grip on Elisha's arm tightened. Elisha patted her hand comfortingly, but said nothing.

Once at the house, she sat in the kitchen, unable to do anything. Elisha had gone to his room where the child was still lying on the bed, and closed the door. He had not allowed her to come in with him, and she had not dared to insist. She could hear him walking about the room, hear the creak of the bed, hear him walking again – it seemed to be a cycle. She counted.

At the end of the seventh repetition, the mother heard a sneeze and leaped to her feet. She met Gehazi, who had come to call her, and pushed past him to Elisha's room.

And there he stood, the child of Elisha' promise – alive, fully healed, and bubbling with his usual joy. She knelt and held out her arms, the boy ran to her embrace and, tears at last streaming down her face, she nodded to Elisha who was wreathed in a smile. He had not told her lies after all. The promise had been kept!

[2 **Kings 4:** 8-37; **8:** 1-6; see **(The) SHUNAMMITE MOTHER**]

# The SIDONIAN WIDOW
## and the Last Meal-Cake

The widow looked again into the meal jar. There was just as much, or as little, as there had been the last three times she had looked this morning – enough for one largish cake she and her son could share, with just enough oil in the jug to hold the meal together so it could be baked.

She glanced at the sky, inverted over her head like a vast, blue bowl with a brazen sun blazing in it, drying everything it touched. The well had not failed, yet, but there was no extra water to sustain even small crops, had anyone had any seed to plant them. Zarephath, all Sidon, in fact, was in dire straits, and no one could say when the rains would come again.

There was a rumor that the drought was the work of their neighbors' God. That Israel had failed to obey Him and this was His punishment. But no one in town knew if that were true – or what to do about it if it were. Surely, if His own people had not been able to move Him, strangers could do nothing!

The widow looked at the meal and the oil again. She was lucky to have this much, she realized; lucky that she had scrimped and saved all along instead of wasting what she had, assuming the rains would come. But she had reached the end and there was no more to be bought, and no money to buy it with if there were.

So, after this last meal they would die, she and the boy. It was a leaden thought, but shuddering wouldn't make it go away, and wishing wouldn't add meal and oil to her stores. "Better get a couple of sticks for the fire," she thought, "and get on with it, before we both grow so weak we can't even eat – or the rats and weevils get the meal!"

That thought made her angry enough to move briskly to the area around the city gates to gather her wood. Absorbed in her troubles and focused on finding her wood, she did not at first realize that the old Israelite approaching was speaking to her. Then, as she turned away, he called her, "Could you please bring me a cup of water to drink?"

She nodded and was turning away again when he added, "Oh! And could you also bring me a chunk of bread?"

At that the widow stopped short, then turned to face the beggar. Her eyes blazing, she answered, "As the Lord God, *your* Lord God, lives," she exclaimed, "I have no bread baked that I can bring you. I only have a single handful of meal in my jar and a couple of swallows of oil in my jug. The reason I'm out here picking up sticks is so that I can go home and make a cake out of what I have left for my son and me to eat. And then we shall die!" While her words were polite enough, her tone made it clear that she considered all this to be his fault. Head up, she awaited his reply.

The old Israelite winced, but said, "All right. Go and do what you have planned, but before you do, make me a little cake with the meal and oil and bring it to me. Then you can make something for yourself and your son." Then suddenly, he straightened up, his voice growing deeper. "For behold! The Lord God says your jar of meal and jug of oil will not run out before the day He sends rain to the earth!"

The widow felt a chill wash over her. Plainly this was a Man of God, and he spoke not his, but his God's words! She backed away from him, then turned and ran to her house. Swiftly she shaped a small cake from the meal and oil, and when it was done, took it up in a napkin, filled a cup with water and brought both back to the Man of God, watching him eat and drink with appetite.

The widow told him she had an upstairs room for him, if he had nowhere to stay. He followed her to the house where she made the cake she had planned for herself and her son. There was enough meal and oil – and the cake was the same size it would have been had she not taken a third of it for the Man of God!

All fell out as the Man of God, Elijah she learned was his name, had promised. The three of them ate, every day, and the meal jar and oil jug were never finally emptied, though they never looked any fuller than they had the day Elijah had met her.

Disconcerting as it was, the widow did not dare to say so to Elijah. If the Lord God was going to feed them for the rest of the drought, why not fill jar and jug? This way, she didn't ever *know* there would be enough for the next day. She just had to trust this Lord God, day to day, and He wasn't even *her* God! Well, she concluded, He *was* Elijah's God, and He thought enough of His man that He had provided for him through the drought. So as long as Elijah was in her house, it would be all right. It would have to be.

And it was, until the day her son got sick. At first the widow thought little of it – boys could be counted on to get sick at inconvenient times, she knew, but they always got better. Except he didn't. He just got slowly sicker and sicker, as she went from irritation, through concern, to absolute panic. Nothing she did helped. Nothing anyone did helped.

Soon the boy turned his face to the wall and died. The widow stood by the bed in shock. Furiously, she rounded on Elijah. "Why do you hate me so, Man of God?" she demanded. "Did you come here just to pay me back for my sins and kill off my son?"

Elijah went white. "Bring your son to me," he said in a whisper and, receiving the corpse, carried it to his room and laid it on the bed. The woman could hear his anguished prayer through the ceiling. "Lord God, *my* God!" he prayed, his desperation matching hers, "Please! Does this widow who's taking care of me *have* to suffer the death of her son?"

The widow heard an odd creaking, as though Elijah had laid himself down on the bed. "Lord God," he prayed at full volume, "let the boy's spirit, his life's breath, return to his body." She shivered, feeling her heart join with the prayer. Then she thought she heard the Man of God rise. The maneuver, whatever it was, and the prayer were repeated twice more, by which time the widow was weeping without restraint.

Hearing Elijah's feet on the stairs, she looked up – to see her son in his arms and a smile on his weathered face that made him glow all over. "Here is your son!" he said to her, handing her the boy. "He's alive again!"

Hugging the child so tightly he squealed and wriggled until she put him down, she let her tears fall and smiled through them like the sun through rain. "Truly," she said when she could speak, "you *are* the Man of God! The word of His truth comes out of your mouth!"

Then, wiping her eyes, she turned to the jar of meal and jug of oil to make still another "last" meal cake for them all to share.

[1 **Kings** 17: 7-24; **Luke** 4: 25-26; see **SIDONIAN WIDOW from Zarephath**]

# SUSANNA
# and the Weighty Word

"It was all a dream!" exclaimed Susanna, as she opened her eyes to the rising sun, splashing gold on the walls. "Oh, Lord God, thank You! It was only a dream!" She reached out to give Joakim, her husband, a hug and stiffened as her hand met only cool undisturbed linen. Where had Joakim – and then it came back to her. The whole sordid business, ridiculous in the abstract and terrifying in the flesh, was *not* the dream she had wished herself into believing it was, but real.

"Horribly real!" she murmured, the tears starting again. She had thought herself dry of tears forever last night, falling asleep, alone for the very first time in this room of her bliss, but evidently that was not so.

"This will never do!" she chided herself, and sat up in bed. No one in the house was awake yet, for the incidents of yesterday had thrown the whole household, servants included, into disarray. She would have to wait for her maid to come and help her with her clothes and hair – "if she deigns to come! Well, at least I have time to think in peace. Now, what can I do, what do I *need* to do, to save myself?"

"There's nothing *anyone* can do," the inner voice that sounded always like her grandmother's told her. "They've got you completely trapped. There are two of them, to begin with, and they are the elders, chosen by the people to be the judges for this year. It's their witness against yours."

"False witness!" Susanna interrupted her thoughts. "They are slimy liars, the two of them!"

"Mayhap," responded the voice, "but their office gives them credibility. Besides they are accusing you of what they say they saw you *do*, so unless you have witnesses who can prove they're lying, you haven't a chance. With only your own word, you know, you can't prove you *haven't* done something. No one can prove a negative."

Susanna thought about that. It was true – she had only herself to bring as witness to her innocence, and no one would believe her word against the elders' charge. *Why* had she dismissed her maids? She had gone into the garden with them, had them return with the scented bath oils – why had she not let them stay?

"Because I wanted privacy," she answered herself bitterly. "Because I had no *idea* those two – crawling *snakes* even knew I existed, let alone lusted after me and were hiding in *my* garden to trap me!"

She shuddered, remembering their sudden emergence from the shrubbery once her maids had departed, shutting the garden gate as she had ordered. "Ancient, stringy, filthy *perverts!*" she said under her breath. "They had to sustain each other even to approach me! These are not *men!*"

"Nevertheless," the voice reminded her.

Susanna blew out her breath in frustration. The voice was right. However despicably, they *had* trapped her. They'd demanded she lay with each of them, right then and there, or they would open the gate and scream that she had closed it to be with a young man hiding in the garden.

"I wouldn't have lain with a handsome, charming man who came to me on his knees bringing jewels, let alone those two smelly *jackals!*" she fumed. "Not if I were a hundred and ten with no hope and no way left to eat unless I did!"

"But," said the voice.

"But," she agreed. "I couldn't kill them – old as they were, there were two of them. And I had nothing to fight with – not even an eating knife! If the maids had left the jars with the bath oils, I might have managed something – but they had taken them back to the house once they had prepared the bath. Oh, I knew then that I was trapped, for if I gave in to them, I would be stoned, rightly, for adultery, but if I resisted, they'd lodge their lies as charges, back them with the weight of their word as judges, and I'd die anyway."

"You were very brave, though," the voice reminded her judiciously. "You told them all that, then said you'd rather risk death under their power and keep your innocence than give in to them and go to the Lord God stained with guilt. Then, while they were grinding their teeth, you screamed as loud as you could for help. That's all you could have done – all anyone could have done."

"And it did me what good?" she returned tartly. "It didn't change anything! They screamed right along with me, accusing me of adultery, and one of them ran to open the gate. Then, when the servants came, they said they'd caught me in the act, and the young man was too strong for them and had fled through the open gate. And everyone *believed* them – on no evidence! And in spite of the fact that I've never, never, never even *looked* at a man besides my husband! And Joakim! He just *stood* there. He ought to have horsewhipped that pair! He should at least have *listened* to my side of things, let my word have the deciding weight."

"Should, certainly," the voice agreed. "But couldn't. You *know* that. He's never really *believed* how much you love him, never believed an *old man*, as he sees himself, could fully satisfy a wife as beautiful and alive as you are. So the elders had only to make their accusation, and he was convinced. Not that he blames you. He blames himself for *tying you down* in a marriage you must certainly find dull, if not hateful. No, Joakim couldn't have helped you."

Susanna shook her head. "No. And when it comes to trial," she thought, "it'll be the same story. Oh, what shall I do?"

The maid's entrance at that moment, bearing a steaming cup and a woeful expression, answered her. She would drink the herbal tea, dress in her best clothes, veil herself properly and, when summoned, go to the court she knew would be convened in the reception hall.

"Your mother and father send their greetings, my lady," the maid reported, handing her the cup and moving to the closet to take out her best gown. "They said to tell you they would have all your relatives dressed and ready to go, whenever you are sent for. And the children are up and being dressed now by their maids. Everyone is very angry at the elders, for everyone knows you simply *couldn't* have done what they accuse you of."

Having delivered her messages, the small maid nodded firmly and clamped her lips shut, rather pink in the cheeks. It was the longest speech Susanna had ever heard her make, and she was moved and startled in equal parts.

"Thank you, Miriam," she answered, feeling her heart lift in spite of what her head had been telling her. Surely, *surely,* someone would listen to her in the court. Surely *someone* would weigh the elders' word against the testimony of her own blameless life and discern their guilt! Surely!

When the summons came, the procession formed as promptly as if everyone had been practicing the maneuver for days. Wearing blinding white, veiled from head to foot and carrying herself like a queen, Susanna took her place, and together she and her retinue, all of them in tears, proceeded into the makeshift court.

"Strip her!" shouted one of the elders. There was a gasp from the assembled community.

"Take off that veil!" shouted the other, giving his partner a dig in the ribs that elicited an "Oof!" and an injured look from the man. "Let everyone look on this shameless woman who has so dishonored her noble husband!" he finished.

And it was done, though very gently and by a man who had tears in his eyes and whispered an apology to her.

With a satisfied smirk at her, the two accusing elders moved to Susanna, placed themselves on either side of her and each placed a hand on her head. She felt her skin crawl in revulsion at the double touch, and her eyes flashed, but she was not given the chance to speak before the elders told their story; the same one they had threatened her with and then told in the garden.

And the court believed them. Before she could draw breath, they had condemned her to death. Beside herself with fear, grief, and frustrated fury at her own helplessness, she took a deep breath. "Lord God!" she shouted at the top of her lungs, "You know everything – all the hidden things of the past and of the future! You know these two men have lied about me! Are You now going to let me die, though I am innocent of everything these wicked men have claimed against me?"

Her words crackled in the sudden silence, but there was no answer, and Susanna found herself being marched out of her own house, into the public street and toward the place of execution.

And then it happened. Moved by the Spirit of the Lord, young Daniel, standing by the side of the road, began to shout, "I will not share in taking this woman's life!" The procession stopped short, and the people began to ask him what he was talking about. His answer was brisk – they were fools to condemn the woman without having solid evidence for her crime, and without examining the case. The witnesses had been lying! They were to return to the court at once!

The people turned back eagerly. The lying judges, hemmed in by the crowd, were forced to return with them.

Once in the court, the rest of the elders invited Daniel to sit with them, for his wisdom was obviously from the Lord God. Daniel agreed, and had the witnesses separated. He examined them independently before the whole court, asking them under what tree they had surprised Susanna and her "lover," and when one said "an oak" and the other "a mastic," the crowd rose up and dragged the liars, convicted out of their own mouths, to suffer the punishment they had tried to inflict on Susanna.

Susanna, held tightly in Joakim's arms and weeping with him for joy at this glorious, impossible rescue, joined her family in praising the Lord God who had saved her. He whose single weighty word had rebalanced the world.

[**Daniel 13:** 1–64 or Apocrypha **Susanna** 1–64; see **SUSANNA, daughter of Hilkiah** (see also **Susanna, daughter of Hilkiah's MOTHER** and **Susanna, daughter of Hilkiah's MAIDSERVANTS**)]

# TABITHA
# and the Other Side of the Journey

No one asked me, you know – no one here, I mean - whether I wanted to come back or not. If they had, I would have said no.

Well, really, it would probably have come out, "NO! Are you out of your *minds*? Come back for what? So I can do some more sewing for the poor? I HATE sewing! And there's certainly nothing else in all of Jaffa – no, make that the whole Roman Empire! The whole world, in fact! – that would move me one quarter of a footstep back in its, or his, or her, direction, if once I could get OUT of here and be HOME at last! You think this is *fun* – being a poor, childless widow with no one to care about me but the community, and that only for as long as I can contribute – *sew* for the poor? And then become a burden on everyone when I can't? If you think *that* is worth leaving heaven to come back to, you are seriously in need of instruction – or the healers!"

So it's just as well I died so suddenly they didn't have a chance to ask me – not that it would have occurred to them to do so; they knew dead was dead, just as well as I did! But that would really have been a hateful dose to have dumped on them, and they wouldn't have understood a word of it. After all, *I* didn't!

But that is how I felt then, before I died, when I saw only one side of the journey we are making together. It took getting to the end – My! That was *something!* – to see the other side, the one I had missed. And *then* coming back wasn't a penance or a punishment but a mercy, the greatest I have ever known, and one nobody could have ever imagined.

I guess that all sounds very mysterious to you? I don't mean it to be. I've come to see that my experience was given to me because so many other people need it, and that the way I thank God for it is to tell anyone who wants to listen all about it.

Would you like to hear? Well, I warn you, I'll have to go back to the beginning. It was back when the community in Jaffa was young, though fairly well established, that this all happened. Cephas – Peter, you know? The one Jesus left in charge of His Church? I find *Cephas* slides more easily off my Greek tongue; I still find it odd to answer to the Hebrew Tabitha when I've been Dorcas since I knew I was me!

Sorry – I do ramble now! Never used to – I always accounted for every second, and never wasted one of them that I could help. You get a lot done that way – *tons* of sewing, I promise you – but you miss a lot, too. Mainly people, and that's what's important, loving them with your service. If you don't, what you're *doing* for them becomes something else – not love (which is the point) but, maybe, control? Making yourself feel good because you're doing all this for these poor souls who can't do for themselves? Getting credit with the local church? I was doing all of that, and didn't have a clue.

Anyway, Cephas was still around the local churches; this was well before he went off to Rome and got himself killed by Nero. He happened to be in Lydda visiting the church there when I died – I was five years into my widowhood at that point.

But wait. Before I get to that, I have to tell you how it was with me. I'd been married to Jonah only three years, and we hadn't had any children when he died. Just like that. Gone. His death devastated me, but once the formal mourning was over, no one seemed to want to talk about him, or listen to me, or help me out of the swamps of sadness and hopelessness I seemed to be living in.

So I shut my mouth and looked around for a way to be useful to the community – seemed only fair. They would be taking care of me in my old age, I knew, and even at that point, they were providing my food and shelter. True, I had sold our house and given the community all the money, but – look. I was never stupid. I could always add – and subtract. I knew exactly how long that money would pay for my keep – and how soon I would become a flat burden on everyone else.

I found that sewing, my very *least* favorite of all the things they teach women to do, was what was needed. There were people, much poorer than I was, who needed clothing – good sturdy stuff for work. And you know children. They grow out of their clothes every two blinks, and there's only so much you can do with letting down and letting out. There was plenty of work to be done and I was the best in the group, so I wound up doing most of it.

Actually, I was grateful. So I didn't like it – too bad! It was needed, doing it let me feel I was giving back to the community and, best of all, *it filled the time so full I didn't have room to think.* You have no idea how important that was for me then. Not having time to think and brood kept me from drowning in my own misery. It kept me focused and in touch with real people – who were annoying enough from time to time to strike sparks in me and keep me alive in mind.

Another thing about the sewing – the fact that I didn't like it, but did it anyway and did it well, was a plus religiously, as I saw things then. Jesus says we each have to take up our cross every day and carry it if we want to follow Him and then be with Him forever, and I figured sewing covered that nicely and left some room to spare!

But what I *really* wanted, with all my soul, was to go Home – to die and be OUT of this world where no one loved me *personally* and I had no one to love. Meanwhile, I used work as my refuge.

Every day I would take a pile of garments to be made or repaired and count the jobs in it. I'd examine each garment to see what needed to be done, then cut and stitch it as quickly and well as I could. Then, when I had it finished, I'd check it off in my mind and grab the next. I was impatient for the pile to diminish and disappear – but when it did and everything was checked off, I'd feel my stomach drop and a weight settle on me. I had nothing to do! So I'd run quickly to get another pile, and the check-off process would start all over.

In short, I was never happy – not working and not idle – and I had no idea what was wrong. I thought that was the way real life *was* – so the sooner out, the better! No one knew that, of course. They all thought I loved to sew and that I was working so hard because of my devotion to Jesus Whom I served in the poor.

Frankly, that last part never entered my mind! Oh, I *knew* the *Whatsoever you do to the least of My brethren, you do to Me* saying – but somehow I never made the connection with what my hands were doing, day after day. I was too busy checking things off to pay attention to them as they were being done. I wasn't living in the *now*, in the present moment, but either in the future or in the past. And I wanted the whole thing to be *over.*

I suppose you think that was profoundly foolish of me? Oh, it was, but that's where I was then, and that was all I could see, so that's what I did. That's all you *can* do, you know. That's all anyone can do.

Anyway, the day I died. It was an odd kind of day – all bits and pieces, you know? – and I really couldn't seem to settle to anything. I took my usual pile of sewing and worked on it, but I felt – strange, I guess. And then the fever started, sudden and high. I fainted. I know because I woke up on the floor! They helped me to bed, put cool compresses on my head, gave me willow-bark tea – all of which felt nice but did nothing.

The fever kept on going up, and then I was floating up above the bed, looking down on myself, seeing the women come in, find me, run out to get the doctor, weep and pray. I saw the doctor check me over and close my eyes – but I could still see, up there above the bed. The women were laying me out when I lost interest and looked up. I saw something like a long tunnel of light, so I kind of floated into it, and began to speed up to get to the end.

And there – well, I can't really describe it. There was a Presence and a warmth. A welcome for me *just because I was me!* I'd never had such love, except from Jonah, and this was a thousand times – more.

Then I saw my life as I had lived it, *with* the half of it I hadn't known enough to live. It was like having a street half in sunlight and color, half in the dark of night with everything gray and black. And God told me – not in words, but I knew – that everything I had *done* was fine, and that He was very pleased. That was the part in sunlight and color.

But the part in night dark – that was what I had *been*, or rather, *not* been while I was busy *doing*. He showed me how much He loves me – can't explain how. He just *did* – and told me that everything I *was*, every breath I drew, every single minute *could* have been a receiving of His love and a returning of it to Him, in what I *did,* directly and by way of the people around me.

He showed me the people – and I could SEE Him in them, see Him in need, see Him loving *me* – and told me I could have had all that love if I had only been listening and watching for it! And *then* He told me that that was the way it was, the way *He* was, with everyone! He said that's how His world works. Or should.

Well! I was stunned – so filled with joy at His love and with delight that He was pleased with me and my work, and so filled with sorrow at all the wealth of love I had missed; so amazed at the way He had made us, and meant His work – and our getting Home to Him – to work that, for once, I had nothing to say!

And that's when He asked me if I'd be willing to go back! I tell you, I jumped at the chance!

Just then, I looked back down at my body and saw that Cephas was kneeling beside it, praying. Then he stood up and looked down at it. "Tabitha!" he said. "Get up!"

And I found myself back in my body, starting to sit up! As if he had done this every day of his life, Cephas took my hand and helped me stand, then opened the door, called the community (who were jammed together in the hall just outside) and stood there beside me with this odd smile.

Well, I don't need to tell you the rest – word spread through town like wildfire, and from church to church just about as fast. We had a real party, of course – and then – well, then I started to live the other side of my journey, and I'm still at it. That's what – thirty years ago now? Amazing! It doesn't feel that long!

[**Acts 9:** 36-42; see **TABITHA (in Greek, DORCAS)**]

# TAMAR
# and the Long Way Around

Have you met my grandsons? I have eight – all boys! My twins, Perez and Zerah, have done me proud – such good boys they always were, and now they take wonderful care of me! Yes, I have everything a woman dreams of – but let me tell you, it wasn't easy!

You see, my first husband was Er – Judah's firstborn of Shua's daughter, his Canaanite wife? Anyway, poor Er offended the Lord God seriously, and the Lord God saw to it that he died shortly after we were married. Since he had not given me children, Judah gave me his second son, Onan, so that he could beget an heir for his brother.

But Onan – well! He didn't like the idea of begetting children who wouldn't be considered his, but he had no way to refuse. Do you know what that – *sneak*, did? He'd get rid of his seed before sleeping with me! He thought no one would know, and I'd be judged barren, but the Lord God knew – and killed him for it. Again, there was no child for Er, and again, it wasn't my fault.

Now, Judah knew he was supposed to give me his third son, who was still a boy, for a husband, and he *really* didn't want to, but he wasn't about to defy the Lord God outright. So what he did was to send me home to my family as a widow, promising me as soon as Shelah was grown up he'd send him to me as husband.

And I believed him! Well, he *was* Jacob's fourth son by Leah, and Jacob was the Lord God's chosen, and he *had* already given me Onan in place of Er, so I went off peacefully to wait. Little did I know that all he wanted was to be rid of me! Judah was terrified that Shelah would die as Er and Onan had – and he might have, if he'd decided to do what his brothers had done – and that would leave *him* without an heir. There was no way Judah was going to risk having that happen. But of course I didn't know that while I was waiting.

Ten years passed and nothing happened. I began to get suspicious. I knew Shelah had to be seventeen, plenty old enough to father a child – and I wasn't getting any younger – but there was no word from Judah. It was as if I had fallen off the edge of the earth as far as he was concerned. I started to get a little frantic. What was I supposed to do now?

Then, I learned first that Judah's wife had died, and second, that he was going up to Timnah for sheep-shearing. Suddenly, the way the sun burns the fog away, my blind darkness cleared and I saw exactly what I could do – had to do, if we were all to obey the Lord God.

I scouted around and found a huge cloak, thick as a rug almost, stripped off my mourning clothes and wrapped myself in the cloak so that it covered my face. Then I went to the place where the roads to Enaim and Timnah fork, and sat there. Sure enough, here he came, and Shelah, well-grown as I'd known he would be, was with him. I was furious, but I said nothing, just sat there.

Judah stopped, planted himself in front of me, grinned and said, "Come here, woman! Lay with me!" Well! I was so shocked, I almost fell over! Dignified Judah! But this was just what I had planned – better, in fact!

"What will you give me?" I said, dropping my voice and slurring the words. I was sure he hadn't recognized me, but I didn't want to take chances.

He cocked his head and smiled slyly. "A kid from my flock?" he asked. "I'll send it to you."

"Oh, no you don't!" I thought. "What will you give me to hold until the kid gets here?"

At that he laughed out loud. "What would you like me to give you?"

I laughed too. "Uh – how about – your seal and cord, and – your stick!"

Still chuckling, he gave them to me, and then – well.

When it was over, he went his way, and I slipped off home, put my mourning clothes back on and hid Judah's seal on its cord and his stick in the cloak and waited. Of course, no kid arrived (and Judah told me later he had sent one with his friend Hirah), for no one knew who I was or where I had gone.

In a month, I knew I had conceived; in three months, so did everyone else. Naturally, some busybody rushed to tell Judah that I had been whoring around and gotten pregnant – sweet people! – and instantly he ordered, "Burn her!"

So they rushed to my house and dragged me out, but I gave one of them the cloak with the stick, cord and seal wrapped in it and sent him to Judah with the message, "The man who got me with child is the one who owns these things. Examine the seal and cord and the stick and tell me whose they are." We all waited for the answer.

The man I sent told me later that Judah put the cloak on a table and unwrapped it angrily, ready to take the man apart once he knew who it was that had dishonored me, and himself – and turned white as washed sheep's wool when he found his own seal, cord and staff. But I'll give him this – he didn't try to get out of it. "This is my fault, not hers," he said. "I should have given her Shelah for a husband, as I promised and the Lord God willed, and I did not."

He received me back into his household, and when the twins were born, he raised them as his own.

So you see, when you follow the Lord God, He takes care of you, and you get everything He wants you to have – though sometimes, you have to go the long way around!

[**Genesis 38:** 6–30; **Ruth 4:** 12; **1 Chronicles 2:** 4; **Matthew 1:** 3; see **TAMAR, mother of Perez and Zerah** (see also **BATHSHUA**)]

# TAMAR
## and the Broken Bread

Absalom's blood-sister, the virgin Tamar, was concerned. Her half-brother Amnon, King David's firstborn, was very ill – so ill that the King, her father, had sent for her and told her to go to Amnon's house to prepare food for him. Apparently, he had told his father that he would only eat what he had seen her prepare with his own eyes.

That struck her as odd, for Amnon had the best cook in the family in his household, "and if she can't please Amnon, how does he think I can?" she asked herself in consternation. "I only know how to make simple things – bread, stew, fruit compote!"

She sighed and continued dressing. "If that's what he wants, that's what he'll get," she thought. "But it doesn't make sense!"

Arriving at Amnon's house, she was brought directly to the fireside where Amnon was lying on a couch, eyes on the flames. At her step, he looked up suddenly, and Tamar took a step backward. The look reminded her of the fierce glower of a falcon, just landing with its prey, and she shivered.

"I'm so glad to see you, my sister," he said, hooding his eyes and lying back on the couch, in seeming weakness. "Would you be good enough to make me some bread?"

Relief brought color to Tamar's cheeks. That she could do! "Of course, brother," she said, and gathered the flour, salt, oil and a large bowl and set to work. For once, everything cooperated, and the flat cakes of bread peeled off perfectly. When the platter was full, she brought it to him, but Amnon refused to eat.

Tamar looked at the bread cakes, puzzled. They were fine – better than she had ever made before. Was Amnon really sick after all? She had not seen any signs of the illness he claimed, and had wondered if he were testing her wifely skills for some reason. But this was very odd!

Before her thoughts could go further, Amnon was clearing the room of all his servants and extending his hands to her. "Bring the bread and come to my room. You can feed it to me there." Slowly, with apparent effort, Amnon rose and retreated to the private room where he slept.

Tamar, now really worried, followed him in, carrying the platter. He collapsed on the bed, leaned back against the pillows and patted it to indicate where she should sit so that she could reach him. So she sat, put the platter on the table, broke off a piece of the top bread cake and reached with it toward Amnon. As the broken bread touched his lips, Amnon sat up, grasped her wrist with one hand and her opposite shoulder with the other and pulled her toward him.

"Sleep with me, sister!" he panted hoarsely, his eyes devouring her.

Dropping the broken bread from numbing fingers onto the bed, Tamar opened her mouth to speak in her shock, but found no words. Then, her heart pounding as Amnon pulled harder, she protested, "No, brother! Don't – take me this way! Men in Israel don't do such things! Don't commit this unforgivable crime! Please! Don't – force me! You'd shame me totally – and where could I go then? And you yourself would be rejected by all of Israel! Look, if you want me for a wife, just go to the king and ask – you know he'll say yes!"

But Amnon was past hearing her. Swept away by his lust, he pulled her over on top of him, rolled over her on the bed and raped her, heeding neither her struggles nor her cries.

When at last he had finished and rolled off her, he looked at her as though she had crawled out of a sewer. "Get out of my sight!" he commanded her coldly. "Go! Now!"

Tamar, stunned, curled into herself on the bed, and he reached for her and flung her to the floor.

"Get out!" he repeated.

Quickly, Tamar gathered her blood stained gown around her and shrank away from the enraged man she no longer knew.

Amnon raised his voice, calling for his servant. When the man came, he pointed to Tamar, now crouched in the corner of the room, shielding her body with one arm and her head with the other, and commanded, "Get rid of her. Now! And bar the door behind her!"

The servant, contriving to look as though he had never seen Tamar before, lifted her up, marched her to the door and, opening it, shoved her out into the street. The door-bar fell into place with a solid thunk she could feel in the pit of her stomach.

Desperate, sobbing aloud, Tamar was beside herself with grief and shame. She raked her garment to ribbons with her fingernails as she trailed down the middle of the street, stooping from time to time to pick up a handful of dust and pour it on her unveiled head. Her tears made clean tracks through the dust on her face, and she stumbled along, reaching the door of her blood-brother Absalom without knowing how.

"How is she?" Absalom asked the old woman who had been nurse to both of them.

"Broken, poor lamb," the woman replied with a sigh. "I think she will not mend. You did right to tell her to put it behind her, that being taken by a brother was not – seriously harming to her honor, but she could not hear you."

Absalom's eyes blazed. "I'll kill him," he declared. "If my father the King will do nothing to harm his firstborn, I will. I will have his life for this – rape, this shattering of my sister."

"That will not help her, and will harm you," she told him seriously, "though certainly it will make you feel better. But Amnon's death will not make her whole. Bread once broken, you cannot again make the loaf whole."

"Nevertheless!" said Absalom.

He was as good as his word. Two years later, he had Amnon killed at a banquet – and found his nurse had been right. There was no change in Tamar, and he had to flee for his life to Geshur, carrying his father's enmity with him.

"So another loaf is broken," he mused, "and there will be no mending of this one, either. I'm not sorry – I was right, and my father was wrong – but the fragments of this loaf will bring us all to our deaths. Would it could all have been different."

[2 Samuel 13: 1-32; 1 Chronicles 3: 9; see **TAMAR, daughter of King David**]

# The WISE WOMAN FROM ABEL
## and the Obvious Solution

"What's going on?" demanded the middle-aged woman of one of the elders of the city.

"King David's chieftain, Joab, is erecting a mound around the city. He's going to besiege us."

"I can see that for myself!" she replied sharply. "What I want to know is why? What's going on?"

"I don't know," her informant admitted. "Abel Beth-maacah has never given offense to King David; it has been a faithful and loyal city. There's no reason for this attack!"

"Then why is it happening?" the woman asked in a reasonable tone.

"I don't know!" the elder repeated a little desperately.

"Well, have you *asked?*" she said impatiently.

"How?" the elder retorted. "I don't think Joab's accepting visitors, and we're certainly not going to surrender the town to find out! And that's what we'd have to do to get him to listen to us, and then it would be too late!"

"But if we found out *why* Joab's attacking, we might be able to stop him *without* either a surrender or having the town destroyed. What's the matter with you? Surely that's plain enough!"

Goaded past politeness, the elder snapped, "If you know a way to find out and stop this thing, go to it! And when they kill you, I'll see to it that you get a decent burial!" He turned on his heel and stamped his way across the square.

"Useless!" she muttered under her breath, then turned to the city walls. If she stood on top and faced Joab's army – "That'll do it!" she thought and headed for the guards' stairs, choosing the sector where her nephews were standing guard.

"Aunt?" they chorused as she appeared between them.

"I need to speak to Joab," she told them. "Which one is he?"

The elder sputtered, "You can't do that, Aunt!" but the younger simply smiled and reached for her hand.

"Come over here," he said. "It's the best place to shout from – something about the way the land falls makes sound really carry. Just say – "

She squeezed his hand. "Not to fret, nephew! I have my lines!" She went to the position he had pointed out and, taking a deep breath, projected,

"TELL JOAB TO COME HERE! I NEED TO TALK TO HIM!"

The sound rolled around the valley, shaking men from their labors, and soon a flurry to the left and a boil of soldiers resolved itself into a tall, armored and helmeted man. "What do you want?" he shouted back and she nodded.

"You're Joab?" she asked, still at full projection.

The soldier removed his helmet so she could see his face and nodded. "I am!"

"My lord Joab! Listen to me, I beg you!"

"I'm listening," he answered, but from his tone, she knew it wouldn't be for long.

"There's an old saying – if they think loyalty has died in Israel, let them ask in Abel or in Dan! Why are you trying to flatten us? Abel is an ancient city in Israel! Why are you trying to destroy the Lord God's property?"

"I'm not!" Joab replied indignantly. "I'm not trying to destroy anything! I don't want to ruin Abel! All I want is Sheba, Bichri's son, from Ephraim's hills. He's hiding in your city with his men and he has rebelled against King David. Give him to me and I'll go – gladly!"

The woman nodded, her eyes gleaming. "All right!" she said. "We'll throw his head over the wall to you." With a sigh of satisfaction, she headed past her nephews, the elder stunned, the younger grinning at her, for the stairs. The elders met her at their foot.

"You heard the man!" she snapped at them. "Get Sheba, Bichri's son, and cut off his head. Then we throw it over the wall to Joab and he goes away! And don't waste time arguing! Joab is NOT a patient man!"

The elder to whom she had spoken first shook his head in admiration. "I never thought you could do it," he began, but she cut him short.

"Sheba?" she reminded him. "Now! Talk to me later!"

And they did. In less time than it takes to tell, they had rousted Sheba from his enclave, bound him hand and foot, cut off his head and brought it back in a basket to the wall where the woman waited. "Hurry!" she urged them. "Up the stairs after me, and throw that," and she made a face pointing to the head, "to Joab. I'll show you who he is!"

On the wall, she gestured to the helmetless soldier, who caught sight of her and raised his hand. "Catch!" she shouted, and they tossed the head in its basket to Joab who caught it neatly, grinned, bowed to the woman, then had the horn blown to disperse his army, while he returned to Jerusalem.

Watching them depart, the woman smiled, then turning to the elder, said, "You'll never learn anything unless you ask, you know!"

[**2 Samuel 20:** 14-22; see **Quick-Witted WOMAN from Abel**]

# The WOMAN
# and the Shattered Jar

Thoughtfully, the woman rubbed the alabaster jar with a soft cloth. It glowed under her polishing and, remembering, she smiled sadly. This had been the gift of the one man in her life who had, she believed, truly loved her both for herself and just as she was. With him alone, she had found herself whole at last, completed in his love as he'd said he was completed in hers.

They had been going to marry – but, as always, not just yet. There were the children to consider, and the children's mother - the wife he had married when they were both too young. The wife who would consider it a favor if he were to divorce her, freeing her to marry her own love. But he couldn't leave her, not just yet, not with the children to raise. Then she wasn't well, and the children were too young, still, to understand this – change, and so …

And so it had never happened. Her expression moved from simply sad to bitter. He had died, far too young, in a freak accident – she preferred *not* to think of it as an act of God – and had left her, fragile and empty, to make her way as she had before he had come on the scene, in a dark world that had no center and no pattern.

As at first, she had again been profligate with her love – or with her longing to be loved; she couldn't quite tell – giving it, pouring it and herself out wherever she caught the hint that it might be needed and would be welcomed. But now, even at the moment of giving, she felt little – certainly not whole again – for it seemed to her that her power of feeling love, either as she gave it or as it returned to her, had been sealed in the alabaster jar. What was left to her was just a dark hunger, never satisfied. So in a way, the coming of the dawn, with the inevitable vanishing of the present man back into the seamless fabric of his own life, in which, of course, there was no place for her, was more relief than pain.

As she grew older, experience taught her to pass up both the younger men who sought only their own pleasure and used her as a convenience, and the divorced (who, whatever they *said*, never could seem to break from their first families) in favor of widowers. They were settled, unattached and often as lonely as she; invariably they were courteous – or the ones who came to her were – and their quiet, domestic love-making was a comfort to them both, even if it did not reach, much less fill her, still sealed in alabaster.

That, really, was why she had not married. For to marry, still sealed in, and by love for the man who had loved her and given her the alabaster jar, still unable to receive the love of her husband, would have been the worst of lies. Instead, she went on searching for another man who would love her so well he would free her, at last. In the mean time, she bore her loneliness with patience and in hope.

That was until this year, she remembered, and her first encounter with Jesus of Nazareth, the Prophet. She bit her lip and, moving carefully, placed the alabaster jar on its usual shelf, out of range of the curious cat who shared her living space and allowed himself to be fed regularly and petted from time to time. This Jesus was – different, and she knew she would have to do something about Him, and about what He was saying.

She could still hear His voice as He spoke, it seemed directly to her, though she was veiled and stood in the thick of a crowd.

*Be compassionate,* He had said, *as your Father in Heaven is compassionate. Do not pass judgment on others, and you will not, yourselves, be judged. Give! The measure you use in your giving is the one that will be used to measure out to you what you will receive.* He had said, *No good tree can put forth rotten fruit, nor a rotten tree good fruit,* and declared, *Whoever listens to Me, and does what I say, builds his house on solid rock.*

As she listened, she had felt her eyes open, and the alabaster around her heart begin to crack. After that, it was as though He were speaking directly to her, and she remembered every word. Unwillingly, fascinated, she had followed Him with the crowds, watching and listening, learning of other things He had said and done before she had joined the group. It was one of those events, the healing of a paralyzed man whom his friends had gotten past the crowds to Jesus by the effective expedient of opening up the roof and lowering him on his mat to Jesus' feet, that was working in her now.

For before healing the paralysis, Jesus had forgiven the man's sins – which, everyone agreed, only God could do. Then He had healed the man's body *as a sign* that He *could* forgive sins – which meant either that He was God (but how could that be so? All Israel knew God was One!), or spoke with God's personal assurance that He would be heard. God had not struck Him down when He forgave the man's sins, and had healed the man at Jesus' command, so ...?

"So," she thought, "I have to decide." What she had to decide had just grown into a question, a problem, since she had been following the crowds around Jesus. "Be honest!" she commanded herself. "You've been following Jesus, not just going along with the crowds! And that's because – "

She stopped. Because why? Because He was a prophet? Maybe. Because He was the Messiah? Well, He probably was – that would explain how He could claim to forgive sins and prove the claim with a cure no one else could have done, ever. But that wasn't why.

Because He *could* forgive sins?

That was getting closer, and that was part of the problem. For up to this point, she had not considered anything she had ever done as sinful – only as giving love which she, and everyone she shared it with, had needed more than food and drink. But the Law called it fornication, or adultery, and said these things were sinful. She still didn't *feel* that what she had done was evil, but – was this good fruit or the rotten stuff that only bad trees produced?

The question was the more troubling in that, with Jesus' voice sounding in her ears and His eyes looking into her soul, she had no answer. Easy to say, yes, yes, it was sinful, and throw herself at His feet begging for cleansing, but for her that would be a lie, for she didn't believe loving ever was sinful – and she somehow *knew* one couldn't lie to Him. But it would be harder to say, no, no, it wasn't sinful, and, if He disagreed, to leave His company. For she knew, if He said she shouldn't be seeking love, she would have to choose. And that choice would be agony.

So far, she had been pushing the question aside, waiting for Him to say the one thing that would, at last, clarify the matter. Meanwhile, she let the reality of His love be, hoping. For, though she had never gotten nearer to Him than three rows back in any crowd that surrounded Him, she *knew* that He knew she was there and that He was reaching out to her, that He loved her just as she was, and maybe, just maybe ....

"So what do I do?" she asked herself, moving restlessly to pick up the alabaster jar to polish again. "I can't go on this way. I *have* to choose. And I can't choose both His way and mine, or neither. I simply cannot. Well, maybe – maybe I could ask *Him* how to choose? Ask Him about loving and sin, and good fruit and rotten, and how to find someone to love me for myself and just as I am, and set me free to receive his love, the way ...."

Her voice trailed off as she considered the alabaster jar in her hands. She had never broken it open to release the perfumed ointment it contained. Her one love had given it to her for a wedding present, he said, and she had saved it, and her hope with it, for that night. Then when he had died, it had become her last link with him, and the pledge of his promise and his love. Shattering the jar would end that dream in her, as the falling block of stone had ended it in him – and might shatter the alabaster enclosing her own heart. Then what would happen to her? She did not know.

But — what if she brought it to Jesus? What if she showed it to Him and then asked Him about love and sin, and feeling and forgiveness. Ask if He thought she needed it? Surely He would understand! Surely He would help her to do whatever it was she needed to do to be whole again?

Unbidden, the words she had heard in passing in the market place that morning came to mind. "He's been invited to Simon's house, the Pharisee, you know? For a banquet! Everyone will be there — not us, of course, but all Simon's important friends. I wonder what He'll say to them!"

It would be the perfect opportunity, she thought. She knew Simon — had known him forever, it seemed. It was a connection which, though innocent, Simon was not likely to have publicized, or to want known, but it gave her a real advantage in this situation. For she knew Simon's house, too, and she was known there by his chief steward as well as by his doorkeeper. So she could slip in by a side door, get into the banqueting room before anyone else arrived and, if she were lucky, ask her questions and be gone before the guests knew she had been there. That way, she would not embarrass Simon — though her arrival would, she knew, make him nervous, poor thing. He worried so about appearances! But finally everything would be *settled,* and she would have some peace.

She nodded. Yes, that would do. Swiftly, she whipped her cloak around her, adjusted her veil and picked up the alabaster jar, wrapping it in her polishing cloth and concealing it in the cloak's folds. Gauging the level of the sun, she calculated she would be in place in Simon's house well before the banqueters, and smiled her satisfaction. This was going to work out well!

As it happened, however, the banquet had been set for early afternoon, and she arrived to find the house full and the banquet winding down. Nodding to the doorkeeper, she slipped in to the house, surveyed the banquet hall and found Jesus' couch. At this point, everyone was fairly expansive. Voices were raised and everyone was talking loudly to those nearby. No one was paying much attention to Jesus, and she saw, to her indignation, Simon had not even had the servants wash Jesus' feet. What was he playing at? How dared he!

And then she noticed how tired He looked and how sad. No one was talking to Him, much less listening to Him, and He shifted restlessly on the dining couch, His eyes moving from person to person, finding not a single one who was willing, or able, to allow Him the contact, to respond to Him. He was being shunned. In the politest way possible, He was being told that He did not matter; that no one cared what He said or did; that He might as well dry up and blow away; that He was useless and that what He was trying to do, whatever it was, was hopeless folly. She felt Him wince at the multi-level rejection she had felt so often, and saw a shadow of pain in His eyes. He loved these people! He wanted so much to bring them to the Father Who loved them, too – and they were refusing Him. They weren't even *seeing* Him!

The woman found herself kneeling at the foot of Jesus' dining couch, weeping for His pain, longing to bring Him some comfort. Her tears fell on His feet and, shrugging off her veil, she unbound her hair and began to wipe them clean of the road dust Simon had ignored, grieving for Him and with Him, trying to give Him the love He longed for and she longed to pour out, by kissing His feet, over and over. He stirred under her hands and she looked up through her tears to see Him, caught between His own tears and a smile, nod to her and see – oh, everything that was inside of her!

The alabaster casing around her heart, so long a part of her she no longer felt it as something separable from her self, cracked and shattered in that look! Joy, fountaining within her, demanded release, and with a sound between a laugh and a gasp, she grasped the alabaster jar in its cloth, broke off its neck and poured out the ointment on His feet, rubbing it in.

"Simon!" Jesus called to his host, who had been staring at the woman with a look of suppressed horror. "I've got a case to propose to you."

"Yes, Rabbi!" answered the Pharisee, startled back to good manners and to his guest. "Say on!"

"There was a man who had lent money to two men," said Jesus. "One owed him five hundred silver coins, and the second owed him only fifty, but, as neither man could pay what he owed, the lender canceled both debts. Now, which one, do you suppose, would love him more?"

"I guess the one who had the larger debt forgiven," said Simon, frowning slightly, for he did not see where this question was going.

"Right you are!" said Jesus approvingly. Then He turned, gesturing to focus the attention of the now silent diners on the woman who was rubbing in the last of the ointment and giving His feet a last kiss.

"Do you see this woman, Simon?" He asked.

Simon nodded warily.

"When I came in to your house, you didn't provide a splash of water to wash my feet – but she has been washing them with her tears and drying them with her hair. You didn't offer me the kiss of welcome, but she has been kissing my *feet* ever since she came in. You didn't use a drop of oil to anoint my head – but she has been rubbing costly ointment into my feet. So I tell you, *her* many sins must have been forgiven, for see how much she loves! The man who loves only a little has only been forgiven a little."

The woman, mouth open, cheeks still wet with tears, was staring at Him intently, hope in her eyes. He smiled, and she felt herself grow whole at last at the touch of His love – love for herself alone, just the way she was – God's love, she knew. And this love would never fade, never die. "Your sins are forgiven," He said to her softly. "It is your faith that has saved you. Go now, in peace!"

And she rose, transfigured in her joy, bowed deeply, smiled at Him, and made her way home, carrying the fragments of the shattered, healing, alabaster jar.

[**Luke 7:** 36–50; see **Sinful WOMAN Who Anointed Jesus' Feet** (see also **Matthew 26:** 6-13; **Mark 14:** 3-9; **John 12:** 1-11; **MARY, sister of Martha** and **MARY MAGDALENE**); see *MARY and the Costly Nard*]

# The WOMAN
# and the Stone Unthrown

"Well done, Samuel!" said the black-clad figure stepping into the darkened room toward the bed, as his companion threw open the shutters.

"Thank you, Joshua," answered the man, rising with a smile and a slight bow. "I'll clear out now, shall I? Wouldn't want to interfere with your business!" He headed for the door, then, turning back to the bed, he said, "And thank *you*, my dear!" and departed with a wave and an amused grin.

Stunned, the woman lay still for an instant. Then, eyes widening in horror and dawning disgust, she glared at Joshua who simply laughed.

"We've been watching you, my girl," he said, knives in his voice.

"And now you have me," she spat. "But it won't do you any good. I'm not interested in you – not in either of you," she added, catching sight of Abinadab, who had retired to the shadow beside the door. "If you're offering me – love, I already have that. If it's gold you think to buy me with, I don't need it. If you're threatening me with shame, it won't work. Samuel loves me as I love him and we shall marry, there's nothing you can do about it."

"Nothing we can do about it?" Joshua repeated with a smirk. "Oh, but you're wrong! We have already done something about it. Or, rather, you have done something for us!"

"What do you mean?" she protested. "I've done nothing for you! I've done – what I've done for Samuel! Samuel loves me!" she repeated, more to herself than them. "And I love him! How does that serve you?"

"Samuel!" exclaimed Abinadab. "He was laughing as he left here!"

"No!" she insisted. "He wouldn't! He loves me!"

Joshua intervened, shaking his head. "I'm afraid not," he said, a note of triumph sounding in his words. "Samuel is ours, first and last, my girl. We sent him to you – told him to make it believable or he wouldn't get anywhere. We do learn, you see!"

"Looks like he did a better job than we paid him for," Abinadab remarked slyly, then laughed openly at the chagrin on the woman's face.

"Enough!" said Joshua briskly. "Put on your robe. You're coming with us!

"I won't!" she said defiantly.

"Suit yourself," he shrugged. "Dressed or not, you're coming with us. Now!" And he took another step toward the bed, his hands outstretched.

"Why? Where are you taking me?" the woman asked as her hands, independent, scrambled for her robe and put it on. Abinadab tossed sandals at
her and she caught them, rising and stepping in to them before Joshua or
he could touch her.

"You'll see!" growled Abinadab, dropping a veil over her head.

"Where do you think?" asked Joshua. "You know the penalty for being
caught in adultery as well as anyone. And Samuel – Samuel who *loves* you
– is happily married. To my niece!"

The woman's mouth sagged open, and her shoulders drooped. "No!"
she whispered.

"Yes!" hissed Joshua in triumph. "Now come along!"

One on each side, the two Pharisees dragged her, silent in despair, out the
door and down the street to the town center, where a huge crowd plugged
all access to the center. The crowds meant nothing to Joshua and Abinadab,
who simply shouldered the people aside. The woman noticed that the people
seemed to shrink back from contact with the black clad pair, and the scribes
and Pharisees who had attached themselves to the party and followed along,
as though their touch were poison.

"And they're right!" she thought, wishing she could melt from their
grasp as easily as the bystanders had cleared their path.

Finally, Joshua and Abinadab plowed through the ring of people standing closest to the circle's center, and in that empty space they stood her in
front of the one who was the crowd's focal point. This must be the Jesus of
Nazareth everyone was talking about, she thought, eyeing Him from the
shelter of her veil. No one else could draw a crowd like this.

Joshua stepped forward, removing her veil with a flourish, so that her
unbound hair floated free in the afternoon breeze and she was exposed to
the gaze of her enemies and the rest of this restless crowd. Stripped of the
veil's protection, the woman raised her eyes defiantly to face whatever it was
her tormentors had decided on, since they had left her no way to hide.

The eyes she met belonged to the Man around whom all these people
had gathered, and she felt her mouth dropping open again, this time in wonder. For she met in the Man's gaze, not contempt, not anger, not even pity,
but her own pain – love rejected and betrayed, powerlessness in the face of
malice, despair. And in his gaze, her pain was transformed somehow, so that
hope and life and love, real love, were somehow underneath and around and
through everything else. She had never seen anyone like this Man, and she
knew she had been waiting to see this very look for all of her life.

In what had suddenly become the background, the woman heard Joshua, laying his charge against her. "Rabbi," he said, his contempt for this poor preacher barely concealed, "we have a case for you! Here is a woman we have just taken in the act of adultery. Now the Law of Moses says she must be stoned. What's your verdict?"

The woman froze, understanding the dilemma that Jesus faced. If He said she should be set free, Joshua, Abinadab and the rest of the scribes and Pharisees there would accuse him of breaking the Law, and that would be real trouble. If He said she should be stoned, she would die at once, for Joshua and his allies were already holding the stones they would throw to put her to death. But then the crowd would attack Jesus – or simply turn away in disgust, and that would be the end of the good He could do. The Romans, who had forbidden their Jewish possession to administer capital punishment, might also take a hand, but their punishment would probably fall on the leadership, not on this itinerant preacher, so that was probably not a factor

Jesus simply looked at the accusers, seeming to see into their very souls. Then, with an infinitesimal shrug, He squatted and began to write in the dust next to her, so that she had to turn sideways to the crowd. The woman could not read the writing, but she suspected the men standing over Jesus could. It was in their heightened tension and the darkening of their expressions, especially when they glanced her way.

At last, when the tension had everyone at the snapping point, Jesus stood easily and, locking eyes with Joshua and Abinadab, announced his judgment. "Let that person among you who has no sin be the first to cast a stone." His eyes moved swiftly from man to man in the group of accusers, making the kind of contact with each one that caused him to shrink, to pale or to redden according to his nature. Then, deliberately, He squatted again and resumed his writing.

Joshua bit his lips, then furious, dropped his stone on the ground, flung himself away from the group at the center and made for home, the woman judged. Doing the same, Abinadab followed. Then, one by one, the rest of her accusers turned away, dropping their stones as they went, filtering through the crowd and disappearing. The crowd members, looking first at her and then at the still-writing Jesus, did the same.

A bird sang, its notes startlingly loud in the silent town center, now empty except for the stones. Jesus stood again and looked at the woman, eyebrows raised. "Where have they all gone?" He asked her. "Did no one condemn you?"

She turned in a circle, checking the area, then shook her head. "No one," she answered, and waited, eyes fixed on his.

For a long moment, there was silence. Finally, Jesus nodded. "Then I do not condemn you either," he told her gently and watched life rise again in her eyes as she straightened and arranged her veil properly. "Now," He said, and she turned to Him, her heart in her eyes, "go! And do not sin again!"

She nodded, heart too full to speak, then suddenly bent to pick something up. She showed it to Him with a smile of gratitude that lit up the universe. It was the single stone he had used to save her life, the stone that was not thrown. As one, they nodded, and the woman went her way, her heart-healed.

[John 8: 3-11; see **WOMAN Taken in Adultery**]

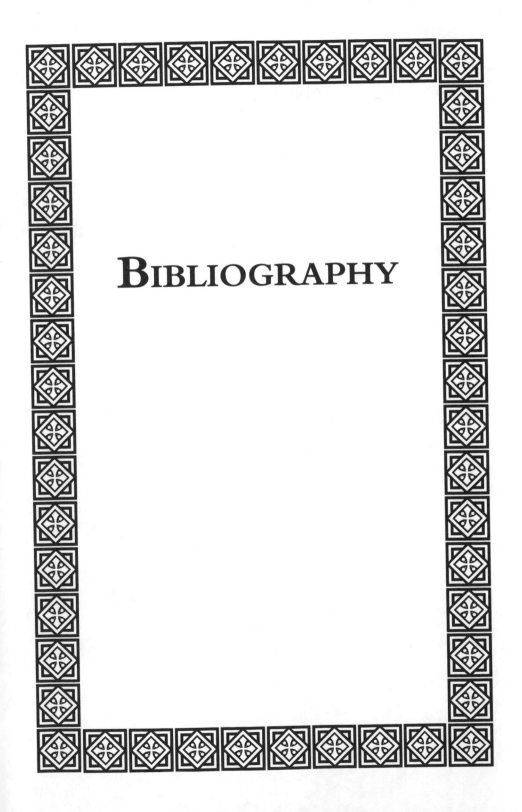

# BIBLIOGRAPHY

## Biblical Sources

**ANC** – *The Anchor Bible*
Albright, William Foxwell and David Noel Freedman, General Editors. *The AnchorBible.* Garden City, New York: Doubleday & Company, Inc., 1964–ongoing series. On the death of William Foxwell Albright, an Editorial Board, consisting of Frank M. Cross for Old Testament works, Raymond E. Brown, SS, for New Testament works and Jonas C. Greenfield for Apocalyptic works, was formed to assist David Noel Freedman.

The Anchor Bible is a work in progress. Each book of the Bible appears in a separate volume or group of volumes and is prepared by an expert scholar who provides translation, notes and commentary. New editions of previous volumes are sometimes prepared by other scholars. The following volumes were consulted:

1   *Genesis,* E. A. Speiser, 1964
2   *Exodus 1-18,* William H.C. Propp, 1998
4A  *Numbers 21-36,* Baruch A. Levine, 2000
6   *Joshua,* Robert G. Boling and G. Ernest Wright, 1982
6A  *Judges,* Robert G. Boling, 1975
7   *Ruth,* Edward F. Campbell, Jr., 1975
7A  *Lamentations,* Delbert R. Hillers, 1972
7B  *Esther,* Carey A. Moore, 1971
7C  *Song of Songs,* Marvin H. Pope, 1977
8   *1 Samuel,* P. Kyle McCarter, Jr., 1980
9   *2 Samuel,* P. Kyle McCarter, Jr., 1984
10  *1Kings,* Mordechai Cogan, 2001
11  *2 Kings,* Mordechai Cogan and Hayim Tadmor, 1988
12  *1 Chronicles,* Jacob M. Meyers, 1965
13  *2 Chronicles,* Jacob M. Meyers, 1965
14  *Ezra, Nehemiah,* Jacob M. Meyers, 1965
16  *Psalms I (1-50),* Mitchell Dahood, SJ, 1965, 1966
18  *Proverbs, Ecclesiastes,* R.B.Y. Scott, 1965
19  *Isaiah 1-39,* Joseph Blenkinsopp, 2000
20  *Second Isaiah (34-35; 40-66),* John L. McKenzie, SJ, 1968
21  *Jeremiah,* John Bright, 1965
23  *Daniel,* Louis F. Hartman, CSsR and Alexander A. DiLella, OFM 1978
24  *Hosea,* Francis I. Andersen and David Noel Freedman, 1980

26  *Matthew,* W.F. Albright and C.S. Mann, 1971

27  *Mark,* C.S. Mann, 1986

28  *The Gospel According to Luke, I-IX,* Joseph A. Fitzmyer, SJ, 1981

28A *The Gospel According to Luke, X-XXIV,* Joseph A. Fitzmyer, SJ, 1985

29  *The Gospel According to John, I-XII,* Raymond E. Brown, SS, 1966

29A *The Gospel According to John, XIII-XXI,* Raymond E. Brown, SS, 1970

31  *The Acts of the Apostles,* Johannes Munck, rev. William F. Albright and C.S. Mann, 1967

38  *Revelation,* J. Massyngberde Ford, 1975

39  *The Wisdom of Ben Sira,* Patrick W. Skehan and Alexander A. DiLella, OFM, 1987

40  *Judith,* Carey A. Moore, 1985

42  *1 & 2 Esdras,* Jacob M. Myers, 1974

43  *The Wisdom of Solomon,* David Winston, 1979

44  *Daniel, Esther and Jeremiah, the Additions,* Carey A. Moore, 1977


**JB** – *The Jerusalem Bible*

Jones, Alexander, LSS, STL, ICB, General Editor. *The Jerusalem Bible.* Garden City, New York: Doubleday & Company, Inc., 1966.


**LV** – *The Latin Vulgate,* Weber, Robert, OSB, Editor; Boniface Fischer, OSB, John Gribomont, OSB, H.F.D Sparks and W. Thiele, Assistants. *Biblia Sacra iuxta Vulgatam versionem, Tomus II.* Stuttgart: Wurttembergische Bibelanstalt, 1969


**NAB** – *The New American Bible*

Hartman, Rev. Louis F, CSsR, Rev Msgr. Patrick W. Skehan and Rev. Stephen J. Hartdegen, OFM, Editors-in-Chief. *The New American Bible [1970] with Revised New Testament [1986].* New York: World Bible Publishers, World Catholic Press Division. 1986.


**NRSV-HC** – *The HarperCollins Study Bible — New Revised Standard Version*

Meeks, Wayne A., General Editor, with the Society of Biblical Literature. *The HarperCollins Study Bible: New Revised Standard Version with the Apocryphal/ Deuterocanonical Books.* New York: HarperCollins, Publishers, 1993.

## Other Works Consulted

*Catechism of the Catholic Church.* New York: Doubleday Image, 1995.

Deen, Edith. *All the Women of the Bible.* New York: Harper & Row, 1955.

Hartdegen, Rev. Stephen J., OFM, General Editor. *Nelson's Complete Concordance of the New American Bible.* Collegeville, Minnesota: The Liturgical Press, 1977.

Josephus, Flavius. *The Jewish War,* G. W. Williamson, trans.; revised E. Mary Smallwood. New York: Dorset Press, 1985

Kinkead, Rev. Thomas. *An Explanation of the Baltimore Catechism of Christian Doctrine, Baltimore Catechism No. 4.* Rockford, Illinois: Tan Book and Publishers, Inc., 1978 (1891, 1921)

May, Herbert G., G.N.S. Hunt and R.W. Hamilton; revised John Day. *Oxford Bible Atlas,* Third Edition. New York: Oxford University Press, 1984.

McBrien, Richard P. *Lives of the Saints, from Mary and St. Francis of Assisi to John XXIII and Mother Theresa.* New York: HarperCollins at HarperSanFrancisco, 2001.

Meyers, Carol, Editor. *Women in Scripture: A Dictionary of Named and Unnamed Women in the Hebrew Bible, the Apocryphal/Deuterocanonical Books and the New Testament.* New York: Houghton, Mifflin, 2000.

*Nelson's Complete Book of Bible Maps and Charts, Old and New Testaments.* Nashville, Tennessee: Thomas Nelson Publishers, 1993.

Packer, J. I., Merrill C. Tenney and William White, Jr. *Daily Life in Bible Times.* Nashville, Tennessee: Thomas Nelson Publishers, 1980, 1982.